A General Police System

POLITICAL ECONOMY AND SECURITY
IN THE AGE OF ENLIGHTENMENT

Edited by:

**George S. Rigakos,
John L. McMullan,
Joshua Johnson
& Gulden Ozcan**

Red Quill Books | Ottawa

ISBN 978-0-9812807-0-7

Printed on acid-free paper. The paper used in this book incorporates post-consumer waste and has not been sourced from endangered old growth forests, forests of exceptional conservation value or the Amazon Basin. Red Quill Books subscribes to a one-book-at-a-time manufacturing process that substantially lessens supply chain waste, reduces greenhouse emissions, and conserves valuable natural resources.

Library and Archives Canada Cataloguing in Publication

A general police system : political economy and security in the age of enlightenment / edited by George S. Rigakos ... [et al.].

Includes bibliographical references.
ISBN 978-0-9812807-0-7 (pbk.)
ISBN 978-0-9812807-1-4 (bound)

1. Social control--Philosophy. 2. Police--Philosophy. 3. Internal security--Philosophy. 4. Internal security--Economic aspects. 5. Police--Europe--History. 6. Enlightenment.

I. Rigakos, George

HV7903.G45 2009 303.3'601 C2009-904837-X

 Red Quill Books is an alternative publishing house. Proceeds from the sale of this book will support future critical scholarship.

Table of Contents

Introduction   1

Sir William Petty   35

Johann von Justi   53

Joseph von Sonnenfels   101

Sir John A Fielding   137

Adam Smith   149

Cesare Beccaria   163

Wilhelm von Humboldt   187

Jeremy Bentham   219

Patrick Colquhoun   243

Georg W.F. Hegel   277

Introduction:
Towards a critical political economy of police

George S. Rigakos, John L. McMullan, Joshua Johnson & Gulden Ozcan

The Enlightenment period of the late seventeenth to early nineteenth centuries is celebrated as an era of European ascendance. Amid internecine state wars, colonial exploitation and imperial campaigns, Europe blossomed in physics, architecture, political philosophy, economic theory and international trade and finance. This post-feudal period laid foundations for the economic progress and accompanying scientific and political rationalities that are considered the bedrock of contemporary 'western' civilization. Scholarly analyses of this *longue durée*, however, are typically silent on the relationship between the then important debates about the role of emerging states, the efficiency of bureaucratic systems, and the most economical and 'scientific' means of governance within a science of police. As a result, we have not sufficiently attended to notions of police established in works of early state theory, commerce or human nature written by authors such as Sir William Petty, Adam Smith, Wilhelm von Humboldt and Georg Hegel. Nor, by the same time token, have we sufficiently examined issues of wealth creation in works by legal theorists and police thinkers such as Cesare Beccaria, Jeremy Bentham and Patrick Colquhoun. These Enlightenment intellectuals (and others included in this anthology) applied themselves to fashioning or *re*-fashioning a *police science* –often directly formulating proposals aimed at imposing market, population and class forms of social control. In this volume, we examine this genealogy of police in its historical context in order to contribute to a critical understanding of contemporary debates about security.

The purpose of this anthology, therefore, is threefold. First, at a theoretical level, we aim to demonstrate the intimate yet overlooked conceptual connections between notions of social order and commerce in key political and economic works of the Enlightenment period. By mapping the economic and administrative projects of prosperity and police we can revive and add to a critique of the political economy of security. With few exceptions (e.g. Neocleous 2000; Pasquino 1991), such critiques have fallen through the disciplinary cracks of radical political economy, critical criminology and critical sociology. The result has been a silencing or abdication of "police science" to instrumental criminology. Critical scholars, perhaps unwittingly, have delimited this idea of police and, in particular, the police functions of classification, regulation and the management of the poor and labouring classes. This has led to critical interventions that are based on a partial appreciation of the longstanding and enduring connections between police, liberty, security and social order. Not surprisingly, some of the most important and well reasoned contemporary critical interrogations of security have overlooked this genealogy of police. As a result of this absence, such analyses have tended to (re)discover the liberal impulse to decentralize social control as 'net widening' (Cohen 1985); or, have lamented how the proliferation of 'securitization' (Loader 2002) permeates almost all facets of planning and commerce; or, have argued that our current epoch is the epoch of the 'camp' because security has, only recently come to trump liberty as the "state of exception" (Agamben 2005); or, have seized on the idea that the need for calculable foreknowledge has in the last four decades, produced a 'new risk society' (Beck 1999). Such perspectives are apt to lack an adequate engagement with the broad historical project of police. Second, we wish to provide a stronger political foundation for critical engagements with contemporary debates about police, surveillance, security, liberty and the current economic crisis. For us, modern issues ranging from policing a major recession, to the proliferation of surveillance technology, to post 9-11 security culture, and even liberal anxieties about the best "balance" between liberty and security are more analytically recognizable and intelligible when aided by an historically informed critique of security. Third, at a more modest level, this book aims to be a resource text for scholars and students seeking to engage in intellectual, theoretical and genealogical analyses of the police. This volume is by no means exhaustive. Nor can it be argued that the intellectuals we have selected are part of a single, coherent, tradition or project. Subsequent examinations of police will surely re-analyze, expand and amend our list of scholars. Nonetheless, we have done our best to produce a compilation of theoretical and practical works that can "[disturb] the obviousness of the present of modern western policing" (Hunt and Wickham 1998:128) and thus aid in furthering critical scholarship on policing and security.

The astute reader will detect that our approach to police entails more than studying uniformed peace officers and other current law enforcement functionaries. We aim to explore the "pre-disciplinary" form (Neocleous 2006:19: McMullan 1998) of police or policing "before the police" (Zedner 2006). Such an approach is rare (see also Dodsworth 2008). Typically, the notion of police is presented as a nineteenth century project doggedly pursued by forward-thinking reformers such as Sir Robert Peel (e.g. Critchley 1967) or, as a class-based initiative (e.g. Storch 1975) aimed at the moral and political control of an increasingly unruly urban proletariat. Sometimes students are provided with conservative and revisionist versions of police (see Reiner 1992) but they are unlikely to see policing as a grand intellectual project linked to state formation, prosperity and security in Enlightenment thought. Because this is our project, we are challenged with the issue of police etymology and with debates concerning the role, breadth, and function of police. Fortunately, Enlightenment thinkers have supplied us with clear definitions about how the police *ought* to be defined, how they *ought* to be deployed, and with whom they *ought* to be concerned. This approach to the subject of police has much to offer. It requires that students consider *inter alia* the very recent and contentious history of modern public policing; the entrepreneurial precursors of policing in the English context; the Continental roots and theoretical antecedents of the broader project of police aimed at general welfare; the far-reaching connections of police to political philosophy and the role of the state; the peculiar English intellectual xenophobia about Continental policing; the liberal philosophical basis for narrowing the roles and functions of police to crime detection and prevention; and the unambiguous link between the need for order in bourgeois Europe and the formation of a police system for administering the indigent and working poor.

Etymological considerations, therefore, alert us to three important themes of police thinking. First, we need to note the gradual *narrowing* of the concept of police from the seventeenth century to the nineteenth century. This has had several consequences for an understanding of police. To start, many contemporary scholars have uncritically accepted liberal definitions of police and ignored early mercantilist and cameralist conceptions. This has created disciplinary silos and has downgraded 'police science' from a master discipline aimed at the preservation and extension of the means of the state to a technical sub-discipline of instrumental criminology. Regrettably, police science has been "transformed beyond anything recognizable to earlier writers on police powers" – it has become a "backwater" field (Neocleous 2006:17). Second, English notions of police were based on a foreign, *Continental* 'other' viewpoint which significantly shaped considerations of the role of police and the legitimacy of the state. In this sense, debates about 'what the police ought to be' were also debates about 'what the state ought to be.' The project of police, when viewed from this etymological characteristic, is implicated with the project of nation-building since police seemed tied to national self-identity and wealth creation. To a great degree, this liberal compulsion still haunts national identities today – e.g. the westward marching RCMP, the friendly 'Bobbie', the nation-forging Carabiniere, etc.. Indeed, if and when state police monopolies are threatened, new calls emerge for their re-consolidation in order to defend or re-establish the 'public good' (Loader and Walker 2001). Third, while the contemporary notion of police is said to have emerged in the fifteenth century with the French-Burgundian policie, the term police is derived from the Greek word "city" and connotes all the problems of order maintenance that classical Hellenic city-states encountered. The constant re-animation of this etymological root in the works of political economists, political philosophers and police thinkers is fortuitous in that it directly equates, in definitional terms, the *problem of police* with the *problem of the city*. As we know, mass urbanization spawned dispossessed "sturdy vagabonds and masterless men" (McMullan 1998) who sent shivers through the ascendant bourgeois world in European capitals from Paris to London (Emsley 1999a; 1999b). The police project, therefore, is mainly an urban project.

The authors included in this anthology are considered scholarly giants in areas ranging from political philosophy to legal theory, political arithmetic and economics. We have selected their works for their intellectual prominence in shaping Enlightenment thought, their availability in English[1] and their contributions to police, security, and social order. Our 200-year time frame was daunting, as was determining the start and end point of the Enlightenment epoch. However, two significant and broad-ranging characteristics shaped our considerations. First, the collapse of the feudal system and the intense social disorganization that early capitalism unleashed created widespread instability and crises of order. This internal instability was coupled with a renewed external stability achieved through the 1648 Peace of Westphalia which ended the Thirty Years War and the Eighty Years War and the signing of the 1659 Treaty of the Pyrenees that ended the war between France and Spain. These treaties solidified the notion of state sovereignty and signalled a European-wide search for a new domestic order in the wake of extensive external warfare. The economic and political needs for stable trade and commerce, and for centralized power systems capable of enabling capitalist growth and imperial conquest resulted in new state experiments for adequate systems of order maintenance to guarantee prosperity through the maintenance of productive workforces – this was a direct impetus for the search for an adequate science of police. Second, the emergence of police science coincided with the defining characteristic of the Enlightenment period: the birth of the scientific method. The works collected in this book demonstrate the imperatives of this method: collecting as much empirical information as possible, attending to all constituent parts of a whole, and using knowledge to calculate and analyze in order to predict events with regularity. The birth of "political arithmetic" and the invention of statistics allowed for the study of the "body politic" in the form of "population." Foucault (1979) points to this intellectual re-casting of political subjects into aggregate objects of analysis as an essential step in making police science possible – what he called *bio-power*. These methods were often applied to a new science of prosperity achieved through managing populations for the benefit of the national wealth. Enlightenment scholars, we shall see, positioned their thinking between police, security, liberty, human nature and economic policy and established new institutional mechanisms and new forms of social relations in emerging political communities. It is a peculiar

---

1   For example, the important French work *Traite du Police* (1707) by Nicolas de La Mare is still unavailable in English.

condition of Enlightenment thought that individual freedom and the pursuit of security were seen as two sides of the same coin – one leading inevitably to the other. The guarantee of both liberty and security often came down to some level of state *force*, the exacting details of which were a matter of considerable debate. As Marx (1904:Div. I, part I) puts it: "[a]ll the bourgeois economists are aware… that production can be carried on better under the modern police…"

In what follows, we overview the relative contributions of police thinkers in this anthology. They are listed chronologically by the original publication date of their contribution as evinced in the Table of Contents. Broadly speaking, these contributions concerning police may be divided into three general schools: 1) mercantilism, which encouraged protectionist economic policy and whose general propensity was that of placing *capital in the service of the sovereign*; 2) cameralism, the closest German equivalent to mercantilism, which sought to create a science of *maximizing the collective welfare* of all through state regulation over, among other aspects, trade and commerce, and finally, 3) liberalism, which advocated the individual over the collective and reversed the logics of mercantilism by placing the *state in the service of capital*. Despite our grouping of these thinkers into three broad political approaches, we must concede that there are sometimes as many variations within these schools as between them. On the rather divisive issue of state reach, for example, liberal thinkers take familiar political positions but may disagree about the acceptable breadth of police practice. On the specific issue of police mandate, for example, thinkers such as Patrick Colquhoun and G.W.F. Hegel sometimes sound more like cameralists than liberals. When these variations emerge we point them out as best we can but the reader would do well to note that the three schools we have identified are not as insular as they may first appear. In what is to follow, we successively overview each school in chronological order bold-facing the authors' names whose works we include in this anthology when they are initially discussed.

Mercantilism

As a young student in Paris, **William Petty** studied with the political philosopher Thomas Hobbes and developed a close intellectual relationship. Of course, Hobbes' impact in the development of modern political thought is well known, so given the close relationship between Petty and Hobbes, it is important to discuss the major tenets of Hobbes' arguments. While Hobbes is frequently cited for his dismal view of human nature, it is rather his methodological approach which, in our opinion, makes him important in the history of social and political thought about police. The sixteenth and seventeenth centuries witnessed a scientific revolution: Descartes called for a new method of inquiry to ascertain truth, generating the basis for materialist and empiricist thinking. Bacon announced his inductive method and Galileo Galilei had provided mathematical rules of nature. Hobbes, of course, was affected by these new events. He constructed a language of political inquiry to corresponded to a proper empirical science that was grounded on principles similar to the study of geometry. He emphasized the importance of definitions and argued that the individual was the smallest element of a political community (Hobbes 1985:4:12,19) – a claim which is of central concern for understanding mercantilist conceptions of police. For Hobbes, science was defined as "the knowledge of consequences, and dependence of one fact upon another, by which, out of that we can presently do, we know how to do something else when we will, or the like, another time." To this he adds, "when we see how anything comes about, upon what causes, and by what manner, when the like causes come into our power, we can see how to make it produce the like effects" (Hobbes 1985:5:17, 25). Thus, methodology is paramount for sound epistemology (Hobbes 1985:5:20, 26). This was to be achieved through the meticulous defining of terms, the proper ordering of consequences, and the ability to produce the desired outcome in a predictable and reconstructable fashion. In his words: "*reason* is the *pace*; increase of *science*, the *way*; and the benefit of mankind, the *end*."

It is from this tradition that Petty learned to apply mathematical calculations to explain, control and estimate the nature, wealth and order of a political community. In so doing, he established the early science of statistics or "political arithmetic" which laid the foundations for all of political economy (Rigakos and Hadden 2001:64)· Even Marx (1904:Appendix A: Historical Notes... fn. 2.) wrote of Petty's "audacious genius" for so early recognizing that the source of wealth under capitalism was labour-power. Petty proposed transporting "all of the movables and People" of Ireland and Scotland to Britain in order to increase productivity (Petty 1690:225). More recently, Linebaugh (1991:48) noted that Petty "found in Ireland that people were not willing to work more than two hours a day" so he deduced that "by expropriating the people from the land and forcing them to migrate" he could produce "spare hands" to produce millions for the economy. His desire to render the scientific socially useful is apparent in "The Petty Papers," where he insisted that, in order to prevent the abuse of law and society, a battery of measures could be taken to render individuals accountable and statistically transparent. He grasped the surveillance needs of an emerging capitalist economy by calling for everyone over 18 to be "enjoyed to have a seal, on which let be engraved his name and time of birth; the colour of his eye, and hair, and shape of nose, in cabula, whereby it may *semper constare de persona*" (Petty 1927b:XXIII, 142:204). In discussing the provisions for the poor, Petty sought to obtain as much information as possible about them, from an exact account of each person within every parish, to their relations, where they were born and bred, and ultimately, which class of poor they can be assigned to (Petty 1927b:XXIII, 145:210). He justified the need for statistical data by describing its benefits for preventing crimes. He proposed "[t]hat all men be bound to keep accounts of their receipts and issues, gain and lose, debts and credits, cattle and goods, and where they were at noon and at night every day in the year; with mention of what deeds he had made or witnessed" (Petty 1927b:XXIII, 145:211-212). Clearly, his preventive measures were to be achieved by rendering the identities, actions, and movements of all persons statistically visible. This attention to ethnographic detail along with his prescription that highways be guarded, that no house stand alone, and that "cattle be disposed of in markets and fairs," reveals the logic of Petty's political arithmetic, namely a detailed ordering of society and the formation of new types of social control in the wake of the demise of feudal arrangements.

The drive to perfect social control is perhaps nowhere more evident than in Petty's "London Wall" project, where he laid out a plan to encircle the city with a "wall of 100m foot in circumference, 11 foot high, 2 brick thick, in a fortification figure, with 20 gates, worth 20£"(Petty 1927a:II, 11:32). The multiple functions of the wall included acting as "a certain visible boundary of property and impositions," functioning as a mechanism to "take an account of all persons and things going in and out of the city," to "increase the value of enclosed lands," and, ultimately, operating as "a foundation of liberties, securities, and privileges." What is strikingly impressive about Petty's vision of social control is his willingness to leap from issues of criminality to economy; from banishment to regulations and to develop wealth and enforce order without distinguishing between the two. As Rigakos and Hadden (2001:70) put it: "the structure of the city, in Petty's vision, is best regarded as a monolithic, panoptic, instrument of data collection designed to measure, calculate and accrue wealth." Mykkänen (1994:75) observes, that this is perhaps the first instance in which city gates were to be "guarded not by sword but by pen". So, by pursuing the Hobbesian principle that politics ought to be rendered a science, Petty developed a technique of social analytics that drew the borders of the city, divided it in small pieces, then built a new complex one again. The ultimate objective was a totality whose every component was known in detail so that planning for the future was imminently possible. In the end, Petty developed an early technique of social control that emphasized inspection, registration, surveillance, the accumulation of wealth and the ongoing monitoring of social problems.

Cameralism

The idea that techniques of social control should simultaneously be techniques of wealth accumulation was also an idea that was central to the first police sciences of the German cameralists. **Johann von Justi's** studies of *staatswirthschaft* and *polizeiwissenschaft* in the mid eighteenth century is exemplary. For von Justi, the business of the ruler is divided into two functions, the first being the preservation and expansion of the means of the state, and the second being the proper application of these means "both in use and in thrift." Statecraft, *policey*, commercial sciences, and economic sciences all referred to the former, while "cameralism proper" referred to application of the means of the state (von Justi 1755:53). The fundamental principle of cameralism is best expressed as follows: "In all transactions with the 'readiest means' of the state, the aim must be to seek the common happiness of the ruler and the subjects" (von Justi 1755:24). The underlying objective of stateship for von Justi was calibrating mutual obligations, or rather the social contract, between the people and the sovereign while avoiding conflicting interests which were not necessary and made little sense.

> ...for when the subjects have placed over themselves a supreme power (sic), from which they demand that it shall promote their happiness, they are naturally bound to conform to those arrangements which that supreme power adopts for their happiness, and to promote them in every way, otherwise they would obstruct their own ultimate purpose. (von Justi 1755:333)

Thus, von Justi's understanding of social contract diverged from Hobbes and Petty. While Petty's understanding of social contract led him to argue that the techniques of good government were the exclusive purview of the state and its institutions; and that the population was a passive object to be known, von Justi's understanding followed Rousseau which led him formulate a 'welfare of the state' as well as a 'welfare of the people.' Contrary to Petty's Hobbesian vision, von Justi conceived the state as omnipotent but within the context of civilian obligations and responsibilities and thus more collectivist than individualistic. So, at bottom, the state for von Justi, was formulated as a single unity, a cohesive whole that did not recognize interest as a pluralized or individualized concept.

The state had as its ultimate end the common happiness, but this begs the question: what is common happiness? For von Justi, it is a condition wherein subjects enjoy reasonable freedom, and attain the goods required for satisfactory living, the measure of which, however, was contingent upon social standing. Three factors were specified by von Justi: "freedom, assured property, and flourishing industry" (von Justi 1755:65-70). Freedom entailed a hefty degree of security, both from without and from within and, for von Justi, this marked the role of statecraft [*staatknust*]. Assured property and flourishing industry, evinced the idea of a state of living where prosperity went hand in hand with security. As Neocleous (2000:13) observes, in the wake of the Thirty Years War and the Peace of Westphalia (1648), the modern state was faced with the challenges of modernizing warfare and international relations, which necessitated a sound fiscal footing for security, and a sound cameralist conception of freedom for the state to develop. For von Justi, it made little sense to separate the good of the sovereign and the good of the subject, since the state required increasing wealth for its own security and the good, or happiness, of the subjects were tied to the development of wealth. There is no separation between political and economic spheres in cameralist thinking.

If statecraft concerns itself with security and wealth, the police sciences [*Polizeiwissenchaft*] were primarily concerned with the preservation and extension of the means of the state on which the security and happiness of all depended. Von Justi (1756:437) sought to enhance the power of the republic through the proper cultivation of land, improvement of the labouring class, and the maintenance of order and discipline in the community. But for him, the line between *polizeiwissenchaft* and *staatknust* could not be too finely drawn. While both goals were separated, policey was "the ground of genuine cameral science, and the police expert must sow if the cameralist is to reap" (von Justi 1756:437). *Policey* was inherently engaged in an effort to manage economic cultivation through direct government action. Similar to the British mercantilist Sir James Steuart (1767) who early on argued for 'national security,' von Justi insisted that a country ought to produce its own goods for need and comfort within its own protectionist borders. He added: "everything that the land produces shall, so far as possible, be worked over to its complete form, and shall not be allowed to leave the country in a raw and unfinished state" (von Justi 1756:446-7). In this view, the more finished goods were exported, the more surplus-value had been added to them, the more labour was employed in their production, the higher the concentration of wealth to the nation. The government thus had an obligation to obtain precise information pertaining to tariffs, excises, licence sheets, and all exported goods in order to properly manage its function of *policey*. In the name of encouraging the development of wealth, *polizeiwissenchaft*, the first of the police sciences, was directly concerned with the accrual of wealth and had this as one of its fundamental objectives.

Acording to Albion Small, the cameralist era closes in the mid to late eighteenth century with the philosophy of **Joseph von Sonnenfels**. Familiar cameralist impulses were developed in Sonnenfels work, including the inseparability between the interests of the state and the subject and the unremitting pursuit of common happiness. Sonnenfels, however, elaborated on von Justi's notion of common happiness and, in keeping with the empiricism of the times, he chastized him for not developing a quantifiable measurement of the concept. In contradistinction to von Justi, Sonnenfels argued that civil society is constructed by individuals who seek to advance their personal safety and their powers for satisfying needs and wants. Two people united were more secure and productive than one, and three more so than two. Thus, the greater the population, the more secure and productive the state, the greater the general happiness of all. While Sonnenfels' argument seems Hobbesian, it differs from the latter's individualism. For Hobbes, individuals came together to form a political community not because it was safer for the collective, but because it was an unfortunate necessity for the protection of each against the other. The contractual power of the sovereign for Hobbes was an unavoidable individual necessity born out the fear of one's own neighbour. Sovereign power, for von Sonnefels, was rather a manifestation of the competitive yet collective will of domestic subjects against the intrusion of outsiders. Put simply, that which increases the population increases the general happiness, and that which diminishes the one, diminishes the other.

The politics of happiness was the ultimate end of *Staatwissenschaft*, and *Polizeywissenschaft* was a subordinate science designed to support and advance this end through the preservation of internal security. For Sonnenfels, the definition of *Polizey* included defence against "intentional" or "fortuitous occurrences" of a "harmful nature," as well as anything that did not contribute to the ultimate purpose of the state. So, everything from proper religious education and duties, acceptable civic education, censorship, and the cultivation of a requisite adulation of laws fell within the purview of Sonnenfels' *polizey*. He also cautioned that *polizey* should not foster "excessive" spying and house-visitation, but it should prevent public indecency by restricting occasions for drunkeness and lodging with strangers, which might corrupt the moral character of subjects. Thus, for him, the number of dram shops should be limited in order to control drunkenness, and the number of feast days should be lessened, as time spent at labour is time rescued from vice and excess. Sonnenfels (1765:§138) also emphasized the importance of deterring the rise of factions able to challenge the "forces or means" of the state "in the exercise of its powers [which] consist[ed] of *wealth, of the strength of a stratum of society, and of privileges.*" Managing wealth, as well as managing labour was thus inherent to the police purview of cameralism.

Polizeywissenschaft seems to take on a modified meaning in Sonnenfels' thought when compared to von Justi's. The latter centred his science on economic questions by stressing the importance of the means of the state. He downplayed the "means" of the state and separated *polizey* more sharply from the management of gainful occupations and the raising of revenues necessary for the expenses of the state. While Sonnenfels acknowledged that commerce is the foundation of public welfare, and that the multiplication of the means of subsistence is the basis for the quantitative measurement of general happiness, *polizey* was only one of four subordinate sciences that fell under the general umbrellas of *staatswissenschaft*. While the specific nature of *polizey* was economically restricted, in von Sonnenfels vision it was still part and parcel of the larger picture of developing a state of prosperity. Thus, from the cameralist tradition in continental Europe there emerged a conception of police science that was intrinsically bound to both the means of the state and the development of wealth.

Liberalism

While the cameralists of continental Europe developed a theory of the state which encompassed all aspects of the lives, securities, and economies of its subjects, the English writer, **Sir John A. Fielding** articulated his own conception of an interventionist state based on the liberal notion of commercial self-interest and the need for crime prevention. There was a natural distrust of the concept of police in England in the eighteenth century and his brother, the novelist, Henry Fielding avoided the term in his *Enquiry into the Causes of the Late Increase of Robberies* (1751), which is generally regarded as the first significant work on preventative police in England. Henry Fielding's work was referred to in "police literatures" by later authors, clearly influencing their thinking (see for e.g. Blizard 1785; Colquhoun 1800b; Hanway 1775). Indeed the "Bow Street patrol" that he and his brother John established was called a "new kind of police" by John Brown (1757) in his discussion of the morals and manners of the times. John Fielding, however, was likely the first Englishman to write a work concerned with police in his *An Account of the Origin and Effects of a Police Set on Foot* (1758). In this work and in his earlier pamphlet *A Plan for Preventing Robberies within twenty miles of London* (1775), he went to great lengths to identify the "lower orders" as the source of riots, immorality, tumultuous assemblies and crime and to dispel any authoritarian images in his Henry's project for the Bow Street Runners (Fielding 1775:2). Fielding praised the efforts of his brother and various thieftakers associated with him for their bravery and effectiveness in crime fighting and for developing a police strategy the value of which was to create a situation wherein a magistrate could react to any robbery, outrage or violence by calling together "brave and reputable men, always ready to pursue and attack the most daring villain" (Fielding 1775:3). While acknowledging that "now and again a single street-robber or house-breaker may be successful" he emphasized that it was important to engage in prevention so that it would always be "impossible for a number of them to form themselves into a gang." Fielding (1775:4) admitted that crimes were indeed committed by thieftakers themselves who "prostituted" their services by "procuring both public and private rewards, at the shameful and shocking price of innocent blood" but he downplayed this official form of crime, saying that permanent officers charged with the prevention of crimes were not as dangerous as criminal gangs. Fielding insisted, in the end, that an agency of crime prevention was a valuable and necessary service to society.

To make his case, he described what he called the dismal state of affairs surrounding London, where more robberies occurred per year than any other part of the kingdom, and where not one in one hundred of the robbers were apprehended (Fielding 1775:7-8). Fielding had several strategies for the prevention of crime including stricter censorship of public activities, tougher regulations regarding the drink trade, money lending and pawn broking, closer inspection and supervision of itinerants, vagrants and paupers and more enlightened civic training and tutelage of the lower orders. His central focus, however, was to create a standing provision of magistrates and thieftakers able to detect and apprehend burglars; and a crime control system whereby information concerning burglaries could quickly and efficiently be communicated and disseminated throughout local communities. A community watch was envisioned that could distribute relevant information regarding the offender, the horse used, and the property stolen to proper authorities (Fielding 1775:12). This information would then be relayed to appropriate community alehouses, public inns, stable-keepers, and pawnbrokers. The first two locations presented the likelihood of immediately identifying the person, while the second two offered the possibility of tracing a criminal who rented a horse or attempted to sell stolen goods. The medium for the exchange and dissemination of information was the daily paper: *The Public Advertiser* (Fielding 1775:18).

In addition to crime advertising, investigation and surveillance, another essential feature of Fielding's policing plan was that the Bow Street office should become the administrative nerve-centre for policing. He set out principles, instructions, procedures and powers for police work, reorganized paid patrols of part-time constables in and around the streets of London, increased the number of principal police offices in the region, and created a small policing bureaucracy for the city of London that standardized police training, record keeping and communications and cultivated work morale among both private thief-takers and paid constables. As Fielding (1758) remarked, "When the constables are collected together, known to each other and bound by connection of good fellowship, friendship, and bonds of society, they.... are a formidable body." John Fielding's vision of police was based on market interests as well as state reform and it did not radically alter the existing character of the English civil power. His ideas intensified surveillance by harnessing the voluntary principle to self-interest and to money. Police still relied on their private hires to pay fees or inducements for services as their principal form of remuneration and so the growing networks of police offices were also stock exchanges in policing provision. As McMullan (1996:104-5) puts it, "the new improved monied police" were hybrids that were not mostly the planned result of official state policy but instead were often creatures of the market in the selling and trading of information created by the spread of private rewards, the commercial compromise of the state and the appeal to public spirit to fight crime.

The Fielding's emphasized a proactive preventative police alongside a detective strategy. Their idea of police, however, was never fully realized. While they received funds from state coffers to implement a plan for the metropolis of London, John Fielding's grand vision for police reform for all of England by means of a systemized and centralized public knowledge and vigilance of crime was not realized. While their efforts resulted in greater surveillance over the metropolitan population of London, the idea of a nationally linked police force was seen as too far reaching because it was too costly, perceived as a threat to local government, and seemed unpopular with the public who were reluctant to act as information brokers of crime (McMullan 1996:102). Nevertheless, John Fielding's "great preventative machine" commodified policing in the late 18th century while simultaneously encouraging a state service function. It comprised many of the nascent principles of the modern concept of police, subject of course, to the discipline of the market-place and not yet under the eye of a single authority.

Adam Smith's contribution to police theory is perhaps best seen in his early work which straddled the intellectual traditions of cameralism and liberalism. While he is most famous for his *Inquiry Into the Nature and Causes of the Wealth of Nations* (1776), it is his earlier *Lectures on Justice, Police, Revenue and Arms* (1763) that reveal his ideas of police and its appropriate applications. Smith identified police as his second general division of jurisprudence and noted that the word originated with the Greeks. Neocleous (2000:24) suggests that Smith's attention to this detail was part of a strategy to legitimate the idea of police by associating it with the positive virtues of ancient Greece rather than the negative values of European absolutism. Indeed, the Greek origin of the term police was also referred to by the cameralists. Smith defined police as "the regulation of the inferior parts of government, viz: cleanliness, security and cheapness or plenty" (Smith 1763:154). It was the latter economic function of police that was the most important for Smith because, in his view, "the most proper way of procuring wealth and abundance" went a large distance in providing for security and cleanliness. Smith directly linked crime to poverty and argued if crime was the effect of poverty, then poverty was the effect of dependency and this necessitated a type of work-place police that would ostensibly free individuals from their dependency. In his words: "Nothing tends so much to corrupt mankind as dependency, while independency still increases the honesty of people. The establishment of commerce and manufactures, which brings about this independency, is the best police for preventing crimes" (Smith 1763:155-6).

For Smith, the primacy of commerce and manufacture in countering crime could not be overemphasized, and this meant reforming outdated feudal notions of production. Under feudalism peasants had no motive to increase their wealth when a capricious landlord could simply consume their surplus produce. "Thus there could be little accumulation of wealth at all," explained Smith (2004 1763:220), "but after the fall of the feudal government these obstacles to industry were removed, and the stock of commodities began gradually to increase." Smith (2004 1763:223-4) insisted that the accumulation of wealth required not only the development of a more elaborate division of labour, but also the creation of a sufficiently strong government that was "so great as to defend the produce of industry." Feudalism was at odds with civilized society in Smith's mind because civilized society had a broader role to play in arranging its economic relations to foster commerce and industry through the division of labour and the creation of wealth. While he pointed out errors of police, such as when the police prohibit the exportation of corn, the general idea of the police was crucial to the development of national wealth.

A remarkable change occurred in Smith's idea of police with the publication of *Wealth of Nations* (1776). In what was to become a classic economic text, Smith discussed labour power and the necessities and conveniences of life supplied by it and the balance between production and consumption which, in his words, should "in every nation be regulated by two different circumstances;" first, by labour's "skill, dexterity, and judgment" and second, by the proportion of those "employed in useful labour" with "those who are not so employed" (Smith 1776:2). Smith signalled that his main concern would be labour and, in particular, productive labour, both in its quality and its quantity. It is in this context that the concept of police was reformulated as a source of criticism rather than a positive development. For example, Smith referred to the 'English Statute of Apprenticeship,' which stipulated that nobody should exercise any "trade, craft, or mystery" without having first served an apprenticeship for seven years and noted rather derisively that "[t]his limitation has given occasion to several distinctions, which, considered as rules of police, appears as foolish as can be imagined" (1776:88). He then contrasted this state of affairs with the situation in Scotland, where no universal laws had been imposed upon corporations, and commented approvingly: "I know of no country in Europe, in which corporation laws are so little oppressive." Interestingly, and in a clear break with cameralism and his own earlier works, Smith distinguished positive and negative economic intervention by the state, and argued that property resided in individual's labour, which is the foundation for all other property. Suddenly, in Smith's work, the state is seen as overstepping its powers and duties by tampering with the conditions by which a person is "free" to sell their labour:

> The patrimony of a poor man lies in the strength and dexterity of his hands; and to hinder from employing this strength and dexterity in what manner he thinks proper, without injury to his neighbour is a plain violation of this most sacred property. (Smith 1776:88)

Smith stated his contempt for the police forcefully: "The affected anxiety of the lawgiver, lest they should employ an improper person, is evidently as impertinent as it is oppressive." Of course, his endorsement of the freedom of labourers to dispose of their property as they pleased should not be mistaken as an argument for a full, rounded concept of liberty. Smith's primary concern remained that of properly deploying labour to its maximum potential, and his exhortation of freedom ends with an economic calculus. Apprenticeships are not only unnecessary, given the simplicity that machinery makes of labour, he wrote, but they also tend to corrupt the spirit of young workers by withholding from them the recompense of their labour. This regulation and policing of labour, Smith (1937, orig. 1776:89) asserted, will create a general aversion to work and, moreover, those who are committed to the longest apprenticeships are more likely to be "very idle and worthless." In the end, Smith's critique of the police function within the economy had much to do with the police propensity to deprive the nation of valuable productive assets. What is to be done with the labourer? Smith's lamentation of the conditions of the apprentice is reminiscent of an earlier argument where he described the labour of a country worker, who is was "almost always slothful and lazy, and incapable of any vigorous application, even on the most pressing occasions" (Smith 1776:6-7). Smith attributed the unproductive nature of the country worker to the fact he had to change tasks over the course of a day, arguing through this example for the superiority of a specialized division of labour. For Smith, police were not really required to increase the quality of labour; this was achieved through the division of labour, which maximized dexterity, eliminated wasted time, and calibrated the use of machinery. With the *Wealth of Nations*, Smith theorized the idea of police to the margins of society. The market, he insisted, will produce its own forms of social control and guarantee a wealthy nation.

While Smith was honing his doubts about the role of the police, **Cesare Beccaria** published his treatise *Of Crimes and Punishments* (1764). If Smith sought to undermine the intellectual basis for state intervention in the economy, Beccaria provided a theory on the state's need to adequately punish criminals on behalf of society. Beccaria developed his critique of the European penal system in the philosophical doctrine of the social contract., but he positioned his thinking as well in the liberal tradition pioneered by Jean-Jacques Rousseau. Becarria (1996 1764:11) explained:

> Laws are the conditions under which independent and isolated men united to form a society. Weary of living in a continual state of war, and enjoying liberty rendered useless by the uncertainty of preserving it, they sacrificed a part so that they might enjoy the rest of it in peace and safety.

The twinning of liberty and security was not surprising given the necessities of coercion and social control implied in the latter and the total absence of the same in the former. While this coupling caused little concern for the cameralists,

Beccaria faced a unique challenge because he connected his notion of liberty to radical individuality, a notion that was altogether denied in the cameralist school and unflinchingly subverted in Hobbes. Like Hobbes', egoism and self-interest are intractable realities of the social contract. No person, he said, gives up their liberty for the sake of the common good alone. Such a chimera "exists only in romances" (Beccaria 1764:12). To the contrary, people avoided their compactual responsibilities if they had the opportunity to do so. He remarked: "If it were possible, every one of us would prefer that the compacts binding others did not bind us; every man tends to make himself the center of his own universe" (Beccaria 1764:11). For Hobbes, this egoism was suppressed through the strong mechanism of the commonwealth, but Beccaria barely acknowledged the threat of "the despotic spirit, which is in every man" or discussed how it could be managed through punishments to infractions of laws. What separated Beccaria (1764:12) from Hobbes and the cameralists was his insistence that the liberty taken from the individual must be minimal:

> It was, thus, necessity that forced men to give up part of their personal liberty, and it is certain, therefore, that each is willing to place in the public fund only the least possible portion, no more than suffice to induce others to defend it. The aggregate of these least possible portions constitutes the right to punish: all that exceeds this is abuse and not justice; it is fact but by no means right.

Smith's economic liberalism was mirrored in Beccaria's liberal discourse regarding crime and punishment where state authority and expertise was viewed suspiciously. While Smith lamented the unnecessary economic intrusions of the state, Beccaria deplored its overextension, irrationality and harshness, especially in the sphere of punishment. Torture, he said (Beccaria 1764:30-2), failed to achieve any good, because it tended to absolve "robust scoundrels" who were able to withstand the pain, and were therefore punished less than they ought to by being released, and to condemn innocent persons if they happen to be weak in body and mind. Beccaria also denounced the death penalty from a Rousseaunian perspective, stating that the sovereignty of laws emanates from the surrender of the private liberty of the subject. He asked: "Was there ever a man who can have wished to leave to other men the choice of killing him?" Not likely, and so Beccaria (1764:45) responds, "The punishment of death, therefore, is not a right." In contrast to Petty, who had no qualms about using the death penalty to achieve social goals, Beccari questioned the state's powers and inisisted on the separation of forces within the state in order to have checks and balances between legislation, executive power and juridicalism.

When it came to punishment, prevention was preferred over pain. Beccaria explained: "It is better to prevent crimes than to punish them. This is the ultimate end of every good legislation, which... is the art of leading men to the greatest possible happiness or to the least possible unhappiness." While this was a noble aim, Beccaria (1764:93-4) also distanced himself from the cameralists by arguing that the state should not be overzealous in limiting social actions that may eventually lead to crime. He observed: "To what should we be reduced if everything were forbidden us that might induce us to crime! It would be necessary to deprive man of the use of his senses." On the one hand, Beccaria confronted the egoism and self-interest inherent in basic liberal principles, on the other hand he refused to abandon a commitment to the sacredness of individuality. Prevention for Beccaria (1764:94) was allied to the quality of the laws per se, and was best directed at individuals qua individuals: He wrote: "See to it that the laws favour not so much classes of men as men themselves." His liberal individualism replaced class divisions and, according to Borkenau (1976:463), through this legal fiction class struggle was "brought down to the level of.. individual material interests." Thus, the liberal tenet of hedonistic calculus upon which Beccaria based his penology "knows only the egoism which strives for power and knows only one difference: that between its permissable and its impermissable manifestation." When the laws are clear, Beccaria argued, and "the entire force of a nation is united in their defence," no persons are left who would seek to subvert them. For Beccaria, the proper use of law had a universalizing effect for individuals and was connected to another important preventative measure: namely, the civilizing impacts of education that accompanies liberty. Beccaria (1764:95) pronounced: "no enlightened person can fail to approve of the clear and useful public compacts of mutual security" when weighing the "portion of the useless liberty he himself has sacrificed" with the totalities of "liberties sacrificed by other men, which, except for the laws, might have been turned against him."

The message was clear. For Beccaria, if people were sufficiently aware of the advantages to law-abiding behaviour then crime would not be a problem. The best measure for preventing crime is achieved through perfecting civic education and morals. Thus, population control and police took another form in Beccaria's plan to prevent crime. It became less a matter of the state concerning itself with the affairs of the nation so much as the state's ability to properly orientate people so that they conceived themselves as willing subjects of their own interests. This liberal tenet of self-correction based on knowledge of civic responsibility and deterrence through a minimal state was the cornerstone of what Foucault (1991) later identified as liberal *governmentality*. Obedience in this view was not achieved through pastoral confessions or the righteous wrath of divine sovereigns but rather through a rational system that disciplined individuals and populations through routine surveillance and civic education. Beccaria expressed an important attribute of liberalism that resonated across Europe and influenced the works of his English contemporary Jeremy Bentham. In this vision of social order, the state served its purpose best by narrowing its reasons for being and by accepting the proposition that the more it is forced to punish and police the more it revealed its impotence.

We have seen in Smith's and Beccaria's writings the emergence of a liberal tradition of police that distrusts the mechanism of the state in both the economic and criminal justice fields. The German thinker **Wilhelm von Humboldt** nicely reflected this ambivalence in his work on the *The Limits of State Action* (1792). He begins his work with the premise that man's ultimate goal is the "development of his powers to a complete and consistent whole," (von Humboldt 1792:16) and he demarcates his position from the cameralist tradition by arguing that man may be best conceptualized as a "whole" unto himself, without reference to the state. This is not to say that man is not social; rather, for Humboldt, individuals required both freedom, the "first and indispensable condition" of life, and mutual cooperation, "the second condition", where personal independence was combined with intimate relationships to allow individuals to experience and possess the qualities of others. As von Humboldt (1792:32) explained, "men are not to unite themselves in order forgo any portion of their individuality, but only to lessen the exclusiveness of their isolation." He adopted the early liberal idea that people were not inherently social, but that they need a social environment to fulfil their vital needs and desires. For Humboldt, society was not natural but rather a conventional necessity for expressing and furthering people's free existence. This conception of human individuality guided the central question of his work concerning the limitations of state action.

von Humboldt's project revolved around the instances where the state *can* legitimately intervene in the lives of individuals. For him, the state's prerogative to act is tied to security. "Without security", he wrote, "it is impossible for man either to develop his powers, or to enjoy the fruits of so doing; for without security, there is no freedom" (von Humboldt 1792:43). Security, of course, was not unfamiliar to the cameralists, and was central to the *staatknust* of von Justi and the *staatskugheit* of Sonnenfels. However, the narrowness of von Humboldt's definition of security, when compared to that of von Justi and Sonnenfels is noteworthy. Security, for von Humboldt, is operationalized as individuals in conflict with other individuals and their rights. "Positive welfare," the attempt to shape a citizen's outward life to forestall actions contrary to the state's intentions, or to hold sway over thoughts, opinions and feelings of others, was displaced in his work by the "negative welfare" of the citizen. It is worth remembering that positive welfare actively promoted the conditions of its members by formulating and implementing policies directed towards improving agriculture, industry, and commerce. But von Humboldt (1792:24) was sceptical and argued that these measures do more harm than good, engendering a spirit of dependency, stunting creativity, and ultimately weakening the vitality of the nation. For him, the bonds forged by the civil compact offer greater space for growth and ingenuity than the relations and institutions spawned by a supra-societal state. Moreover, von Humboldt was confident that dangerous occupations and industrial manufacturing worked best when they were self-regulated. "Agreements to this kind," he said, "are infinitely to be preferred to any state arrangements." When economic regulations spring from the vested individuals, they are likely to be more wisely applied, more rigidly observed, and be less harmful to the character of the citizen. He proferred: "[t]he best efforts of the State should therefore aim at bringing men into such a condition by means of freedom, that associations would arise with greater ease, and to take the place of political regulations in these and many kinds of similar instances" (von Humboldt 1792:91). These "similar instances", he noted, include education, religious doctrine and public morality: all of which were foundational pillars for cameralist science, and all of which were now placed outside the purview of state action by von Humboldt.

In discussing the police, von Humboldt argued that the state should only be allowed to restrict those actions of individuals which infringed on others. He conceived of harm in narrow terms and argued that to harm a person an infringement of an individual right must occur. As he put it:

> In order to provide for the security of its citizens, the state must prohibit or restrict such actions, relating directly to the agents only, as imply in their consequences the infringements of others' rights, or encroach on their freedom or property without their consent or against their will. (von Humboldt 1792:90)

Any other type of action relating to persons that might encroach on an individual freedom, he said, should be outside the object of state intervention. The term "rights" was not well defined by von Humboldt but he twinned property with freedom as did other social contract theorists such as Smith and Beccaria and he argued that the interests of civil society were deeply connected to property, its policing and protection.

While the continental liberals attempted to curtail the state's role and legitimacy in civil society, the English liberal reformer **Jeremy Bentham** argued that population control was quite properly a matter of state action. *The Panopticon Writings*, published in 1787, aimed at reforming penology so that it was economic, efficient, and effective. At the centre of Bentham's scheme for prison reform was a technique of surveillance that rendered itself ambiguous to the objects under surveillance. Control was achieved through a circular architectural structure where cells occupied the circumference with an inspector situated in a lodge at the centre of the prison. Blinds and partitions located in the lodge and the careful use and manipulation of lighting, would allow the inspector invisibility from the prisoners in exterior cells, while simultaneously making all prisoners transparent at all times to the gaze of the guard. For Bentham (1787:letter V), the essence of the panopticon lied "in the *centrality* of the inspector's situation, combined with the well-known and most effectual contrivances for *seeing without being seen.*" The final product of this panopticon was an occupant who could neither confirm nor deny the fact of their own surveillance. "[T]he *apparent omnipresence* of the inspector (if divines will allow me the expression)", he wrote, combined with the extreme facility of his *real presence*" (Bentham 1787:letter VI) makes prisoners and guards transparent. According to Foucault (1977), the technical, rational and architectural replacement of the 'eye of God' signalled the making of the liberal subject as the bearer of their own surveillance. While Foucault (1980) was reticent to claim the panopticon was a metaphor for modern surveillance society, Bentham was not so reserved. Perhaps as a result, Bentham's panopticon has been widely cited as a metaphor for understanding contemporary post-modern societies (e.g. Bogard 1996; Dandeker 1990; Gandy 1993; Lyon 1994) Bentham's list of possible applications of the panopticon is impressive and, by Bentham's own account, more accurately reflects a discourse on general social control than just prison reform:

> No matter how different, or even opposite the purpose: whether it be that of punishing the incorrigible, guarding the insane, reforming the vicious, confining the suspected, employing the idle, maintaining the helpless, curing the sick, instructing the willing in any branch of industry, or training the rising race in the path of education: in a word, whether it be applied to the purposes of perpetual prisons in the room of death, or prisons for confinement before trial, or penitentiary-houses, or houses of correction, or work-houses, or manufactories, or mad-houses, or hospitals, or schools...(Bentham 1787:letter I)

Bentham also suggested that he had found a satisfactory answer to the most puzzling of political questions: "*quis custodiet ipsos custodies* (who will guard the guards themselves)"? He explained that his panoptic plan was "not less beneficial to what is called *liberty*," as it made coercion less necessary by acting "as a controul upon subordinate power" thus providing "a shield to innocence, than as a scourge to guilt" (Bentham 1787:letter VI). Of course, a final interesting claim here was that this technique of surveillance was simultaneously a technique of liberty. Like Beccaria and von Humboldt, security and liberty for Bentham were also difficult to disentangle. In *Principles of the Civil Code* (1843), he argued that "a clear idea of liberty will lead us to regard it as a branch of security" (Bentham 1843:302,

307). Thus, surveillance was not only beneficial for controlling delinquents, but it also protected those under surveillance by expanding surveillance to those who were not even under suspicion of wrongdoing—a remarkable notion, given the liberal tradition's purported disdain for an overzealous state. Liberty, for Bentham, required not a small measure of security, but an all pervasive gaze by the state not necessarily to detect and punish the guilty but to testify to innocence – an eerily familiar refrain in contemporary post-9/11 North America.

The idea of surveillance as a method of social control resonated with Bentham's contemporary, **Patrick Colquhoun**. Like Bentham, Colquhoun was not as much interested in the punishment of criminals as in developing a system where crime could be anticipated, managed and prevented. In *Treatise on the Police of the Metropolis* (1795), the role of the police was designated in the preface with a broad mandate:

> Police in this country may be considered as a new science; the properties of which consist not in the Judicial Powers which lead to Punishment, and which belong to Magistrates alone; but in the Prevention and Detection of Crimes, and in those other functions which relate to internal regulations for the well ordering and comfort of civil society.

Colquhoun saw much lacking in the existing state of affairs at the end of the eighteenth century, and he identified a host of improvements that could be made, including the reform of punishment, a better system of hulks, and the establishment of a proper penitentiary house for the reformation of convicts. Most importantly, like the Fieldings, he called for a nationally unified police service capable of data collection, information dissemination, crime detection and crime prevention (see also Colquhoun 1799; Colquhoun 1800b:24-7).

Colquhoun was especially concerned with the causes of crime and he connected crime to social, moral and economic conditions associated with poverty. He was quick to point out, however, that by "poor" he did not mean those whose poverty forced them into labour. "Labour", he declared, was "absolutely requisite to the existence of all Governments; and it is from the poor only that labour can be expected, so far from being an evil, they become, under proper regulations, and advantage to every country" (Colquhoun 1800b:366). The "evil," of poverty, as he put it, was "to be found only in indigence," which included those unable to obtain subsistence due to disease or age, as well as those who were willing to work, but were unable to find employment. For Colquhoun, the economic system that generates wealth must by necessity produce poverty. Colquhoun remarked that, "the poor" did not include "the whole mass of the people who support[ed] themselves by labour" but rather those who by "necessity" were compelled "to exercise their industry." For Colquhoun (1800b:365), those compelled to work

class of criminals.   Socially and economically, Colquhoun (1800a:13) called for the personification of panopticism in the form of a general police able and willing to provide an improved state of society where the conditions of "constant vigilance and attention" prevailed.

Throughout his *Treatise on the Police*, Colquhoun stressed that because the lower classes had grown apart from their rulers and communities and the "force of religion or the influence of moral principle" no longer governed them, they were in need of new technical police operations – a central board of police, a pauper police institution, a registry of all lodging houses and their occupants, a system of licenses for all traders a compendium of criminal offenders, a criminal intelligence and exchange centre, a police gazette, an office of public prosecutor, and a police of the river Thames – all of which would ensure the "blessings of true liberty", the "enjoyment of property" and the "preservation of public order" (Colquhoun 1800b:preface).   Police, he opined was linked to the process of governance, part of what he called "the art of conducting men to the maximum of happiness and the minimum of misery."   As McMullan (1998:111) notes, Colqhuoun's emphasis on paid police, police commissioners, and special police forces evinced his "profound belief in the need for a formalized concept of the police, concerned with the domain of security, yet removed from the magistracy (whom he thought incapable of monitoring security), and divided from the general tasks of domestic administration".   Yet, police for Colquhoun was not simply about safety and the protection of the individual citizen, it also implied the protection of commerce, a notion of police that he learned from Adam Smith and Adam Ferguson (1767), both of whom had presented lectures on police and political economy but neither of whom had developed the concept intellectually. Colquhoun thus committed himself to creating a radical new system of police aimed unapologetically at fabricating a social order to ensure productive workers for capitalism.

Colquhoun thought his theory of police was one which could benefit commercial interests in trade, manufacturing and transportation, especially along the river Thames where acts of fraud, theft, pillage and depredation were common.   He claimed that the Thames was the jugular vein of the British Empire and that by the turn of the century the port of London had an annual traffic of over 13,000 vessels and a commercial trade worth £60,000,000.   Shipment delays were common and moored ships and cargo on the bank side quays were attractive targets for crime.   In *Police on the River Thames* (1800) Colquhoun developed his plan for the protection of property and production on the river. He noted that the core of the crime problem was largely internal to the river work force.   He claimed that 700 out of 1200 Revenue Officers employed on river duty had "more or less" profitted "by excessive plunder, which seems to have been more or less general in every line of Commerce" (Colquhoun 1800a:178).

This organized form of thievery was attributed to the lack of workforce controls and deterrence since punishment went no further than dismissal and there were no means of detecting and tracking offences and offenders (Colquhoun 1800a:171). Colquhoun (1800a:170) argued that pilfering was connected to "the increasing expense of livelihood" which, in turn, contributed to the development of delinquency. Surveillance was part of his solution to river crime. Through the eyes "of a watchful Police for the purpose of controlling, by its influence, the turbulent and unruly passions of such a multitude of dissolute characters," (Colquhoun 1800a:252) he believed he had effectively reduced the plunder. He sought to demonstrate this by impressively providing statistical tables demonstrating that once "[t]he Various classes of offenders perceiv[ed] that every vulnerable point was guarded" and "felt for once the power of the Law" exercised by a "well-regulated Police", they became "resigned to the alternative of abandoning their evil pursuits" (Colquhoun 1800a:210-11).

Indeed, Colquhoun (1800a:268) boasted that his police force reduced losses to West-India properties to one-fiftieth of its former depredations and "placed all the other branches of Commerce nearly on an equal footing." Colquhoun's success was not realized by large scale interjections into the economy, nor though transforming religious, civic, or moral attitudes. Rather, his Thames Police revealed that a simple mechanism of regulation, inspection and surveillance went a long way in preventing crime.

Of course, the police role in the class-based functioning of economic prosperity can hardly be overlooked. The logic used by Colquhoun was utilitarian; the port of London stood to loose upwards of £60 million, whereas the cost of maintaining his police force amounted to only a fraction of that cost. Likewise, his conception of police extended "security to Commercial Property", where he claimed that "the privileges of innocence will be preserved, and the comforts of Civil society eminently enlarged" (Colquhoun 1800a:38). Colquhoun clearly realized that social control was geared to the benefit of a particular class of property holders, which was consistent with his emphasis on managing the various classes of persons who he said threatened commercial interests.

This class politics was especially obvious in his work for the Thames shippers and London merchants where he set about instituting a system of surveillance that eliminated customary compensation outside official lumping rates (wages). Colquhoun skilfully created and enforced a wage labour system at the precise time and place where international capitalism demanded it most – the heart of Imperial England. The lumping rates were arrived at so that "honest labour could be procured for daily wages" in order that lumpers would not resort to "plunder" (Colquhoun 1800a:619). Rates were publicly posted at the Thames Police office. Master lumpers (dock foremen) were scrutinized by the police; clothing used to conceal customs and payments in kind such as wide trousers, jemmies, and concealed pockets were banned; lumpers were searched; all ships, contents and manifests were registered and their contents guarded. Thus, while Beccaria envisioned a perfected set of laws that would ostensibly benefit "not so much classes of men as men themselves," Colquhoun's police machine was indeed directed to class discipline by uplifting the indigent poor and fabricating the working conditions for a 'useful' poor.

Other than Colquhoun, few thinkers have been as direct about the necessity of policing the poor than **G.W.F. Hegel**. Yet Hegel's contribution to police has been both significant and undervalued, even though an entire section of the *Elements of the Philosophy of Right* (1821) was dedicated to this topic. According to Schroeder (1998), Hegel's theory of property marked liberalism's sublation because Hegel neither accepted nor dismissed the liberal emphasis on individuality and civil society. For Hegel, sublation was not simply the negation of something; it was also its preservation. He explained: "it means to preserve, to maintain, and equally it also means to cause to cease, to put an end to" (Hegel 1812:107). Hegel, of course, did not wish to deny liberal philosophy, but rather he sought to intellectually restructure the liberal emphasis on civil society.

In the course of this essay we have seen how 'civil society' within liberal discourse challenged, and even subverted the role and actions of the state. Hegel also wanted to grant a place for individuality. He demarcated civil society from the family, where he insisted one's self-consciousness was subsumed not as an individual but as a member (Hegel 1821:§158). The family, while providing a potentially gratifying ethical life, did not enable individuals enough to confront the subjectivity and freedom inherent of the modern world. "The concrete person," Hegel offered, "as a totality of needs and a mixture of natural necessity and arbitrariness, is his own end, is *one principle* of civil society." We are presented with the familiar picture of individuals whose ultimate ends have no vantage point other than self referral. Of course, all individuals stand in relation to others. They try to acquire their ends through their mediation with each other and this constitutes the second principle of civil society (Hegel 1821§158). The system of needs that results, however, is arbitrary and capricious and universally in the form of the market economy. The study of the relationships that comprise this rationality, for Hegel (1821§189), is the science of political economy. The freedom and subjectivity of the individual was located in the market, which manifested its objective existence, at least partially, through the rubric of property (Hegel 1821:§232). While this formulation was in part liberal, Hegel departed from the economic tenets of Adam Smith, for example, and asserted that the market, despite an inner rationality, can never fully protect those people existing within it. Thus, unlike Smith, Hegel conceived the police broadly as "crimes which the universal authority (Macht) must prevent or bring to justice" because the uses of property can escape the control of individuals and harm or wrong others. He observed the "differing interests of producers and consumers" often "come into collision with each other" requiring adjustments to be "consciously regulated by an agency which stands above both sides" (Hegel 1821:§236). Furthermore, because branches of industry were dependent upon "external circumstances and remote combinations," the police must monitor not only criminal behaviour, but also regulate the economy to make sure that the market and the freedom of civil society did not become threatened or subverted. Hegel thus prescribed a much more expansive role for his police including providing for street-lighting, bridge building, the pricing of daily necessities, and the oversight of public health.

Despite police intervention in the economy, the dialectic of the market drives a certain class towards poverty and immiseration. As Hegel observed: "despite an excess of wealth, civil society is not wealthy enough – i.e. its own distinct resources are not sufficient – to prevent an excess of poverty and the formation of a rabble" (Hegel 1821:§245). The rabble, for Hegel, were a distinct class of poverty similar to Colquhoun's indigent poor. The rabble were created by feelings of lost honour associated with the deprivation of self-sufficiency which, in turn, incited rebellion against the wealthy and the government. These conditions led to the "evil" said Hegel (1996, orig. 1821:§244) of a "rabble [which lacked] sufficient honour to gain their livelihood through their own work, yet claim[ed] that they [had] a right to receive their livelihood." While poverty could not be avoided, the rabble must be managed, or policed, and Hegel seemed to mirror Colquhoun by suggesting that the key to police success lay in preventing the poor from becoming a rabble. Hegel (1821:§241) prescribed that the Macht take on not only a poor family's "immediate deficiencies" but also attend to "laziness, viciousness, and the other vices to which their predicament and sense of wrong give rise." The role of the police was to keep civil society from imploding by keeping a watchful eye on the poor and by actively managing those who had fallen into poverty so that they did not become an organized force that threatened the rest of society, especially those who own enough property to remain self-sufficient and enjoy freedom from toil. While it might be tempting to associate Hegel's police with the cameralists of the mid-eighteenth century, it is important to note the importance Hegel assigns to civil society and the notion of class. While von Sonnenfels, for example, mitigated the idea of class by having police manage the wealthy as well as the poor, Hegel provided no such assurances. For him, police was imbricated with security and wealth issues, but it was also correctly an instrument deployed by a particular class against the poor.

Conclusions

The police project has a broad and sophisticated intellectual lineage. Police science permeated discussions of human nature, family, civic morality and state purview in Enlightenment thought. The notion of police both theoretically and practically connected state, citizenship, wealth, and welfare. It is a concept that, in the Enlightenment period, was equated with considerations as high-minded as national security and as practical as the maintenance of sewer flows. Police is inextricably connected to the birth of modern-day surveillance, political economy, population control and the management of labour. In short, we have seen that police comes to conceptually bind social order and commerce.

In 1843, Marx (1978) wrote: "Security is the supreme concept of bourgeois society" and it is tempting to suggest that this prescient statement about police has perhaps never been more salient than in today's security-obsessed society. Security thinking has trumped, or literally colour-coded – as in the case of the Bush administration's threat assessments – almost all facets of social life. It has acquired a fetishistic quality that suffuses its content on almost every commodity (Spitzer 1987). It has provided the rationale for international military "policing" operations (Hardt and Negri 2001), curbed the playing fields of our children (Furedi 1997), increased the scope and types of aural, visual and data surveillance technologies (Coleman 2004; Gandy 1993; Lyon 1994), and has rebranded welfare as social security, hunger as food security, defense as national security, crowd control as public security and disease as health security (Neocleous 2008).

The fulcrum around which security functions is *knowledge*. As Neocleous (2006:37) observes, "security uses its claim to knowledge as license to render all aspects of life transparent to the state." He cites the recent example of London Metropolitan Police Commissioner Sir John Stevens who spoke out in favour of a national identification card system for Britain because, as he put it, "we don't actually know who is in London at the moment." "[J]ust imagine", ponders Neocleous, "a system that allowed the state, police, and security services to know exactly who was in London at any one time." What is striking about Stevens' statement in favour of a national identification system is the remarkable correspondence of his comments to the three-hundred year-old proposals made by Sir William Petty we have examined in this volume. Petty's design for a London wall was "[t]o take in accompt of all persons and things going in and out of the Citty" (1927a:II, 11:32-33) and his suggestion that all men be issued a "peculiar Seale" with "uncounterfeitable Tickett[s]" of identification seems eerily similar the Commissioner's call for an account of all subjects in the city today. Our own knowledge of this very long lineage of police power, its connection to class discipline in the writings of foundational thinkers, and its circumlocution in contemporary police scholarship forms an important basis on which a critique of security and a critical political economy of police can be developed. In this way, we believe that the fulcrum of knowledge upon which security and police power now mobilizes may also be the fulcrum upon which an informed critique may be mounted.

References

Agamben, Giorgio. 2005. *State of Exception*. Chicago: University of Chicago Press.

Beccaria, Cesare. 1996, orig. 1764., orig. 1764. *Of Crimes and Punishments*. New York: Marsilio Publishers.

Beck, Ulrich. 1999. *World Risk Society*. Malden Mass.: Polity Press.

Bentham, Jeremy. 1843."Principles of the Civil Code." in *The Works of Jeremy Bentham, Vol. 1*, edited by Sir John Bowring. Edinburgh: William Tait.

—. 1995, orig. 1787. *The Panopticon Writings*. London: Verson.

Blizard, William. 1785. *Desultory Reflections on Police: With an Essay on the Means of Preventing Crime and Amending Criminals* London.

Bogard, William. 1996. *The Simulation of Surveillance: Hypercontrol in Telematic Societies*. Cambridge: Cambridge University Press.

Borkenau, Franz. 1976., orig. 1934. *Der Übergang vom Feudalen zum Bügerlichen*. Weltbild, Darmstadt: Wissenschaftliche Buchgesellschaft.

Brown, John. 1757. *An Estimate of the Manners and Principles of the Times*. London: L. Davis and C. Reymers.

Cohen, Stanley. 1985. *Visions of Social Control*. Cambridge: Polity.

Coleman, Roy. 2004. *Reclaiming the streets surveillance, social control and the city*. Cullompton UK: Willan.

Colquhoun, Patrick. 1799. *A General View of the National Police System, etc*. London: J. Mawman.

—. 1800a. *A Treatise on the Commerce and Police of the River Thames*. London: Joseph Mawman.

—. 1800b., orig. 1795. *Treatise on the Police of the Metropolis, etc*. . London: Mawman.

Critchley, T.A. 1967. *A History of the Police in England and Wales, 900-1966*. London: Constable Press.

Dandeker, C. 1990. *Surveillance, Power and Modernity: Bureaucracy and Discipline from 1700 to the Present Day*. Cambridge: Polity Press.

Dodsworth, F.M. 2008. "The idea of police in eighteenth-century England: Discipline, reformation, superintendence." Journal of History of Ideas, 69(4): 583-605.

Emsley, Clive. 1999a. *Gendarmes and the State in Nineteenth-Century Europe*. Oxford: Oxford University Press.

—. 1999b. "A typology of nineteenth century police." *Deviance et Societe* 3:29-44.

Ferguson, Adam. 1995, orig. 1767. *An Essay on the History of Civil Society*. Cambridge: Cambridge University Press.

Fielding, Sir John. 1758. *An Account of the Origins and Effects of a Police* London.

—. 1775. *A Plan for Preventing Robberies Within 20 Miles of London*. London: A Millar.

Foucault, Michel. 1977. *Discipline and Punish*. New York: Vintage Books.

—. 1979. "Omnes et singulatim: Toward a criticism of political reason" Presented at The Tanner Lecture on Human Values, Stanford University, October 10 and 16.

—. 1980. *Power/Knowledge: Selected Interviews and Other Writings*. New York: Pantheon Books.

—. 1991."Governmentality." Pp. 87-104 in *The Foucault Effect: Studies in Governmentality*, edited by Graham Burchell, Colin Gordon, and Peter Miller. Chicago: University of Chicago Press.

Furedi, Frank. 1997. *Culture of Fear: Risk Taking and the Morality of Low Expectation*. Harrison PA: Continuum Publications.

Gandy, Oscar H. 1993. *The Panoptic Sort: A Political Economy of Personal Information*. Boulder: Westview Press.

Hanway, Jonas. 1775. *The Defects of Police the Cause of Immorality, and Continual Robberies...* London: J. Dodsley & Brotherton and Sewell.

Hardt, Michael, and Antonio Negri. 2001. *Empire*. Cambridge MA: Harvard University Press.

Hegel, Georg .W.F. 1929., orig. 1812. *The Science of Logic*. London: George & Allen.

—. 1996, orig. 1821. *Philosophy of Right*. Amherst NY: Prometheus.

Hobbes, Thomas. 1985., orig. 1651. *Leviathan*. Toronto: Penguin.

Hunt, Alan, and Gary Wickham. 1998. *Foucault and Law: Towards a Sociology of Law as Governance*. London: Pluto.

Johnston, Les. 2000. *Policing Britain: Risk, Security and Governance*. Harlow: Pearson.

Linebaugh, Peter. 1991. *The London Hanged: Crime and Civil Society in England*. London: Allen Lane.

Loader, Ian. 2002. "Policing, securitization, and democratization in Europe." *Criminal Justice* 2:125-153.

Loader, Ian, and Neil Walker. 2001. "Policing as a public good: Reconstituting the connections between policing and the state." *Theoretical Criminology* 5:9-35.

Lyon, David. 1994. *The Electronic Eye: The Rise of Surveillance Society*. Minneapolis: University of Minnesota Press.

Marx, Karl. 1904. *A Contribution to the critique of Political Economy* Chicago: C.H. Kerr.

—. 1978., orig. 1843. "On the Jewish Question." Pp. 26-52 in *The Marx-Engels Reader, 2d.*, edited by Robert C. Tucker. New York: W.W. Norton and Company.

McMullan, John L. 1996. "The new improved monied police: Reform, crime control, and the commodification of policing in London." *British Journal of Criminology* 36:85-108.

—. 1998. "Social surveillance and the rise of the 'police machine'." *Theoretical Criminology* 2:93-117.

Mykkänen, Juri. 1994. "'To methodize and regulate them': William Petty's governmental science of statistics." *History of the Human Sciences* 7:65-88.

Neocleous, Mark. 2000. *The Fabrication of Social Order: A Critical Theory of Police Power.* London: Pluto Press.

—. 2006."Theoretical foundations of the "New Police Science"." Pp. 17-41 in *The New Police Science: Police Power in Domestic and International Governance,* edited by Markus D. Drubber and Mariana Valverde. Stanford: Stanford University Press.

—. 2008. *Critique of Security.* Edinburgh: Edinburgh University Press.

Pasquino, Pasquale. 1991."Theatrum politicum: The genealogy of capital - police and the state of prosperity." Pp. 105-118 in *The Foucault Effect: Studies in Governmentality,* edited by Graham Burchell, Colin Gordon, and Peter Miller. Chicago: University of Chicago Press.

Petty, Sir William. 1690. *Political Arithmetick.* London: Robert Clavel.

—. 1927a., orig. circa 1690. *The Petty Papers: Some Unpublished Writings (Vol. 1).* London: Constable.

—. 1927b., orig. 1660-1669. *The Petty Papers: Some Unpublished Writings (Vol. 2).* London: Constable.

Reiner, Robert. 1992. *The Politics of the Police, 2nd edition.* Toronto: University of Toronto Press.

Rigakos, George S., and Richard W. Hadden. 2001. "Crime, capitalism and the risk society: Towards the same olde modernity?" *Theoretical Criminology* 5:61-84.

Schroeder, Jeanne L. 1998. *The Vestal and the Fasces: Hegel, Lacan, Property and the Feminine.* Berkeley: University of California Press.

Smith, Adam. 1937, orig. 1776. *The Wealth of Nations.* New York: Random House.

—. 2004, orig. 1763. *Lectures on Justice, Police, Revenue and Arms.* London: Kessinger Press.

Spitzer, Stephen. 1987."Security and control in capitalist societies: The fetishism of security and the secret thereof." Pp. 43-58 in *Transcarceration: Essays in the Sociology of Social Control,* edited by John Lowman, Robert J. Menzies, and Ted S. Palys. Aldershot: Gower.

Steuart, James Sir. 1966, orig. 1767. *An Inquiry into the Principles of Political Economy.* Chicago: University of Chicago Press.

Storch, Robert. 1975. "The plague of the blue locusts: Police reform and popular resistance in Northern England 1840-1857." *International Review of Social History* 20:61-90.

von Humboldt, Wilhelm. 1993, orig. 1792. *The Limits of State Action.* Indianapolis: Liberty Fund.

von Justi, Johann H.G. 1755. "Staatswirthschaft." in *The Cameralists: The Pioneers of German Polity*, edited by Albion W. Small. New York: Burt Franklin, 2001 (orig. 1909).

von Justi, Johann H.G. 1756."Grundsätze der Polizeywissenschaft." in *The Cameralists: The Pioneers of German Polity*, edited by Albion W. Small. New York: Burt Franklin, 2001 (orig. 1909).

von Sonnefels, Joseph. 1765. "Grundsätze der Polizei, Handlung und Finanzwissenschaft." in *The Cameralists: The Pioneers of German Polity*, edited by Albion W. Small. New York: Burt Franklin, 2001 (orig. 1909).

Zedner, Lucia. 2006."Policing before the police: The historical antecedents of contemporary crime control." *British Journal of Criminology*, 46:78-96.

Sir William Petty (1623-1687)

Artist: Johann Baptist Closterman.
Dibner Library of the History of
Science and Technology

William Petty was born on May 26, 1623, in the Hampshire village of Romsey. As a young man, he studied at a Jesuit academy in Caen. He supported himself by teaching English to locals and later joined the Royal Navy. When civil war broke out in England, he moved to France to studying medicine at the University of Paris. Here he encountered and befriended the English philosopher, Thomas Hobbes. The two studied anatomy and read Vesalius together, and when Hobbes wrote his "Optics" in 1644, Petty drew up the optical schemes. By 1651, Petty was a professor of Anatomy at Brasenose College, Oxford, and professor of Music in London. Petty's rise to prominence followed his decision to travel with Oliver Cromwell's army to Ireland in 1652 as a physician general. While there, he secured a contract to chart Ireland for the sake of repaying in land those who had funded Cromwell's army. Petty was handsomely rewarded for his services, receiving roughly 30,000 acres of land in southwest Ireland, and £9 000.

Back in England, Petty successfully ran for Parliament in 1659 and was knighted in 1661 by Charles II. A year later, Petty published his first book dealing with economics, entitled *Treatise of Taxes and Contributions*. The concept of productive labour, and an associated social division of labour, likely find their first articulation in this work. This and subsequent works solidified Petty's oft ascribed title of father of political economy and founder of classical political economy. He is also considered an early statistician and the founder of political arithmetic, the latter of which he defined as the art of reasoning by figures upon things relating to the government. In *Essays in Political Arithmetic and Political Survey or Anatomy of Ireland* (1672), Petty was able to present a rough but uniquely calculated set of estimates regarding population and social income in Ireland. Moving to Ireland in 1666, Petty's focus shifted from medicine to economics and social sciences, as he sought to explain and remedy what he saw as Ireland's backwards condition. He remained in Ireland for much of the rest of his life, moving back to London in 1685 but dying only two years later, on December 16, 1687

Works Referenced:

Amati, Frank and Aspromourgos, Tony. "Petty Contra Hobbes: A Previously Untranslated Manuscript." *Journal of the History of Ideas* 46, No. 1 (January - March, 1985), pp. 127-132.

Masson, Irvine and Youngson, A.J. "Sir William Petty, F.R.S. (1623-1687)." *Notes and Records of the Royal Society of London* 15, (July, 1960), pp. 79-90.

Strauss, E. *Sir William Petty: Portrait of a Genius.* The Bodley Head Ltd: London, 1954.

Selections from: "A Treatise on Taxes and Other Contributions", Chapter X: Of Penalties in the *The Economic Writings of Sir William Petty*. Edited by Charles H. Hull. (pp. 67-73) (London: Augustus M. Kelley, 1899)., orig, circa 1660.

A Treatise of Taxes and Contributions, Chapter X: Of Penalties
The usual Penalties are Death, Mutilations, Imprisonment, Publick disgrace, Corporal transient pains, and great Tortures, besides the Pecuniary Mulcts. Of which last we shall most insist, speaking of the others but in order to examine whether they may not be commuted for these.

2. There be some certain Crimes, for which the Law of God appoints death; and these must be punished with it, unless we say that those were but the Civil Laws of the Jewish Commonwealth, although given by God himself; of which opinion certainly most modern States are, in as much as they punish not Adulteries, &c. with death, as among the Jewes, and yet punish shall Thefts with Death instead of multiple reparation.

3. Upon this supposition we shall venture to offer; whether the reason of simple Death be not to punish incorrigible Committers of great faults?

4. Of publick Death with Torments, to affright men from Treasons, which cause the deaths and miseries of many thousand innocent and useful people?

5. Of Death secretly executed, to punish secret and unknown Crimes, such as Publick Executions would teach to the World? Or else to suffocate betimes some dangerous Novelties in Religion, which the patient suffering of the worst man would much spread and encourage.

6. Mutilations suppose of Ears, Nose, &c. are used for perpetual disgrace, as standing in the Pillory is for temporary and transient; which and such other punishments have (by the way) made some corrigible offenders, to become desperate and incurable.

7. Mutilations of parts as of Fingers, are proper to disable such as have abused their dexterous use of them, by Pocket-picking, Counterfeiting of Seals and Writings, &c. Mutilations of other parts, may serve to punish and prevent Adulteries, Rapes, Incests, & c. And the smaller Corporal pains, serve to punish those, who can pay no pecuniary mulcts.

8. Imprisonment seems rather to be the punishments of suspected then guilty persons, and such as by their carriage give the Magistrate occasion to think, either they have done some smaller particular Crime, as Thefts, &c. or that they would commit greater; as Treasons and Seditions. But where Imprisonment is not a securing men untill their Trialls, but a sentence after Triall, it seems to me proper onely to seclude such men from conversation, whose Discourses are bewitching, and Practices infectious, and in whom neverthelesse remains some hopes of their future Amendments, or usefulnesse for some service not yet appearing.

9. As for perpetual Imprisonment by sentence, it seems but the same with

death it self, to be executed by nature it self, quickened with such Diseases, as close living, sadness, solitude, and reflections upon a past and better condition, doth commonly beget: Nor do men sentenced hereunto live longer, though they be longer in dying.

10. Here we are to remember in consequence of our opinion, [That Labour is the Father and active principle of Wealth, as Lands are the Mother] that the State by killing, mutilating, or imprisoning their members, do withal punish themselves; wherefore such punishments ought (as much as possible) to be avoided and commuted for pecuniary mulcts, which will encrease labour and publick wealth.

11. Upon which account, why should not a man of Estate, found guilty of man-slaughter, rather pay a certain proportion of his whole Estate, then be burnt in the hand?

12. Why should not insolvent Thieves be rather punished with slavery then death? so as being slaves they may be forced to as much labour, and as cheap fare, as nature will endure, and thereby become as two men added to the Commonwealth, and not as one taken away from it; for if England be under-peopled, (suppose by half) I say that next to the bringing in of as many more as now are, is the making these that are, to do double the work which now they do; that is, to make some slaves; but of this elsewhere.

13. And why should not the solvent Thieves and Cheats be rather punished with multiple Restitutions then Death, Pillory, Whipping? &c. But it will be asked, with how manifold Restitutions should picking a pocket (for example) be punished? I say, 'twere good in order to the solution hereof, to enquire of some candid Artists in that Trade, how often they are taken one time with another practising in this work? If but once in ten times, then to restore even but seven-fold, would be a fair profit; and to restore but ten-fold, were but an even lay; wherefore to restore twenty-fold, that is, double to the hazard, is rather the true *ratio* and measure of punishment by double reparation.

14. And surely the restoring two, three, four, and seven-fold mentioned in *Moses* Law must be thus understood, or else a man might make thieving a very fair and lawful profession.

15. The next question is, in such multiple Restitutions how many parts should be given to the sufferer. To which I answer, never above one, and scarce that, to oblige him to more care, and self-preservation, with three parts to discoverers, and the rest to publick uses.

16. Thirdly, in the case of Fornications, most of the punishments not made by pecuniary mulcts and commuted, are but shame, and that too but towards some few persons, which shame for ever after obdurates the Offender, what ever it work upon such whose fames are yet intire: Of all which men take little consideration, standing upon the brink of such precipices as makes them giddy; and when they are in danger of such faults as are rather madnesses, distempers, and alienations of the minde and reason, as also insurrections of the passions,

then deliberate acts of the understanding.

17. Moreover, according to that Axiom of, *In quo quis peccat, in eodem puniatur;* if the *Ratio formalis* of the sin of *Concubitus Vagi,* be the hindering of procreation, let those who by their miscarriages of this kinde are guilty thereof, repair unto the State the misse of another pair of hands with the double labour of their own, or which is all one, by a pecuniary mulct; and this is the practice of some wise States in punishing what they will never be able to prevent: Nor doth the Gospel specifie any punishment in this world, onely declaring they shall not be received into the joyes of the next.

18. I could instance in more particulars, but if what I have already said be reasonable, this little is enough; if not, then all the rest would be too little also: wherefore I shall adde but one instance more, as most suitable to our present times and occasions, which is the way of punishing Heterodox Professors of Religion.

19. That the Magistrate may punish false Believers, if he believe he shall offend God in forbearing it, is true; for the same reasons that men give for Liberty of Conscience, and universal toleration; and on the other side, that he may permit false Worships, seems clearly at least by the practice of all States, who allow Ambassadours their freedom (be the Worship never so abominable) even when they come to negociate but upon temporal and small matters.

20. Wherefore, since the Magistrate may allow or connive at such Worships as himself thinks fit, and yet may also punish; and since by Death, Mutilations, and imprisonments of the Subjects, the State not onely punisheth it self, but spreadeth the Pseudodoxies; it follows, that pecuniary Mulcts are the fittest wayes of checking the wantonness of men in this particular: forasmuch as that course savours of no bitterness at all, but rather argues a desire to indulge, provided such indulgence may consist with the indemnity of the State; for no Heterodox will desire to be tolerated longer then he keeps the Publick Peace; the which if he means to do, he cannot take it ill of the Magistrate, to keep him steddy unto that his duty, nor grudge to contribute towards so much charge for that purpose as himself occasions.

21. Moreover, as there seems a reason for indulging some conscientious misbelievers, so there is as much for being severe toward Hypocrites, especially such as abuse holy Religion to cloak and vizzard worldly ends: Now what more easie and yet effectual way is there to discern between these two, then well proportioned pecuniary mulcts? for who desiring to serve God without fear, and labouring then hours *per diem* at his Calling, would not labour one hour more for such a freedom? even as religious men spend an *hour per diem* more then the looser sort do at their Devotions; or who weaving Cloth of one and twenty shillings the yard, would not be contented with that of twenty shillings, for the same advantage of his liberty in Worship? Those that kick at this, being unwilling either to do or suffer for God, for whose sake they pretend so much.

22. It may be here objected, that although some bad Religions might be tolerated, yet that all may not, viz. such as consist not with the Civil Peace. To which I answer.

First, that there is no Schisme or Separation, be it never so small, consistent with that unity and peace as could be wisht; nor none so perfectly conscientious, but may also be civilly most pernicious: For that *Venner*[1] and his Complices acted upon internal motives, the most free exposing of themselves to death may evince; and yet their holding the King to be an Usurper upon the Throne and Right of Jesus Christ was a Civil mischief neither to be pardoned or parallel'd.

23. And yet on the other hand there is no Pseudodoxy so great, but may be muzzled from doing much harm in the State, without either Death, Imprisonment, or Mutilation: To make short, no opinion can be more dangerous, then to disbelieve the immortality of the Soul, as rendring man a beast, and without conscience, or fear of committing any evil, if he can but elude the penaltie of humane Laws made against it, and letting men loose to all evil thoughts and designs whereof man can take no notice: Now I say, that even this Misbeliever may be adequately punished if he be kept as a beast, be proprietor of nothing, as making no conscience how he gets; be never admitted in Evidence or Testimony, as under no obligation to speak truth; be excluded all Honours and Offices, as caring onely for himself, not the protecting of others; and be withal kept to extream bodily labour, the profit where of the State is the pecuniary Mulct we speak of, though the greatest.

24. As for opinions less horrible then this, the Mulct may be fitted to each of them respectively, according to the measure of danger which the Magistrate apprehends from their allowance, and the charge necessary to prevent it.

25. And now we are speaking of the wayes how to prevent and correct Heterodoxies in Religion, which we have hitherto done by designing punishments for the erring sheep, I think it not amiss to adde, That in all these cases the Shepherds themselves should not wholly scape free: For if in this National there be such abundance of Free-Schools, and of liberall Maintenance provided in our Universities and elsewhere for instructing more then enough in all such learning as is fit to defend the established Religion, together with superabundant Libraries for the purpose. Moreover, if the Church-preferments be so numerous and ample both for Wealth, Honour, and Power, as scarce any where more; it seems strange that when by the laziness, formality, ignorance, and loose lives of our Pastours, the sheep have gone astray, grown scabbed, or have been devoured by Wolves and Foxes, that the Remedy of all this should be onely sought by frighting those

---

1   Thomas Venner, the London wine-cooper, who led the revolt of the Fifth Monarchy Men, 6 Januay 1661. See A relation of the Arraignment and Trial of those who made the late Rebellions Insurrection in London, 1661, in Somer's Tracts (1812), VII. 469-472; Howell, State Trials, VI. 105-120, 67-70 n.; Burnet, Own Time, I. 160-161.

that have strayed from ever returning again, and by tearing off as well the skins as the wool of those that are scabbed; whereas Almighty God will rather require the blood even of them that have been devoured, from the shepheards themselves.

26. Wherefore if the Minister should lose part of the Tythes of those whom he suffers to dissent from the Church, (the defector not saving, but the State wholly gaining them) and the defector paying some pecuniary Mulct for his Schisme, and withal himself defraying the charge of his new particular Church and Pastorage, me thinks the burthen would be thus more equally born.

27. Besides, the judicious world do not believe our Clergy can deserve the vaste preferments they have, onely because they preach, give a better accompt of Opinions concerning Religion then others, or can express their conceptions in the words of the Fathers, or the Scriptures, &c. Whereas certainly the great honour we give them, is for being patterns of holiness, for showing by their own self-denials, mortifications and austerities, that 'tis possible for us to imitate them in the precepts of God; for if it were but for their bare Pulpit-discourses, some men might think there is ten thousand times as much already printed as can be necessary, and as good as any that ever hereafter may be expected. And it is much suspected, that the Discipline of the Cloisters hath kept up the Roman Religion, which the Luxury of the Cardinals and Prelates might have destroyed.

28. The substance therefore of all we have said in this discourse concerning the Church is, that it would make much for its peace, if the Nursery of Ministers be not too bigg, that Austerities in the Priests lives would reconcile them to the people; and that it is not unreasonable, that when the whole Church suffers by the defection of her Members, that the Pastours of it by bearing a small part should be made sensible of the loss; the manner and measures of all which I leave unto those unto whom it belongs.

Selections from: *The Petty Papers.* **Vol I. Nos 10-17 on the "London Wall", "Plague", and "Emprovements" (pp. 30-42) and Vol. II, No. 145 "A scheme for the Provision of the Poore (1687)" and No. 146 "Crimes and Punishments" (pp. 210-213). Edited from the** *Bowood Papers* **by the Marquis of Landsdowne. (London: Constable and Company, 1927)., orig. cira 1660.**

No.10 Of London, Westminster, Southwark, Fortifyed &C.

By London is meant an ovall piece of ground, whose length is from Blackwall to Vauxhall, and whose breadth is half of the said length.

This ground contaynes about 7500 acres, whereof about 1500 is built and 6000 field, worth 40s per acre at least.

There are on this ground 80^m houses, worth 20£ per annum one with another.

There are above 500^m soules inhabiting the same, among whom are above 80^m able to fight.

The sayd ground contaynes all the shipping &c.

It spends 300 chaldron of coales brought in from the sea.

Is supplyd with water from Ware, the Thames, and springs within the said ground.

It contaynes Merchants and artisans of all sorts, fit for war or peace, and all provisions for the same.

One half or 700^m of the King's Revenue arises and is payable from thence.

A Wall of 12 miles or 65^m foot about, will fortify the said ground artificially.

10m men will man the said wall at 6 foot to a man.

The forts at Sheereness, Tilbury, the Tower and Windsor will countenance (?) the river, which must have a new bridge at Lambeth.

100^m£ will defray the charge of this wall, which may be finished in one sumer.

His Majesty's present forces of 2000 horse and 3000 foot will suffice for the Citadells of the said wall, and the charge thereof will be 120^m£.

The Merchants of London do ingrosse all the seamen of England and Navall provisions.

5000 horse moving in the country, and 20^m foot which London can raise, can do anything in England.

The 3 cittyes of London, Westminster, and Southwark, are governed actually by the King.

No papist to live with [in] the wall, nor approach.

Otherwise Liberty of Conscience, and the people to pay their priests and parsons as they please.

Law-suits for within this ground shortned.

The land and housing to bee embanked, and the credit thereof let to Interest.

Every 200 men in London to send a member to each House of Parliament, or the Council of Trade; sending in all about 80 or 90 members.

London to bee divided from Westminster by a line run North from the Temple to the wall, with [a] small wall thereon.

Exact accompts to bee kept of the peoples, trades, religion, wealth, sex ages, marriages, births, burialls, housing, wealth, shipping of the Citty or 3 Cittyes,[2] with a perfect rule to raise taxes by.

One common Council for the 3 Cittyes, and freedomes renewd.

The expence of the 500m people in London is about 1/3 of the whole nation, which is 45 millions, (for the expence of London is 1/3 of the whole). Besides the expence is 10 times the house rent which is 1500m. Wherefore London can at one 20th part of the expence beare 750m per annum and 2/3 of the customes which [is] 260m more. Besides 90m is received there as small branches of the revenue. In all 1100m; enough to defray the whole government.

London embanked is security for 15 millions which at 1 per cent yields 150m per ann., enough to defray the guards of London.

The 6000 field acres of London will rise to double, and bee good for 4000 villas of pleasure.

No. 11 London Wall

A wall of 100m foot in circumference, 11 foot high, 2 brick thick, in a fortification figure, with 20 gates, worth 20m£.

To bee a certaine visible boundary of property and impositions.

A small defence and enforcement to approved men (?) and banishment.

For wall fruite.

For a fence to 20m acres of ground.

To take an accompt of all persons and things going in and out of the Citty.

To plant necessary garden stuffe [for] food, milk and cowes.

To denote the Citty of London.

To have a list (?) of a furlong without houses next the wall, to be all garden for the Kitchin.

To increase the value of enclosed lands.

A foundation of libertyes, securityes, and priviledges.

Priviledge to Inhabitants within the Wall

No hay nor corne to grow within it.

Men for crimes may bee put out of it.

---

2   i.e., London, Westminster, and Southwark, ut supra

Even man of 21 yeares old to have his voice in electing the Minister [and] Justices. Traynbande men. [To] License beggars. Provide for Impotents. Prison Keeper. (The owners of the ground upon which the wall stands to pay half; and the owners of all unpaid (?) ground to pay the other half by the acres.)

The justices so elected to choose parliament men.

[Inhabitants] Not to be sued but within the walls.

To have the benefit of hospitalls and work houses.

To exercise any trade, with exclusion to such as are not free or inhabitants.

Mony to be ascertained and preserved from abuses.

Not to be imprisoned, but put to servitude.

Infected with the plague to bee carryd out.

To borrow mony upon responsible security and interest.

Tythings to enforce for their members.

Care for Easements, Annoyances &c.

Ban within the wall, who to beg or perish (?).

No. 12 *An Essay For The Emprovement Of London (1687)*

Although many good conjectures have been made of the people, housing, burialls, &c. of London which onely authority can ascertain, Wee shall (in order to the emprovement of London) proceed upon the severall suppositions as following concerning the same: vizt:

1. That in the 137 parishes already contayned in the bills of Mortality, and in [the] parishes of Deptford, Greenwich, and Bow, hereafter to bee added, there are 108^m houses or 120^m families.

2. That a wall of 100m feet will encompasse all the said 137 parishes and 20^m statute acres of land, and may be built strong enough for one man within to defend against 2 without, for 10s. the foot.

3. That the full ground within the said 137 parishes is 2500 acres, and that the streets, foreyards, backsides, and gardens belonging to the same, is as much more. In all 5000 acres.

4. That the Rent of the said 5000 acres, and the 15,000 acres to bee enclosed, is 400^m per annum, worth 8 millions; and the rent of the superstructure 1000^m, so worth 10 millions.[3] In all 1400^m per annum for the said 108^m houses, at – each one with another.

5. That the number of registered burialls within the said 137 parishes are 24000, of registered christenings 15000, and of marriages 4000 per annum.

6. That the People of the same, men, women, and children, are 720^m; whereof 180^m are males of between 16 and 60 yeares old able to beare arms, the 1/10 whereof may be of the Traynbands, and 54^m of the experience favorable, within the wall above mentioned, to defend [it] against above 100^m beseigers.

---

3   Petty apparently calculates land at 20 and houses at 10 years purchase.

7. Of the said 720^m soules, 140 are teeming women of between 16 and 45 years old, who may beare 40^m children per annum or above double the present number.

8. Of the said 720^m, 600^m are above 10 yeares old, and able to do some kind of work.

Upon these suppositions, and that the late charter of London is now lost and other circumstances; it is proposed:

1. That the ground within the wall bee made a Diocese, consisting of 400 parishes of 300 familyes in each; to have one common service and prayer, with liberty of worship and opnion in matters purely spirituall, with a more certain way for Maintenance of the lazy and Poore therein.

2. That the same bee made a County, with uniting the common Law and Chancery, without termes (?) and the speedy tryall of criminalls.

3. That for every parish be a Justice [of] the Peace. That 400 Justices chose 40 parliament (?) men or Aldermen for governing and representing the Citty, out of which 40 a mayor and 2 sheriffs are [to] bee chosen, and that this common Council choose the 18000 to be of the Militia.

4. That there bee a Generall of all the force and arms and fortifications relating to the Citty.

5. An admirall, who is to keep an exact account of all shipping belonging to, or trading with the Citty, of all Watermen &c., and of all Navall provisions and ordnance, and to be judge of all maritime cases and navall matters with fit assistants, one to regard all seamen and Naval rations (?).

6. That there bee a Bank Master to manage usury and exchange and coynage, upon the fund of the ground rents.

7. A Surveyor Generall of buildings, pavings, lights, bridges, streets, common shores,[4] highways and scavenging, and carriages.

8. That there bee a Council of Health viz. for the Plague, acute and epidemicall diseases, aged foundlings, as also for persons and houses of correction, and all sorts of hospitalls and women in child-bed.

9. A Council of Trade for regulating plantations, manufactures, land and water carriage, enforcing dutyes upon goods, excise &c., and also for all forain Trades and the ballances thereof.

10. A Council of arts, Mathematicall, Mechanical, Natural extending to all artisans and artists whatsoever, to answer the ends of a Royall Society and all the Trademen's Halls.

The King to have an immediate correspondence and influence with and upon the Governors property, and other of all the said 10 Councils and authorities.

---

4   Sewers

The advantages which may bee expected from the above reformation and assessment of London are:

1. The ground rent of the said 20^m acres of London will be advanced enough to defray the charge of the wall, gates, and a New Bridge nere Lambeth, and perhaps to new pave the Citty in a better manner.

2. The bounds of the Citty and all impositions will by the wall bee ascertayned, and the meanes had of knowing who goes in and out, and of taking such tolls and dutyes as shall bee allowed, as also for defence and saving it from bomb[arding].

3. The bank of 8 millions may yield a profit 300^m per annum.

4. The administration of the law will save the people in expence &c. some— per annum.

5. The forces of London, with the force of each particular county, is able to defend England from any foran invasions and suppresse any intestine commotion.

6. If the plague can be lessened, the profit thereof will bee half a million per annum at a medium.

7. On the multiplication of mankind by the marriage of teeming women, 900^m£ more.

8. The charge of the Clergy lesse, and poore better cared for.

9. All Arts and Trades advanced.

10. An example [for] representing [to] the rest of the nation.

No. 13 The Emprovement of London: 1687

If London (viz. 120^m families and 20^m acres) bee enclosd, a new bridge made, and an hospitall for 1000 sick instituted. These advantages will follow, vizt:

To the people; by making the same by bounds & defence
A Dioceze.
A County.
An Universitas.
An Emporium.
A Corporation
For lessening the Plague

To the King; by making it
A speciall fund or branch of his revenue.
A Citadell to the whole state.
A Magazin for land and sea forces, and provisions.

To the King's subjects and Undertakers
A Bank of creditt for 7 million of money.
An emprovement of the ground rents of 20^m acres
The building of the Wall, Bridge, and hospitall.
The honor of effecting the same.

No.14: Of the Plague
  Of the intervalls of Plague.
  The quota that dye.
  The numbers of the people.
  The value of the same.
  Of shutting up and Pest houses.
  Of the time of rising and falling.
  Of water.
  Of leaving the cittye and wide roomes.
  Of Rich people and undertakers (?).
  Of Medicine in the Plague.
  Of 10^m small separate houses with 15 miles of Citty.
  Of carriages to and from these houses.
  Of chosing these houses and substitutes.
  Of burialls.
  Of discovering the Plague, and time of removalls.
  A theory of the Plague, Pneumatic (?)
  A tax for the poore within the wall, and who shall bee retained.
  Q. How many dyed of the Plague within 20 miles of London, when there dyed 97^m within it, and in what quota?
  That which dye above 24^m do dye of the Plague.
  And what dye fewer than 164^m were saved by this contrivance.
  Take an accompt of the people, ground, and houses, among which the Pest houses stand, and of their extra and ordinary burialls in the same.
  N.B.—A *Civitas* about London of 18 miles radius contaynes as many people as London.

No. 15 Plague (Pest Houses)
  1. Let there be a circle of ground about London (20 measured miles, equally distant from the Monument), and a list of the parishes which, or the greater part of them, lye within the said circle.
  2. Whereas probably there bee 30^m houses within the said circle, let 6^m of them bee chosen out as fittest to receive persons supposed to bee sick of the plague, and an appointment made where the dwellers in the same shall go, when their houses are called for for the cure of the plague.
  3. Let the just prices bee settled for the hire of such houses, out of which the dwellers are to bee removed, and those whereto they are to go.
  4. Let cariges bee provided to carry the infected from London to their Pest Houses respectively, begining with the nearest, or as the patient desires.
  5. Let matrons and chirugions bee agreed with to attend the sick so removd; the charges to bee general.
  6. Let Medicaments bee generally approvd by the best advice.

7. Let removalls bee made from London, not onely when any person is dead of the Plague, but when the manifest symptomes appeare.

8. Let the dwellers in the infected familyes of London go to severall pest houses, if they please.

No. 16 Concerning The Plagues of London

1. London within the bills hath 696^m people in 108^m houses.

2. In pestilential years (which are one in 20), there dye 1/6th of the people of the Plague and 1/5th of all diseases.

3. The remedies against spreading of the Plague are shutting up suspected houses, and [making] pest houses within ½ a mile of the Citty.

4. In a circle about the centre of London of 35 miles semi-diameter (or a days journey), there live as many people and are as many houses as in London.

5. Six heads may bee caryd a days journey for 20sh.

6. A family may bee lodged 3 months in the country for 4£, so as the charge of carying out and lodging a family at a medium will be 5£.

7. In the greatest Plague wee feare, scarce 20^m families will be infected, and in this new method but 10^m; the charge whereof will be 50^m pounds.

8. The People which the next Plague of London will sweep away will be probably 120^m, which at 70£ per head is a losse of 8,400^m, the half whereof is 4,200^m.

9. So as 50^m£ is ventured to save 4,200^m, or about one for 84.

10. There was never a Plague in the champagne of England by which 1/6th of the people dyed.

11. Poore people who live close, dye most of the Plague.

12. The Plague is about 3 monthes rising and as much falling, which cold weather hastens.

13. Killing dogs, making great fires in the street, nor the use of medicaments are considered sure; for which everyone by common directions may bee theire owne Physicians.

14. In the circle of 70 miles diameter, choose 10 large wide roomey disjoined houses, with water and garden to each; the Inhabitants to remove at 7 dayes notice.

15. Convenient wagons or coaches to bee prepared to carry away the suspected.

16. A method to furnish the pesthouses with medicines for theire money.

17. Bookes of devotion for every house.

Proposalls.—When 100 per week dy, the Plague is begun. If there dye fewer than 120^m out of the bills, of all diseases within a yeare after, then W.P. is [to} have 20sh. per head for all lesse and to pay 10sh. per head for all above it.

Every family removed being to provide 10£ for the charge of going and coming, and of 4 monthes rent. Or a gratuity of 2000£ with W.P. his ensurance.

(*Endorsed.* "Of Lessening the Plagues of London, October 7, 1687")

No. 17 The Uses of London

How by the present greatnes & state of London, to make it supply the use of forain Travell to the Youth of England.

It is expected that the 134 parishes already calld London, & 2 or 3 more, will contayne in all perhaps 800^m people, 120^m familyes, in 108^m houses; will be encompassed with a Wall of about 20 miles about, enclosing 20^m acres of Land, and that the same Enclosure shall bee made a county & diocese, and that hospitalls of all sorts will be erected within the same &c. I then say:

1. That within a Wall or Citty contayning 800^m heads, 'tis more likely to find able men by nature & art than in any lesser number.

2. That by the liberty of Conscience, there will bee a further discussion of all Theologicall matters & better Experiment made of the effect of severall faiths & persuasions than elsewhere.

3. The Hospitalls, gardens, & laboratryes of this place may well exceed any in the world in order to the art of Medicine.

4. This Citty will have Courts of Municipall, Civill, Common & Sea Law, of Equity, of honor, of Conscience, concerning mony, Lives, limbs, libertyes, lands & personall Equity, and the art of governing so vast a people in peace & plenty.

5. The Exchange of London will furnish men every day who have fresh concerne & correspondance with all parts of the knowne world & with all the Commodityes growing or made within the same.

6. In this Citty will be found store of men skild in all languages of the world, in all speculative sciences & practicall arts, among the great numbers whereof some must bee very excellent.

7. At the Royall Societymathematicall, mechanicall, & Naturall learning will bee much emprovd.

8. There [will] bee all Examples (?), Playes, Entertainments, of the shows of Nature & Art.

9. There will [be] the Court of the King of 3 Kingdoms, & [men] who have dominion & Interest in all the 4 quarters of the world, & Ambassadors from all Princes & States.

10. There are faire Collections of all natural & artificiall rarities, with coments upon them and applications of them.

11. All that belongs to Shipping & Gunery may bee exquisitely learnd, & other military discertations.

12. This Citty contaynes People—neere the Court, neere the Exchange, neere the Inns of Court, in St. Giles in the field, St. Giles Criplegate, Spittlefields, Southward, Wapping &c.—as different as in 8 severall cittyes or nations.

13. There is no place perhaps upon Earth where one may enjoy all Meates, drinkes, & Clothings, which the whole world affords & at better rates than at London.

14. In no Cittyes There is greater liberty at the Court, in St James & Hide parks, in Churches, at Theaters & elsewhere, to see beautifull Women with & without Impunity.

15. In no place so great variety of drinks: viz. of sorts of waters, beeres & ales, syder & juices of fruite, of wines from all Countryes & of distilled spirits & essences, than at London, and also of bathes & medicinall springs.

16. Such rivers, villes, so healthfull ayre & temperate weathers.

17. So great convenience for boates, Coaches, postage, & travelling from London to the other great cittyes.

No.14 A Scheme For Provision For the Poore. 1687

1. Let the exact accompt bee made of Every man, woman and child within each parish.

2. Let all that please, or others for them, make knowne their wants and cause of the same; and what kindred and relations they have; and where borne or bred.

3. Let those who are admitted to reliefe bee distinguished into 3 classes.

(i)   Impotent in whole or in part.

(ii)   Who can work, but want employment.

(iii) Who are able bodyd, but know not how to work.

As to reliefe

1.   Let some be sent to their country & friends.

2.   Others have work and Masters assigned them.

3.   Others receive proportionable almes.

4.   Others have a Badge & licence to beg.

Let an exact accompt bee made for the last 7 yeares of all receipts & payments made for the poore, and first for the last yeare itselfe.

No.146 Crimes And Punishments

This paper, though in the original headed "Bankrupts," deals (as will be seen) with various forms of crime, and their punishments. From its general tenor, and its suggestion that prisoners should be kept in Ireland, it may have been intended to apply to malefactors in that country, rather than to criminals in England.

Helps whereby it may bee knowne:

Whether any Bankrupt doth not pay his debts:

Because hee concealeth his effects,

Because hee hath vainly spent his estate and Creditt,

Because he hath lost the same by negligence, Ignorance, and Credulity,

By Inevitable Cawses.

How Robbing upon the Highway may bee prevented.

The same of Burglary & Burning of Howses.

Of Stealing Horses, Oxen & Sheep.

Of other portable goods.

Forging of Deeds.

Of foisted, changed and vitiated Deeds.

Of cheates & frawdes.

How the Persons guilty of all and every the aforementioned Crimes, may bee known and detected.

How being detected they may bee taken or kept safe as Prisoners within the Island of Ireland till they be taken.

Proper & proportionable punishments to each of the said Crimes, in order to Right and Reveng.

Some of the helps to the premisses:

1. That all men bee bound to keep Accompts of their Receipts and Issues, Gayn and Losse, Debts & Credits, in mony, Cattle & Goods, and where they were at noon and at night every day in the yeare; with mention of what deeds hee hath made or wittnessed.

2. That no howse stand alone, nor without call of some other howse. But that 10 Howses may stand neer together, and as neer as may bee in some Highway; and that one of the said Howses bee an Inn, and the Keeper thereof a Custable, tything man or other officer, with good security for his good behaviour.

3. That every man have and cary about him an uncounterfitable Tickett, expressing his name, the numero of this Howse, his Age, Trade, Stature, Haire, eye, and other peculiar marks of his Body.

4. That every man of—have a peculiar Seale.

5. That the High-ways bee guarded.

6. That all Cattle bee disposed of in marketts & fairs.

7. That speciall Ports & vessells bee appointed for going in and out of the Kingdome.

8. That an office bee instituted for recording the peculiar marks of any Deed or writeing, without knowing the Contents of the same.

9. Where a crime is committed by many, That pardon be offerd to one who shall discover the fact, within 3 monthes & not before one month.

10. Upon what grounds Accompts may be suspect.

Of punishments

Pecuniary mulcts ⎫ for damage to the publiq.
Forfeitures   ⎬
                   ⎭
Banishment – for useless persons & cowards.
Servitude & Slavery – for spendthrifts, bankrupts, debauchers.
Corporall paynes – for fornications, quarellers, cheates.
Exposd to shame & ridiculous habits – for Lyers, cheates, bawds, pimps.
Secluding Imprisonment – for plotters, heretics.
Castration.
Incapacity of Office, Trust, Testimony – for Judges, Officers, Witnesses.
Exposd to Military danger – for homicides, hesters (?).
Branding & Stigmatizing – for Thieves, rogues, blasphemy.

Simple death of severall kinds – for murther, great robbery, burglary, bankrupts (?).

Dismembring – hands, eyes & eares. Thumbs for forgers, Testicles [for] P ... eyes [for] adultery Eares for Plottes sedition.

Torture & death – for repeated murthers.

Bedlam – for witches, Scepticall hereticks (?).

Johann von Justi (1717-1771)

There is some confusion over Johann Heinrich Gottlob von Justi's birth, though it is generally thought that he was born on Christmas night, 1717 in Brücken. In 1741 von Justi joined the army and began a career as a soldier during the Austrian War of Succession (1741-42). It is in the army that Justi came under the influence of Colonel Wigand Gottlob von Gersdorff, becoming his personal secretary and something of a protégé. From Gersdorff, Justi was imparted a love of science and given the means to attend the University of Wittenberg. In 1744, Justi defended his thesis, entitled *De Fuga Militiae*, on the punishment for military dissertations. Moving to Austria in 1750, Justi began to shift his focus to economics, publishing on his own experimentations on a colorant from local plants to serve as a cheaper substitute for indigo. He was given a professorship at the Theresanium, where his inaugural lecture entitled 'The Connection Between the Flowering of the Sciences and the Means which Make a State Powerful and Happy,' reflected the cameralist tradition which he would come to symbolize.

Justi's career saw him developing and teaching cameralist sciences, establishing academic journals and commercial industries, as well as courting political prestige, gaining the respect and trust of the Purssian King, Fredrick the Great. He was to become embroiled in political intrigue during the Seven Years War (1756-1763) by plotting against the Jesuits and by later criticizing the allied Empresses of Austria and Russia. He was also taken to court over an outstanding debt and then failed to deliver on a promise to the Prussian King to supply the territory with an abundance of metal sheets. These missteps ultimately landed Justi under arrest in 1768, and he spent the rest of his life in Fortress Küstrin. He continued to write and publish from jail until his death on July 21, 1771.

Johann Von Justi is said to be have epitomized the German brand of mercantilism known as cameralism. According to Erik S. Reinert, "it is probably fair to say that he was the man who first systemized the science of economic policy and administration." Justi captured the essence of an era, publishing 67 books, some of which have been translated into five languages, on such wide ranging topics as metaphysics and philosophy, minerals and fossils, and economic sciences. His somewhat eclectic repertoire is reflective of the scope of the cameralist tradition, which in turn laid the foundation for the economic and state sciences that nurtured the creation of the European nation-states and the Industrial Revolution.

Works Referenced:

Reinert, Erik S. "Johann Heinrich Gottlob von Justi: The Life and Times of An Economist Adventurer." In *The Beginnings of Political Economy: Johann Heinrich Gottlob von Justi*. Ed, Jürgen G. Backhaus and Frank H. Stephen. Springer: New York, 2009.

Small, Albion W. *The Cameralists: Pioneers of German Social Polity* (1909). Kessinger Publishing: Montana, 2009.

Tribe, Keith. "Justi, Johann Heinrich Gottlob von (1720-1771)." In *The New Palgrave: A Dictionary of Economics Vol.2*. London: Macmillan, 1987.

Selections from: *Staatswirthschaft* in *The Cameralists: The Pioneers of German Social Polity* by Albion W. Small (New York: Burt Franklin, reprint 2001, orig., 1909)., orig. 1756

Note: Enumerated notes following section ranges (e.g. §§72-82) are summary translations provided by Albion Small. Some referencing has been changed or omitted.

Preface to the First Edition
    §xi: People have always been obliged to observe appropriate rules in exploiting their estates, and rulers of republics have found themselves constrained to adopt expedient measures both for organizing the state and for thrift and order in the same. This is the essential in the economic and cameral sciences.

* * *

    §xxii: There are very few positions of responsibility in the state in which expertness in the economic and the cameral sciences would not be the chief matter, if the duties of the position were fulfilled and good service to the state performed.

* * *

    §xxxvii: [The book] contains in a coherent system the chief principles of all economic sciences. First of all the chief theorems of statecraft [*Staatskunst*] are presented. Then the police administration is explained, which in a broad sense includes the science of commerce. These two sciences occupy the first book. The second book teaches principally the immediate duties of subjects, in which duties are involved the grounds of financial science, and then follow the general rules of management, with the chief theorems of agricultural science.

Introduction
    §3: Hence follows the first and universal principle, namely: all the governmental activities of a state must be so ordered that, by means of them the happiness of the state may be promoted.

* * *

    §10: Not the division of the Empire, as many writers on history believe, caused the fall of Rome, for both empires remained after the division stronger than the most powerful realms. We must seek the true cause of the fall of both empires in the insecure occupancy of the throne and in the irregular succession, etc.

* * *

    §24: In respect to the finances, Germany has been very careless for several hundred years. Only at the end of the last century were manufactures to some extent re- established through the Protestant French refugees, and the former king of Prussia, who was himself a very great administrator [*Haushalter*], by good management, increased his revenues by one-half, and he gave equal attention to manufactures. The present great and wise Prussian monarch has not only retained the former management, but by forming great maritime trading societies he has laid the foundations for sea commerce, etc.

First Book

§33: Our times are so fortunate that almost all rulers are eager to secure for their states a nourishing trade, and for their subjects all kinds of subsistence and temporal welfare. I do not venture to say that this providence always springs from genuine sources, that is, from love for the subjects and from paternal impulse to make them happy. Self-love is here and there the chief motive. Yet there is rather satisfactory consciousness on the part of princes in general that they cannot be great and powerful if they have a land that is poor and resource less. All courts accordingly use language consistent with the genuine sources of motive for political action. It is our business to set in order the principles of these governmental sciences, which the nature of things, truth, and sound reason demand. These principles must be derived from the ultimate purpose of the state. What then is a state, and in what does its ultimate purpose consist? It is usually asserted that republics have been derived from fear of incursions. It is more probable that they grew out of the governing skill of families; that is, the patriarch must necessarily have had a certain prestige and power over his children and servants, which descended at his death to his eldest son, until in the course of time it amounted to a real rulership. We have many evidences that this was the fact, but of course they do not account for great empires, which have always been formed by force of arms.

§34: A republic or state is a unification of a multitude of people under a supreme power, for the ultimate purpose of their happiness; or we may say, a republic consists of a multitude of people who are combined with each other by means of a general interdependence and certain fixed institutions, in order, with their united energies, and under a superimposed supreme power, to promote their common happiness. Republics are accordingly distinguished from *Gesellschaften* or *Societaeten,* which, to be sure, have a certain best, and sometimes happiness in general, as their aim, but have never subordinated themselves to a supreme power. The supreme power in the state accordingly originates without doubt from the people; a principle which today is as universally recognized as true as it was formerly regarded as dangerous by little minds.

§35: The ultimate aim of each and every republic is therefore unquestionably the common happiness. It is unnecessary to enlarge upon the proposition, therefore, that the subjects do not exist for the sake of the ruler.

§36: All republics or forms of government are classified into the three types: (1) The monarchy or autocracy, in which the power resides in one alone; (2) the aristocracy, or the government of the better class [*die Vornehmen*]; (3) the democracy, or the rule of the common people. Then there are mixed forms.

* * *

§38: It is easy to prove that the monarchical form of government is far preferable to all others, in consideration of the rapidity with which it can grasp the means of happiness of a state, and became many domestic disturbances and discords are thus prevented. It is also certain that a single good monarch can do more good than free republics could bring to pass in centuries.

§43-44: (1) The fixed form of succession is necessary to the happiness of a state, because otherwise the state can expect nothing but unrest, wars, and disruption; (2) the territorial possessions, and the freedom of those classes that are not harmful to the welfare of the state must be preserved; (3) no new liberties and privileges must be conceded which interfere with facile control of the means of happiness of a state; (4) various realms and lands belonging to a monarch must be combined in a union and a general organization, because separation hinders the use of the full powers of the state, prevents complete employment of means of revenue, especially in commerce, and leads to antipathy and jealousy between the different territories.

* * *

§47: A monarch or ruler [*Regent*] is the supreme head of the state, or of the republic, who possesses the highest power in order that by means of it he may take care of all the affairs of the community and may apply efficient means for promoting the common happiness... The chief duty of the monarch consists therefore in guardianship of the happiness of the subjects.

§48: We should limit the supreme power much too narrowly if we should make it consist merely in laws, ordinances, penalties, etc. To the means and powers of the state belong not only all sorts of goods, both fixed and movable, within the boundaries of the country, but also all the talents and abilities of the persons who reside in the country. The reasonable use of all these things, then, and the prerogative of such use, is therefore the supreme power.

* * *

§55: From the combined welfare of the ruler and the subjects alone springs the real strength of a state. This strength consists principally of the reciprocal trust and love which the wise ruler and the fortunate subjects of a considerable state have for each other, while they endeavor with united energies to preserve and extend the resources of the state. For neither the well-filled treasury and the formidable army of the ruler, nor a land living in riches and abundance makes this strength. Such a condition, however happy it appears to be, is by no means sufficient against all accidents. History is not empty of examples of the most powerful and flourishing realms which unexpectedly came to destruction. A monarch has accordingly met with a great loss if he no longer enjoys the love and confidence of his subjects.

* * *

§60-62: The chief purpose of *Staatskunst* is to assure complete security for the community, both against external and internal dangers. The immediate reason for this purpose is that these dangers threaten the common welfare, and weaken the resources and powers of the state. Statecraft thus obviously seems to preserve the resources of the state. *Policeywissenschaft* is concerned chiefly with the conduct [*Lebenswandel*] and sustenance [*Nahrung*] of the subjects, and its great purpose is to put both in such equilibrium and correlation that the subjects of the republic will be useful, and in a position easily to support themselves. The name "commercial science" is applied to two distinct sciences. The one teaches the ways and means of conducting commerce, and the composition of goods with which commerce is carried on. The other treats of the measures by means of which commercial enterprises may be established and made to flourish, so that as a result the sustenance of subjects may be more ample and the resources of the country may be increased. The latter presupposes knowledge of the former, so that it is not dependent merely on the reports of traders themselves, and it (the latter) is peculiarly appropriate for those persons who are charged with the government of the state. Accordingly it may be called, in distinction from the first, civic-commercial-science [*Staatscommercien-wissenschaft*]. Fundamentally it is a subordinate science of *Policey*, and it is a subject which we shall presently discuss. It is evident that this science, too, ends with extending the resources of the state. Management [*Haushaltungskunst*] is particularly devoted to showing how the resources of private persons may be preserved, increased, and well used: and since rural thrift is of great importance to the state, this branch of science, after referring to all classes and vocations, gives special attention to the ways and means of cultivation. The more thrifty the private persons, the greater and securer the resources of the state. Again there can be no doubt that the science of management is tributary to the preservation and extension of the resources of the state. Since the co-operation of ruler and subjects is necessary for these ends, the subject-matter of these sciences involves two chief considerations, viz.: (1) What means and measures has the ruler to adopt, in order to preserve and increase the resources of the state, and thus to promote the happiness of his subjects? (2) What duties have the subjects in order to lighten the responsibilities of the ruler?

§§72-82:

1. A republic enjoys external security when it is fortified against conquest and even against the excessive power of a neighboring state.

2. Interest is the moving spring of all actions of states, and when two peoples insist on their irreconcilable interests war is the consequence.

3. Hence two things are necessary: first, discreet conduct toward other free powers; and, second, a sufficient army.

4. Discreet conduct toward other states involves: first, knowledge of all other European states; second, adequate knowledge of the home state, its physical and personal make-up.

5. A state must perfectly understand the nature of its relations to other states, the previous history of those relations, etc.

6. The so-called "balance of power" in Europe is an academic invention. If there were such a system no one would have less cause to conform to it than the house of Austria.

7. A state must observe natural law, the law of nations, and the social duties toward other states.

8. A state must seek to discover the movements and intentions of other states.

9. For the foregoing purpose the most able and discreet men must be selected as ambassadors.

10. But no pains must be spared to get the necessary information by secret means.

11. No state should invent schemes for the disadvantage of others which would be disgraceful if discovered.

12. When a state discovers such secret machinations, it often performs a good service by informing the court of the country in whose interest the plans are made, that the plot is known. This usually leads to abandonment of the scheme.

13. When the plan is abhorrent to natural and international law, or to fidelity and faith, it may be made known at other courts.

14. Discretion demands that the blame be put on the ministers, not on the sovereign.

15. A state must be particularly on its guard against another state in which such a plot has been discovered, even though it was dropped. The same animus is likely to hatch another.

§§83-101:

16. Measures for the foregoing purpose consist usually in advantageous alliances, which are of two sorts, offensive and defensive, each of which requires its own sort of consideration.

17. Allies against a hostile power must be sought among those whose interests and policies are identical with ours.

18. Guarantees, and other treaties, by which free powers promise aid in stipulated cases, are also means of security for a state.

19. Another protection against outbreak or extension of war, is the treaty guaranteeing the neutrality of a given territory.

20. Frequently some European power, under a particularly energetic prince, threatens to subordinate the rest of Europe. Then a wise monarch is both privileged and bound to adopt means to keep such a prince within proper limits.

21. Such measures vary according to circumstances, but they must not include treachery.

22. Discreet conduct toward the other free powers is not a guarantee of external security, but other means of defense will be required.

23. The chief of these is an adequate army.

24. Recruits from the inhabitants of the state are preferable to foreign mercenaries.

25. The army must be in constant readiness for war.

26. There are three ways to make an army brave and invincible: (1) By honors and rewards, together with appeals to love of country, after the example of the Romans; (2) by granting license to plunder and ravish, as in the case of Tamerlain, Attila, etc.; (3) by maintaining discipline through fear of punishment. The third only is to be recommended.

27. In a well-ordered state the military budget must take precedence of everything else.

28. The monarch should be commander-in-chief of the army.

29. Fortifications are another means of security.

30. Maritime nations also require a fleet.

§§102-114:

31. Incidental to these latter, various munitions of war must be collected.

32. Resort must be had in extremes to troops furnished by allies, and to mercenaries.

33. It is most advantageous when the allies make separate invasions of the enemy's territory.

34. It is a question whether subsidizing revolt in an enemy's territory is a permissible means of security.

35. It is permissible to destroy an enemy's trade and commerce.

36. Non-permissible means of defense are: assassination of the hostile monarch or his ministers; bribed incendiaries, murder, or similar treacherous violence; poisoned weapons; violation of truce.

37. The domestic security of a state consists in such a well-ordered constitution of the same that all parts of the civic body are held in their appropriate correlation, and in the consequent repose, while the persons and property of individuals are protected against all injustice and violence.

38. For the above purpose each class in the state must be required to keep its appropriate place.

39. The relation which subjects must observe toward the state, as well as toward each other, is based on a moral foundation. A wise government therefore will have a care for the religious faith which the people profess.

40. The state must care for the administration of justice.

41. The state must protect the subjects against frauds and violence.

42. No one should be permitted to gain so much power and wealth that he might be dangerous to the state or to his fellow-citizens.

43. The ruler has nothing to fear from the wealth of his subjects if it is not too unequally distributed.

44. The ruler must first of all give his attention to securing the best talent for the high offices of state and of the army.

45. No officer should be allowed to gain enough power to be dangerous to the state.

§§114-125:

46. Hence no officer should be in trusted with lettres de cachet.

47. Offices should not be hereditary.

48. Neither at court nor in the state should there be different parties.

49. No special class, family, or single person should be allowed to gain so much power that disobedience to the supreme power would be safe.

50. No one should be permitted to possess fortifications or maintain an armed force.

51. Subjects should not be allowed to attach themselves to foreign powers.

52. No privileges should be permitted to subjects which are harmful either to the state or to other subjects.

53. No class should be permitted to monopolize the riches of the country.

54. The ruler must not disregard the feelings of the subjects toward himself or his ministers.

55. The ruler must use all the wisdom possible in governing his conduct in case disorders arise.

56. The moral condition of the subjects must be such as will accord with the welfare of the state [*Wohlfahrt des Staats*], and promote internal security.

57. The ruler must not allow his own religious opinions to be the sole criterion of the goodness or badness of the religion of his subjects; but he must always treat that religion as true which has been introduced by the fundamental principles and constitutions of the state or by the treaties of his predecessors.

58. The regent must nevertheless attempt to establish unity of faith among his subjects.

59. On the other hand the welfare of the state must be preferred to unity of faith.

60. The ruler must prevent the introduction of opinions about religion which are blasphemous and disgraceful, and which tend to demoralize the character of the subjects.

§§126-140:

61. For the forgoing reason, a censorship of books must be established.

62. The ruler must try to stimulate the intelligence of his subjects.

63. The ruler should use the thousand means which are at his disposal to put premiums on personal virtues of all kinds.

64. Yet the ruler must not go so far as to pry into the family life of unsuspected persons.

65. The ruler must not deny the subjects innocent pleasures.

66. The supreme power must adjust strife between subjects over property, pursuits, and transactions, and the decision must rest on the constitution of the republic and on the principles of morals.

67. The administration of justice is to be distinguished from the science of law. It belongs partly to statecraft, partly to Policey.

68. The laws must correspond with the condition of the community, with the character of the various groupings of the subjects, and with the particular purposes which a wise government proposes.

69. The laws must be plain and intelligible.

70. The laws must be brief and simple.

71. Good laws will be in vain unless the government selects men of high character for judges.

72. Even then the judges cannot be trusted without careful supervision.

73. Before all things the administration of justice must be non-partisan.

74. The judicial procedure must be prompt and brief.

75. It would promote justice if the costs of court procedure should be defrayed by the state and not by the litigants.

§§141-151:

76. Domestic security demands that the persons and goods of subjects shall be safe.

77. This safety must be assured both against domestic and foreign violence or fraud.

78. Nations frequently regard the traders of another nation as legitimate booty.

79. Nations sometimes kidnap, the subjects of other nations for soldiers.

80. Nations sometimes encourage special sorts of lotteries, or other fraudulent schemes for obtaining the property of the subjects of other nations.

81. The worst sort of domestic violence is nocturnal robbery and murder, whether on country roads, the streets of cities, or in private houses.

82. If we seek the sources of these evils, they are to be found chiefly in the defective education of youth, and in the consequent excesses of adults, the scarcity of food in the country, or the defective impulse to perform remunerative work, the oppression of the land under heavy taxation and other wrongs of government.

83. A wise ruler would not have much difficulty in adopting measures which would remove these conditions.

84. Meanwhile the minor civic officials must be required to keep sharp watch of criminals.

85. Frequent visitations of roads, forests, and suspicious houses, and the use of the militia on country roads and at night in the streets of towns, are advisable. Also the closing of public houses at an appointed time, and sharp watch of them

after that hour, while the watchmen themselves must be subject to the severest punishments, if they take bribes to allow criminals to escape.

86. Thieves are on the whole more dangerous to security than robbers and murderers, and must consequently be zealously traced and punished.

87. Vagabonds of all sorts must be driven from the country.

88. Watch must be kept at the boundaries against such classes, and householders must he required to report the names and circumstances of the people who lodge with them.

89. It is a question whether a wise government should tolerate Jews. They surely cause much harm by their usury and sharp practices. Yet it is also a question whether they have not been forced to these and even criminal practices by the policies of governments toward them. Probably if they were admitted to all means of gaining a livelihood they would be as useful to a land as other subjects.

90. A wise government must finally punish with severity all other kinds of violence, such as duelling, outbreaks of apprentices, and all ways of taking private steps to supplant the law in meting out justice.

§§151-157:

91. To prevent these evils, the law itself must efficiently treat the conditions which they are intended to correct.

92. Besides security, sufficient wealth is necessary to the happiness of a state.

93. By the wealth of a country we understand a sufficient supply of goods to satisfy the needs and conveniences of life, and by means of which the subjects by diligence and labour may find adequate sustenance.

94. Such being the nature of wealth, if a land yielded an abundance of such useful things, and had no trade relations with other lands, we might call it rich, even though it contained no trace of gold and silver.

95. Because of international transactions we need a ware [*Ware*] which is rare, to which all peoples assign equal value, which is durable and easily carried, to be used as a universal means of payment.

96. Gold and silver possess these qualifications. Consequently a land cannot be regarded as rich today unless it possesses a sufficient supply (*hinreichende Menge*) of these metals.

97. Token currency is in no proper sense an addition to national wealth, although it may be a means of increasing wealth.

98. If a ruler could circulate token currency at will, he could gradually absorb the whole national wealth.

99. Such currency ought not to be used unless a definite term is fixed for its redemption.

100. We must distinguish (a) the wealth of the ruler; (b) the wealth of private persons; (c) the wealth of the land.

101. Gold, silver, and costly ornaments stored in the treasure-chests of the monarch are of no use to the country and would not alone tend to remove the land from poverty.

102. The same is the case if there are many rich persons in a country who either hoard their wealth, or keep it in foreign banks.

103. The true conception of national wealth then is that it consists of an adequate supply of money, distributed among the subjects, employed in gainful pursuits, and constantly passing from one hand to another.

104. In order that the people may be able by labour and diligence not only to support themselves but to supply the needs of the state, the ruler must see (a) that all measures are taken which secure the necessary means of increasing wealth; (b) that all necessary means are used to insure the constant employment of this wealth in gainful ways, and the circulation of it from hand to hand.

105. A state cannot increase its wealth without guarding what it already possesses. The first rule of a wise government therefore should be to prevent by all possible means the unnecessary removal of money from the country.

§§157-168:

106. This involves stopping, by the court, of purchases of foreign goods and discouragement of customs which tend to take the money of private persons out of the country.

107. The second fundamental rule of a wise government must be that there should be constant effort to increase the wealth of the state, for a land cannot be too rich.

108. On the other hand riches must not be increased at the cost of oppressing other peoples, for such means of obtaining wealth demoralize those who so obtain it. The chief cause of the fall of thePersian and Roman monarchies is to be found in their disregard of this principle.

109. There are three chief ways of increasing the wealth of a land: (1) the increase of population; (2) foreign commerce; (3) mining.

110. Increase of the population increases the means of a country both because the newcomers bring goods into the country, and because they stimulate circulation of money.

111. It is thus certain that large population makes a state prosperous provided its constitution is beneficent. The talents of the persons in the republic, indeed the persons themselves, are among the resources of the state. The larger the number of people living in the country therefore, the greater will be the means and power of the republic. Hence the duty of the ruler to promote increase of population.

112. It is often asked whether a population cannot become too great, so that some will obstruct the happiness of the rest. Nothing is so unfounded as this objection. Given flourishing commerce, manufactures, and trades, with well-administered police and government in general, and there is no good reason

why the population should stop at any particular point. Holland and China are evidence to this effect.

113. There is no reason to fear that population could overtax the food supply. Europe could feed six times its present population.

114. If we had wise police and economic administration, there would be no need of allowing emigration to America.

115. To encourage increase of population the government in the first place must be beneficent and mild.

116. As a particular under this generalization, reasonable freedom must be permitted to the subjects.

117. The growth of population is scarcely possible unless the ruler permits complete freedom of conscience.

118. Freedom of conscience must be distinguished from complete freedom of religious liberty. The latter is to be granted only under approved conditions. The former, consisting of rights of belief and household worship, should be allowed in so far as it is not harmful to the state.

119. A wise ruler will not leave the food supply and employment of subjects to take care of themselves, but will see that they are systematically made abundant.

120. Still further, the government must encourage the immigration of rich and talented people of all kinds, and may resort to titles, honors, positions, and privileges as premiums to them.

§§168-180:

121. So far as possible, the government should relieve newcomers who wish to build, of the taxes, building-permit fees, etc.

122. Special encouragement must be given to skilled foreigners who wish to introduce into the country desirable industries.

123. The ruler should see that the laws are favorable to the marriage relation.

124. A wise Catholic ruler will try to limit the growth of the clerical orders, for they arc largely responsible for the unfavorable contrast in population between Catholic and Protestant countries.

125. A wise ruler will consider seriously the point of view of population, before entering into war. He will especially encourage all means of diminishing sickness and of preventing plague.

126. A wise government will check drunkenness and other demoralizing vices.

127. The art of medicine must be brought to the highest efficiency.

128. Surgery, midwifery, and pharmacy must for the same reason be encouraged and regulated by the government.

129. Provision must be made for assuring purity of foods.

130. The cleanliness of cities must be assured, and this requires attention to the building regulations.

131. Commerce is transactions in means of sustenance in which the goods and wares are exchanged with advantage either against gold and silver, or against other wares, and by this process the needs and conveniences of human life are satisfied. This explanation includes everything which belongs to the nature of commerce and to comprehension of it.

132. Only foreign commerce can increase the wealth of a land.

133. The first principle of commerce must be that more gold and silver shall be brought in than carried out by it.

134. The first distinction to be made is between goods produced at home and those obtained from abroad.

135. When commerce is carried on with domestic wares, the wealth of the land always gains something by it, but this kind of commerce may nevertheless be very disadvantageous to the state; for if the wares are carried from the country in the raw and untransformed condition, or are drawn from foreign nations, the land loses considerably from the earnings and support of subjects which might have been enjoyed from the same.

§§180-188:

136. When commerce is conducted with foreign wares alone, this is either because these wares are to be consumed at home, or because they are to be traded, with profit, to other nations. The first sort of commerce is wholly harmful to a country; for although the special traders, certain commercial cities, and the tariff and excise accounts of the ruler may temporarily profit, the land as a whole cannot gain anything by such trade. On the contrary, if it has no other sources of wealth, it must gradually lose all its gold and silver, and this harmful trade must at last stop from lack of means of payment.

137. The second sort of foreign trade is incomparably more profitable for the state.

138. There is a great difference in goods with respect to the source, or the lands from which they are derived. The trader must know all about the differences, and he must know whether he receives them from the first, second, or third hand, and where they can with profit be sold. The cameralist, however, must know them so far that he can judge what sorts are most advantageous for the entire system of commerce, and for domestic manufacture, or with which kinds the land may most easily carry on profitable trade.

139. Another difference in wares springs from their essential nature and composition. That is, they may be rough or fine, useful or useless, superfluous or necessary, genuine or spurious, fresh or spoiled, etc. Of all these differences, a trader must be fully informed. A civic official in the commercial department must also be somewhat intelligent about these things, in order to promote the transportation of the wares, and properly to assess the duties and excises.

140. There are also differences with respect to their external and accidental condition; i.e., packed or unpacked: to be counted, weighed, or measured;

salable or unsalable and contraband—the latter only temporarily and in time of war forbidden. Both merchants and cameralists need to be informed about these details.

141. These various sorts of goods occasion many sorts of trade; e.g., the customary classification is: (1) Cloth; (2) Silk; (3) Spices; (4) Groceries [*Materialien*]; (5) Hides and furs [*Pelz-handel*]; (6) Gold, silver, or jewels; (7) Books. This however is merely an approximate classification, for there may be as many sorts of trade as there are separate sorts of wares. Indeed it is advisable for a trader not to deal in too many wares. If he dares to confine himself to a single one he can more effectively master the conditions of that trade. Small traders who have to look out merely for cost and sale may carry a miscellaneous stock.

142. Trade comprises two chief types of transactions: (a) obtaining the wares; (b) marketing them.

143. All domestic goods come either from cultivating the earth, or from stock- breeding, or from industries [*Gewerbe*]. As to agriculture, a wise merchant will either himself engage in it, or by advancing loans, storage, and favorable contracts will seek to get the wares at a good price. As to products of stock-raising, he may, by cash payments, by courteous conduct and minor attentions [*eines kleinem Ergötzlichkeit*], get the good-will of the shepherds and other country folk who have such things for sale. The wares, however, which come from the trades, are procured best through the establishment of manufactures and factories. Sometimes advances to the manufacturers and hand-workers will secure the goods. A wise government, on the other hand, will always see to it that all these domestic wares are supplied at the required quality and price, in order that the favorable balance in other countries may be retained.

144. As to obtaining foreign wares, they come either by wagon or by boat from neighboring lands, and in such cases the factors involved are essentially those just named; or they are brought from long distances across seas. For that purpose the merchant must either have ships of his own, if commerce is free to all, or he must buy shares in trading associations, or in the great auctions he must provide himself with the needed wares.

145. By "shares" [*Actien*] we understand those participating parts which a great privileged trading society at its organization sells at a fixed price, in order thereby to bring in the sums which must be used in the trade of the society. These shares, which thereafter may be resold, rise or fall in price, according to the success of the society.

146. Since seafaring is beset with many dangers, a wise merchant will never risk his whole resources, or a large portion of them, at one time upon the waves. Consequently it is not only customary for many merchants to join in fitting out ships, but many forms of contract have been invented, such as shares in ships, insurance, etc. The most important of these is insurance; that is, another party undertakes to assure the cargo of a ship for a payment of 3, 5, 10, 20, 30, or more

per hundred, according to the degree of danger to be feared, and in case of loss to make it good.

147. The second chief type of transaction, sale, depends principally upon good correspondents, who protect the merchant by giving him timely notice of rise and fall of prices and other circumstances which affect his trade. A good merchant must be able to distinguish between a correspondent who can be relied upon to serve his employer's interests and one who is seeking chiefly his own advantages. The bourse, a house where in great trading centers the merchants daily meet to transact business, is very prolific of such reports, but they cannot be regarded with much confidence.

148. Actual sale is of various kinds: e.g., for cash payment, on credit, on installments, on exchange, on venture, or on speculation [*a l'aventure ou en l'air*], or by means of commission merchants, factors, fairs [*Messen*] or similar devices. A merchant must be well instructed about these different sorts of trade, together with the cost of transportation, tariffs, probable dangers, and the prices to be expected, in order that by weighing these items over against one another he may be reasonably assured of profits. He must also assure himself about the reliability of the persons intrusted with the transportation, also concerning the warehouses and other circumstances of the towns and roads through which the goods must pass.

149. To keep all these things straight, bookkeeping is necessary. It is customary to use the following books: The inventory book; the manual, or memorial, or chief book; the journal; the debt book; the credit book; the treasury book; the secret book; the stock book; the expense book. All of these must be kept in the greatest order, and they must exactly correspond with one another. For this reason, in large concerns a special bookkeeper is appointed.

150. The ultimate purpose of all these transactions is, on the side of the republic, to export goods produced in the country, and not needed, and therefrom to gain increase of wealth, as well as to provide the land with all those goods which are required for the needs and convenience of human life. On the side of the merchant, however, gain is the single purpose of all his endeavor. In view of the service which he renders to the state, of the danger which he incurs, and of the labours which he undertakes, we should not begrudge his gains. They consist in the increase of his goods and of his means. The amount of his goods depends entirely on the value which they have in terms of gold and silver. Consequently the single aim of the merchant is to increase, his resources in gold and silver, or in goods which in comparison with these metals have a great value.

§§189-199:

151. Gold and silver is also in fact the ground (sic) of all commerce carried on in the world or at least among civilized or somewhat intelligent peoples.

152. Because merchants have constant occasion to transfer gold and silver to one another, a large number of devices have been invented to serve their purposes.

Thus the important exchanges, and the system of bank credits, whereby gold and silver are transferred only in imagination, yet with the same advantage to the merchant as though the metals were actually delivered. The essence of the matter is that one gives to a third party notice that the sum due can be drawn at a certain place. This simple and natural way of payment is then by the laws, by the different moneys, and other circumstances, surrounded with a multitude of formalities and special details, which today compose a considerable part of the science of commerce, not only for the merchant, but also for the cameralist.

153. A bank is a public institution of the state in which merchants and other private persons may at will securely deposit sums of money, in such a way that they may withdraw the same any hour, or may use their deposits for payment to other persons by means of the bank-credit system. Banks of this sort are called deposit [*Giro*] or exchange banks, in distinction from loan banks.

154. Those rulers who coin depreciated money miss their calculation in expecting to gain by it. Foreigners will take it only at its true value, and even something less. The bad money therefore returns to the land that coins it. It is paid back by the subjects into the treasury of the ruler, and he deceives himself if he supposes he has in the treasury more than the actual gold and silver. This flattering idea disappears as soon as the attempt is made to purchase abroad. Meanwhile the subjects who have received the money from the ruler at the imaginary value, and who must make foreign purchases, suffer.

155. The persons engaged in trade are either principals, subordinates, or auxiliaries. The duties of each of these classes must be treated in the special textbook on commercial science.

156. The fundamental principles of merchants must be distinguished from the measures and purposes of the government. While the merchant aims only at gain, and is not always concerned whether his gain corresponds with the advantage of the state, a wise government, on the contrary, must give the chief attention to this latter consideration. Hence the merchants may be much dissatisfied with the regulations of trade. Domestic manufacture and trade are far less inviting to them on this account than the welfare of the state demands. It is not to be assumed, however, that the advantage of the whole state is incompatible with the prosperity of the merchants. The former may, however, require that the advantages enjoyed by the latter shall be less than at some other periods. Even in this case the merchants may offset the restrictions by interesting themselves in promoting mining, manufactures, etc.

157. No European country is entirely without foreign commerce, but some of it is very harmful, and cannot continue without adequate increase of wealth from other sources.

158. The establishment of commerce presupposes that it will obtain a condition which promises permanence with advantage to the state.

159. The founding of commerce is not a mere matter of appointing and encouraging fairs and markets.

160. If at these markets more foreign than domestic goods are sold, then they are only a great vortex from which more gold flows out than comes in, and the town where the fair is held is the only gainer, and it consequently holds on to its advantage as long as possible, in spite of the general poverty of the country.

161. Prohibition of the exportation of money does not secure profitable commerce. In the first place it cannot be effective, in the second place it would deprive the subjects of many things which their present standard of life requires, and in the third place it could accomplish nothing of itself in the direction of establishing commerce.

162. The first principle of advantageous commerce with foreign nations is, that more gold and silver shall come into the country as a result than goes out, and on this principle must all measures for establishing useful commerce be founded.

163. Since commerce must be carried on either with domestic or foreign goods, and since the mere importation of foreign goods cannot possibly constitute an advantageous trade, there follows naturally another principle, viz.: The value of the domestic products exported must exceed the value of foreign wares imported. The inferences from these two principles will give us all the measures necessary for the establishment of commerce.

164. The excess value of exports over imports can be secured in only two ways: first, the quantity of imported foreign wares must be diminished; or, second, the gaining and exportation of domestic products must be increased.

165. In fact these two methods must be combined in order to assure the result.

§§199-212:

166. For this purpose a wise ruler must inform himself precisely about the exported and imported wares and their aggregate values. These facts must be exhibited in tables drawn from the tariff and excise registers, so that they can be reviewed at a glance. For greater exactness the contents of the tariff and excise registers may be tabulated separately and compared with each other. To be still more certain, all merchants, artists, manufacturers, and artisans may be required to report what kinds of wares they imported during the previous year, and what domestic products they sent abroad. By these three processes together the facts may be somewhat exactly ascertained.

167. We call this casting the general trade balance. The special trade balance is a similar showing of the imports and exports between the home and a specified foreign country. A wise government will every year keep both accounts.

168. A wise ruler or his ministers will study these tables to discover whether among the imports there are any which could be produced at home, and thereupon it must be made a fixed rule that nothing which can be produced at home shall be imported. The necessary measures must then be adopted to promote production of those wares.

169. In this connection all kinds of textiles call for attention, since they are for clothing and are accordingly necessaries of life. Every land either has materials for these, or can easily get them. Silk-weaving is also possible in northern countries. Wool may be grown everywhere, and the fine wool to be mixed with it may be had through trade, as the English importation of Spanish wool. Hence such manufacture ought not to be omitted.

170. Yet foreign trade in such fabrics is not to be expected. Our neighbors, England, Holland, France, and Wales, have already too long start of us. But it will be advantage enough if we check the import of foreign textiles.

171. The only variation from the last conclusion is in case we can invent such improvement in the fabrics, that we can make foreigners our debtors.

172. The same principle holds in the case of every sort of ware which might be produced at home. As everything cannot be done at once, beginnings should be made in the case of those wares which are most used at home, and for which the largest sums are now sent abroad.

173. A second rule must be kept in mind along with the first, viz.: preference should be given to those industries which would employ and support the most men.

174. A third rule should also be followed, viz.: to prefer those industries for which the raw materials arc produced at home.

175. On the other hand, those industries must be stimulated which will produce goods that foreign nations need.

176. In order to exploit these resources it is necessary for the government to rouse a commercial spirit among the subjects.

177. No monopolies in such domestic products, and no similar privileges should be granted.

178. Assuming such measures for promoting domestic production, a wise government must give its attention to measures for inducing foreigners to take the wares. Two factors must be assured: (1) The wares must have the desired quality; (2) the price must be satisfactory. It may be added that the beauty of the wares is also a factor.

179. In order to insure the quality of wares, the government must not merely promulgate certain ordinances and rules, but it must also appoint certain inspectors who will examine the completed wares, and will mark with a distinguishing sign those which conform to the standards and those which do not. In case, as is certainly advisable, complete freedom from tax shall be permitted to exports, this immunity should extend to those wares only which satisfy this test.

180. It is also often necessary to stimulate production by certain prizes and rewards, and when the court learns that science or skill is lacking for the production of certain wares, every effort must be made to attract people with the necessary qualifications, or by the necessary money payment to get the lacking information from a foreign artist, since everything may be had for money.

§§214-225:

181. If the wares are to be supplied at a favorable price, not only must the articles requisite for supplying the necessities of life be purchasable at moderate prices, for on this depends the amount of the wages of the labourers, but the raw material of the wares must also not be dear. The ruler must accordingly take all possible care that not only agriculture but all the industries that supply the necessities of life shall be in good order, so that no scarcity shall occur, as one industry always sustains another. Before all things, however, those crafts which deal with the necessities of life must be held under strict supervision, in order that they may not raise prices by charging excessive profits, or by buying up the supply, and other underhanded means.

182. When so much has been done for stimulation of domestic production, it is time to establish fairs and great markets.

183. But flourishing commerce must be described as something more than enough to sustain fairs and markets established under the foregoing conditions. The expression is properly used only when flourishing trade in all sort of wares is carried on with all parts of the world. This is hardly to be thought of unless it is in connection with extensive merchant marine and foreign trade.

184. Assuming that the land borders on the sea and has good harbors, or at least the possibility of making them, or is crossed by a navigable river which is at the command of the country to its mouth, the beginnings of sea-trade may be made by the formation of a great trading society, which can collect the guarantee or the capital for its transactions by the sale of a certain number of shares.

185. In order to induce both natives and foreigners to take shares, either very great privileges must be granted to the society, or the bad condition and management of foreign companies must furnish the necessary stimulus, or the court must offer the company material support.

186. The success of such a company depends principally upon I good management of its affairs. The court must consequently do; its best to insure the election of directors whose insight, talent, diligence, and integrity are grounds for confidence; and the minister of commerce and marine, who should possess all these qualities in the highest degree, must know how to lead these directors in accordance with his purposes.

187. Such a company must be guarded against dangerous enterprises and needless outlay. A few unfortunate investments will not only ruin the company, but it will be much harder for the state afterward to bring about the formation of a new company.

188. The power and prestige of the monarch go far toward the success of such a company. Other nations that carry on foreign trade look with jealous eyes on such a company, and try in every way to put obstacles before it. The power of the monarch, however, restrains them within such limits, that they cannot openly antagonize it.

189. It is proper that possession of a certain number of shares should be a condition of sitting and voting in the meetings of such a company. It is not so certain that a similar condition should hedge election of directors, because it is not at all certain that wealth enough to own shares is combined with the necessary qualifications for such an office.

190. It is a prime condition of success that such companies start with sufficient capital for large operations.

191. It must be insisted that the predominant effort of such companies should be to sell domestic goods in foreign lands. If they only bring in goods directly from foreign lands which have previously been bought from middle-men, a saving of middle-men's profits and of transportation charges of foreign ships is made, to be sure; but nevertheless the money to defray the first cost of the goods goes out of the country.

192. Such a trading society must not count on founding establishments in distant lands at once, but must plan to gain them gradually; i.e., not until they can pay good dividends to the shareholders, and until there is a comfortable capital in reserve, so that the cost of foreign establishments may be covered out of the reserve without diminishing the dividends (p. 221). Such gains take large fractions of the capital; societies formed by other countries, and already operating there, conduct minor warfare with competitors, and the monarchs cannot regard their quarrels as sufficient grounds for actual war. If one such society is ruined under these conditions, it is all the harder for subsequent ones to succeed.

193. When the trade of such a commercial company becomes flourishing it is possible to organize other companies to operate in the same territory in particular lines of goods. It is preferable, however, to sell more shares and expand the operations of a single company. This prevents harmful jealousies, cross-purposes, and manifold loss of advantage by the home company.

194. After all, such companies are not absolutely essential to the promotion of foreign commerce. Even if they have been used to establish trade, the time may come when expansion of trade will be best assured by opening it freely to all mariners and merchants.

195. First of all we must name among the conditions of promoting commerce, a mild government, and reasonable freedom of conscience and action, as in the case of domestic prosperity. People engaged in foreign trade must for special reasons enjoy these immunities, because they have special facilities for withdrawing their wealth from the country.

§§226-237:

196. Second, a wise ordering of the tariff and excise system is the principal means by which a wise government can guide foreign commerce according to its purposes. Instead of being detrimental to trade, since traders always have their own interest in view more than that of the state, and it would be ruinous to leave the ways and means of commerce to their enterprise, no trade can be carried

on in a way that is advantageous to the state which is not in this way guided, controlled, and to a certain extent promoted.

197. For purposes of tariff and excise, wares are of three classes: (1) for export; (2) for import; (3) for transport. Wares of the first class are either fully manufactured, or in raw or partially manufactured condition; those of the second class are either indispensable or dispensable. Accordingly the tariff and excise laws must take account of five classes of wares, and this makes five primary rules necessary.

198. RULE 1.—All exports of manufactured goods must be burdened with light imposts. The one profitable kind of trade consists in commerce of this class, and a wise ruler must not merely take care that the goods themselves are of high quality, but he must see that foreigners are stimulated to take them. It is poor encouragement to foreign buyers to lay a tax on such goods. The exportation is of itself such an advantage to the state, that it is unnecessary to burden it with imposts which make against the ultimate use of exportation.

199. The only exception to this rule is in case the home products are so cheap, or transportation is so cheap and easy, that the exports can undersell competing products of foreign countries. Even in this case, export taxes should not be imposed on articles the home production of which is capable of indefinite expansion. It is better to give the home merchants the opportunity to make the profit, so that they will be stimulated to increase the volume of trade to the utmost.

200. Another corollary from this rule is that very low imposts should be placed on raw materials when they are moved from one part of the country to another for the purpose of being manufactured.

201. RULE 2. — Export of raw material which is a home product must either be heavily taxed or entirely prohibited.

202. RULE 3. — All imports of dispensable wares must carry heavy imposts; for if they are really dispensable the importation brings the country great harm by useless foreign expenditure of money.

203. RULE 4.—Imports of indispensable wares should bear only light imposts. Tariff and imposts should not be the ordinary way of collecting tribute from the subjects. They are justified as a source of revenue only by some subsidiary purpose. Their main purpose should be to direct the course of commerce.

204. It follows that foreign raw material needed for chief or subordinate purposes in home manufacture should be free of import duties.

205. RULE 5. — Goods in transport should be free of imposts, with the exception of trifling tolls.

206. The only exception to this rule is when the carriage of an article through the country takes a market away from a home product, in which case we must be sure that imposition of high taxes would not lead to reprisals.

207. All the servants of the taxing system must be held under strict discipline, both against peculation, and against needless vexation of travelers.

208. Commercial treaties with foreign countries are the next most important means of promoting commerce.

209. Next in order are good harbors and roads, and passable rivers and canals.

210. A well-organized system of posts, boats, and land carriers is a further desideratum.

§§240-252:

211. The coinage is an essential factor of flourishing trade.

212. Unpartisan and prompt rendering of justice in all trade litigation greatly promotes business.

213. To this end special commercial courts, both original and appellate, should be organized. They should be composed in part of legal experts, in part of merchants, capable of bringing the most exact technical knowledge to interpretation of the laws.

214. The most flourishing commerce is hardly possible unless the ruler organizes a special bureau of commerce. This must be composed of members who, along with proved integrity, fidelity, and wisdom, possess complete knowledge of trade, and especially of civic-commercial science; and it is particularly advisable that no merchants should be members of the bureau, because their purposes are often different from those of the state. In the largest countries a special subordinate bureau may be organized for manufactures. In this bureau former merchants and mining experts may be useful. In both bureaus individuals must be placed in charge of divisions of operations with which they are particularly acquainted, and consequently only the most important and general matters should be handled by the whole body. In every important seaport or commercial center there should be at least one commercial councilor, to supervise commercial and manufacturing relations at that point under the provisions of the two bodies.

215. Finally, a wise government must take care to remove all obstacles which may embarrass commerce. These may come either from foreign or domestic causes. Thus, under the former head, war between other powers, with incidental hindrances to our commerce; secret machinations of other powers against our foreign traders, etc. Among domestic hindrances may be named: Scarcity of materials for shipbuilding and other production; lack of capital in the country; existing privileges of certain lands and towns in the matter of imports and exports of staples; the envy and jealousy of certain lands and towns toward one another, etc.

216. Precious metals should be mined with the aid of governments even at a loss.

217. This is not a loss for the state as a whole. The sums expended remain in the country and support many people. The country as a whole will be richer by the amount of gold and silver that is taken from the earth.

218. In case of the other metals, even a small profit should justify mining. By furnishing material to be sold abroad they add to the nation's wealth as truly as the mining of gold and silver.

219. The measures to be adopted by rulers for promoting mining fall into three groups: (1) for stimulating the population to engage in mining; (2) for standardizing the operation of mines; (3) for promoting mining science.

220. Although all mining rights belong to the ruler, yet he cannot work them, because that would too greatly enlarge his budget, and make his income uncertain. The first requisite, then, is proclamation of free mining rights, subject to the laws of the land, at least to citizens, with reserve of the rightful royalties to the government.

221. The ruler should give assurance that he will not himself, or through his ministers, engage in mining.

222. The ruler must take care in many ways that those who operate mines shall be free to carry on their enterprise under the most favorable conditions.

223. The government must assist unprofitable mines, by remitting dues, etc.

224. Many changes in the mining laws are necessary, especially because the introduction of machines, etc., has changed conditions.

225. An area of "at least two miles" should be assured for the operations of a new mine.

§§253-376:

226. This plan is recommended only for the precious and base metals.

227. For salts, coloring matter, and clays, commercial societies are preferable.

228. Schools of mines should be founded to train future managers of mines.

229. It will be useless to count on mines as a permanent source of wealth unless provision is made for keeping up the supply of wood.

230. It is not enough that there should be wealth in the country, but the ruler must take care that this wealth is constantly active in the trades, and that it passes from hand to hand, for the true wealth of the country depends wholly upon this. In this way the subjects are put in a position not merely by diligence and labour to provide for their need and comfort, but also bear their share toward supplying the needs of the state. In fact it is quite natural to represent a republic under the figure of a human body. Wealth is the blood, the trades are the arteries, and the government is the heart, into which from time to time the wealth circulating in the arteries flows, and thence again pours into all parts of the civic body through the outlays of the state. We have now to treat of the means by which this circulation is promoted.

231. The chief means of promoting circulation of money in the trades are four, viz.: (1) that the sources of subsistence shall be kept in good correlation; (2) that the land shall keep its credit high; (3) that manufacture and artisanship shall be kept prosperous; (4) that idleness and beggary shall be abated.

232. The nature of a republic necessarily involves common and harmonious obligations, for when the subjects have placed over themselves a supreme power (sic), from which they demand that it shall promote their happiness, they are

naturally bound to conform to those arrangements which that supreme power adopts for their happiness, and to promote them in every way, otherwise they would obstruct their own ultimate purposes.

233. By subjects we understand all those who enjoy the protection of the state. This brief proposition gives us the clearest idea of the essential characteristics of a subject, and in fact no more essential finding mark can be determined than the enjoyment of protection.

234. The right cannot be denied to a ruler to demand that all those who possess estates in his land shall either be permanently domiciled upon them, or shall sell the estates to some person agreeable to him.

235. Subjects owe their duties to an unlimited monarch only when he does not act as an enemy of the people. This situation may never have occurred, because even the greatest tyrants had apparent excuses, and it is consequently never quite clear that an autocrat is acting as the enemy of his people.

236. Under mixed forms of government the subjects owe duties not to the monarch alone, but also to the whole state, and to the fundamental laws of the same. Consequently duty to the monarch is not a valid plea in extenuation of action harmful to the estates.

237. Duties of subjects are accordingly of two classes: (a) immediate duties to ruler or state, springing from the essential nature of the relation of subjects; (b) mediate duties toward ruler and state, i. e., such as subjects owe primarily to themselves, and thus secondarily to ruler and state.

238. The immediate duties of subjects toward ruler and state are those which are necessarily connected with the ultimate purposes of the republic and with the relation of subjects, and which subjects owe to the supreme power in the state alone.

239. These immediate duties fall into three chief classes: (a) exact obedience to the laws, commands, and ordinances of the supreme power; (b) unimpeachable loyalty to the same; (c) contribution according to ability to the support and best welfare of the state.

240. Loyalty [*Treue*] consists of complete devotion, attachment, and reverence toward the supreme power, with careful endeavor to avoid, and so far as possible to assist in preventing everything which might be harmful to the external and internal security of the state and of the person of the ruler.

§§397-457:

241. Subjects are released from loyalty to a ruler (1) through absorption by conquest or otherwise into another country; (2) when the ruler abdicates.

242. In order to treat at length of the mediate duties of subjects, we must elaborate the whole housekeeping art [*Haushaltungskunst*] since the obligation to operate well with our resources can be fulfilled in no other way than through the rules which this *Haushaltungskunst* teaches. But *Oeconomie* belongs in the system of the sciences which we have undertaken to expound, because through the

exercise of the same the resources of the state are maintained and increased. On that account it is the more evident that all the sciences pertaining to government and to the large management [*Wirthschaft*] of the state hang together most exactly in a single system. Attempting therefore to treat of *Haushaltungskunst* completely and thoroughly, so far as the limits of the present work permit, we shall in the first place present the general doctrines of the same, then we shall treat particularly the two chief topics of *Oeconomie*, viz., urban economy and rural economy, and shall apply to them the general rules.

243. The name *Haushaltungskunst* or *Oeconomie* may really be applied to two distinct sciences. When we speak of the *Oeconomie* of the country, or of the great management [*Wirthschaft*] of the state, all the sciences are involved which we treat in this book. When we talk of *Oeconomie* or *Haushaltungskunst* simply, we mean that science which we are now about to explain, and which is concerned with the goods and with the gainful occupations of private persons. Haushaltungskunst is, however, a science of so ordering the gainful occupations and the thrift in town and country that means [*Vermögen*] will thereby be preserved, increased, and reasonably used, and the temporal happiness of private persons will be promoted; or more briefly expressed, it is the science of applying our "means" to the promotion of our temporal happiness.

244. One sense of "means" [*Vermögen*] signifies everything that is within our power, or that which we are able to bring to pass. In ordinary thinking "means" signifies all goods and aptitudes which we possess and which we may employ in order to provide for ourselves the necessities and conveniences of this life. In the narrower sense we understand by "means" the possession of a sufficiency of movable or immovable goods, which put in our hands, according to our social position and make-up [*Beschaffenheit*], all the conveniences and advantages of life. When we here use the term "means," it is in the two last senses, principally in the third.

245. Except through accident, no obtaining of "means" is possible unless our aptitudes and already-possessed goods are the beginning and ground of the acquisition.

246. By "goods" we understand in Haushaltungskunst only those things which have a certain value and use for the need and convenience of human life, and which at a certain value or price can be transferred to others; i.e., things that have a money value.

247. Credit is to a certain extent to be reckoned among goods, for it can be used as the ground and beginning of "means".

248. By "aptitudes" we understand those acquired capabilities and skills by which we may be useful to others and to ourselves in business and trades, or in social life in general.

249. All "means" must be gained either by services [*Dienste*], or by trades [*Gewerbe*]. The former require only "aptitudes;" the latter require "aptitudes" and goods together.

250. Services are a certain compact between the principal and the servant, by which the latter, in return for a certain salary or compensation, promises to apply his "aptitudes," in certain assigned occupations, for the benefit of the principal. These services are either honorable or menial; they are also morally legitimate or illegitimate.

251. The two great classes of gainful occupations are (1) those that procure livelihood in the town; (2) those that procure livelihood in the country.

252. From services or trades come "earnings" [*Gewinne*]. This is the advantage which accrues to us from a thing after deduction of our applied outlay and effort. The justification of earnings must have at its basis the revenue which the other can, and probably will derive from the thing, for we are surely entitled to demand that the other shall allow a just portion of the return to accrue to us which he would not have acquired without our co-operation.

253. In order to gain "means," one must first of all make a plan of his mode of life, and of the ways by which he is to acquire earnings. In this plan account must be taken of his aptitudes and goods. Most men make the mistake of making no plan, and of seeking their fortune in a merely haphazard way. Still others fail because they draw back in fear from every obstacle.

254. Further it is necessary to know all the details involved in the success of our plan.

255. This knowledge will enable us to choose the necessary means for carrying out our plan.

§§458-496:

256. It is further necessary to combine these means in a skilful way.

257. By this skilful combination of "means" it is often possible that one may at the same time accomplish several sorts of purpose, and earn in several ways.

258. But one will not acquire "means," either by service or trade, if one has not learned to save.

259. In order to exercise this great art of saving, the first thing in every establishment must be a budget or correct estimate of income and outlay.

260. The savings must then be used further to increase "means".

261. After all, the increase of "means" will be a tedious process unless one takes some reasonable chances, and occasionally exposes a part of his "means" to the hazards of fortune.

262. Those who make such ventures should first possess considerable "means," so that they could lose what they risk without being reduced to want.

263. Then the anticipated gain should be in proportion to the danger to which one is exposed.

264. The reasonable use of "means" is the chief purpose of acquisition and of *Haushaltungskunst*.

265. "Means" contribute not a little to the end of a social happy, and virtuous life. One is thereby much more qualified for service to the community, and one

can fulfill the duties of social life in a much higher degree than those who have no means.

266. The reasonable use of means depends upon three chief rules: (1) The "means" must be so used that the substance (sic) of the same will not be impaired; (2) one must apply one's "means" to the support of one's life and to the promotion of one's temporal happiness, according as the social position and constitution of each demand, and as the condition of one's "means" permits; (3) besides using our "means" for our own needs and the convenience of our life, we must devote them also to the use of our needy neighbor, and to the advantage of the republic.

267. The life of towns has the most intimate connection with human society and with the constitution of the republic. The towns both form the bond of connection between the rural sustaining system and the whole sustaining system of the country, and in them quite unique occupations are pursued, which have immediate influence on the weal of the state. The fundamental rules of management can be applied here therefore only in a general way, because otherwise it would be necessary to discuss each particular occupation. In the case of rural management, on the contrary, there must be specific application of the general rules.

268. A town is a combination of societies, families, and single persons, who live in a guarded [*verwahrten*] locality, under the oversight and direction of a police bureau, or other persons charged with administration of the police system, in order with better success to maintain the operation and co-operation of those gainful pursuits which are immediately demanded both for the needs and conveniences of the country and for the unification of the whole sustaining system. The protection [*schutz*] is the essential finding mark of the town, without which no locality can be called a town, however large and well built it may be.

269. The essential difference between towns depends therefore on the fact that one kind must be guarded by art, that is, by walls and ditches, another kind by nature, that is, by oceans, seas, rivers, and inaccessible mountains, so that entrance may be had only at certain places called gates or portals expressly designated for that purpose. Otherwise the requisite police arrangements for the chief purpose of the town are not available.

270. Towns must accordingly be classified in various ways: (1) Into (a) commercial towns; (b) manufacturing towns; (c) mining and salt towns; (d) brewery and distillery towns; (e) market towns; or (2) into (a) residence towns (i.e., of the court); (b) university towns; (c) fortified towns; (d) border towns, etc.; or (3) into (a) large; (b) medium; (c) small; or (4) into (a) capitals; (b) provincial towns.

§§497-523:

271. At bottom there are two principal types of occupation for towns; first, the assembling of persons capable of carrying on the various pursuits; second, the accumulation of all sorts of wares and goods, and to this end all their establishments, measures, and endeavors must be directed.

272. Since we are here exclusively concerned with the economy of private persons in towns, we have to do principally with two subjects, viz.: (1) What the general rules of management have to say about management and organization of the sustaining occupations; (2) how management itself, without reference to occupations in the town, may best be conducted.

273. Rural management is a complex of sustaining occupations' to the end that through agriculture and stock-raising the resources of the soil may be best used, and that all sorts of raw wares and materials may be extracted from the same for human need and convenience. The rural sustaining occupations consequently differ from those of towns principally in this: in the former the effort is to produce raw wares and goods, in the latter men are chiefly engaged in transforming the raw wares and materials. While this latter purpose requires unified societies and efforts, with police supervision, the former can be carried on by separate families either scattered at considerable intervals, or living in village groups.

Second Book: On the Reasonable Use of State Revenues in General
§§3-30:

274. To recapitulate: The common happiness, the ultimate purpose of all republics, for attaining and realizing which the supreme power exists in states, demands that the care and endeavor of this sovereign power shall be directed chiefly toward two great activities, viz.: first, securing and increasing the "means" of the state; second, the reasonable and wise use of the "means." The great management of the state consists then of these two chief employments. Part I having been devoted to the former of these, Part II will deal with the latter.

275. The "means" of the state consist not merely in all sorts of movable and immovable goods, possessed primarily either by the subjects or by the state itself; but rather in all talents and skill of the persons who belong to the republic. Even the persons themselves must in a certain sense be included, and the general use of these means of the state constitute the supreme power. All ordinances of the supreme power have for their object therefore the wise use of the means and forces of the state for the realization of the common happiness.

276. In the widest sense, the reasonable use of the "means" of the state includes all the rules laid down in Part I. In the special sense we understand by the reasonable use of the "means" of the state the wise measures of the ruler, to the end that the general "means" of the state may be made to yield certain revenues, and constantly available resources, without impairing the "means," and in accordance with the demands which from time to time the essential needs of the state may enforce.

277. The first condition of reasonable use of the "means" of the state is adequate knowledge of them.

278. The wise ruler has a conception of a true happiness of the subjects and of the state constantly before his eyes, and he has a correct judgment of the relative proportions of the different needs.

279. The wise ruler must take no steps for the welfare of the state without taking care that "means" enough are devoted to the purpose to insure its success.

280. For the purposes of the state, great sums must be expended. These "means" are mostly in the hands of private persons. The portions necessary for the purposes of the state must be obtained from the individuals in ways which will not impair the substance of their "means," i.e., they must be taken from earnings [*Einkommen*]. Enough, however, must be left so that the subjects can live from their earnings.

281. The "means" so obtained must be at all times available in the form of money, and we call it then "the readiest means" of the state.

282. This "readiest means" of the state is the great subject-matter of cameral or finance science proper, in so far as the same is regarded as a subordinate science under all the economic and cameral sciences required for the government of a state. All measures and transactions of cameral science have to do merely with this "readiest means," and have for their aim either the systematic raising of the same or wise application or administration. Otherwise expressed, cameral or finance science is an adequate knowledge and facility [*Erkenntnis und Geschicklichkeit*] in those transactions whereby "the readiest means" of the state, for promotion of the common happiness of the same, are well and economically managed.

283. We easily see that cameral science is closely connected with all other economic sciences which are treated in this book. It teaches not merely how to use wisely and for the good of the state those "means" of the republic which are founded, preserved, and increased by *Staatskunst, Policey, die Commercienwissenschaft und Oeconomie*, but in the great management of the state it conducts, so to speak, the internal management, to the effect that without its co-working no governmental business of any kind can be undertaken; because for all such undertakings "readiest means" are necessary. In short, cameral science is absolutely indispensable to the happiness of the state, because the greatest "means" of the state would yield nothing, without skilful administration. Hence it has its ground in the common fundamental principle of all the sciences which pertain to the government and general management of the state. It is particularly based however on *Staatskunst und Policeywissenschaft*, since it must derive its chief working principles from them. Moreover it must make use of Haushaltungskunst and jurisprudence as principal auxiliaries. The former will furnish the elementary rules of managing "means," the latter will guard against unjust procedure.

284. The fundamental principle of cameral science is this: "In all transactions with the 'readiest means' of the state, the aim must be to seek the common

happiness of the ruler and the subjects".

285. The rules of raising the revenues without harm to the subjects, and from current earnings, must also be applied to provinces, so that the chief division of the state will not be favored at the expense of minor divisions.

§§39-66:

286. The theory of cameral science may be divided into three chief parts. We accordingly divide this second part of the *Staatswirthschaft* into three books: (1) On the raising of revenues; (2) on the disbursements of the state; (3) on the organization and administration of cameral business. This classification leaves nothing lacking which is necessary for a beginner in cameral or finance science, and in general about the reasonable use of the "means" of the state.

287. A state often finds itself in need of resources which are not supplied by the rules already given for raising the "readiest means." This book is devoted then to the problems which those extraordinary requirements involve.

288. The problems of cameralism accordingly fall into three chief divisions: (1) The establishment of the "readiest means" — which calls for the greatest skill and strength of the cameralist; (2) the raising of the regular income of the state from the sources that are common to almost all states; (3) the raising of emergency funds.

289. Establishing the "readiest means" of the state depends first upon developing a populous land, with the maximum amount of wealth circulating in the gainful occupations.

290. A second and more immediate foundation is necessary, viz., either certain estates the proprietorship of which belongs immediately to the state and to the ruler, and the whole revenue of which accrues to the "readiest means," or certain rights reserved to the supreme power. The proper name of these rights is the regalia.

291. The foundation of the revenues of the state is laid then, first, in good management of the estates immediately appertaining to the state or to the ruler.

292. In the case of the regalia, the desideratum is a reasonable use of the rights, in consideration of the common "means" of the state, and of the common welfare of the ruler and of the subjects.

293. The best standard of taxation is the persons of the subjects in general, according to a just proportion of their immovable "means" and industry, and especially the labourers and assistants employed in such gainful occupations. In such case the commerce, the industry, and the freedom of the subjects would not suffer the slightest hindrance, as the number of the persons employed could not possibly be concealed.

294. It is possible for the state to raise so little revenue by taxation that the total "means" of the state will fall far below the normal level, and the welfare of the subjects will be harmfully restricted.

295. The Regalia should be so administered that the welfare of the state and the convenience of the subjects would remain the first consideration, and the revenues the second.

296. A reasonable cameralist will accordingly follow two rules: (1) Direct management by the administration of complicated economic processes must be avoided by arranging with competent Entrepreneurs (sic) to carry on the enterprises at their own risk, at a certain rate of dividend on the proceeds; (2) all needless extra expense, such as unnecessary employees, must be avoided.

297. Subsidies from foreign rulers are not to be rejected, especially if they do not entail more costs than they amount to.

298. The best and surest increase of the revenues of the state comes from encouraging the labouring class.

299. A cameralist should at the same time be a police expert and an economist.

300. The first care of the cameralist must be for the development and cultivation of unimproved and thinly populated sections. A considerable budget must therefore be annually at the disposal of the bureaus.

§§67-103:

301. Even without such capital the domains may by good management be made to yield large revenues.

302. Returning to the Regalia—the most harmless increase of revenues through extended use of the Regalia occurs (1) when they are used in places where they had previously not been enforced. Hence the intelligent cameralist must be on the watch for such undeveloped sources of revenue; (2) through improvements of public works affected by the Regalia; (3) through increase of the rate of impost and of prices of products covered by the Regalia.

303. The problem of increasing the revenues of the state in the form of contributions, taxes, and other payments by the subject can be solved only by improving the condition of the labouring class, and by increasing the population, but this just portion of revenue should be collected only when the needs of the state call for it.

304. The only exception is when a new impost may restrain or cure a police evil, or may evidently benefit and enlarge the labouring class.

305. The second chief responsibility of the cameralist is the raising of the ordinary revenues of the state. By the ordinary revenues we understand the established arrangements for covering the ordinary needs of the state by levies upon designated objects.

306. Following the Roman law, it has been customary in Germany to distinguish between Fiscum and Aerarium. Under the former are classed the revenues of the cameral estates and of the Regalia. These are supposed to be for the support of the person of the ruler and of his family, court, and servants, with all other expenses necessary to maintain the princely dignity. It is the traditional

idea that the cameralists were to deal especially with these revenues, and they are accordingly known as cameral revenues. The revenues of the Aerarium are supposed to be especially for the protection and security of the country, and for promoting the general welfare of the state.

307. This distinction is groundless.

308. Knowledge of the distinction is necessary, however, in order to understand certain existing survivals and consequences of the distinction in the present cameral organization.

309. It is best to divide the revenues of the state according to their four chief sources, viz.: (1) Those from the crown estates, the cameral estates, or the domains (as they are variously named); (2) those from the Regalia; (3) those from payments by the subjects, in general taxation; (4) those which indirectly accrue in the course of attaining other chief purposes.

310. The three chief sources of the necessary income of the state are: (1) the contributions; (2) the taxes; (3) the excises paid by the subjects. The domains and the Regalia are not sufficient to cover the expenses necessary for the welfare of the state, especially in the present armed condition of Europe. The magnificence of courts has also greatly increased. To cover these costs the subjects must contribute from their private means.

311. There can be no doubt that the subjects owe this contribution to the great expenses of the state. In so far as all subjects, in respect to their common welfare, are in close unity with one another, and represent a single body, or moral person, their private means are at the same time the general, although mediate "means" of the state.

312. It is a fundamental rule to seek such ways and means of levying the taxes now in mind, that the subjects will pay them with willing and happy hearts, and at their own initiative. This is possible even in monarchies, if wise use is made of the passions of the subjects; e.g., if the people, with the exception of nobility and scholars, are divided into classes, according to the amount of tax which they pay; or, if certain lucrative occupations are permitted only to persons who pay a certain minimum tax, as is stipulated for example in the case of brewers in Frankenhausen, Schwarzburg, etc.

313. A second fundamental rule is that the taxes must not interfere with the reasonable freedom of human conduct, with the credit of merchants, with the trades, and shall in general not be oppressive to the industrial system or to commerce.

314. A third rule is that the taxes must be levied upon all subjects with righteous equality, since all are equally under obligation in this connection, and all share in the protection and other benefits of the state. Yet the application of this rule must have due respect to the second, for, although all subjects should pay taxes in just proportion to their means, yet the nature and purpose of the different species of goods does not permit that all objects can bear equal rates of taxation.

315. A fourth rule is, that the contributions and excises shall have a sure, fixed, and unfalsified ground, and consequently should be levied upon objects not only upon which they may be promptly and certainly collected, but in connection with which fraud and concealment is not easy for the subjects, nor peculation for the officials.

§§104-136:

316. A fifth rule is, that the taxes shall be based on such objects as will permit limitation of the number of collectors' offices, and therewith of officials.

317. The sixth and last fundamental rule is that payments must be made as easy as possible for the subjects, and hence must be divided into convenient parts, and made payable at appropriate times.

318. It is not easy to hit upon an impost which satisfies all these requirements. Vauban, Schröder, and others have proposed a royal or general tithe, which should combine all desirable qualities. Tested by above rules, however, the plan will be found wanting. Others have proposed a combined poll and income tax, etc.

319. The nearest approach to application of the rules will be through selecting three classes of objects for taxation, viz.: first, immovable goods; second, the persons of the subjects; third, the gainful occupations.

320. The propriety of taxing land rests on two facts: first, it is mediately a part of the general property of the state; second, the revenues from it are least concealable. Nor is there any hardship in liability of the land for a portion of the expenses of the state.

321. Lands of the different kinds, e.g., meadows, vineyards, forests, etc., must be divided into three classes, good, medium, and bad; and houses must also be classified as large, medium, and small. Again, the regions in which the lands lie must also be classified, and in like manner the towns which contain the houses. A calculus of these different factors will give the rate of taxation.

322. The productiveness of the land must be precisely reckoned, and the tax must be levied accordingly.

323. The revenues of the houses should also determine the amount of levy upon them; and it should correspond with the just rate upon the interest which would be derived from the selling value of the same.

324. An important duty of the bureaus relates to remission of the taxes in case of providential losses by fire, flood, storm, drought, etc.

325. It is a mistake for the ruler to reward services by grants of freedom from taxation.

326. The second chief taxable object is the person of the subjects themselves. Not all subjects possess immovable goods. All are however members of the community, and enjoy its benefits; all consequently owe something in return. Personal payments to the state even by those who also pay land taxes are therefore proper, if they are rightly graded.

327. The personal tax may be the chief tax of a country, virtually summing up all the forms of income tax, or it may be an accessory of the principal forms of taxation.

328. There is no adequate standard of personal taxation.

329. Personal taxes may be regarded as a means of collecting a portion of their dues to the state from subjects who otherwise would be wholly or partially exempt from taxation.

330. Poll taxes on Jews are to be specified as one of the forms of personal tax. They are levied at the same rate upon rich and poor alike, and they are left to equalize the matter among themselves. Usually the whole Jewish community is held responsible for payment of an aggregate sum reckoned in proportion to the numbers. Since it is the choice of this unfortunate race to remain aliens among us, we need not bother ourselves about strict propriety and exact justice.

§§137-160:

331. In some countries protection-money [*Schutzgeld*] is paid by those subjects, or aliens, who possess no immovable goods. It is sometimes reckoned by families, sometimes by polls. In either case it is to be reckoned as a personal tax. This is an undesirable levy in addition to a poll tax.

332. Various other taxes have been levied as personal, which are really occupation taxes or excise.

333. In the same way, salt and tobacco taxes have been levied as personal taxes.

334. The chief duties of the cameralists in connection with these personal taxes consist in so administering the same that the system will be reasonable, conducive to the welfare both of the subjects and of the state, and duly respective of the equality of the subjects. In this respect a cameralist has an opportunity to show great skill and wisdom. Decisions must be rendered as to cases in which personal taxes should be remitted. The ground for this concession should be services. Particularly must the cameralists take care that personal and other taxes are collected by the same officials, so that the expense of separate employees shall be saved.

335. Since immovable goods can be burdened with taxes to the extent of only one-fourth or one-third of their earnings, and since no very considerable sum can be raised from personal taxation, the gainful occupations must be the next source of revenue.

336. Occupations may be taxed (a) on the materials which they use, and on their output (excise); or (b) directly, according to the extent of their operations.

337. The former method is almost universal in Europe.

338. The latter has a minor place.

339. Various causes contribute to the vogue of excises in Germany: thus (a) the limitation of tariffs by the laws of the Empire gave occasion for excises as the most convenient and productive substitute. Again (b) it was observed that large

industries were growing up in the towns without paying much into the national treasury; (c) they are means of getting revenue from individuals who have no immovable goods.

340. It is not true that the owners of real estate can make the taxes which they pay fall upon other subjects, because customary price defeats this shifting of the incidence of the tax.

341. A further reason for the use of excise is that it gives the ruler a much freer hand than in levying land taxes.

342. Excise is either universal—falling upon all articles without exception which are used for the support of life or come into the channels of trade; or particular—falling upon selected articles of consumption or wares.

343. Excise does not conform to the rules above given for taxation; for (1) it limits the reasonable freedom of human action; (2) it is detrimental to crafts and commerce; (3) it does not spread the burden of taxation equally; (4) it has no secure basis, since fraud and peculation are afforded large scope; (5) its collection requires many officials and large expense.

344. The claims for excise are insufficient; viz.: (1) It puts a share of the common burdens upon all; (2) by limiting his expenditures each may ease the burden at will; (3) it calls for only a fraction of earnings a little at a time; (4) but almost without the knowledge of the subjects it increases the "readiest means" of the state; (5) no sheriffs' process (execution) is required to enforce it; (6) aliens must bear their share; (7) it is a means of controlling the commerce of the country, and of promoting manufactures.

345. Since immediate abolition of excise is hopeless, the rules for its employment must be stated, viz.: (1) All the sales previously laid down in the case of tariffs, etc.; (2) excise rates must respect the rate of earnings of the different occupations, and must call for only a small fraction of the earnings of those that deal in the necessities of life; (3) in order that moderation of excise be not misused for unwarranted increase of profits, the police must interfere and fix the price of necessities; (4) larger demands may be made upon luxuries; (5) but the three grades of luxury must be respected; (6) excise is surely excessive when it amounts to more than the remaining earnings of the craft, or when it amounts to a half or two-thirds of an article on sale; (7) excise must vary according as the transactions are first, second, or third hand, and whether a craft contributes or not to the completion or improvement of a thing.

§§163-251:

346. Occupation-taxes [*Gewerbesteuer*] might be introduced, in harmony with the fundamental rules of taxation, and to the advantage both of ruler and subject.

347. The essential principle of this type of tax is adjustment to the scale of income of the occupation.

348. These revenues may be called accidental in a double sense: First the sovereign power finds occasion to raise certain revenues without making the revenues themselves the ultimate purpose, and at the same time without prejudice to the actual ultimate purpose of the state; second, these revenues may be called accidental because they are based merely on accidental arrangements and certain incidents, either of the whole republic or of the supreme power; or of those subjects who contribute to these revenues. Such occasional circumstances are so various that some of them are likely to be present always, and their revenues consequently aggregate an appreciable sum.

349. These accidents may be grouped in five classes, and we may arrange them in the order of their probable value in yielding revenue, viz.: (1) Revenues from over lordship of the state over certain properties, to be distinguished from the Regalia; (2) rights of revenue that are incidents of the administration of justice; (3) the revenues accruing through administration of the police system; (4) revenues incidental to the war-making power, including subsidies; (5) revenues from sovereignty over the ecclesiastical system.

350. In case of war, or other crises, exceptional demands for money arise. It is not for the cameralist to decide whether the occasion actually demands the exceptional sums, but if the ruler has so decided it is the task of the cameralist to find the ways and means. These are chiefly two: (1) Extraordinary contributions of the subjects; (2) the credit of the ruler and of the country.

351. There are two ways of levying extraordinary contributions, viz.: (1) By increasing the rates of ordinary contributions and taxes; (2) by levying a new sort of contribution. The preference is to be determined by the circumstances of the state. If the sums to be raised are not too great, if there is no need of instant payment, and if the ruler can assure the subjects that the increase will be only temporary, the former method is preferable, because the technique for raising such contributions is already in operation. The existing taxes must, however, be at such rates that they do not absorb one-third of earnings, or the other form must be adopted.

352. The best form of extraordinary levy is a tax on social position [*Würdensteuer*], that is, all subjects, lay and clerical, are to be arranged in classes and subdivisions, and the higher the social rank and dignity the higher must be the rate of this tax. Thus the levy falls to a considerable extent upon persons who were not burdened before, and who have the ready means of payment.

353. One of the first rules of a wise government must be to preserve its credit, and this depends, first, on integrity in its transactions; second, on prompt payment of interest.

354. The establishment of a bank is also a useful means of obtaining control of extraordinary sums.

355. Another means is the provision of annuities, the capital of which falls to the state on the death of the annuitants.

356. So-called "Tontines," invented in France, and named after their originator, Tonti, are also to be considered.

357. Lotteries may also be used when exceptional sums are needed.

358. Scruples about the fundamental morality of annuities, tontines, and lotteries are not sufficiently valid to stop the state from losing them.

359. Although it is impossible to exclude aliens from investment in annuities, tontines, and other forms of state debts, yet so far as possible subjects should be preferred as investors, so that the interest will not go out of the country. Whether money should be borrowed abroad for the sake of winning other nations to our interest is another question which belongs to Staatskunst.

360. When the credit of the country makes borrowing difficult, then one of the more common devices is to farm out certain fixed revenues, and to obtain advances from the parties to whom they are farmed.

§§252-267:
361. A similar device is to make over certain domains or other revenues of the state to a lender.

362. A still more desperate device is the pawning of domains or even provinces.

363. A cameralist will today scarcely recommend the absolute alienation of territories and people for the sake of money.

364. The second chief responsibility of the cameralist is with the disbursements of the state, and this is quite as important as responsibility for the revenues.

365. Instead of being expended for the common happiness, the means of the state are (1) often wasted; (2) used with shortsighted niggardliness; (3) applied at the wrong point for the best results; (4) unsystematically administered.

366. In order to avoid these errors, the rules laid down in the introduction must be applied, viz.: (1) Outlays must be in accordance with the circumstances and revenues of the state; (2) the "readiest means" of the state must be used for no other purpose than the best good of ruler and subjects.

367. From the previous fundamental principles we derive the first rule of wise expenditure, viz.: No outlay must be undertaken without the most thorough previous consideration, and estimate of the involved cost, and of the income likely to accrue from the same to the state.

368. The second rule is, that the outlay should never exceed the income.

369. Rule three. — For all outlays the "readiest means" must be already in hand, and in no case should a start be made with a debt.

370. Rule four. — All expenditures of the state must be made certain.

371. Rule five. — No outlay should be made which tends permanently to diminish either the available or the total "means" of the state.

372. Rule six. — So far as possible, outlays should be so ordered that the money will be expended within the state, and will get into circulation in the sustaining system of the country.

373. Rule seven. — The importance of every proposed outlay must be measured by the amount of income that it is likely to return for the welfare of the state.

374. Rule eight. — Outlays must be arranged in the order of their usefulness for the common good of ruler and subjects.

375. The great management of the state bears much similarity to the housekeeping of private persons; hence the rules that are valid in private housekeeping apply, with changed details, to the use of the "means" of the state.

§§278-454:

376. Rule nine. — The necessities of the state must take precedence of all other demands, and necessities must be reckoned in the following grades, viz.: (1) Those on which the stability of the republic depends; (2) those which are of qualified necessity, i.e., from omission of which the community would suffer great harm, such as loss of industries through failure of proper promotion; (3) those which might be omitted without positive injury, but without which the maximum happiness of the state cannot be reached.

377. Even expenses of the first grade should not be covered so extravagantly that outlays of the other grades would be impossible.

378. Rule ten. — Only when all the necessary expenses are provided for can the means of the state be appropriated to conveniences.

379. Rule eleven. — After all outlay is provided for which is required for the needs and conveniences of the state, attention may be given to comfort, dignity, display, and ornamentation.

380. Rule twelve. — The aim should be to put the finances of the country in such condition that not merely the necessities and conveniences, but also the comforts and elegancies may be secured.

381. Rule thirteen. — If the government is to be in a situation to make fair appropriations of all kinds, it must in all its outlays observe reasonable economy.

382. Rule fourteen. — Care must be taken that economy be not turned into greed, especially through contempt of the ruler for certain needs of his subjects, while his passions lead him to favor other outlays.

383. Rule fifteen. — The finance bureau must constantly have the most exact information about the condition of all the funds.

384. Rule sixteen. — No disbursements should be made except upon strict account.

385. Rule seventeen. — Entrepreneurs should be used in all cases which involve employment of a large number, and many minor outlays.

386. Rule eighteen. — Nothing which can be obtained with a lump sum should be subject to several charges.

387. Rule nineteen. — The persons expending the money of the state should not themselves make additional costs necessary.

388. Rule twenty. — Everything must be supplied at the proper time, with foresight and advantage, and by cash payments; and when it is profitable stocks of goods needed by the state should be kept.

389. Rule twenty-one. — Strict accounts, in perfect order, must be kept of the outlays of the state.

390. After provision for the military budget, and for the court budget, the cameralistic expenses proper may be divided into eight groups: (1) Moneys for the civil-list and dowries; (2) appropriations for the various administrative expenses; (3) the expenses of levying and collecting the revenues, and of maintaining the sources from which they are derived; (4) the salaries and pensions of all civil servants in the state, finance, police, and justice bureaus; (5) the expenses of bringing land under cultivation; (6) the expenses of buildings for the use of the state; (7) the support of the ecclesiastical and school systems; (8) expenses for the comfort and adornment of the country.

391. The organization and the correlation of the cameralistic system, and of the bureaus belonging to it, is one of the most important elements in the government of a state. The whole management of a community rests upon it, and to a certain extent its whole internal constitution rests upon it. The administrative police institutions of the state are a part of the cameral system. At all events the two are inseparable, because the former constitute the ground of the "readiest means" of the state and must in turn be supported by the same. In this most general signification of the cameral system, it comprehends not merely all police institutions and measures, and consequently the commercial and agricultural administration, but also the administration of justice, at least so far as concerns the technique of the same, and the nature [*Beschaffenheit*] of the laws, as well as the management of the military system. There remain therefore only foreign affairs, which may be contrasted with cameral business, and which constitute the second essential element in the government of the state. Important as the constitution of the cameral system is then in itself, it is especially so on account of the peculiar traits of our times. Since the European powers have placed themselves on a constant war footing, since they have made it a part of their programme to encourage commerce and manufactures and the sustaining class, as well as the general culture of their countries, the cameral system has taken on a quite other form. Those states in which the rulers two or three hundred years ago either left the finances to their consorts, or intrusted them as a minor duty to a privy council or court, now have various great and important bureaus for the administration of the same, and meanwhile the revenues have increased five, six, and ten times.

Selections from: *Grundsätze der Polizeywissenschaft* [Principles of Police Science] in *The Cameralists: The Pioneers of German Social Polity* by Albion W. Small (New York: Burt Franklin, reprint 2001, orig., 1909)., orig. 1756.

Note: Enumerated notes following section ranges (e.g. §§2-3) are summary translations provided by Albion Small. Some referencing has been changed or omitted.

Preface to the First Edition

This book is the first installment of the promise to write textbooks on each of the cameralistic sciences. It is the outline of a course to occupy one semester. It is the first complete treatment of *Polizeiwissenchaft*. The common error has been to boil this subject in one broth with *Staatskunst* (the art of government). We have a countless number of books which contain the elements of *Staatskunst*, but they do not assort their material. *Staatkunst* has nothing for its purpose but the internal and external security of the state, and its chief attention must be given to the conduct of states toward each other, to increase of the power of the state in relation to other states, and especially to wise conduct toward other states. In like manner *Staatkunst* is concerned, on the other hand, with adjusting the conduct of subjects toward one another and toward other states. *Polizeiwissenchaft*, on the contrary, is concerned with nothing but the preservation and increase of the total "means" of the state through good internal institutions and with creating all sorts of internal power and strength for the republic: e.g., through (1) cultivating the land; (2) improving the labouring class; (3) maintaining good discipline and order in the community. In the last task it is the total of *Staatknust* in maintaining inner security. Other books have treated *Policey* in connection with principles of *Cameral- oder Finanz-Wissenschaft*, to the disadvantage of each science, though they are nearly related. *Policey* is the ground of genuine cameral science, and the police expert must sow if the cameralist is to reap; yet each science has its fixed and indisputable boundaries. The one seeks to get from this the "readiest means," without harm to the former.

In other books, *Policey* is treated along with *Oeonomie*; e.g., Zink, both in his *Grundriss* and in his *Anfangs-Gründe*, starts with certain general principles of *Oeconomie*, and then of *Policey*. And then treats of more special economic questions first from the economic, second from the police standpoint. This leads to constant repetitions. Moreover, *Policey* cannot be completely treated in this way, because it has a much wider scope than economic subjects. In his *Anfangs-Gründe*, which is very diffuse, Zink either wholly forgets many important police subjects, or gives them only a few lines.

The late Herr Canzler von Wolff wrote a large number of books, and as, according to his profession, he wanted to be a system-writer of all sciences, it was to be expected that he would write a *Policey*. But the social life of human beings was the mistaken chief subject of his work, which did not fit into the proper boundaries of the sciences. His book therefore contains many valuable teachings about *Policey*, but consistently with his ultimate purpose he mixed them with so many principles of moral philosophy, of the law of nature, and of prudence, in general, that the work is of no use as a system of *Policey*. Sciences must be separated from each other to be complete, because many useful doctrines will be overlooked if they are treated together.

Of the few books that remain on *Policey* proper, we name none until the present (eighteenth) century. There has been, until late years, no adequate idea of Policey, as is proved by such examples as Boter, *Gründlicher Bericht von Anordnung gutter Policey*, Strasburg, 1696; Schrammer, *Politia historica*, Leipzig, 1605; Reinking, *Biblische Policey*, etc.

Others in this century have a correct idea of *Policeywissenschaft* but are not at all complete: e.g., Law, *Entwurf einer wohleingerichteten Policey*. The author was not equal to his undertaking. With the exception of certain observations about the *Policey* of various states, the book contains little that can be used. Again a pseudonymous "C. B. von L." published (1739) *Ohnverfängliche Vorschläge zu Einrichtung guter Policey*. It is not a system, and contains much that is chimerical and not pertinent to the science. Lucas Friedrich Langemack published *Abbildung einer vollkommenen Policey*, Berlin, 1747. In this brief work the fundamental principles are very well and philosophically presented, but on the whole it is not specific enough for a system. The Mecklenburg *Hofrath* Velter published several monographs on *Policey*: e.g., *Unvorgreiflichien Gedanken von Einrichtung und Verbesserung der Policey*, 1736; more important was *Unterrichi van der zur Stoats und Regierungswissenschaft gehörenden Policey*, 1753. The author flatters himself, in the prospectus of the latter book, that he is the first to treat this science systematically, but no one with an orderly mind will admit this. The book is not only confused, but leaves out much that should be included, and has much affectation of wisdom from the ancients, while betraying defective judgment.

The English and French have produced nothing better. De la Marc's *(sic)* *Traité de Police* contains certain excellent and useful things, but has no well-grounded and connected system.

It has been said that Zink's book is more available as a text, because it describes the police systems of other lands, and applies the general principles of *Policey* to this or that particular state. On the contrary, this ought not to be expected of such a textbook. We should rather require of a textbook on the *oeconomischen Wissenschaften* only the general principles, without this or that concrete application.

In this book I have followed my usual rule of not citing other authors. A dogmatic writer must present the subject conclusively, and if he does this he does not need the authority of earlier writers. Such citations smack of pedantry, unless they contain historical facts, or unless some special circumstances call for them.

Introduction

§1: The name *Policey* comes from the Greek word (πολις) a city, and should mean the good ordering of cities and of their civic institutions.

§§2-3: Two uses of the term *Policey* are common today: first, and most generally, "All measures in the internal affairs of the country through which the general means [*Vermögen*] of the state may be more permanently founded and increased, the energies [*Kräfte*] of the state better used, and in general the happiness of the community promoted. In this sense we must include in *Policey die Commercienwissenschaften, die Stadt- und Landöconomie, das Forstwesen,* and similar subjects, in so far as the government extends its care over them for the purpose of securing general correlation of the welfare of the state. Some are accustomed to call this *die wirthschaftliche Policey-Wissenschaft.* This name is a matter of indifference so long as it is not supposed to designate a particular science.

§3: In the narrower sense we understand by *Policey* everything which is requisite for the good ordering of civic life, and especially the maintenance of good discipline and order [*Zucht und Ordnung*] among the subjects, and promotion of all measures for the comfort of life and the growth of the sustaining system [*Nahrungsstand*]. We shall treat here the general principles and rules of *Policey* according to the comprehensive idea. In the special elaboration we shall not stop to consider those things which are the subject-matter of other economic sciences, and meanwhile we shall discuss chiefly the objects of *Policey* in the narrower sense.

§4: The purpose and consequently the essence of all republics rests upon promotion of the Common happiness. The general "means" of each republic is the resource which it must use for promoting its happiness. Hence the general "means" must be assured, increased, and reasonably used, i.e., applied for the promotion of the common happiness. This is the content [*Inbegriff*] of all the economic and cameral sciences. The maintenance and increase of the general "means" in relations with other free states is the affair of *Staatskunst Policeywissenschaft,* on the other hand, has for its object the maintenance and increase of the same general "means" of the state in connection with its inner institutions, while cameral and finance science has for its task to raise from the general "means" of the state, by a reasonable use of the same, the special, or "readiest means," and to put into the hands of *Staatskunst* and *Policey* the means of accomplishing their purposes.

§5: The purpose of *Policey* is therefore to preserve and increase the general "means" of the state; and since these "means" include not merely the goods, but also the talents and skill of all persons belonging to the republic, the *Policey* must have constant care to have in mind the general interdependence of all these different sorts of goods, and to make each of them contribute to the common happiness.

§7: *Policeywissenschaft* consists accordingly in understanding how, under existing circumstances of the community, wise measures may be taken to maintain and increase the general "means" of the state in its internal relations [*Verfassung*], and to make the same, both in its correlation and in its parts, more efficient and useful for promotion of the common happiness [*gemeinschaftliche Glückseligkeit*]. More briefly, *Policeywissenschaft* consists in the theorems for preserving and increasing the general "means" of the state, and for so using them that they will better promote the common happiness.

§8: The general principle of *Policeywissenschaft* is accordingly: *The internal institutions of the community must be so arranged that thereby the general "means" of the state will be preserved and increased and the common happiness constantly promoted.*

§§9–16: Hence follow three fundamental rules, viz.:

1. *Before all things the lands of the republic must be cultivated and improved.*

The development of the territories may take place in two ways: (a) through external cultivation; (b) through increase of the population, which may be called the internal culture of the lands. The second sort of culture must be of three chief kinds: (1) Through attraction of foreigners as settlers; (2) through means which promote increase of the native inhabitants; (3) through prevention of sickness and premature death.

2. *Increase of the products of the country and the prosperity of the sustaining system* [*Nahrungsstand*] *must be promoted in every possible way.*

3. *Care must be given to securing among the subjects such capacities and qualities, and such discipline and order, as are demanded by the ultimate purpose, viz., the common happiness.*

Book I: The External Cultivation Of The Land

§86: All external improvement of a land would be of little avail, if the same were not satisfactorily settled and populated. This populating is the internal cultivation which must give to external cultivation its soul and life. Hence increase of population is the second main aim in the cultivation of countries, and just as the sustaining system will always be more flourishing, the more people there are in the country, so we must regard it as a fundamental theorem in this division of the subject that *a land can never have too many inhabitants.* It is easy to protect this theorem against all objections.

On Agriculture

§109: The promotion of the sustaining system in the country demands in the first place that a sufficient number of rural products shall be gained. To that end the rural *Policey* must constantly pay great attention to those sources through which rural products are derived. Here then the rural *Oeconomica* come first to attention, as the chief means through which the raw materials for the products of the country are brought into existence. These are: agriculture, the exploiting of natural and cultivated forests, the mines, and the thereto appertaining smelting and refining works. In this subdivision we deal first with agriculture.

On Manufacturing and Factories

§152: A wise government must consequently have two theorems constantly before its eyes, viz.: (1) Everything required by the need and comfort of the inhabitants of the country is to be produced as far as possible within the country itself; (2) the government shall see that, in the interest of the sustaining system, and of foreign commerce, everything that the land produces shall, so far as possible, be worked over to its complete form, and shall not be allowed to leave the country in a raw and unfinished stale. To this end the government must have precise extracts from the tariff, excise, and license sheets, on such points as (a) all imported goods, in order to judge which of them might be produced within the country; (b) all exported goods, in order to discover whether domestic products in the form of raw materials, or partially manufactured, are exported.

On the Circulation of Money

§223: If money and goods are to retain a constant ratio to each other, no change should occur in either; and if such change could be totally avoided, it would be a matter of entire indifference whether there were much or little money in a country. A state which had no relations whatever with other peoples, and whose inhabitants consumed all that they produced, would have a constantly unbroken circulation of money. It would have all the power and strength of which it was capable, and it would be as fortunate as another state of like population with ten times as much gold and silver. But since no state in our part of the world is in such circumstances, changes in the value of money and of goods with respect to each other often occur. We must explain the effect of these changes upon circulation.

§224: If the amount of money in circulation diminishes, the price of wares will increase, beginning with the most needless, the influence extending gradually to all. If the quantity of money in circulation increases, the most necessary wares will grow dearer. This stimulates the activity of labourers and has its influence upon all wares. Money becomes less desirable, interest falls, more wares are produced. Gradually wares will again become cheaper, and thereby exportation is promoted, whereby the quantity of money in circulation is more and more increased and the diligence of labourers more stimulated.

§226: Accordingly it must be a first care of the government to prevent diminution of the amount of money in circulation.

§228-230: Lack of confidence and external dangers are prime causes of diminished circulation... Unfavorable trade balance is the most effective cause.

Book II: On The Moral Condition Of The Subjects And Maintenance Of Good Discipline And Order

§270: If the means of the state in its internal constitution are to be used for the promotion of the common happiness, the subjects, apart from the cultivation of the land and the promotion of the sustaining system, must also themselves possess such qualities, capacities, and talents that they can contribute their part to the realization of the common welfare. In this view religion deserves first to be considered. The members of a community are made by religion incomparably more capable of fulfilling their duties as citizens; and a state can hardly attain all the happiness of which it is capable if public institutions of religion [*offentlicher Gottesdienst*] are not introduced. The more this cults harmonizes with the nature and essence of men, and with the paramount purpose of republics, the more excellent will it be, and the more capable will it make the citizens of the state to work for the common welfare.

Book III: The Technique Of Government On The Principles Of Police Science

§382: The law-giving power in police affairs, since the internal arrangement of the state chiefly rests upon it, can unquestionably be exercised by no one but the sovereign power, the destiny of which is to administer the affairs of the state for promotion of the common happiness. In whosesoever hands the sovereign power is lodged, he has also to enact the police laws which are to bind the state as a whole. If now the sovereign power rests not alone in the hands of the ruler, but at the same time also with the estates of the realm, or with representatives of the people, obligatory police laws must be agreed upon and promulgated by these conjointly. On the same principle, the police laws which should affect the whole German Empire should be enacted by the Kaiser and the estates assembled in the *Reichstag.*

§384: Since the territorial sovereignty which the estates of the German Empire possess is nothing else than the sovereign power in each particular state, which finds its limitations merely in the proviso that its exercise shall not extend so far as to prejudice the general coherence and common welfare of the Empire; the estates of the German Empire accordingly possess the law-giving power in *Policey* affairs; and the above limitation does not prevent them from adopting such *Policey* institutions and ordinances as will serve the advantage and prosperity of their respective lands; even if this advantage and prosperity might not harmonize with the interest of other German states. Thus they could ordain that no wares should be imported from neighboring German states for consumption within their own territories. On the other hand, they could not forbid the mere transportation of the wares of their neighbors; because thereby the total coherence of the German states united in a common civic body would be utterly destroyed.

Selections from: *Die Grundfeste zu der Macht und Gluckseligkeit der Staaten oder ausfuhrliche Vorstellung der gesamten Policeywissenschaft* in *The Cameralists: The Pioneers of German Social Polity* by Albion W. Small (New York: Burt Franklin, reprint 2001, orig., 1909)., orig. 1761.

Note: Enumerated notes following section ranges are summary translations provided by Albion Small. Some referencing has been changed or omitted.

Preface

I have often noticed that there are very few people who have a correct idea of *Policey*. That which in the narrowest sense is called *Policey*, namely the *Policey* in the cities, is regarded by the majority as the whole scope of this science. If this very limited signification were the whole, I should have insufficient ground for calling the *Policey* the main defense of states. Both the *Grundsätze* and the present work should make it plain that the scope of the science is much wider.

It will be found that as a rule those who have treated *Staatskunst* have at the same time discussed *Policey* with *Commercien- und Finanz-Wissenschaft*. This is the case, for example, with the latest writer on *Staatskunst*. If our conception of *Staatskunst* or *Politik* made it include not only all knowledge necessary for the government of a state, but also all the details of institutions necessary in civic society, those would be right who include in one system of *Politik, Policey*, the *Finanz-Wissenschaften*, and all the other economic sciences. But, in that case *Staatskunst* would be no special science at all. It would be nothing but a general name for almost all other sciences. *Die Rechtsgelehrsamkeil, dieBergwerks-Wissenschaften, die Mathematik, die Mechanik*, and almost all other sciences would belong to *Staatskunst*. For all these furnish knowledge which is applicable in the government of a state, and necessary for the institutions and practices of civic society. In a word, they all contain knowledge of means whereby the state may be made powerful, and the citizens happy. That is the explanation which Baron von Bielfeld gives of *Politik*.

It [Policey] *is that science which has for its object permanently to maintain the welfare of the separate families in an accurate correspondence and proportion with the best common good...* The best common good [*das gemeinschaftliche Beste*] is the ultimate aim of all civic institutions. But, we can imagine no best common good without the welfare of the separate families. To make these correspond with each other is accordingly in fact the main defense of the state, out of which its power and happiness must chiefly arise.

Perhaps we find here a lack in our *Policey*. It is without doubt the duty of the *Policey* to look out for the quality of wares and work, and to set the standard below which work shall be regarded as entirely unfit, and to be made good to the person who suffers injury from it. I doubt, however, if there is a country in which a standard of passable quality in printing is enforced. The more our publishing system becomes a staple ware (*sic*) the more will such laws be necessary.

[General fundamental principle of *Policeywissenschaft*] *In all the affairs of the country, the attempt must be made to put the welfare of the separate families in the most accurate combination and interdependence with the best common good, or the happiness of the whole state.*

First Part of the Book
§25: The strength and the permanent happiness of a state rest principally upon the goodness of the climate and soil of the country.

* * *

§27: Economic trade is always based on the stupidity and laziness of other peoples. So soon as a people perceives that it does better when it gets its wares from the first hand, it is all over with this economic trade. Upon quite as uncertain ground rest the manufactures of such a country. A wise and industrious people will always seek to manufacture its own raw materials. Hence this source of riches rests on the stupidity and laziness of other peoples, and so soon as these peoples get their eyes open, they will no longer furnish to the trading nation a source of riches. A nation which, by virtue of its good and well-cultivated soil, exports a great quantity of domestic products is also in a situation, according to the nature and course of commerce, to draw to itself much easier and to retain even the economic trade, than another nation which has few domestic products. From all this it is clear in my judgment, that the success and permanent happiness of a people rest in a very important degree upon the good character of its soil and climate, and that a people which itself produces all its needs and many domestic goods is incomparably more powerful and happy than a nation which must obtain its necessities and wares for consumption from other peoples, and thus is in a certain sense dependent upon them. These considerations lead us to two theorems which will be of great importance in the whole treatment of *Policey*. First, *a prudent nation must always take care to put itself in such condition that it is not under the necessity of obtaining its most important wants* [Bedürfnisse] *and materials from other peoples;* second, a *nation must seek in every possible way to cultivate the area which it occupies and to improve its climate.*

§30: Since there can never be complete cultivation of the soil without dense population, our second working theorem is, that *a state must in every way promote population.* These theorems are insufficient without a third, viz.: *If a state has only inhabitants devoted to cultivation of the surface of the earth, its population can never be dense...* Consequently we have the third fundamental principle: *that government must constantly pay the strictest attention to the building and growth of cities and villages.*

* * *

§32: *The Policey must devote itself to works and institutions for the comfort of the inhabitants and the ornamentation of the land.*

Joseph von Sonnenfels (1732-1817)

Artist: engraved by Joahann David Schleuen (17th century), Aeiou Encyclopedia

Born in 1732 in Nikolsburg, Moravia, Sonnenfels received his elementary education from his father, a Hebrew Scholar who had converted to Catholicism as the price of acceptance into Western society. Sonnenfels then studied at Piarist College in Nicolsburg, a school that placed heavy emphasis on Latin and religion. From 1745-1759, his education continued in the University of Vienna, where he learned philosophy and linguistics. The education was fairly irregular, however, and Sonnenfels found himself ill-equipped to pursue a higher vocation. He thus turned to the army, joining as a long-serving private in the famous *Deutschmeister* infantry regiment in 1749. His five-year stint in the regiment was a successful one. He rose to the rank of corporal, serving in Styria, Carinthia, Hungary, and Bohemia. During this time, it is reported that Sonnenfels was able to learn nine languages, picking up the dialect of foreign deserters, local girls, and whatever books he could lay his hands on.

After leaving the army in 1754, Sonnenfels studied law at the University of Vienna. He practiced law for several years thereafter, also gaining a reputation as a writer and journalist. His finances were poor, however, and he was forced to take a post as bookkeeper, which he secured through connections he had made in the army. By 1761, Sonnenfels had been made chairman of the notable cultural association *Deutsche Gesellschaft*, and it was ultimately his wish to be appointed to the prestigious chair of German literature at the University of Vienna. Sonnenfels was unable to secure this position, however, and he was instead made the first professor of *Polizei-und Kammeralwissenschaften* (loosely translatable as applied political sciences) in 1763. Sonnenfels made the position significant in relation to political reforms by instructing at the Theresianum, a college largely devoted to training nobles in government services. He wrote several textbooks, acted as a government consultant on a variety of judicial and economic reforms, and was assigned in 1770 the task of literary censorship of the theatre. He served various councilor positions, including councilor on police problems in 1779, and is considered largely responsible for bringing the abolition of torture in Austria.

With the death of the empress in 1780, Sonnenfels' career began a slow decline, as he was disliked by Joseph II. While his assignments became less prestigious, his stature grew with external distinctions such as the title of baronet, the High Order of St. Stephen, and an honorary citizenship of Vienna. He was also the dedicatee of Ludwig van Beethoven's Piano Sonata No. 15, Op. 28, which was published in 1801. Sonnenfels died on April 25, 1817.

Works Referenced:

Kann, Robert A. *A Study in Austrian Intellectual History from Late Baroque to Romanticism.* Frederick A Prager Inc: New York, 1960.

Small, Albion W. *The Cameralists: Pioneers of German Social Polity (1909).* Kessinger Publishing: Montana, 2009.

Selections from: *Grundsätze der Polizei, Handlung und Finanzwissenschaft* [Principles of Police, Trade and Financial Science] in *The Cameralists: The Pioneers of German Social Polity* by **Albion W. Small** (New York: Burt Franklin, reprint 2001, orig., 1909)., orig. 1765.

Note: Enumerated notes following section ranges (e.g. §§28-31) are summary translations provided by Albion Small. Some referencing has been changed or omitted.

General Introduction For Three Volumes

§1: The isolated human being is not the human being in the state of nature; his condition would be a condition of constant helplessness. But he feels his lack. He feels that he is capable of remedying the lack, of improving his condition. Reason, which distinguishes him from the beasts, enables him to perceive the means by which he may reach an improved condition. This means *is* socialization with his kind [*Vergesellschaftung mit seines Gleichen*]. The natural condition of man is thus the condition of society: the domestic, the conjugal, the paternal society, are so many steps whereby he comes nearer to the great society, which includes all others, and which, since the minor groupings direct their gaze toward the weal of the separate members, has adopted as its aim the best good of all societies.

§2: The great society is the state. The transition into the same has given the members a new name, has put them into new relationships. The human beings have become citizens, beings who, through the nature of their self-chosen (*sic!*) status, have now, as parts, their relationship to a whole, are united as members in a moral body. The effect of this unification is *unity of ultimate purpose, unity of will, unity of force.*

§3: *Unity of ultimate purpose,* or of welfare, of the best, which now is called the best good of the community [*das gemeinschaftliche Beste*] whereby the best of the single member, that is, private advantage, remains constantly subordinated to the former, and cannot be otherwise brought into the account than in so far as it constitutes a part of the common best of the whole body. In case their private advantage could not be reconciled with "the common best," the former must necessarily be subordinated to the latter. Fortunately, however, in the precise sense, there can be no thought of a contradiction between the true permanent private welfare and the general welfare. For upon closer examination it will always appear, either that what is regarded as private advantage ceases to be such so soon as it works in opposition to the general advantage; or frequently that a supposed limitation of the common weal is not actually such. The welfare of the parts is based upon the welfare of the whole; but at the same time the welfare of the whole springs only from the welfare of the parts.

§4: *Unity of the will,* which, in case something is involved whose effects extend to community interests, suspends all contradiction, upon the principle that no one can at the same time will and not will, and makes the separate will of the individual subordinate to the community decision.

§5: *Unity of force.* In so far as the individual energies are necessary for the attainment of the ultimate end of the community, they should be exerted in no way except that toward which the community energy is devoted. Whoever withdraws his share of this energy, in case the common ends require a given quantity of force, leaves the general activity too weak; but if he turns his energy against the general purpose the disadvantage is doubled, because the energy of another person is thereby nullified.

* * *

§9: In these three forms of government [democracy, aristocracy, and monarchy] nothing essential to society is modified, but merely the form in which the common will expresses itself, i.e., either through the majority or through the élite, or through the autocrat. Thus, just as the decisions of all were binding upon each individual, the same must be the case with the decisions of those who take the place of all. This obligation on the one side implies on the other side the right of compulsion, and irresistibility, and thus the relations between rulers and ruled, between subjects and the supreme power, were more specifically determined.

§10: Originally the use of the combined forces was determined by the will of all the citizens. Since now the supreme power combines in itself the community will, its prerogative is likewise to determine how the community energies shall best be used for the common welfare.

§11: The ultimate purpose for the sake of which men enter society is that best which they possess neither enough moral nor physical power to attain alone; which in itself considered is, to be sure, the separate best of each member. Since, however, this separate best is sought by each at the same time, and each by promoting the best of the other thereby also confirms his own, it is called the community best. The ultimate purpose of men entering into combination might be expressed therefore as the *individual best;* the ultimate purpose of combined men as the *general best.* In civic societies this best, this ultimate purpose, has been security and convenience of life, which combined constitute the *public welfare.*

§12: [Security is] a condition in which we have nothing to fear. The condition in which the state has nothing to fear is called public security, that in which no citizen has anything to fear is called private security. When the state is safe against attacks from without, the condition is called public external security, and if no danger threatens from its own citizens, there exists public internal security. If neither the state, from within nor without, nor the citizens have anything to fear, this fortunate condition is called the general security.

§13: The convenience of life is the facility of providing one's support by diligence. Diligence will find its support the easier the more diversified the gainful occupations. The general convenience of life depends therefore upon diversification of the gainful occupations.

§14: The general welfare cannot be maintained without cost. The ruler must be provided with revenues, which must be in proportion to his dignity. This outlay is made for the best good of all the citizens. It is therefore proper that the expense should be borne by all the citizens, but that it should be drawn from them in a way that will promote the ultimate purpose.

§15: From manifold observations and experiences it is possible to refer the various rules through which the general welfare may be maintained, to reliable fundamental principles, and to give them the form of a science, which is *Staatswissenschaft* in the most comprehensive sense; that is, the science of maintaining the welfare of a state, the science of governing. We are convinced that the problematical and the variable do not reside in the principles of the science, but in the circumstances and occurrences to which the principles are to be applied. The mere empiricist in politics is therefore as little to be regarded as a statesman as the empiricist in the healing art is to be regarded as a physician.

* * *

§17: The ultimate purpose of states may be divided into four cardinal subdivisions, which are connected with one another, to be sure, and must join hands with one another, each of which stops, however, with a subordinate end. *Staatswissenschaft* has accordingly been divided into four sciences, viz.: external security; internal security; diversification of gainful occupations; and raising the revenues necessary for the expenses of the state.

§18: [The first of these sciences is called] *Staatswissenschaft* in the special sense; otherwise known as *Staatsklugheit* or *Politik*.

§19: The second is *Polizeywissenschaft*.

§20: The third is called *Handlungswissenschaft*.

§21: The fourth is *Finanzwissenschaft*.

§22: Natural science [*Naturlehre*] in all its parts, the mathematical sciences, physical geography [*Erdbeschreibung*], the history, laws, languages, are to be regarded partly as an indispensable preparation, partly as reinforcing auxiliaries of the theory of *Polizey, Handlung,* and *Finansen*. But the man of affairs, in actual administration, must know the customs, habits, and statutes of peoples, the reciprocal advantages and disadvantages of lands, the political conditions of states, and if he is to participate with advantage in law-giving, he must know men.

Fundamental Principle of Civic Science, and Its Branches

§24: The only one who has referred *Staatswissenschaft* with all its branches to a universal principle is, so far as I know, Justi. He assumed as such a principle the promotion of general happiness. That is a true, hut not a conclusive principle. The promotion of general happiness is the object of all states, to be sure, in the period of their origin, and it is their perpetual aim; for that very reason, however, it cannot be taken as a principle of verification, or as the general fundamental, *because by means of this fundamental the goodness of the measures, which consists in their harmony with the ultimate purpose, must be tested.* In his [Justi's] *Staatswirthschaft* when a law is to be given, or any other device is to be derided on, about which it is doubtful whether it would be advantageous for the state, the question is, "does the proposed law promote the general happiness?" Hereupon it must be tested by that principle, as the moral touchstone, and when the judgment of benefit or injury is reached, the ground for the judgment is given through that principle (i.e., general happiness). In case, therefore, the promotion of general happiness is assumed as the chief fundamental principle, the decision will amount to this: "It promotes the general happiness because it promotes the general happiness."

§25: Observation of how civic societies have arisen, and through what means they have reached their end, will more surely guide to the real fundamental principle. The isolated man was at the mercy of every attack by a superior power. His security was not greater than the forces with which he could defend himself against the attack. Two men whose physical strength exceeded his own were already dangerous to his security. He therefore sought to increase his strength by combination with others. The isolated man felt wants for the support of his life, sufficiency to satisfy which was within the compass neither of his strength of body nor of soul nor yet of his time. He sought to satisfy these wants by putting his diligence at the service of the wants of other men, from whom he received as compensation the supply of necessaries which he lacked. The isolated man was deprived of a thousand comforts, the lack of which he felt, the possession of which would make his external condition more complete. He sought the comforts through socialization [*Vergesellschaftung*] with others. The larger the society into which he was merged, the greater was the quantity of the resistance which he could exert in every case, and thereby assure his security. The more numerous the society, the more frequent its wants, the easier he found ways, by supplying what was lacking to somebody, to get from the same person what he wanted. The more numerous the society, the more various were its products, and the easier was it for him to supply each of his wants and comforts. Through the enlarging of the society therefore, and according to its bulk, was the aim of civic societies reached, viz., *the security and comfort of life.* In later times this aim remains ever the same. The same means will also remain effective.

§26: *The enlargement of the society* thus contains in itself all subordinate special means which in the aggregate promote the general welfare. So soon then as it is proved of an institution [*Anstalt*], or of a law that it makes for the enlargement of the society, or at least does not hinder the same; this proof at the same time carries the higher conclusion, viz., that the measure promotes, or at least does not hinder, the general welfare either on the side of security or of comfort. I take, therefore, *the enlargement of civic society, through promotion of the increase of population,* as the common fundamental principle of *Staatswissenschaft,* with its included parts: and the validating principle [*Prüfsatz*] of every measure which is adopted for promotion of the general happiness is this: *Does it lend to increase or diminish population?*

§27: I must seek to avoid indefiniteness. The population contains all the means which the common welfare [*gemeinschaftliche Wohlfahrt*] demands. All institutions of the ruler should accordingly be directed toward maintaining and increasing the numbers of the population. This number, nevertheless, has its limits, or a so-called maximum: and these limits are drawn by the nature of states, by the political and physical situation, and by the circumstances. Genoa will never reach the populousness of France. The bare rocks of Malta will never maintain as many inhabitants as fertile Sicily, the sandy Mark Brandenburg never so many as Bohemia. This, however, should not, on the other hand, prevent the Senate of Genoa, the Order of St. John, the King of Prussia, from using all means to assure for their territories the largest population which they are capable of supporting. If man with all his efforts can never be quite perfect, yet it always remains nevertheless a principle of morals that man must strive for the highest perfection! In politics, as in morals, if small states, less favored than others by nature, never can become as populous as those which combine larger area with rich soil, this does not invalidate the principle, *the government should always concern itself with promoting population to its highest level:* that is, the highest level which the means at its disposal make possible. This explanation will remove most of the objections which can be made against the fundamental principle of population. I come then to the application of this principle to the separate branches of *Staatswissenschaft.*

§§28-31: The greater the number of the people, the greater is the quantity of the resistance upon which the external security rests. The smaller states are consequently of their own strength capable of no high degree of external security. They combine with others, so that with the same, in respect to the ultimate purpose of defense, they may constitute a numerous society. Even the promptness of diplomatic action is affected by the amount of power at the command of the conferring parties. Then follow the conclusions:

(1) Hence the fundamental principle of *Politik.*

(2) The greater the number of the people, upon whose ready assistance one may count, the less has one to fear from within— hence the fundamental principle of *Polizey.*

(3) The greater the number of people, the more the needs, hence the more various the gainful occupations within the society. The more hands, the more abundant the products of agriculture and industry, the stuff for external exchange. Hence the fundamental principle of *Handlungswissenschaft.*

(4) The greater the number of citizens, the more are there to help bear the public expenses. The smaller therefore is the share of each taxpayer, without decreasing the total amount of the public revenues. Consequently the fundamental principle of *Finanzwissenschaft.* The knowledge of population is therefore, in all parts of public administration, indispensable. The means of surveying it, as a whole and in its parts, belong therefore to no branch of *Staatswissenschaft* exclusively. They belong as introductory knowledge to all.

Volume I: Polizey
Introduction: The Simplest Concepts of Polizey and Consequently an Outline in Accordance with Which They Will Be Treated

§43: When these measures and devices are assembled, and referred to certain principles derived from the nature of the social purpose, there results the science of founding and maintaining the internal security of the state; that is, die *Polizeywissenschaft.*

§44: By this formula I take issue with all authors who have previously treated the subject. To a certain extent I give *Polizey* an entirely different meaning. Perhaps I should say, my reason is because the formulas hitherto offered seem to me too vague, too ill-defined, some of them too limited, not including all which belongs within the scope of *Polizey;* others too general, embracing much which does not belong in *Polizey.* My intention is not, however, to repudiate other formulas, but by means of my own to draw the proper boundaries of *Polizey* according to my own views, and to exhaust the concept. I think I have a right to demand that after the work itself has been read the judgment should be passed whether I have acted in accordance with my intention. This intention is to treat the internal constitution of a state in its interdependence, and in all parts of the public administration, and at the same time to investigate the sources of law-giving. Consequently I shall frequently use the words *Polizey* and *Gesetzgebung* as synonymous.

* * *

…in a certain sense *Polizey* is principally defense against either intentional or fortuitous occurrences of a harmful nature; second, every occurrence which hinders the accomplishment of the ultimate purpose of society must be regarded as harmful; third, from this point of view *Polizey* regards every transaction which does not *promote* this ultimate purpose as harmful. In order to perform a harmful act, the will and the ability must coincide. The law-abiding man has constant opportunities to perform harmful acts, but he does not want to. The imprisoned criminal has the will to perform harmful acts, but he is deprived of ability. Hence *Polizey* falls into two parts, first, directive, the intention of which is that no one shall wish to perform harmful acts; second, preventive, which seeks to make it impossible for anyone to commit harmful acts even if he has the desire. The will of the actor is determined by impulses [*Beweggründe*], and the more certainly and effectively the oftener the impulses toward or against an action occur, or the greater the weight of the single impulse which operates upon the actor. This is the invariable principle of will, in which alone the great secret of law-giving resides. If the law-giver only knows how to offer his people preponderating impulses toward the good, he may be assured that he may lead them as he will. The impulses to action are of two sorts—first, *attractive* [*einladend*]; second, *preventive.* Again, the nature of the advantages or disadvantages to be anticipated from actions divides impulses into *general* and *special.* The general impulses include all actors and actions. For that reason they deserve the first rank in law-giving. There is another reason, viz., there are actions in connection with which it is difficult or impossible to discover a special attractive or preventive impulse. In such a case there remains for the lawgiver only the motive power of the general impulses, which may be grouped in two classes: *morals,* and *the high idea of the excellence of the laws.* Morals, in the relation in which they are regarded by the law-giving authorities, are devotion to the general order. As Toussaint well says, "they very well supply the place of laws, but nothing is capable of supplying the place of morals." Devotion to the general order is the effect of combined institutions, which enlighten the understanding of the citizen to the end that he may pass correct judgments upon everything which affects the general order, which guides the inclinations, which controls the passions and directs them to worthy actions. The whole system of devices to this end I refer to under the phrase *attention to the moral condition.* Next in importance is effort to propagate *a high idea of the excellence of the laws;* that is, to raise it, among all the citizens, to the rank of an accepted, incontestable principle, that whatever the laws command is good; that is, with respect to the whole, necessary; and with respect to each individual, profitable. Whenever the supreme power succeeds in establishing this presupposition, it is the most reliable guarantee for the observance of the laws, through the violation of which each will then believe that he will harm himself. But given the willingness to obey the laws, insight into the special actions that would conform to the laws is not thereby assured. The ruler must consequently supply this lack by laws which specify what is to be done and left undone. This is what Hume had in mind when he said that the laws are to be regarded as reinforcement of the insight of the individual. The subject-matter of these laws is internal *public* and internal *private* security. As previously defined, internal public security is a condition in which the state, that is, the public administration whatever the governmental form, has nothing to fear from the citizens. Voluntary obedience to the law, and thus public security, is brought about through the devotion above discussed. Compulsory obedience springs from the consciousness of weakness against the superior powers of the sovereign, or from impossibility of resistance. What Montesquieu in another connection makes the fundamental principle of a civic structure [*Staatsverfassung*] may be applied here with great accuracy, viz., "it is essential," he says, "that through the order of nature one force holds another in check;" that is, the quantity of possible powers of resistance on the side of the citizens must always be smaller than the quantity of the powers of coercion on the side of the state. Hence the chief attention of the *Polizey* and law-givers is demanded to prevent any stratum or single citizen from attaining to such power that the public authorities may be successfully opposed.

* * *

§52: All good, which can accrue to the citizen, all bad, whereby his happiness may be endangered, may be traced back to his business, his person, his honor, and his goods.

Attention to the Moral Condition

§61: Morals are a common subject-matter of religion, of ethics, and of law-giving; but each treats them in the light of its own purpose; the first two as an end, the last only as a means, satisfied if correspondence of conduct with the laws can be procured not by the most lofty motives, but also merely by hope of an advantage or by fear of punishment. Hence arises the idea of *political virtue*, which differs from the concept of virtue demanded by *ethics* and *religion*. *Political or social virtue is the facility of ordering one's conduct in correspondence with the laws of the society.* The motor machinery, whereby this correspondence is procured, does not fall within the scope of the present explanation, since virtue of a higher order is not to be dispensed with. Meanwhile there is no ground for the anxiety that *political virtue* may be dangerous for religion and ethics [*Sittenlehre*]; that would be the case if political virtue and religious virtue were in antithesis with each other: but this is by no means the case. For the purpose of the law-giver, to be sure, the first is enough; yet the second is not thereby excluded," but to a certain extent it is presupposed by the first. A wise law-giver will always seek to base social virtue [*Gesellschaftstugend*] upon moral virtue, yet from inadequacy of the means at his command he cannot always discover whether each member of society in practice bases his social virtue upon moral virtue. He must therefore be content to take knowledge simply of the body of the transactions, and he leaves it to the spiritual teacher to introduce the vitalizing spirit of religion.

* * *

§63: The chief and most effective means for the building-up of morals are *religion, education,* and the *sciences.* Among these religion deserves the first place. Religion is the gentlest bond of society. Religion instructs through her venerable teachings in goodness. Religion stimulates to the application of the same through promises. Religion deters from evil actions by threats. Religion brings about thorough repentance, which she produces in the sinner, and forgiveness, which she offers to the penitent, the improvement of the vicious. Religion increases therefore the determining as well as the deterring motives. Law-giving would in countless cases find itself inadequate, if religion did not beneficently come to its aid. Whenever the eye of the law-giver, and consequently also the penalty of the judge, fails to accomplish the end, the exalted principle of the omnipresent God, as witness and judge of all, even the most secret evildoers, is the sole means of arresting evil undertakings. The whole world is consequently in agreement with Warburton, that *the doctrine of a future life of rewards and punishments is utterly indispensable for every civic society.* The ruler may not disregard this leash [*Leitriemen*] given into his hand, and he must take care that every citizen in the state has religion.

§64: From this point of view freethinking appears as a political crime, because to a certain extent it robs the state of the means of guiding its citizens most completely. The chancellor Bacon, and President Montesquieu have never been under suspicion as persecutors, yet the former writes: "No one denies God, except those who have an interest in there being no God;" the latter: "From the opinion that there is no God comes our independence or our revolt." Accordingly to them the atheist becomes either a criminal or a disorderly citizen. Consequently the concord and happiness of the state depend on intolerance of the declared *freethinkers;* and circumstances might often make it necessary for the public authorities to demand of everyone a visible sign of the religion "to which he adheres."

§65: From the necessity of religion, even for the temporal happiness of the citizens, and the common security, are derived the right and the obligation of the *Polizey* to extend its attention to the education of the people in religious duties, to prevent abuses, and to watch over the external order of religious functions and worship. The instruction in the duties of religion, in the rural regions particularly, is worthy of so much attention, because with the rural population religion must largely take the place of education, and at the same time it is the only means of making an impression upon their ways of thinking. The first object to which the care of the *Polizey* should be given in this respect should be sufficient and skilful curates.

* * *

§70: After religion, education has the greatest influence upon morals. It is, to be sure, a peculiar duty of parents; but not only a son, a citizen is also to be educated. Education can therefore, on account of its connection with the common welfare, not be a matter of indifference to the law-giver, and cannot be left by the state to private whim.

§71: Parents must be compelled to give their children the necessary education.

§72: In order that dependent children may be educated, academies, foundling and orphan asylums are necessary.

§73: It is desirable that public schools should be attended by children of the upper as well as of the lower classes, for the sake of making these classes acquainted with each other.

* * *

§122: All that can be demanded of a reasonable *Polizey* is, not that its attention shall be carried to the extreme of increasing its numbers for the purpose of spying and house-visitation, nor that by excessive severity toward weaknesses it shall give occasion for greater and more dangerous crimes, but that the *Polizey* shall restrict itself to preventing public indecency, and outbreaking offenses, and that it shall co-operate with parents, relatives, married people, who make complaints about seduction of their relatives, or disturbance of domestic order. Beyond that, religion, education, and reduction of the number of the unmarried must do the most toward the restriction of an evil which it will be possible for no foresight entirely to uproot.

§123: The *Polizey* must, however, exert itself to remove all occasions through which, directly or indirectly, moral disorders of another sort may be increased. Here belong, for lessening drunkenness, and the evils that flow from it, the restriction of the number of dram shops; the ordinance that after a certain hour (at night) nothing more shall be sold in such shops, and at no time to intoxicated persons; exemplary punishments for confirmed drunkards; prohibition of lodging strangers except in recognized inns; and further, measures approved by monarchs of insight, and readily granted by a head of the church worthy of immortality, viz., for decrease of the number of feast days. For it is certain that all time devoted to labour will be rescued from vice and excess.

On the Means of Awakening a High Idea of the Laws
§124: on the average in a nation high respect for the law will be less a result of persuasion than of antecedently formed opinion, that is, of a favorable prejudice. This prejudice must be aroused and strengthened. It may be weakened or destroyed. The means in either case are in the hands of those who give the laws. In republics, where laws are examined by representations of the people before they are enacted, the presumption of the goodness of the laws springs from the nature of the constitution. That is, it is supposed that the law would have been rejected if its advantages had not been beyond all doubt. In monarchies, that which occurs in republics before the acceptance of a law should occur at the promulgation of the same. This may take place in two ways—first, by giving assurance that consultation with estates, parliaments, councilors, etc., preceded the decree; second, that every law should have a preamble, setting forth the reasons why it was necessary for the public weal and beneficial for the individual. A government which imposes upon itself the rule of accompanying its laws, so far as possible, with reasons, shows confidence in its measures, honors the intelligence and integrity of the citizens, appears less to command than to persuade. The people itself imagines that it obeys less the law than its own insight.

* * *

§128: Even if the law bears only some such legend as 'moved by the public good,' the people will be inclined to believe it.
§129: The conviction which assumes that the laws are good is produced by laws of great age, and the invariability of laws is the condition of their attaining great age.

* * *

§131: Conflicting interpretations of the law by experts weaken the presumption in its favor.
§132: Nothing weakens the prestige of the laws more than a distinction between obligation before the judge, and absence of obligation in conscience.

On Provision for Holding Private Powers in a Subordinate Equilibrium with the Powers of the State

§136: The powers of resistance on the side of the citizens must always be kept inferior to the powers of compulsion on the side of the state.

* * *

§138: The forces or means, which might hinder the state in the exercise of its powers, consist of wealth, of the strength of a stratum of society, and of privileges." "While security of property is one of the principal advantages to be gained by civic society, wisdom seeks to prevent the accumulation of excessive private wealth.

§139: It is not wise to prescribe the limits of wealth which individuals or families may possess; but the state may set precise bounds to the wealth of deathless societies.

§140: This necessity has been recognized in all states, especially since Edward I set the example with his 'amortization laws'.

§141: In case the laws have neglected to provide against too great accumulation of wealth in families, indirect measures may be adopted with advantage to correct the evil; as when Henry VII of England allowed the division of the estates of the nobility among several sons. If he had ordered the division, it would have been resisted. The permission was regarded as beneficent. Similar indirect measures may be taken to limit the growth of deathless societies;

§142: And parallel action is wise in the case of societies, parties, and organizations of many sorts which tend to acquire excessive power.

On Penalties

§352: Punishment is an evil of sensation because of malice of action. This aphorism, handed down from writer to writer, has given a one-sided direction to reflection upon the subject. The viewpoint from which the judge who enforces the penalty regards it, and that of the law-giver who ordains it are quite different. The first punishes because the law was disobeyed. The second threatens a penalty in order that the law may not be disobeyed. With the former the penalty is a consequence of the conduct. With the latter the conduct is a consequence of the penalty. With the first the affixing of penalty is inculpation, with the second it is stimulus. Penalty therefore, considered as an auxiliary, to protect the law, namely, by exerting an influence upon the resolutions of actors, and by supplying the place of other determining motives, is an evil which is attached to the law as a means of influencing against infraction of the same. In determining penalties, attention is to be paid, first, to the quantity; second, to the kind of the same.

* * *

§357: The general means of measuring punishment is, therefore, to be sought only in the motives of the crime. (1) The penalty must be as great as necessary to procure the lawful action or restraint; (2) The penalty must not be greater than necessary to procure the lawful action; (3) The strongest deterring motive, that is, the most effective penalty, will always be that which threatens an evil in direct antithesis with the motive which solicits to the crime.

* * *

§376: Death penalties are contrary to the purpose of penalties.   Hard, incessant public labour promises much more for that purpose, and at the same time makes the punishment of the criminal profitable for the state.

§377: The first question which must be investigated is without doubt in respect to the right. Has the law a right to punish with death? If questions have been raised over this point, it was because writers have fawned upon princes, and have sought the source of this right in no one knows what form of a majesty derived immediately from heaven, and assigned to them an unlimited right over life and death. The source of this awful right is to be sought nowhere except in the individual man, whose combination constitutes the state. Man, thought of in the natural condition, has the right to protect his security in every way, and if the violence of attack cannot otherwise be warded off, it is his right to carry his defense even to the death of the assailant. In civil society each separate member has made over this right of defense to the whole, that is, to the sovereign power that represents the whole; that is, not a right over his own life, which no one possesses, but the right of each over the life of every other who might become an assailant. In that way the sovereign power acquired the right over all.

On Institutions for Maintaining Internal Security

§389: Under the name institutions we include all persons and devices which aim at prevention and discovery of every action harmful to civic security, including the higher as well as the lower stations and functionaries that have to do in any way with guarding the peace, with detecting seditious intentions, or dangerous persons, and finally everything which has to do with punishment of the same.

§390: As the prerogatives of *Polizey* have been treated in this work, the law-giving as well as the executive power lies within the scope of its functions. The supreme administration of the same can consequently be accredited only to the highest station in the state, whatever be the name under which it exists. This is the directing guidance of the state, where the principal laws and ordinances are enacted. Execution, however, is, according to the variety of the objects, committed to subordinate divisions. Moreover, the public administration usually subdivides affairs, and retains for itself law-giving, at least in general affairs of the country, or respecting other more important matters; it turns over the civil and criminal judiciary functions to special bodies, or so-called *Stellen*, and restricts the operations of *Polizey* in the narrower sense to maintenance of the public peace, good order, and discipline, to superintendence over measures, weights, markets, cleanliness of cities, institutions necessitated by the various dangers and accidents, and especially over everything which demands emergency action.

Since mention has already been made of the different judicial offices, it remains for this chapter to treat only of this last significance of *Polizey*.

Volume II: Handlung
Preface

[This] outline of political commercial science was not written for men in business, whose theories have been established by long experience, and have become complete. If I wish to leave the book in their hands, it is only in order that I may be corrected by them if any errors have escaped my knowledge.

My ambition limits itself to the young friends to whom my calling commissions me as a guide. If I have in some measure smoothed their way to their duty, if I have made their preparation for their calling easier, I have accomplished my purpose.

There is no lack, to be sure, of thorough writings on the subject of commerce. The English and the French have always recognized the importance of a subject which may be regarded as the foundation of public welfare [*der öffentlichen Wohlfahrt*], since through multiplication of means of subsistence it is the basis of population.

The greatest men in all sciences, publicists [*Staatskündige*], historians, philosophers, have made contributions to the explanation of commerce. Mathematicians have believed that they were no less useful to the world and to their fatherland when they spoke of the advantages of a cloth factory than when they analyzed the profound theory of the infinite. Their writings meanwhile are rather for the already educated readers than for beginners. It appears that men of such ability have been unable to put themselves on the level of the untrained. Hence the obscurity of their writings. They presuppose knowledge of which the uninitiated have no comprehension. The latter cannot grasp conclusions from principles which they do not understand.

The profound author of the *Elements of Commerce* declares at the outset that he did not write for those who read only to save themselves the trouble of thinking. If Forbonnais would admit only thinking readers, did he reflect that his excellent book would remain almost unread? I take the liberty of confessing that my intention is precisely the opposite of his. I write for those who are not yet capable of thinking for themselves on this subject. This book is to introduce them to it. My purpose is to prepare readers for Forbonnais.

Four books, or eight, if we reckon Becher's *Bedenken van Manufacture in Deutschland*, von Vogemont's (or Bogemont's) *Deutschlands vermehrten Wohlstand*, Boden's *Fürstliche Machtkunst*, and Jörger's *Vota Cameralia*, from all of which no one would be able to gather particularly important information. These are all of these species, however, which Austria up to this time has to show. The rest of Germany is not rich in writings of distinction, while other nations are taught about all parts of commerce and finance by the most excellent works.

* * *

§8: This lack may have its cause chiefly in the difficulty of access to those sources which occasion the speculations of writers, which guide them, which must necessarily be made fundamental by them, in so far as their works are not to remain merely indecisive and mostly inapplicable thoughts. The strength and population, the condition of commerce, of manufactures, the various changes, the occasions of the same, the hindrances, the encouragements, the increase of diligence, the condition of the public revenues, of the national credit, all this is in other states known in detail, either from public registers and tables, or it is readily made known to those who desire to inform themselves about these matters competent men then look upon it as their duty not to withhold from the state their observations about the same, and their advice. In this way, as it were, a whole nation unifies its insight. The number of its councilors is in certain respects not smaller than the number of its thinking patriots. With us such facts are still regarded as state secrets. There may be many important grounds for this reticence, which are unknown to me. Meanwhile I can cite this secrecy in general as the cause of that dearth of political writings, the number of which I wish to increase by publishing these elements. My merit may perhaps be very slight, if a one-sided estimate is put upon the worth of my labour. If, however, judgment is so generous as to consider the intention, the endeavor, to be useful at my post, I have thereby earned at least a certain measure of thanks.

Introduction

§2: The beneficent influence of commerce upon general happiness [*allgemeine Glückseligkeit*] was long overlooked by political philosophy [*Staatsklugheit*]. No attention, no care, no promotion was supposed to be due to this subject. Not as though Alexander, even in the irresistible course of his victories, had not cast a glance upon commerce, and after the destruction of Tyre had not built Alexandria as the emporium of eastern and northern wares: but ministers and monarchs recognized in the son of Philip only the conqueror, and only in that character did he seem worthy of imitation. Charles V, Sully, Elizabeth, Colbert first enlightened, cabinets about the true advantages of commerce. World-wisdom lent statecraft its insight. Men who had received from Providence the calling of being teachers of the nations instructed the world on this subject in deathless writings. Finally, as the principle gained prevalence—*the happiness of the state consists in the number of its citizens* — people began to recognize the worth of a business [*Geschäft*] which, through multiplication of the means of support, contributes such a large portion to this happiness. Thereupon commerce became an affair of the cabinets. Attention was given to the principles *by whose application the largest number of people may be supplied with occupation.* The collection of these principles constitutes the *political science of commerce.* Mercantile [*die kaufmännische*] science is distinguished from this subject, because the private merchant has for his purpose the increase of his own private means, without thought whether thereby anything accrues to the general advantage of the state, or whether the general advantage is endangered. Yet the *political* commerce by no means works against private advantage. The former seeks to use the latter as a tool to subordinate it as a means to the general end: that is, to combine the advantage of the state with that of the individual citizen. The occupation [*Beschäftigung*] of human beings has for its purpose the placing in their hands the means whereby they may provide their support. They derive this support through receiving something as compensation for that which they produce by their occupation. Thus *barter* comes into existence, and this is the business of commerce in the most proper sense.

§3: What one should accept as a compensation for that which one has given must be of such character that one *wants it*. Want [*Bedürfnis*] is here not to be understood in the restricted sense which misanthropic worldly-wise have given to the word. Desire [*Verlangen*] for greater comfort, the means to gratify this desire, the ability to find pleasure in possession and enjoyment of the same, are not without a purpose in the plan of nature. They are, to the same extent, not without a purpose in the plan of *Staatsklugheit*. Want [*Bedürfnis*] means accordingly everything the use of which can give us advantage of any sort whatever, the possession of which is meanwhile desired; and these wants, whether they are real wants, without which human beings could not exist, or imaginary wants, which the customary mode of life, the standard of comfort or enjoyment, the pride of men, have made desirable, are equally an object of exchange through which wants are traded for wants.

§4: If that which one can give for that which is offered were of such a sort that it were everywhere found in abundance, it would have no compensating worth, and by means of it, therefore, no exchange could occur. The object offered in exchange must accordingly be something which he, with whom the exchange is to occur, wants and does not possess, or at any rate does not possess *in the quantity* which he desires. That is, it must be relatively rare. Commerce is thus a business which owes its origin to a reciprocal want. What one may offer to another for the satisfaction of a want, is called a ware [*Ware*].

§5: In the exchange of wares many sorts of hindrances presently appear. It is possible that he who desires to acquire a ware cannot offer for it precisely the ware which the other party wants at the moment, or in the quantity in which it is offered, and the offered ware is either entirely incapable of division, or the division diminishes its worth. In such a case one must seek to secure what one wants through a series of exchanges. Then again, that which one possesses may be of such a nature that it cannot, without difficulty or deterioration, be transferred from one place to another; the want may be so imperative that one cannot wait for the circuit of exchanges. These difficulties presently led men to look around for a means by which the difficulties might be avoided, and exchange be made easy. Something was sought which might, as it were, take the place of all wares, and be regarded as a universal equivalent [*Entgelt*] for the same. Not any stuff whatever could be adopted arbitrarily as such equivalent. Each of the qualities which was sought in the same should be a recourse against one of the indicated difficulties of exchange, and these difficulties pointed to that stuff in which the qualities were found united.

§6: In order to relieve wants in as small portions as was necessary according to circumstances, that which was adopted as the general equivalent must necessarily be capable of very great divisibility without loss of worth. Since, especially after the extension of commerce, the objects of exchange often had to be carried long distances, durability and imperishability were demanded, both in order that in the exchange itself, or in going from hand to hand, it might not be used up, and also in order that, without danger of deterioration, it might be saved up. In order that the carriage should not be difficult it must be rare. In this way a small piece became an equivalent for a considerable bulk of wares. At the same time a great sum could be sent in a small space. But it is probable that only after many unsuccessful attempts would the peoples discover the combination of these qualities in the precious metals, which had elsewhere been sought in vain. And therein lies the cause of the almost universal agreement of the nations about gold and silver, which now are regarded as the representatives of wares, and are called money.

§7: After the introduction of money, to be sure, the turn-over [*Umsatz*] was no longer called barter, but purchase. But this change in the words (*sic!*) did not essentially change the "commerce." The money did not thereby come otherwise into consideration than in so far as it represented those wants, or wares, which at another time could be procured for it. The thing accomplished by the "commerce" is still always the exchange of one ware for another, or for the representative of a ware.

§8: Wares with which exchange is effected are either immediately usable in their original form, or they must be transformed for use by artificial labour. The occupation which devotes itself to obtaining [*Erziehung*] the former is rural management [*Landwirthschaft*]. It embraces the natural produce of the earth, of grazing, and of the waters. The occupation which makes the natural products usable through imparting an artificial form, or which multiplies their use, is called *Manufaktur*. The manufactures are dependent upon land management. The first attention of the state must therefore be given to this latter. What land management furnishes to the manufactures is called raw materials or stuffs.

§9: The original commerce consists therefore in the produce of the earth and of artificial labour, so far, that is, as both come to the assistance of wants; and in those who devote themselves with their produce, who furnish the means, of providing in turn their own wants. This enables us to determine the extent of general commerce. It is equal to the sum of the wants of all consumers [*Verzehrenden*]. In order to extend commerce, either the wants or the consumers must be increased.

§10: The wants of human beings, as already observed, are very limited, if we attach to the word the strictest concept of *real* wants. But in that case the occupations of the citizens will be kept within the same narrow bounds. The multiplication of wants occurs through introduction of comforts and of superfluity, both of which make luxury. All declamations against luxury, therefore, are either not well considered, or the objections which are urged against it are not really directed so much against luxury, as against the one-sided wastefulness on the part of a few, while the other portion of the nation ekes out a miserable existence. Luxury, in so far, on the one hand, as it increases the wants of citizens, and thereby perhaps makes it harder for some to support themselves, increases on the other hand the occupations; thus it incidentally makes gainful occupations easier and more numerous; that is, the superfluity of one satisfies the wants of others. And if here and there a citizen does not know how to limit his outlays by the rules of private prudence, and ruins himself, his wasted resources are, in the first place, no loss for the state, because they merely pass out of one hand into the other, or are transferred to many persons; second, the ruin of the one may perhaps have provided the support of ten families of the labouring class of the nation. With this explanation all, even the most plausible, objections to luxury may be answered.

§11: At the same time, however, the boundaries between useful and harmful luxury may be determined. For without doubt there is a sort of luxury which is harmful. All luxury, for example, is harmful, which contradicts the purpose for the sake of which the state should encourage it, which does not increase the sum of national occupations, but diminishes it. This occurs in the case of unnecessary foreign articles of luxury and also in the case of those which are not made in the country itself, because these foreign wares always take the place of a national ware, and crowd the latter out of the sum of national occupations. One case only deserves to be regarded as an exception, viz., when the foreign article of luxury has come in, not by purchase but in exchange for a ware produced at home. In this instance justice is done in advance both to national consumption and to all demands of the foreigners who wanted to acquire it by purchase or in exchange for wants. In this case, however, it is only the extension of a branch of the occupation. The foreign article of luxury takes the place of the national product.

§12: The outlay that is restricted to domestic products cannot be increased without end. The resources of those who use these products, and their number, constitute their necessary limits. Commerce would thus not be greater than the possible national consumption. There remains, however, the extension of the same on another side, through increase of consumption. Takers of the wares will be sought outside the country. The effort is made to supply other nations with what they need, and through their consumption to increase the sum of national occupation. Commerce thus divides itself into domestic and foreign. Domestic commerce is that which is carried on between the members of a state.

§13: Foreign commerce is carried on with foreigners. It must necessarily be based on domestic commerce, and it must give up something to foreigners only when it has first satisfied the national wants. Thus foreign commerce is carried on only with the surplus; that is, with that which the national consumption can spare. On the other hand a nation will take either only such wares as it really needs, or those to the taking of which it is drawn by powerful stimuli. These two grounds determine takers in general, but a state will be moved to take from precisely *this* nation, inasmuch as the same wares may actually be had from several sides, only through the most advantageous, or the least disadvantageous conditions under which a ware is offered. These conditions affect the price of wares, or their qualities.

§14: Scarcely any state or nation, at least under present circumstances, and with the once introduced mode of life, will be sufficient unto itself. What it does not possess, it must try to get from abroad under the least oppressive conditions. To this end external commerce furnishes its aid, and in accordance with the division of its occupation it is divided into two branches, viz., export and import. It carries out, from the surplus; it brings in for a double purpose, either to use the imported articles itself, or to export them again, with advantage, to other nations.

§15: This last makes a third branch of commerce, re-export [*Wiederausfuhr*], called economic commerce [*ökonomische Handlung*]. If its advantage consisted only in the occupation of persons engaged in trade, and in the increase of navigation or of wainage, re-export would even then be highly important for a state. It would be giving occupation to a part of the citizens at the cost of other nations. But this is not the whole of the advantage, and the re-exporting state increases thereby the national stock [*Nationaleinkommen*] to the extent of the excess of the selling price over the price of purchase, which is always a nation's gain if it may not always be the gain of the merchant.

§16: The less a nation has to receive from others for its own wants, and the more sales it can make to other nations, the more advantageous is its commerce. But the situation in different regions does not always afford to countries either the requisite quantity or the variety of wares necessary for their own consumption and for export. The commercial states, particularly the maritime provinces, turned their gaze in consequence toward the islands, sought to subjugate the same, and to secure possession through settlers transplanted thither, whence they have the name colonies, or settlements [*Siedlungen*]. Thence they may now draw a part of their wants, independent of other states and under self-imposed conditions, and they may increase without limit the stuff to be exported thither.

§17: The wants which are obtained from other states, and that which is sent abroad, must be transported to the place of sale. This transportation, which is denoted by the word "carriage" [*Fracht*], may occur in various ways. The nation receives its own wants through foreign carriage; and foreigners bring that which they are to receive by their own carriage; or the nation brings in by its own carriage what it receives from others, and returns by its own carriage what other nations buy. In the former case the nation loses the whole advantage of the occupation, which reciprocal carriage was capable of creating; and its commerce is thus in a certain sense passive. In the second case the nation appropriates this advantage and its commerce becomes more active. Every nation must therefore seek to receive its wants through its own carriage and to deliver exports to other nations with its own carriage.

§18: Carriage is by land or by water. Land carriage depends on good commercial roads and a well-conducted carrying system.

§19: Water carriage is on rivers or on the sea. River navigation is promoted by making and keeping rivers navigable, and by uniting rivers by means of canals and locks. These arrangements cannot be extended beyond the boundaries of a state. Sea carriage, on the contrary, is of incomparably greater extent. It depends upon a well-organized and supported merchant-marine.

§20: The danger of carrying, especially at sea, would of itself frighten from undertakings, because only few have enough courage to risk their whole resources, or a considerable portion of them, for a gain which is in no proportion to the possible and often very probable loss. The costs of carriage would also mount very high on account of this consideration, because the carrier would take into account the risk which he undertook. The danger of carriage may be approximately estimated, and according to this estimate the goods and ships may be made secure for a proportional compensation. From this making secure the business has the name insurance or assurance, whereby the courage for commercial undertakings is produced and increased.

§21: In the most favorable situation of a state, it is not possible greatly to extend commerce, or to maintain already extensive commerce, without a corresponding sum of money. The presence of money is necessary from two points of view: the state must in general not lack money as a promoter of national exertion; in particular commerce must not lack an adequate fund for its undertakings.

§22: The physical presence of money in a state does not give to enterprise the energy which comports with the purpose of commerce. It is necessary that the money shall do its work, and shall circulate among the members of society. It is therefore a special duty of the state to promote the circulation, and to remove all hindrances which might obstruct the same.

§23: In case, however, for whatever cause, the circulating sum of money is either insufficient, or diminished, means must be sought to replace the deficiency. The work [*Verrichtung*] of money is as follows: *to be to its possessors the reliable representation of a certain quantity of wares, to the effect that whenever it pleases them they may exchange the representation for that which is represented.* If it is possible for a state to succeed in procuring, for verbal consent, or for certain other signs, the same confidence, that, as money represented the wares, these signs represent the money, these arbitrary signs will then accomplish the work of money, and will temporarily make up completely for its absence. No care will therefore be too great which the ruler may devote to the maintenance of public confidence.

§24: If commercial enterprises are to be carried on energetically, they will require great sums. Only a few individual citizens in a state have the means or the credit, and those who have both have not always resolution enough to risk so much in undertakings from which to be sure great gain may be expected, which however are always exposed to an uncertain outcome. Where the means of individuals are not sufficient, an association is formed, each member of which risks only a small sum the more resolutely because in any event the loss would not impair his fortune; and yet the total of these separate contributions procures for commerce the adequate fund. The commercial associations accordingly contribute a large portion to the extension of commerce.

§25: Through export to foreigners and import from foreigners the commercial nations become reciprocal debtors. The discharge of these debts with ready money would be expensive, through the carriage of the money to the place of payment, and also dangerous; the money in carriage would be a considerable time unused, and the business of commerce would be plunged into tedious straggling [*Weitläufigkeit*]. It is possible to avoid these difficulties in whole or in part, if a state exchanges its claims with another, whereby it discharges its debts in so far as the condition of their commerce with each other permits. This exchange of reciprocal claims gave rise to the business of dealing in exchange, which to be sure is only a private affair, but it is always worthy of public attention, because it either facilitates or retards general commerce, and in addition furnishes useful information for the guidance of the same.

§26: In the present situation of science and knowledge, all cabinets are in such wise enlightened about the great influence of commerce that each nation must expect to be crossed [*durchquert*] in all undertakings by the states with which commerce is carried on, or through whose territory the commerce will take its course, whenever it runs counter to their purposes. It is necessary to anticipate these hindrances, and at favorable opportunities, by means of negotiation, to assure advantageous conditions both for oneself and against other rivals. Commercial treaties consequently constitute an important part of *Handelspolitik*.

§27: In order to know the status of commerce in itself and relatively and therefrom to conclude whether the course of affairs conduces to the utmost expansion of population, states compare the amount which they have supplied to others with that which they have received. This comparison of import and export is called the *balance:* the plumb line in the hands of the state to show where and in what parts commerce requires special aid.

§28: From the foregoing merely general concepts we see how numerous and far reaching are the knowledge, purposes, combinations, and plans which must be made the basis of advantageous commerce; and the necessity of controlling this important business through the combined insight of capable men, and incidentally of establishing for the conduct of commerce a special *Kollegium,* or a special *Stellc,* is thus very obvious. The name in itself is a matter of indifference, but this *Kollegium* must embrace in the circuit of its activity everything which can promote the advantage of commerce.

On rural Management (Landwirthschaft)

§30: Rural management is regarded in *Polizey* as the occupation which provides means of life; in its *commercial* functions [*Handelsleistung*] as also providing the material [*Stoffe*]. Considered from the side of the state, the perfection of rural management consists in the best possible utilization of the earth in accordance with the demands of subsistence [*Unterhalt*] and of commerce. From the side of the proprietor, it is the best combination of the largest yield with the least expenditure [*Vorauslagung*].

§31: I, by utilizing all the earth; II, by utilizing it in the best way as respects systems of cultivation; and III, by utilizing it as required by relations to the other connected or dependent occupations. The use of *all the earth,* and the *best* use of the same, coincide in many ways in obstacles and in furtherance.

§32: The earth is either private property, or the means of the state... In order to make full use of private property, the proprietor must have first the necessary power, and second the necessary motives.

§33: Lack of means for rural management may be regarded from two sides; namely, the poverty of the rural folk as a class, or of the particular cultivator. The former condition comes from such unavoidable circumstances as first, wars, loss of cattle, failure of crops, the poverty of the present possessor, or only from his temporary embarrassment.

§§34-41: Each of these types of misfortune is treated as deserving of public attention. Means of extinguishing fires are to be provided by the local administration; the dwellings are to be in village groups, not scattered over the land, and the garden plots are to be located between the houses instead of behind them, the barns to be separated from the houses, etc., in order that there may be the minimum danger from fire with the maximum facility of controlling it. Districts should also maintain systems of mutual fire insurance; proprietors should be made to see that their interests demand such precautions. In case such protection is lacking, the cultivator who is embarrassed must be assisted either by the proprietor or by the state. Mere negative help, which is customary, i.e., remission of the dues, does not meet the case. Active help must be given, e.g., lumber, building materials, farming implements; seed must be furnished gratuitously, or at least on the easiest terms. If the individual proprietors are not in a position to do this, it must be done by the state. The alternative is sterilization of the soil, declining value of the revenues of the state, and diminishing population. To remedy these conditions is more expensive than to prevent them. The direct and indirect consequences of cattle diseases are among the important objects of public attention. To prevent them veterinary schools should be introduced, and the causes of the diseases should be investigated. The price of salt, and provision that farmers shall have easy access to it are important in this connection, and should be carefully looked to by the state. In case of failure of crops, as in case of fire or war, the cultivator must be helped either by the proprietor or the state to raise his crops the following year. The state must take measures to prevent exorbitant or oppressive terms in case of loans by individuals. In case an individual proprietor is too poor properly to cultivate his tract, the state is in danger of suffering loss of a portion of its dues. There is therefore no reason why the state should not have the right to require that the proprietor should permit others to cultivate the land on shares, or to purchase it. The very circumstances which have caused the embarrassment of the proprietor may make such purchaser or farmer hard to find. The flocking of persons of means to the cities leaves the cultivation of the soil to an inferior class of people. In case forced sale is necessary, the state should provisionally take over the property at a fair price, in order that the possessor may not be compelled to make too great sacrifice. Land is often uncultivated, not by reason of the permanent but the temporary poverty of the possessor. It is an unpardonable mistake of the law-making power to aggravate this helplessness by exaction of the usual dues. The proprietor who has allowed the tenant to fall into arrears should be declared to have forfeited the amount. Laws should seek to prevent excessive debt by setting a limit to the amount which may be borrowed. An exception should be made in case the loan is necessary for actual cultivation of the land, and the conditions of loans for that purpose should be made especially favorable, and should be under the oversight of the proper officials. Unthrift on the part of proprietors will be checked by the introduction of supervisors of rural management [*Landwirthschaftsaufsicht*], consisting of the officials of the circuit [*Kreis*] to whom a subordinate might be added, and the private managers subordinated to these.

§§42-43: A second means of preventing neglect of proper cultivation is afforded by the dues to the state. That is, every piece of arable land should be taxed on a moderate estimate of what it would yield if properly cultivated. Thus the occupant will be compelled to cultivate the land or to pay dues for land which yields him no crop, while the industrious cultivator receives as it were a reward for his industry, in being assessed only on a medium rate of yield. If these means are not sufficient to secure good cultivation, a third remains. It seems severe, but it is not if the others have failed, viz.: In case a piece of land has remained uncultivated two or three years, unless the proprietor can offer to the supervisors an adequate excuse, it shall be declared forfeited, and transferred to someone who will cultivate it. Such a provision is based on the claim which the state has upon the private property of the citizens, for proportional contribution for maintenance of the whole. The forfeiture here proposed can no more be regarded as an invasion of property rights than the law of limitations. The security of property is only conditionally assured by the state, viz., in case the private proprietor does not impair the property of the state.

§§44-45: The lack of courage on the part of the cultivator has its ground in the opinion that his labour is lost, and that he will not reap its fruits. The insecurity of property, the rate of taxation, and the excessively favored love of hunting, on the part both of the sovereign prince and of the private owners, may be regarded as the chief causes of this lack of courage, and the multitude of idle days may be added. In case the insecurity of property has its origin in the defective fundamental order [*Grundverfassung*] of a country, it will always be difficult for the laws to limit the evil. If the private possessors considered, however, that such fundamental order made against their own advantage, they would not oppose abrogation of the same. The right which is based on ancient possession is made very questionable through the older and imprescriptible rights of mankind. Where the tenants in a certain sense are regarded only as farmers [*Pächter*] the lords of the soil think they do wisely when they transfer a thrifty farmer to the holdings of a negligent one. Instead of increasing the industry of each, they ruin both. The negligent one shirks work because he is negligent, because this negligence is rewarded, and he keeps hoping for the same reason to be transferred to a better cultivated location. The thrifty one is discouraged and refuses to make improvements which would give occasion for another transfer. Since this right has such great influence upon the condition of rural management in general, we cannot but approve a system which would assure to the peasants a tenure for life at least, and the abolition of this freedom of transfer.

§§45-49: The evictions [*Abstiftungen*] which the officials are sometimes empowered to make must also be reckoned as unfavorable to the security of property. They must consequently never be a one-sided procedure. Even the economic supervisors must have their hands bound in this respect; how much more the private owners. The tiller of the soil will work only hard enough to maintain life, if all the rest of his produce is taken from him by landlord and government. The peasant is most industrious when he is miserable.

§50: The more incentives to labour are presented to the fanner, the greater will be his diligence. The first motive for him is the support of self and family; the second, the tribute [*Entrichtung*] to which he is bound; the third, the desire to lay by something in case of need, for the improvement of his condition, or for his family. The products of the soil must not fall below a value which affords the hope that all three motives may be satisfied. In determining this price the interests of agriculture seem to be to a certain extent opposed to those of other kinds of business [*Handelsgeschäfte*]. If the price of agricultural products is high, the price of every manufactured product must rise, whereby one of the principal qualities of a ware, cheapness, is lost. If the price of agricultural products is low, it is not sufficiently encouraging for the farmer, and he finds it to his advantage to produce less, because from half the crop he can then receive a like sum, and save himself trouble, time, seed, etc. Only the medium price remains therefore where the interests of both branches can be combined. This medium price may be considered in its essence or merely numerically.

§51: In its essence the medium price is always and everywhere the same: the price, namely, which stands in such relation to the condition of commerce in general that thereby land management may get its proportional share of the gain which comes from commerce. This sharing in the general advantage is not only just, it is also necessary. The state is under obligations to observe and maintain equality between the members of society according to the degree of their reciprocal contribution to the general welfare. Where this equality is not observed the neglected part lacks those encouragements which must be the spur to and the real soul of diligence. It is also unavoidably demanded in order that the worth of the agricultural products may procure for the seller adequate means of satisfying his other wants, that—in the degree in which the wants either rise in price, or otherwise, as through the prosperity of commerce, the prosperity of the working class, and with the same the number of their wants increases— the farmer shall find enough in the price of his products to procure either the higher-priced or the more numerous wants. If his way to this result is closed by an arbitrary fixing of the price, it would follow in the one case that his wants would not be satisfied, whereby he would be forced to interrupt his labour; or, in the other case, his condition would be at least relatively more unfortunate than that of the other working classes. The peasant class would consequently be abandoned, because it would be eager to improve its lot by going over to the other classes. Those that would remain in the class would be without means, or would avenge themselves by indolence for the unrighteousness of society.

§52: It is consequently necessary from so many grounds to assure to land management through the medium price its share of the gains of commerce. But the regulation of the medium price cannot occur through the taxes, but through the reciprocal agreements of purchasers and sellers in the market place, if no hindrances are otherwise placed in the way of the freedom of these compacts. If the varying market price of several ordinary years is compared, and the average reckoned, this will be taken as the numerical mean, which is variable according to circumstances.

§53: The state must see that the number of sellers is not too great, and also that a proportional number of customers for agricultural products may be assured.

§54: The state has therefore not merely to moderate the fiscal burdens upon agriculture, but to prevent cheapening of the produce by spreading the payment over various periods.

* * *

§59: Opinions about the advantage of free trade in grain, and about the limits of the freedom, have varied among times, states, and writers. Early times did not consider agriculture in connection with commerce, and fear of scarcity long restricted export of grain. On the contrary, writers of eminence have urged unlimited freedom in this respect at all times and places. The purpose and the effect of free export of grain must be to assure a sufficiently remunerative price for agricultural products without embarrassing national consumption. This combination is secured in a freedom of export which is not directly limited in quantity but by rise of price above an accepted mean. In application this principle will have the expression: *Everyone has freedom to export grain so long as the price at such and such markets does not exceed such and such figures.*

§60: If administrative policy adopts this view, it rests on the principle that the mean price is a sign of adequate supply [*Feilschaft*]. If this is not the case the state is infallibly and immediately informed of it by the advancing price. At the same time the counter-influence begins to work. Export ceases, and the national market contains what had been exported. Thereupon the price falls. The mean price and therewith freedom of export are restored.

§61: England began in 1689 to furnish the other nations an illustration that freedom of foreign trade in grain not only supports the cultivator in this industry, but is also capable of bringing agriculture to perfection. Since that time other nations have tried still harder to promote agriculture, and through this effort foreign trade in grain has been greatly hindered. All the more must the law-giver remove the internal hindrances and must assist the merchants by external means, e.g., premiums on export, etc., so that they can compete with the merchants of other nations.

* * *

§§80-107: In order that the earth may be used to the best purpose in respect to cultivation, it is necessary: I, *that the rural folk shall possess the necessary knowledge of cultivation and of agricultural improvements;* II, *that no hindrances shall stand in the way of applying their knowledge;* III, *land which is devoted to other purposes than cultivation must be managed with skill.*

On Manufactures

§108: Manufactures, in the most extended and literal sense, are all occupations which give a new form to any stuff whatsoever.

§109: Manufacture is the correlation of all the kinds of labour which are demanded in order to make a ware complete, that is, to make it marketable. The manufacturer is accordingly the citizen who guides this correlation. The purpose of manufactures, from the standpoint of the individual manufacturer, is to provide support and gain; from the standpoint of the whole state, to increase the occupations; in other words, through manufactures to give work and employment to a part of the people which land management does not employ. From this point of view, from which manufactures must be contemplated by the public administration, the designation by which the economists mean to depreciate the value of artisanship and of the whole class of manufacturers, is a senseless play on words. The amount advanced to manufactures is called by them "an unproductive outlay" [*unfruchtbare Auslage*]; the class of manufacturers, "the unproductive class," because, in the physical sense of the word, they do not create [*hervorbringen*] anything. The essential thing is, however, not whether manufactures create, but, whether they enlarge occupation, that is, whether they increase the means of support for the people, and herewith the population, the welfare of the state from within, the security and prestige of the same from without. This is the effect of manufactures. They themselves really originate [*erzielen*] nothing; they are however the immediate occasion for the origination of the stuff, which without the transformation of artisanship would have no worth and consequently would not be originated. Without the prospect of linen, flax would have little or no use. Worked into Brabantian lace the price rises to such an extent that the worth of the stuff entirely disappears... [Manufacturers] are the immediate occasion for the enlargement of agriculture, for they increase the consumption of the necessities of life, which would otherwise be reduced to the demands of the cultivating families, and consequently would be without value. They even occasion a real growth of national wealth. For, although, according to the calculation of the physiocrats, in the case of an artificial product all parts of the investment [*Vorauslage*] can be resolved into products of the soil [*Boden*], yet in the case of wares disposed of abroad the gain of the merchant cannot be classified under that head, but is a real addition either in equivalents of wealth [*Wohlhaben*] or in wares taken in exchange. More than that, when the Genevan clock-maker constructs of brass and steel worth perhaps two gulden a clock which he sells abroad for thirty gulden, and then in exchange for the thirty gulden imports fifteen measures of grain, is not his skilled labour quite as fruit-bringing for Geneva as that of a farmer who has got fifteen measures from his field? On the other hand, when a state raises a surplus of agricultural products, but is surrounded by states that are devoted to agriculture, its surplus will find no sale, and because there is no prospect of disposing of it no surplus will be raised. But a silk factory is established. The labourers engaged in it consume the produce of the field. The silks are exported. The state receives in exchange their worth. Is it not indifferent to the state whether it exports grain in its original form, or grain transformed into silk? Only, that the skilled labour obtained a sale which agriculture could not have obtained; only, that the skilled labour furnishes a growth in occupation and so a growth in population.

§110: Manufactures are thus, in the economy of the state, not unfruitful, but a useful and an indispensable enlargement of occupation. In the arranging [*Anordnung*] of manufactures the grades of promotion are to be measured according to their contribution to the purpose of the state, that is, according as the general mass of occupation is enlarged and made more permanent. The general mass of occupation, however, gains only when artisan labour is a means of multiplying the products of agriculture. Those manufactures accordingly deserve the first attention for which national stuff is either actually in hand, or might be had with little trouble. Without observing this consideration, agriculture not only loses a possible sale, and consequently a portion of the occupation which it could appropriate; but the manufacturing labour will be dependent upon those nations which furnish the raw stuff. Therefore the occupation of the people, from this side also, will exist only by favor [*auf Bitten*], that is, only so long as the nation from which the raw stuff is received either does not work it up itself, or it is not taken under more favorable conditions by another nation, or for some reason or other the supplying nation makes the export of the stuff more difficult, or finally for political reasons the supplying nation stops production of this stuff altogether.

§111: It is worth while to draw out the consequences of such a situation still farther, in order to reach conviction of another truth, viz.: that it is less harmful never to have extended occupations above a medium number, than ultimately to lose something from a greater number. In the former case, to be sure, the state will enjoy only a moderate degree of prosperity, but it will maintain itself on that level. In the other case the reversal of its prosperity will be almost without limits. In such circumstances many people lose their occupation. That is, they no longer receive the sum of money which they previously used for their support. Since it is not easy at once to absorb an unemployed number into the ranks of the general gainful agencies, the labourers who have lost their employment will be reduced to the most miserable circumstances, and perhaps find themselves compelled to emigrate in order to find ways of earning a living. I will not follow out the consequences of diminution of the number of marriages and other harmful accompanying effects, but restrict myself to the most immediate.

§112: A manufacture occupies more people in proportion to the amount of preparation necessary before the stuff which it handles becomes complete wares, and in proportion to the generality of its use.

§113: The more common use of a ware depends upon its sale to the greater part of the people; that is, it must be of a quality and price which the small means of the great numbers can purchase.

§114: It would be at bottom to the advantage of manufacturers to give to their wares the four features: cheap price, good quality, external beauty, and variety. Shortsighted manufacturers should be compelled to recognize this principle, so that they would not in the end make foreign purchases more desirable, and thus diminish the amount of home occupation.

§115: In order to be able to sell wares of a poor quality at a high price, the manufacturer must be in a position to control the supply, and it must be something that the public needs. If competitors enter into rivalry, the conditions are reversed. The conjunction of the above conditions alone can insure to manufactured articles those qualities which will multiply their sale.

§§116-132: So soon as an occupation yields profits, it is attractive enough for itself; hence, to promote the active combination of factors above named, not only affirmative means are necessary, but also negative, i.e., removal of all hindrances to industry and zeal, e.g., monopolies, exclusive societies, special privileges, manufactures supported by the prince, exclusive guilds, and disproportionate levies upon a manufacture. Examination of these hindrances in order will call attention to principles which may never be neglected in conducting manufactures.

§133: If the hindrances mentioned are out of the way, the zeal of industry will be unrestrained, and its fortunate consequence will be the perfection of manufactures. Each of the qualities which we have specified as necessary to this perfection springs from a multitude of separate parts, knowledge of which is necessary, and it will not be practicable in considering them not to cast side glances at foreign commerce.

* * *

§136: The price at which the manufacturer can part with his wares comprises the sum of all the separate outlays which were made up to the time of sale, with addition of the profit... [The elements of price upon are] buildings, lumber, and all other common necessities, purchase of material, wages, carriages, insurance premiums, import and export duties, interest on the capital, exchange, in case of wares requiring foreign purchases, and profit.

* * *

§141: Not even for the advantage of a manufacture established in the province is it advisable to put restrictions on removal of raw material to another province. For this outgo will not occur so long as buyers are to be found in the locality of its origin who offer acceptable terms of purchase. If it were desired however to give the manufacturer a one-sided advantage, this would amount to promotion of industry [*Emsigkeit*] at the cost of land management. Then only can the state hope for permanent advantage when it supports both at the same time; so long as the producer can get a proper price for raw material, constraint is unnecessary; so soon however as the manufacturers take advantage of the constraint of export duties and try to oppress the producer, the latter abandons the unremunerative production, and the manufacturer suffers from lack of material.

* * *

§155: For the state, cheapness of manufactured goods is merely a secondary purpose, which must not be opposed to the paramount purpose, viz., the multiplication of occupations. Everywhere, therefore, where the ways to occupation are in such precise equilibrium with the population that the portion of people whose place would be taken by machines could not be utilized for other labour, the introduction of machines would be harmful. This would be approximately the situation of a state which had no foreign commerce of any consequence. The same consideration is to be kept in view in the case of agriculture. The introduction of agricultural machinery would diminish the class of rural folk, and for the state nothing is so desirable as to see this class as numerous as possible.

* * *

§157: Since increase of price in the first instance contradicts the paramount purpose of commerce it is necessary to criticize this theorem. As certain as it is that the revenues of the state must cover the expenditures, so certain is it also that inappropriate means may be selected for raising these revenues. Those objects then will be inappropriate in which the first purpose of the state, viz., to have a large population, is hindered, because the impost has an influence on occupation; in which case what may be gained on the one side may be more than lost on the other, and in which by virtue of their very nature, no fixed basis of assessment can be assumed; in which, finally, the collection of the money revenues is not in accord with the main purpose, for the reason that although large sums are collected the main purpose is not promoted; or if this purpose is reached, the revenues would have to be raised to an impossible amount. All of this may be proved in the case of customs [*Maerkte*].

§§158-165: Consequently the finances purchase their momentary advantage at a much too high price, through the loss of land management whose stuff is in less demand, and through the harm to industry whose earnings are in the same degree lessened.

* * *

§172: A state which in the last analysis possesses only an economic trade, cannot carry exclusiveness [*Häuslichkeit*] in its mode of life too far without provoking other states, whose trade is based upon their own products, to imitate this policy with equal vigor.

* * *

§174: Considered from one point of view, however, these migrations should not be abolished, but better regulated. Only the most talented should be sent abroad, and that with the previous knowledge of the state, and with certain assistance. According to their branch of trade the places to which they should go should be designated, and they should be recommended to the embassies at those places. In this way the emigrations would be profitable in gaining for domestic wares the envied perfection of foreign goods.

On Foreign Commerce

§207: England especially has selected as ambassadors men of fundamental insight into the commercial system; such were *"die Keene, Castres, Fallquener, Porter, Walpole,"* in Spain, Portugal, Turkey, and France.

* * *

§223: In order therefore not to diminish the useful class of merchants, the state should make common cause with them. Instead of granting letters of nobility to rich merchants upon retirement from business it should rather ennoble the merchant only upon condition that he shall continue to carry on commerce, and shall bring up his children to the same occupation. The state should offer nobility to him who, with certain resources, passes from another stratum into the ranks of the merchants. On occasions where distinctions are to be drawn between classes of the people, for instance, at court festivities, the state should include the merchant class among the distinguished. The protection of the state must be extended to the large, as well as to the small trades, etc.

On Colonies

§224: Colonies have the significance and the purpose, first, of promoting *external security;* second, of promoting *commerce;* third, of promoting *navigation.*

§225: The mother state will have the preference over every other country in drawing from the colonies those wants which it will either use itself or again export. And in general, whenever a decision must be made between foreigners and the colonists, the state will seek to secure the advantage for the latter. Whenever, on the other hand, a question arises between the state and the colonies, the state appropriates the advantage to itself, and deals with the colonies in complete accordance with the principles of foreign commerce. That is, everything which the colonies supply will be accepted only in the simplest form. On the contrary, whatever is supplied to the colonies they must consent to take in the most complete form. Thence the mother state derives the increased advantage: it gets its wants in the easiest and supplies the wants of the colonies in the most profitable way, since it increases occupation at home through the consumption of the colonists. These advantages are all the greater since the home government prescribes laws for the colonies, and can exclude all rivals from trade with them. Consequently the merchants of the mother state are to be regarded as to a certain extent monopolists as respects the colonies.

* * *

§228: Such are the chief principles in accordance with which mother states treat their colonies: principles of armed power, against defenseless weakness, to the injustice of which the lust of expansion and the mercantile spirit blind all nations. When the English, who regard private property in their own island as so inviolable, but treat with contempt the property of inoffensive peoples in other parts of the world, when they, even yet in our century, take possession of every island on which they land, in the name of his British Majesty, are they nevertheless in the eyes of mankind the honorable [*achtungsurürdig*] nation in which the concepts of freedom and right seem almost exclusively to have been preserved? But however many the advantages which are drawn from the colonies, their possession will continue only so long as the colonists are kept in the ignorance, out of which time, the efforts of rival nations, and the confluence of favoring conditions, will sooner or later, but certainly, some time remove them, and will put an end to their dependence.

Volume III: Finanzwissenschaft
Preface

These contemptible hirelings of tyranny resemble the hunting-dog that scares up the game for the hunter in order to feed on its entrails. A third type which, to be sure, is very small, aims at a quite different purpose, viz., the honor of standing for the interest of the people [*des Volkes*]. These have to reckon with the ruler, and to challenge every expenditure which exceeds reasonable needs.

In respect to the books to which I have referred in this as well as in the first and second parts, I have this to say: that my intention in such references was not to furnish a literary encyclopaedia. The reader or student does not want a mere list of writings, brought together from catalogues and unreliable journals, without selection and very often without knowledge. He wishes to get acquainted with good writings, from which he may extend the principles which he has gained, and in which he may find further information about this or that subject. With this purpose alone in view I have listed books, and none others than those which I have myself read and of which I can give assurance that they will repay the trouble of consulting or reading them.

Introduction

§2: The more necessary is it, therefore, for those interested in this important part of administration to be guided by well-considered *principles according to which the revenues of the state may be most advantageously raised.* These collected principles are the science of finance [*Finanzwissenschaft*].

* * *

§20: The contribution to the extraordinary expenses must be arranged according to the multitudinous circumstances in which the state finds itself, always however without allowing attention to wander from the *well-being of the citizens,* which remains under all circumstances the ultimate purpose of every expenditure.

* * *

§32: The sources of national income are agriculture and industry [*Emsigkeit*], under which latter everything is included which increases the so-called numerical riches [*numerären Reichthum*] of a state.

On Taxation

§85: I at least lay my hand on my conscience, in order to concede that the community could do without my writings better than it could dispense with the labour of the rustic who produces our bread by the sweat of his brow. But I am treating the matter more seriously than it deserves. Every social stratum contributes after a certain proportion its share to the common well-being. These contributions therefore cancel one another, and the duty to contribute remains the completely equal responsibility of all.

* * *

§91: The concessions of princes are the only remaining ground for the claim. Now, in so far as this exemption is a concession of the ruler, it carries with it, like every concession of this sort, the tacit qualification, *provided the public welfare is not too nearly affected thereby;* in which case it is not alone revocable, but it *must* be revoked, because no power extends so far as to [be free to] harm the community for the sake of an individual or a class.

* * *

§99: The payments of the individual citizen must be reckoned according to a double relation: to his own means, and to the means of the other tax-payers. With reference to the former, this principle must govern: the dues must not be so great as to impair the earning-power of the citizen, or to affect his courage to continue earning. That is, whatever is necessary to the continuance of his earning must be free from tax; e.g., first, the necessary support; second, the advance [*Vorschuss*] or the necessary and useful outlays without which the income cannot be gained at all, or at least in full; third, a portion of income large enough to stimulate the citizen to continued labour. Men whose hearts are of steel and whose temper is hostile to the citizens have tried to make it a principle that *a people will be the more industrious, the more it is loaded with taxes.* The difference between stimulating and discouraging taxes consists in this: the former increase the motives for industry, the latter diminish the motives to labour. Even if the state had a right, therefore, to extend the taxes to the limit of support and advance, the self-interest of the state would forbid use of this right. The greater sum of one year would be purchased too dear at cost of the deficit of the following years through loss of energy and decrease of national zeal for labour [*Arbeitsamkeit*].

§100: Certain writers have ventured to define numerically the fraction of income which may be taken for taxes. Men of insight cannot fail to have seen the impossibility of finding such a general numerical ratio. In order to determine the ratio of the payments for taxes to the means of other tax-payers, this seems to be taken for granted as an infallible principle, viz., the portions to be paid should be to each other as the incomes of those who are liable to taxation.

* * *

§103: One sees that no point can be assigned for even an approximate comparison of the abundance of the one with the misery of the other... Nevertheless one must be fair enough to admit that this striking inequality is not the consequence of the disproportion in the tax, but of the incomparability [*Unebenmasses*] of means, i.e., of the difference in the strata of civic society, and that the demand to reduce to equality, by means of a finance system, this difference which, at least in larger states, is not accidental, would be senseless. The thing to be considered, in the case of definition of the reciprocal relation between citizens, is that this inequality shall not be increased by a disproportionate burden of taxation. This end will be approached as near as possible by applying the following principle: "The sums to be paid shall be to each other as the *net* incomes of the taxable citizens; that is, as the sums which remain to each after subtraction of support and advance."

* * *

§104: The same will have to raise the sum reckoned with reference to the general national income and adequate for the needs of the state, in so far as the domains [*Regalien*] and accidental revenues do not yield" the same according to a provincial apportionment corresponding to the balance of money, from the citizens assessed *without exception, in proportion to their net incomes,* covering short specified periods, at the time which is least inconvenient, through its own system of collection, which must be as simple as possible.

On Financial Schemes

§180: Financial schemes are in great part the offspring of the spirit of selfishness, which clothes itself, however, in the garb of zeal for the public good. This must arouse the distrust of the financial administration, and as the anonymous author of the *Versuch über die Staatseinkünfte* says, always rouse the more suspicion against them the more they promise. Every proposition looking to the improvement of the income of the state is a financial scheme. However they may be dressed up, these schemes fall into three classes: I, those which propose to facilitate collection, and incidentally to diminish cost of collection; II, those that propose to increase the amounts raised on actually assessed objects; III, those that propose to assess new objects. Before dealing with these in detail, the following two observations may be advanced: I, *Every proposition which promises no other advantage than increase of public revenues in general,* or as the hirelings are accustomed to express themselves, *den Nutzen des allerhöchsten Aerariums, deserves no attention.* For the incorrectness of the principle, *the public revenues must constantly be raised,* has been exposed. A proposition which aims at the one-sided advantage of the treasury is a scheme for exaction. II, Every proposition which promises larger sums for the state treasury, in spite of the fact that the payers are to pay less, unless it discovers fraud or incompetence in the collection, is at first glance to be rejected. It promises a numerical increase by means of a subtraction. That is, it promises a monstrosity.

Sir John A Fielding (1721-1780)

Artist: Nathaniel Hone, 1762, National Portrait Gallery, London

Born in London in 1721, John Fielding was the younger half brother of the English novelist Henry Fielding. As a youth, John Fielding joined the navy, but at the age of nineteen suffered an accident in which he lost his sight. He was nonetheless able to open and manage by himself a business called the Universal Register Office. In his spare time, John was taught law by his brother, who himself became a Magistrate and ultimately Chief Magistrate. Discouraged at the unchecked crime throughout London, Henry took on his brother as Assistant Magistrate in 1750, and together the two established a quasi-permanent force of detectives who would investigate crimes, serve writs and arrest criminals. Henry used his house to establish a working office, and John was able to convince the government to contribute towards the expenses of their small force of detectives. With Henry's house situated in Bow Street, the force of magistrates and detectives became known as the Bow Street Runners – often cited as an early precursor to the modern police force. A critical device employed in the service of the Bow Street Runners was the newly created "Police Gazette," which carried the names of known criminals and offered awards and immunity for information regarding their whereabouts.

When Henry was forced to retire in 1754 due to failing health, John took over as Chief Magistrate. John Fielding sought to improve on his brother's work, citing his success at breaking up gangs within London. He sought to establish a horse patrol to fight mounted highwaymen who prowled the outskirts of London. John Fielding was just as anxious to prevent crime as to punish it, insisting that the "gazette" be used to deter crime, as well as seeking to root out the causes of delinquency. To this latter end, Fielding held that poverty was a major contributor to criminal behavior, and he reportedly organized charities to feed and clothe abandoned children, as well as established institutions to help children learn to read. In order to deter corruption within his force, he advocated a system of stipendiary magistracy, which was eventually adopted in 1792. For his efforts, John Fielding was knighted in 1761, though he was perhaps best known by his popular title: "blind beak on Bow Street." "Beak" referred to any person in authority in 18th century argot. Fielding was described by contemporaries as wearing a black bandage over his eyes, and carrying a switch that he used to tap his way in and out of courtrooms. He was reportedly able to recognize the identities of roughly 3,000 thieves simply by their voices. John Fielding published three pieces on policing and crime prevention including *A Plan for Preventing Robberies Within 20 Miles of London* (1775). He remained Chief Magistrate until his death on September 4, 1780.

Works Referenced:

Babington, Anthony. *A House in Bow Street: Crime and the Magistracy, London 1740-1881.* Macdonald and Co: London, 1969.

Pringle, Patrick. *Hue and Cry: The Story of Henry and John Fielding and their Bow Street Runners.* Morrow: London, 1955.

Leslie-Melville, R. *The Life and Work of Sir John Fielding.* L. Williams Ltd: London, 1935.

Selections From: *A Plan For Preventing Robberies Within Twenty Miles of London with an Account of the Rife and Eftablisment of the real Thieftakers. To which is added, Advice to Pawnbrokers, Stable-Keepers, and Publicans.* **(London: A. Millar)., orig. 1775.**

To the Public:

The perfuries of McDaniel and his crew having raised a strong prepossession against thieftakers in general, it seems proper at this time to publish a few facts, relating to the real and useful thieftakers, where-by the public may be enabled to distinguish between those who deserve to be considered with regard and esteem, and those who are most justly the objects of contempt and indignation. As this is one of the principal ends of the following narrative, with which the plan I have proposed for preventing robberies within twenty miles of London is naturally connected, and on which, indeed, the success thereof depends; I doubt not but it will be received with candour by that public, whose true interest will ever be the constant view of,

Their most faithful humble Servant

John Fielding

Introduction

As the method which I here intend to lay before the public, in order to prevent highway robberies within twenty miles of London, is founded on the same principles with that made use of intown, viz. quick notice and sudden pursuit; and as both will generally be executed by the same instruments, namely, the real thieftakers; it will I apprehend, be necessary to give some account of their establishment, and of the means by which they were reduced to a regular body.

The winter after the late Henry Fielding Esq; came to Bow-Street, the town was infested by a daring gang of robbers, who attached several persons of fashion, and gave a general alarm through the City and the liberty of Westminster; and as that magistrate then enjoyed a good share of health, he spirited up a civil power, and sent several bodies of constables, with the advantage of having Mr. Welch at their head, into different parts of the town, by whose bravery and activity those disturbers of the peace were quickly apprehended and brought to justice: and though, the year after, most of these constables were out of office, yet some of them, being actuated by a truly public spirit against thieves, and being encouraged by the said magistrate, continued their diligence, and were always ready , on being summoned, to go in pursuit of villains. The next winter furnished them with the sufficient occasions to try their courage; when Mr. William Pentlow and Mr. Peele, then constables, particularly distinguished themselves, having taken on Lewis in a very remarkable manager, by whose information the whole gang was apprehended. The keeper of New Prison dying soon after, the justices, as a reward for Mr. Pentlow's public services, gave him that place, which he has now enjoyed four years, and in that time has brought several villains to justice, and still continues to act with such vigilance, that no longer ago than last sessions, he was honoured with the thanks of the justices at Hicks's-Hall, for his bravery in attacking, assisted by Mr. Gee a constable, the notorious Burk and Gill, even though Mr. Pentlow and Gee were unarmed, and Burk and Gill had each a pistol in his hand, one of which was fired in Mr. Gee's face.

This encouragement of merit induced several constables and other persons to serve the public in the same way: and as soon as Mr. Fielding was enabled by the government to put his plan in execution, whatever constables appeared willing to go on these hazardous enterprizes, were occasionally employed, together with a set of brave fellows, who had before entered the list; to whose services the public is much indebted. All of these had served the office of constable, except one, a Marshalsea-court officer, and consequently used to the apprehending of common debtors, who are generally of the desperate kind; so that the real thieftakers must all have been housekeepers, and reputable ones too, otherwise they could not have been nominated to serve the office of constable in their respective parishes: and as often as the year comes round, and they are discharged from their offices, some of the bravest of them generally enter the other list, and are ready on all occasions to obey the directions of the active magistrate.

Now when it is considered, that by this means the active magistrate, besides having the whole civil power within his jurisdiction at command, can every day, upon notice given of any robbery, outrage, or other violence committed, call together a number of such brave and reputable men, always ready to pursue and attack the most daring villain, a real thieftaker must be esteemed a valuable servant of the society. Let us only look back on that terrible Irish gang, consisting of thirteen persons, which infested the town about the time that Lord Harrington's cook was murdered, and recollect that all these villains were brought to justice by the real theiftakers, all persons who have served the office of constable: that the great Mr. Parry, who had struck terror into all the squares about St. James's, fell a victim to the resolution of these men, as did several other street-robbers afterwards; and lastly, Walsh, Armstrong, Courtney, and the two desperadoes Gill and Burk: that the persons who shot at and wounded Colonel Schutz, were taken by a pickt party of constables, who seized the bold Mr. Fleming, and several others for the highway.

This, therefore, may serve to show, that so long as the spirit of the civil power is preserved by proper encouragements, the public will never want such thieftakers as one would wish should be employed; and though now and then a single street-robber or house-breaker may be successful, yet it will be always impossible for a number of them to form themselves into a gang.

Indeed, it was the advantages received by these persons, as the just rewards of their diligence, that tempted McDaniel and his hellish crew, to prostitute the useful employment of thieftaker, to the procuring both public and private rewards, at the shameful and shocking price of innocent blood.

And that the subscriptions, raised by the gentlemen about London to prevent robberies, added to this temptation, is clear from the scheme practised in relation to the sham robbery committed on Salmon at Blackheath.

To remove this temptation, by altering the nature of the subscriptions, is the intention of the following proposal.

But before I open it, as I have mentioned McDaniel and his gang, I take the liberty to assure the world that neither he, Berry, Salmon, Egan or Blee, were ever to my knowledge employed by my late brother, or myself, in any shape whatever; nay, so far from it, that I remember this very McDaniel came some years ago wounded to my brother, and swore he had been robbed and shot at by two persons whom he produced; and though he swore positively to them and the fact, yet that magistrate conceived so ill an opinion of the prosecutor in the course of his examination, that the prisoners, though charged with a capital offence, were both admitted to bail, to the great satisfaction of his grace the late duke of Richmond, and several gentlemen then present, and were afterwards acquitted at the Old Bailey.

Another circumstance that may serve to show the very bad opinion which Mr. Fielding had conceived of these people was, that this very Blee, who was evidence against McDaniel and the rest, came to Mr. Fielding, soon after His Majesty's proclamation of an hundred pounds for the apprehending of street-robbers was published, and offered to make an information, nay, brought an information drawn up, in which it was set forth, that McDaniel and others had obtained two hundred and eighty pounds, as rewards for hanging two innocent men; and the reason he gave for making this information was, "that they had used him ill:" but Mr. Fielding had so very bad an opinion of Blee and his accomplices, that he ordered the former to be turned out of his house, and would have nothing to do with the latter. But when he laid his plan to prevent robberies before the right honourable Privy Council, he gave the wickedness of this particular set of men as a reason against the publishing any future rewards, by way of proclamation, for the apprehending of thieves, in order to take away from these wretches their only temptation to perjury and murder. Indeed it was owing to this representation, that these kind of rewards have not been published since, except in one instance only.

Having thus shown the cause and means of forming a regular body of real and honest thieftakers, I proceed to a scheme naturally connected therewith, and dependant upon it, namely,

A Plan For Preventing Robberies Within Twenty Miles of London

That there are more highway robberies committed in one year within twenty miles of London, than in any other part of the kingdom, or perhaps in the whole kingdom besides, will, I believe, be allowed; and that not one in a hundred of these robbers are taken in the fact, is no less astonishing than true; especially when we consider that, within this distance from London, there is scarce a mile without a town or village, and that there are always numbers of people passing and repassing on these public roads. Were there any possibility of these pages living longer than an advertisement, I am afraid I should hardly be believed in the following true story; but, luckily for me, the chief actor in the scene is now alive. A captain of guards was some time ago robbed on Hounslow Heath in a post-chaise, and the moment the highway-man left him, disengaged one of the horses, and pursued the robber; and who will believe it? Though he drove him through a public town at noon-day, crying out highwayman! highwayman! Both being in full view of the populace, yet no one join'd the pursuit, more than if all the inhabitants had been interested in the highwayman's escape. That these kind of robberies have been very frequent, and very disagreeable to the gentlemen who live at a small distance from town, will appear from the pains they have taken, and the many subscriptions they have set on foot, to cause these highwaymen to be apprehended; but, very unluckily, such subscriptions, instead of being an encouragement to honest men, of bold and daring spirits, to pursue, attack, and apprehend robbers, have been a temptation to a body of villains, who disgrace human nature to contrive robberies, and to make robbers, in order to destroy the latter for the sake of the reward; like their master, the devil himself, who first tempts to sin, then punishes, and lastly, feasts on the wickedness he has occasioned.

I believe, when these subscriptions were fist proposed, it was not thought there were men capable of converting them to such abominably shameful and horrid purposes: but as that is become an evil which was intended as a remedy, and the remedy is grown worse than the disease, I have taken the liberty to offer a small alteration in these subscriptions, which would, I apprehend, make them fully answer the end proposed, and put them out of the reach of abuse.

But it may perhaps be thought proper previously to establish the following facts, *viz.* 1st, That those persons who rob upon the highway, within twenty miles of London set out from thence for the purpose; 2dly, That they ride hired horses; 3dly, That they retire thither for shelter; 4thly, That they are generally taken in town; and lastly, that there is a plan fixt in town, and supported by the government, for the apprehending of robbers; in which, if the public do but perform their part, by giving immediate notice of any robbery to that magistrate, who, from experience of its use, daily solicits it by a standing advertisement, it must be impossible for villains ever to escape justice long. The public are desired once more to take notice, that those persons who are entrusted with the execution of this plan, and are commonly stiled thieftakers, are all of them housekeepers, men of tried courage, pickt from among the peace-officers; and moreover, that the moment any one of them commits an act either of cruelty or injustice, he is immediate discharged by the magistrate from the office of thieftaker, and never admitted again.

There are two circumstances relating to these persons, equally deserving of attention, as they render them the properest people in the world for the purpose, viz. 1st, As they have been constables before they were thieftakers, and have been called upon by the magistrates to search houses of bad fame, and take up idle and disorderly persons, they are by that means become acquainted with the bad part of the populace, and their houses of resort: in a word, every man that seems to dress above his circumstances, that occasionally mixes in alehouses, and whose way of living is not known, never misses being inquired after by the persons abovementioned. The fate of Fleming, the late highwayman who was supposed to have subsisted three to four years by the road, is a proof of the truth of this observation; for it was a description of his way of life, told as matter of conversation to Mr. Pentlow, keeper of New Prison, that was the occasion of his being apprehended. 2ndly, As magistrates are often obliged to admit a robber as an evidence, in order to apprehend the gang, who, after the conviction of his confederates, is constantly discharged, and as constantly returns to his former courses; such an evidence, I say, being first apprehended either by the constable or thieftaker, is consequently well known to them, and their eye is always upon him, expecting, as it generally happens, that by the next sessions after the executive of his comrades, he will become the caption of a gang of his own raising. Indeed, after a man has appeared at the Old Bailey as an evidence, he does not, when he is discharged, find a very easy admission among the industrious part of society; and the motive of his turning evidence being rather the fear of death than remorse for his guilt, there is very little hope of his reformation under the circumstances abovementioned. To this may be added, that commonly the greatest rogue in the gang turns evidence. Is it not a pity then, that there is not some provision made for these outcasts, in order to prevent their doing farther mischief themselves, after they have served the public by discovering other criminals? I am of the opinion that if, instead of being pardoned, they were to be transported for a certain term, to break them of their haunts, and to inure them to a life of labour; nay, if they were to be send abroad for life, it would be an equal, if not a great inducement to them to impeach their accomplices.

Now as to the plan which I have to propose:

Let any number of gentlemen, for instance twenty, whose country houses are situated at different distances, from five to twenty miles from London, subscribe two guineas each, which makes the sum of forty guineas, to be lodged in the hands of one of the subscribers, whom they shall appoint treasurer. Let this money be subject to the draughts of all the subscribers, as they shall severally have occasion to employ it; and if any highway robbery be committed in the neighbourhood of any of these subscribers, let the first that hears of it obtain an exact description of the robber, his horse, (if he had one) and whatever is taken from the person robbed: this let him put in writing, always adding, if possible, the name and place of abode of the party robbed; for it sometimes happens, when a highwayman is apprehended, that the prosecutor not being to be found, the former escapes justice, and is let loose again upon the public. Next let a man and horse be immediately hired, and dispatched to Mr. Fielding, in Bow-Street, Covent-Garden, with full authority to that gentleman to advertise the same in what manner he thinks proper, and to receive of the treasurer of the subscription the expence of the advertisements. Mean time let the messenger communicate to all the bye ale-houses, public inns, and turnpikes in his way to and from London, the said robbery, with a verbal description of the man and horse: the more suddenly and quickly this notice is given, the surer is the success. On the messenger's returning to the subscriber who sent him, and producing a testimony from the justice of his having delivered to him the said description, and setting forth the hour of his arrival in town, the subscriber shall give the messenger a draught upon the treasure for such a sum of money, as he shall think his time, trouble, diligence, and expedition deserve: and on such occasions honest men will always be found ready enough, on being paid for their trouble, without any other reward, to go on such a message, though, perhaps, they would not chuse to run any hazard of their persons by attacking a rogue in desperate circumstances. Nay, it has often happened to my brother and myself, that by bestowing a shilling or half a crown on a messenger, without which he would not have stirred one step, more service has been done to the public, than has been done to the public, than has accrued from advertising rewards of an hundred pounds; but when notice is given immediately, the expences on the first instance are trifling; and the messenger, the informer, and apprehender are three different persons, all equally useful, but the two first are the cheapest, because the least dangerous offices. And if any subscriber should hear that highwaymen, housebreakers, or any other species of robbers, lie lurking in his neighbourhood, let him hire a sufficient number of persons to pursue and apprehend him or them, and pay them by draughts on the treasurer as before: but this, perhaps, in the country he might find some difficulty to do.

There is one thing that would, in some respect, make this plan perfect, and in which a very large body of men in this metropolis might render themselves very useful to society; I mean the pawnbrokers, alehouse-keepers, and stable-keepers who let horses to hire. There is indeed, no authority to oblige these persons to perform their parts; yet I should imagine, that when they come to consider that their own reputation, or, what is still of more weight, their interest, is highly concerned in their being active in this scheme, they would do the same things for their particular benefit, which the law requires every individual to do for the good of the whole. There is nothing more true than that these persons, may, indeed, all persons, act with a view to their own interest, and that their differing in opinion arises from their mistaking, not neglecting, that interest. First, as to pawnbrokers, it would be needless to mention the inconveniencies they suffer from taking in stolen goods; and I am sure it would be unnecessary to tell them, that when a shoeblack brings a diamond ring to pawn, there is great reason to suspect he did not come honestly by it. I shall therefore confine myself to that part of their conduct, in which they are supposed to be least on their guard, in order to remedy an error they frequently fall into, from the fear of having actions brought against them. With respect to this, I would have every pawnbroker know, that wherever there is sufficient cause to stop goods on suspicion of their being stolen, the very same cause will justify their stopping the party, and carrying him before a justice; and that the latter without the former, is not only useless, but unwarrantable; and I should ever advise this practice in pawnbrokers, 'till any one shows me he has suffered by it. But, as the remedy of one evil often begets another, so has it happened in this case; for some pawnbrokers having lately stopt several watches that had been taken by street-robbers, and on the highway, this has taught the thieves to be more cunning, and to sell their watches and other goods to wandering Jews, who, to do them justice, will buy any thing they can get a penny by, thought they saw it stolen but the very moment before. The late street-robbers generally left their watches at alehouses for their reckoning, and when once they were pledged there, they were obliged to eat and drink them out. To the alehouse-keepers, therefore, I would speak one word, as the good government of the common people depends greatly on the regulation of their houses: and indeed I wonder, that as keeping an alehouse it not only a reputable, but an advantageous business, some of them are not more cautious in preserving that order and good conduct which is the condition of their licenses: above all, I would have them to avoid taking in pledges for drink; for if a man wants to raise money on any part of his property, let him go to a pawnbroker, whose experience acquired in trade teaches him to know whether that is likely to be the man's property or not. It is likewise a dangerous thing for publicans to appear, in order to give characters at the Old Bailey of men who stand indicted for capital offences, merely because they used their houses. In a word, as it must ever be the interest of alehouse-keepers to detect rogues of all kinds, I hope their best endeavours to do it will never be wanting, and that whenever they are sent for on such occasions by magistrates, they will always attend with chearfulness, and not put them to the disagreeable necessity of using harsher means than a messenger. Lastly, as to stable-keepers, and those who let horses to hire, I dare say they know that when a highwayman is taken upon their horse, such horse is forfeited to the captor; whoever, therefore, lets a horse to a stranger, hazards the losing that horse for the sake of getting five shillings. Moreover, I will tell them a secret, which some of them don't know, viz. the three highwaymen last brought before me kept their horses out several days, though they came themselves to London every night, put up their horses, and lay themselves at an inn some distance from the owner's house. Now if a highwayman were taken in this situation, the horse would be forfeited, as much as if he had been apprehended on the road; and it would be a very good caution to a stable-keeper never to let a horse to a man whom he does not know, unless he comes recommended by some person of reputation, whom he does know; and upon all occasions to book the name of the hirer, the road and distance he is going the day of the month he sets out, with the colour and marks of the horse he rides; and if a stranger offers more than a common price, there is the more reason to suspect his purpose.

Now the peculiar use that I would make of these three bodies of men, is as follows. It is I suppose pretty generally known, that there is a daily paper called

THE PUBLIC ADVERTISER, fixt for the advertising of robberies of all kinds: in that paper, therefore, alehouse-keepers will see the descriptions of the persons of all highwaymen; there, likewise, stable-keepers will see the exact description of highwaymen's horses, and of those horses also that are stolen; and pawnbrokers will there find an exact account of goods in general that are taken on the highway, and otherways stolen. If therefore these three sets of people would constantly take in and read this paper, the first would never harbour a rogue without his knowledge; the second would never furnish a highwayman with a horse, without knowing it time enough to detect him, and save the horse; and as to the latter, they have already found so many advantages from this paper, as to need no other recommendation of it.

Having nothing more to add to this plan, (if so plain and trifling a thing deserves that name) I think it would not be altogether unnecessary to consider the objections that may be brought against it; for objections there certainly are, which, if I do not discover myself, will, I am persuaded, be soon pointed out by the ingenious criticks of this very critical age, at whose tremendous bar I now presume to appear: but in order to save my judges some trouble, I will make a species of confession, and by turning commentator on my own works, rob them of the opportunity of abusing the public's

* * *

A Few Criticisms On The Above Plan
   First Critic
This I think might as well have been called any thing else as a plan. Indeed when I read Mr. Fielding's advertisement, I must confess I expected to see some ingenious performance; but *parturiunt montes,* may very justly be applied here, for this is the simplest and most trifling thing I ever saw.

Culprit
The more it partakes of simplicity, the easier I apprehend it will be executed; and the more trifling it is, *i.e.,* the less there is to do, there will be the more probability of its being done, and the expence of its execution will be so much the less. If therefore it should answer the purpose as well near London, as it does in town, and in all probability it will do so, for the same causes are very apt to produce the same effects, then will this first critic be mistaken.

Second Critic
Methinks I hear Mr. McDaniel say, that this must be a damn'd plan indeed, seeing it offers no reward.

Culprit
Then it offers no temptation for perjury.

Third Critic

I suppose the author's interest is much concerned in the success of the PUBLIC ADVERTISER, otherwise he would not recommend it so strongly.

Culprit

The author has no share in that paper, though his brother had: but the true reasons for his pointing out this paper, are, 1st, Because many of the pawnbrokers, and a great number of alehouse-keepers originally agreed to take it in; 2dly, Because it is pretty well known to be the paper in which robberies in general, and most stolen goods are advertised; and lastly, because the managers of this paper constantly preserve a vacancy to the last hour, in order to insert any occurrence of public utility, and never refuse any advertisement of robberies that I send, whether long or short; but rather leave out a trifling particular advertisement, than run the hazard of stopping the progress of public justice. On the other hand, I must declare that I have frequently had advertisements refused, and others delayed, by the proprietors of another Advertiser, though I have carried them myself, and assured them of the necessity of such and such circumstances being immediately made public. However, I must desire that if any advantage either from this paper, or from any of my endeavours to serve the public, should accrue to me, none would presume to be pleased at it, but those who think my labour deserves encouragement.

Fourth Critic

Would not the raising the hue and cry in the country, be a more effectual method of apprehending thieves, as it has the sanction of authority, than any private subscription whatever?

Culprit

At a great distance from London, I acknowledge it would, and verily believe that if the method of raising hue and cry, together with the penalties upon peace-officers for the neglect of this important duty, was made universally known, by being published in a short manner, and clear light, once every month in all the evening papers, for a year together, it would make this part of their office as easy and familiar to them as any other whatever, and render it absolutely impossible for any villain in the country to escape justice; but near London I apprehend it would lose its effect, not only from the vast variety of passengers on the road, mounted and dressed alike; but if they should not succeed before the rogue reaches London, seeking him there, by means of the hue and cry, would be fruitless indeed. The different effects of a hue and cry near town, and of the notice mentioned in my plan, was the other day proved, much to the advantage of the latter; for a gentleman in Essex was, a few weeks ago, robbed by a single highwayman within a mile of his own house, and about ten miles from London; upon which he went before a magistrate, made an information, and raise d the hue and cry, in despite of which the highwayman lay all night about fourteen miles distant on the straight road, and returned to London the next morning the same way, without any molestation or hindrance whatever: but the gentleman being more active than persons generally are on such occasions, sent out his servants, and having procured as exact descriptions of him and his horse, and other circumstances, as he could, he brought them to Mr. Fielding, and in three hours time a plan was formed from those circumstances, which made his escape impossible, and in about eight and forty hours he fell into the trap, and is now in safe custody.

Fifth Critic

If these real thieftakers, as the author is pleased to stile them, are men of any reputation, why are not their names and places of abode published, that their characters may be inquired into, and the public not put to the necessity of taking the author's bare word for the truth of his own assertion?

Culprit

As the thieftakers are extremely obnoxious to the common people, perhaps it might not be altogether politic to point them out to the mob; and the less they are known, the better able they will always be to executive the purposes of their institution: besides as they are annually increased by the discharge of constables, it might deter them from this useful office, by injuring them in their respective trades; but as one of them lately lost his life in his duty, *viz.* by taking Burk and Gill, and is consequently out of the reach of any father injury, I shall not conceal his name, as its being known may, in this generous kingdom, be of some service to the two children he has left behind him. His name then was Hind, and his chief employment that of deputy-governor of Tothillfields Bridewell, where he farmed the tap and labour of that prison, and carried on a manufacture of chopping rags for the making of paper, which made the Bridewell of great use in employing disorderly persons committed thither, and prevented them from spending their time in wickedness and debauchery, the too common practice of prisoners in other Bridewells in this kingdom. His having the care of a prison, made him also very useful in relation to the discovering of thieves; for as most highwaymen keep company with bad women, who generally spend half the year in the Bridewells about town, they have often impeached their paramours; and persons committed for small offences, have every now and then been the means of destroying gangs of housebreakers, shoplifters, and street-robbers.

Lastly, if any person who is more likely to be an encourager, than the game of a thieftaker, has curiosity to know all their names and places of abode, Mr. Fielding will very readily communicate them, having no intention of concealing any thing that ought, for the good of the public, to be made known.

Adam Smith (1723-1790)

Artist: Etching by Cadell and Davies (1811), John Horsburgh (1828) or R.C. Bell (1872)., Baker Library, Harvard University

Adam Smith was born in Kirkcaldy, Scotland, in 1723, and raised by a widowed mother. At the age of 14, Smith entered the University of Glasgow on a scholarship and would move on to Balliol College at Oxford where he gained an extensive knowledge of European literature. Upon returning home, Smith delivered a series of lectures that were well received. In 1751 he was made chair of logic and a year later, chair of moral philosophy at Glasgow University. In 1764, Smith left academia to tutor the Duke of Buccleuch, with whom he traveled throughout France and into Switzerland. It was here that Smith was brought into contact with the likes of Voltaire, Jean-Jacques Rousseau, and Anne-Robert-Jacques Turgot. With the pension he had received in the service of the Duke, Smith retired to Kirkcaldy where he wrote what was to be his most infamous work, *An Inquiry Into the Nature and Causes of the Wealth of Nations*, first published in 1776. Here, many of Smith's famous ideas are expanded, including his intense opposition to mercantilism, the importance of the division of labour, and the mechanism of the 'invisible hand.' In the book, Smith's exhortations against mercantilism are frequent, and he is highly critical of the cost of British imperialism. He further argues that free trade would allow greater markets abroad and cheaper goods at home. Two years after the book's publication, Smith was appointed commissioner of customs, where he helped enforce anti-smuggling laws, despite having partially defended the practice of smuggling in *Wealth of Nations*. He died in Edinburgh July 19, 1790.

Adam Smith is regarded as a pioneer of political economy and a foundational thinker in western capitalism. Although other writers had dealt with political economy before Smith, his would come to be known as the most systematic and comprehensive study of his day, making him a competitor for the title of the founder of classical political economy. Threads of his thought would resonate in the later works of thinkers as varied as David Ricardo, Karl Marx, John Maynard Keynes and Milton Friedman. Though famous for the *Wealth of Nations*, Smith's other works concentrated on ethics, charity, and jurisprudence. Smith reportedly told a student, while teaching at the University of Glasgow, that his favorite lecture subjects, in order of preference, were natural theology, ethics, jurisprudence, and then economics.

Works Referenced:
Muller, Jerry Z. *Adam Smith In His Time and Ours.* The Free Press: New York, 1993.
Raphael, D.D. *Adam Smith.* Oxford University Press: Oxford and New York, 1985.

Selections from: *Lectures on Justice, Police, Revenue and Arms* [reported in 1763] (London: Kessinger Press., reprint 2004)., orig. 1896.

Introduction

  §1: Of Works on Natural Jurisprudence

Jurisprudence is that science which inquires into the general principles which ought to be the foundation of the laws of all nations. (p. 1)

  §2: Of the Division of the Subject

Jurisprudence is the theory of the general principles of law and government. The four great objects of law are justice, police, revenue, and arms. The object of justice is the security from injury, and it is the foundation of civil government. The objects of police are the cheapness of commodities, public security and cleanliness. It is likewise necessary that the magistrate who bestows his time and labour in the business of the state should be compensated for it. For this purpose, and for defraying the expenses of government, some fund must be raised. Hence the origin of revenue. As the best police cannot give secure unless the government can defend themselves from foreign injuries and attacks, the fourth thing appointed by law is for this purpose.

Part I: Of Justice

  §Introduction

A real right is that whose object is a real thing and which can be claimed a *quocumque possessore*. Such are all possessions, houses, furniture. Personal rights are such as can be claimed by a law-suit from a particular person, but not a *quocumque possessore*. Such are all debts and contracts, the payment or performance of which can be demanded only from one person.

Real rights are of four kinds, property, servitudes, pledges, and exclusive privileges. Property is our possessions of every kind, which if any way lost, or taken from us by stealth or violence, may be redemanded a quocumque possessore. Servitudes are burdens upon the property of another. Thus I may have a liberty of passing through a field belonging to another which lies between me and the highway, or if my neighbour have plenty of water in his fields and I have none in mine for my cattle, I may have a right to drive them to his. Such burdens on the property of another are called servitudes. These rights were originally personal, but the trouble and expense of numerous law suits in order to get possession of them, when the adjacent property which was burdened with them passed through a number of hands, induced legislators to make them real and claimable a *quocunique possessore*. Afterwards the property was transferred with these servitudes upon it. Pledges, which include all pawns and mortgages, are securities for something else to which we have a right. The laws of most civilized nations have considered them as real rights, and give a liberty to claim them as such. Exclusive privileges are such as that of a bookseller to vend a book for a certain number of years, and to hinder any other person from doing it during that period. These rights are for the most part creatures of the civil law, though some few of them are natural, as in a state of hunters even before the origin of civil government, if a man has started a hare and pursued her for some time, he has an exclusive privilege to hunt her, by which he can hinder any other to come in upon her with a fresh pack of hounds.

Division I: Of Public Jurisprudence
§14: Of the Rights of Sovereigns

We shall now consider what duty is owing to the sovereign, and what is the proper punishment of disobedience. Every attempt to overturn this power is in every nation considered as the greatest crime, and is called high treason. It is to be observed that there is a great difference between treason in monarchies and treason in republics. In the one it is an attempt on the king's person, and in the other on the liberties of the people, from whence we may see how the maxim of assassination came to be established in republics, and not in monarchies. It is the interest of monarchies that the person in authority be defended, whatever his title or conduct be, and that no person be allowed to enquire into them. The laws of monarchy are therefore unfavourable to the assassination of tyrants. In a republic the definition of a tyrant is quite clear. He is one who deprives the people of their liberty, levies armies and taxes, and puts the citizens to death as he pleases. This man cannot be brought to a court of justice, and therefore assassination is reckoned just and equitable.

Division II: Of Domestic Law
§5: Domestic Offences and Their Punishments

Infidelity of the wife to the husband is punished with the greatest ignominy. In the husband, it never was punished with death, nor in the woman unless where the greatest jealousy prevails. It would be thought ridiculous in our country to bring a woman to the scaffold for adultery. Forcible marriages and rapes are generally punished with death. Bigamy, as it dishonours the former wife, is punished capitally. As there is the closest connexion betwixt persons in a family, if the wife kills 3 the husband, it is considered as a sort of petty treason, and the punishment by the English law is burning alive. The same is the punishment if a servant kills his master or makes an attempt upon him.

Division III: Private Law
§1: First Way of Acquiring Property: Occupation

Property is acquired five ways. First, by occupation, or the taking possession of what formerly belonged to nobody. Second, by accession, when a man has a right to one thing in consequence of another, as of a horse shoes along with the horse. Third, by prescription, which is a right to a thing belonging to another arising from long and uninterrupted possession. Fourth, by succession to our ancestors or any other person, whether by a will or without one. Fifth, by voluntary transference, when one man delivers over his right to another.

§11: Of Delinquency

Injury naturally excites the resentment of the spectator, and the punishment of the offender is reasonable as far as the indifferent spectator can go along with it. This is the natural measure of punishment. It is to be observed that our first approbation of punishment is not founded upon the regard to public utility which is commonly taken to be the foundation of it. It is our sympathy with the resentment of the sufferer which is the real principle. That it cannot be utility is manifest from the following example. Wool in England was conceived to be the source of public opulence, and it was made a capital crime to export that commodity. Yet though wool was exported as formerly and men were convinced that the practice was pernicious, no jury, no evidence, could be got against the offenders. The exportation of wool is naturally no crime, and men could not be brought to consider it as punishable with death. In the same manner, if a sentinel be put to death for leaving his post, though the punishment be just and the injury that might have ensued be very great, yet mankind can never enter into this punishment as if he had been a thief or a robber.

The greatest crime that can be done against any person is murder, of which the natural punishment is death, not as a compensation, but as a reasonable retaliation. In every civilized nation death has been the punishment of the murderer, but in barbarous nations a pecuniary compensation was accepted of, because then government was weak, and durst not meddle in the quarrels of individuals unless in the way of mediation.

Part II: Of Police
Division I: Cleanliness and Security

Police is the second general division of jurisprudence. The name is French, and is originally derived from the Greek word, which properly signified the policy of civil government, but now it only means the regulation of the inferior parts of government, viz:--cleanliness, security and cheapness or plenty.

Nothing tends so much to corrupt mankind as dependency, while independency still increases the honesty of people. The establishment of commerce and manufactures, which brings about this independency, is the best police for preventing crimes. The common people have better wages in this way than in any other, and in consequence of this a general probity of manners takes place through the whole country. Nobody will be so mad as to expose himself upon the highway, when he can make better bread in an honest and industrious manner.

Division II: Cheapness and Plenty
§1: Of the Natural Wants of Mankind

Nature produces for every animal everything that is sufficient to support it without having recourse to the improvement of the original production... Such is the delicacy of man alone, that no object is produced to his liking. He finds that everything there is need of improvement. In general, however, the necessities of man are not so great but that they can be supplied by the unassisted labour of the individual. As the delicacy of a man's body requires much greater provision than that of any other animal, the same or rather the much greater delicacy of his mind requires a still greater provision to which all the different arts [are] subservient.

The taste of beauty, which consists chiefly in the three following particulars, proper variety, easy connexion, and simple order, is the cause of all this niceness. Nothing without variety pleases us; a long uniform wall is a disagreeable object. Too much variety, such as the crowded objects of a parterre, is also disagreeable.

§2: That all the Arts are Subservient to the Natural Wants of Mankind

Law and government, too, seem to propose no other object but this; they secure the individual who has enlarged his property, that he may peaceably enjoy the fruits of it. By law and government all the different arts flourish, and that inequality of fortune to which they give occasion is sufficiently preserved. By law and government domestic peace is enjoyed and security from the foreign invader. Wisdom and virtue too derive their luster from supplying these necessities. For as the establishment of law and government is the highest effort of human prudence and wisdom, the causes cannot have a different influence from what the effects have. Their velour defends us, their benevolence supplies us, the hungry is fed, the naked is clothed, by the exertion of these divine qualities. Thus, according to the above representation, all things are subservient to supplying our threefold necessities.

§3: The Opulence Arises from the Division of Labour

In an uncivilized nation, and where labour is undivided, everything is provided for that the natural wants of mankind require; yet, when the nation is cultivated and labour divided, a more liberal provision is allotted them; and it is on this account that a common day labourer in Britain has more luxury in his way of living than an [American] Indian sovereign.

In a civilized society, though there is a division of labour, there is no equal division, for there are a good many who work none at all. The division of opulence is not according to the work. The opulence of the merchant is greater that that of all his clerks, though he works less; and they again have six times more than an equal number of artisans, who are more employed. The artisan who works at his ease within doors has far more than the poor labourer who trudges up and down without intermission. Thus, he who as it were bears the burden of society, has the fewest advantages. (p. 163).

§4: How the Division of Labour Multiplies the Product

It is to be observed that the price of labour by no means determines the opulence of society; it is only when a little labour can procure abundance. On this account a rich nation, when its manufactures are greatly improven, may have an advantage over a poor one by underselling it.

The quantity of work which is done by the division of labour is much increased by the three following articles: first, increase of dexterity; secondly, the saving of time lost in passing from one species of labour to another; and thirdly, the invention of machinery.

§5: *What Gives Occasion to the Division of Labour*

It [the division of labour] flows from a direct propensity in human nature for one man to barter with another, which is common to all men, and known to no other animal.

Thus we different genius is not the foundation of this disposition to barter which is the cause of the division of labour. The real foundation of it is that principle to persuade which so much prevails in human nature.

§6: *That the Division of Labour Must Be Proportioned To The Extent of Commerce*

The division of labour is the great cause of the increase of public opulence, which is always proportioned to the industry of the people, and not to the quantity of gold and silver, as is foolishly imagined, and the industry of the people is always proportioned to the division of labour. Having thus shown what gives occasion to public opulence, in farther considering this subject we propose to consider: (1) what circumstances regulate the price of commodities; (2) money in two different views, first as the measure of value, and then as the instrument of commerce; (3) the history of commerce, in which shall be taken notice of the causes of the slow progress of opulence, both in ancient and modern times, which causes shall be shown either to affect agriculture or arts and manufacture; (4) the effects of a commercial spirit, on the government, temper, and manners of a people, whether good or bad, and the proper remedies.

§7: *What Circumstances Regulate The Price of Commodities*

Of every commodity there are two different prices, which though apparently independent, will be found to have a necessary connexion, viz. the natural price and the market price... When men are induced to a certain species of industry, rather than any other, they must make as much by the employment as will maintain them while they are employed.

A man has the natural price of his labour, when it is sufficient to maintain him during the time of labour, to defray the expense of education, and to compensate the risk of not living long enough, and of not succeeding in the business. When a man has this, there is sufficient encouragement to the labourer, and the commodity will be cultivated in proportion to the demand.

The regulation of the market price of goods depends on the three following articles: (1) the demand, or need for the commodity; (2) the abundance or scarcity of the commodity in proportion to the need of it; (3) the riches or poverty of those who demand.

§8: *Of Money As The Measure of Value and Medium of Exchange*

There must of necessity be a common standard of which equal quantities should be of equal values, metals in general seemed best to answer this purpose, and of these the value of gold and silver could best be ascertained. The temper of steel cannot be precisely known, but what degree of alloy is in gold and silver can be exactly found out. Gold and silver were therefore fixed upon as the most exact standard to compare goods with, and were therefore considered as the most proper measure of value. In consequence of gold and silver becoming the measure of value, it came also to be the instrument of commerce.

§9: That National Opulence Does Not Consist in Money

We have shown that rendered money the measure of value, but it is to be observed that labour, not money, is the true measure of value. National opulence consists therefore in the quantity of goods, and the facility of barter.

The more money that is necessary to circulate the goods of any country, the more is the quantity of goods diminished.

It is evident that the poverty of any country increases as the money increases, money being a dead stock in itself, supplying no convenience of life... If we could therefore fall on a method to send the half of our money abroad to be converted into goods, and at the same time supply the channel of circulation at home, we would greatly increase the wealth of the country.

The opulence of a nation does not consist in the quantity of coin, but in the abundance of commodities which are necessary for life, and whatever tends to increase these tends so far to increase the riches of a country.

* * *

§11: Of the Balance of Trade

The idea of public opulence consisting in money has been productive of other bad effects. Upon this principle most pernicious regulations have been established. Those species of commerce which drain us of our money are thought disadvantageous, and those which increase it beneficial, therefore the former are prohibited and the latter encouraged.

The absurdity of these regulations will appear on the least reflection. All commerce that is carried on betwixt any two countries must necessarily be advantageous both.

Again, by prohibiting the exportation of goods to foreign markets, the industry of the country is greatly discouraged. It is a very great motive to industry, that people have it in their power to exchange the produce of their labour for what they please, and wherever there is any restraint on people in this respect, they will not be so vigorous in improving manufactures... By hindering people to dispose of their money as they think proper, you discourage those manufactures by which this money is gained. All jealousies therefore between different nations, and prejudices of this kind, are extremely [hurtful] to commerce, and limit public opulence. This is always the case betwixt France and us in the time of war.

It is to be observed that the poverty of a nation proceeds from much the same causes with those which render an individual poor. When a man consumes more than he gains by his industry, he must impoverish himself unless he has some other way of subsistence. In the same manner, if a nation consume more than it produces, poverty is inevitable; if its annual produce be ninety millions and its annual consumption an hundred, then it spends, eats, drinks, tears, wears, ten millions more than it produces, and its stock of opulence must gradually go to nothing.

§12: Of the Opinion that no Expense at Home can be Hurtful

There is still another bad effect proceeding from that absurd notion, that national opulence consists in money. It is commonly imagined that whatever people spend in their own country cannot diminish public opulence, if you take care of exports and imports.

From the above considerations it appears that Britain should by all means be made a free port, that there should be no interruptions of any kind made to foreign trade, that if it were possible to defray the expenses of government by any other method, all duties, customs, and excise should be abolished, and that free commerce and liberty of exchange should be allowed with all nations, and for all things.

§14: Of Interest

We have only two things further to mention relating to the price of commodities: interest and exchange.

It is commonly supposed that the premium of interest depends upon the value of gold and silver. The value of these is regulated by their quantity, for as the quantity increases, the value diminishes, and as the quantity decreases, the value rises. If we attend to it, however, we shall find that the premium of interest is regulated by the quantity of stock.

Under the feudal constitution there could be very little accumulation of stock, which will appear from considering the situation of those three orders of men, which made up the whole body of people: the peasants, the landlords, and the merchants. The peasants had leases which dependant upon the caprice of their masters; they could never increase in wealth, because the landlord was ready to squeeze it all from them, and therefore they had no motive to acquire it. As little could the landlords increase their wealth, as they lived so indolent a life, and were oppressed by all ranks, and were not able to secure the produce of their industry from rapine and violence. Thus there could be little accumulation of wealth at all; but after the fall of the feudal government these obstacles to industry were removed, and the stock of commodities began gradually to increase.

§15: Of Exchange

Exchange is a method invented by merchants to facilitate the payment of money at a distance. Suppose I owe $100 to a merchant at London, I apply to a banker in Glasgow for a bill upon another merchant in London, payable to my creditor. For this I must also reward him for his trouble. This reward is called the price, or premium, of exchange... In every exchange you must pay the price, the risk, some profit to the banker, and so much for the degradation of money in notes. This is the cause of the rise of exchange.

§16: Of the Causes of the Slow Progress of Opulence

The causes of this may be considered under these two heads: (1) natural impediments and (2) the oppression of civil government.

This is one great cause of the slow progress of opulence in every country; till some stock be produced there can be no division of labour, and before a division of labour take place there can be very little accumulation of stock.

The other cause that was assigned was the nature of civil government. In the infancy of society, as has been often observed, government must be weak and feeble, and it is long before its authority can protect the industry of individuals from the rapacity of their neighbors. When people find themselves every moment in danger of being robbed of all they possess, they have no motive to be industrious. There could belittle accumulation of stock, because the indolent, which would be the greatest number, would live upon the industrious, and spend whatever they produced. When the power of government becomes so great as to defend the produce of industry, another obstacle arises from a different quarter. Among neighboring nations in a barbarous state there are perpetual wars, one continually invading and plundering the other, and though private property be secured from the violence of neighbors, it is in danger from hostile invasions. In this manner it is next to impossible that any accumulation of stock can be made. It is observable that among savage nations there are always more violent convulsions than among those farther advanced in refinement.

Agriculture is of all other arts the most beneficent to society, and whatever tends to retard its improvement is extremely prejudicial to the public interest. The produce of agriculture is much greater than that of any other manufacture.

One great hindrance to the progress of agriculture is the throwing great tracts of land into the hands of single persons. If any man s estate be more than he is able to cultivate, a part of it is in a manner lost. When a nation of savages takes possession of a country, the great and powerful divide the whole lands among them, and leave none for the lower ranks of people.

Besides these there were several other impediments to the progress of agriculture. At first all rents were paid in kind, by which, in a dear year, the tenants were in danger of being ruined. A diminution of produce seldom hurts the tenant who pays his rent in money, because the price of corn rises in proportion to its scarcity. Society, however, is considerably advanced before money comes to be the whole instrument of commerce. Another embarrassment was that the feudal lords sometimes allowed the king to levy subsidies from their tenants, which greatly discouraged their industry. Besides all, under the tyranny of the feudal aristocracy, the land lords had nothing to stop them from squeezing their tenants and raising the rents of their lands as high as they pleased. England is better secured in this respect than any country, because everyone who hold[s] but 40s. a year for life has a vote for a member of parliament, by which, if he rent a farm, he is secure from oppression.

The keeping land out of the market always hinders its improvement. A merchant who buys a little piece of land has it in his eye to improve it, and make the most of it he can. Great and ancient families have seldom either stock or inclination to improve their estates, except a small piece of pleasure-ground about their house. There are many errors in the police of almost every country, which have contributed greatly to stop the progress of agriculture. Our fathers, finding themselves once in every two or three years subject to the most grievous deaths, to escape that calamity prohibited the exportation of corn. This is still the police of the greater part of Europe, and it is the cause of all that dearth it is intended to prevent.

In all places where slavery took place, the manufactures were carried on by slaves. It is impossible that they can be so well carried on by slaves as by freemen, because they can have no motive to labour but the dread of punishment, and can never invent any machine for facilitating their business. Freemen, who have a stock of their own, can get anything accomplished which they think maybe expedient for carrying on labour. If a carpenter thinks that a plane will serve his purpose better than a knife, he may go to a smith and get it made; but if a slave makes any such proposal he is called a lazy rascal, and no experiments are made to give him ease.

§17: The influence of commerce in manners

Whenever commerce is introduced into any country probity and punctuality always accompany it. These virtues in a rude and barbarous country are almost unknown.

A dealer is afraid of losing his character, and is scrupulous in observing every engagement. When a person makes perhaps twenty contracts in a day, he cannot gain so much by endeavoring to impose on his neighbors, as the very appearance of a cheat would make him lose. When people seldom deal with one another, we find that they are somewhat disposed to cheat, because they can gain more by a smart trick than they can lose by the injury which it does their character.

Another inconvenience attending commerce is that education is greatly neglected. In rich and commercial nations the division of labour, having reduced all trades to very simple operations, affords an opportunity of employing children very young... But, besides this want of education, there is another great loss which attends the putting boys too soon to work. The boy begins to find that his father is obliged to him, and therefore throws off his authority. When he is grown up he has no ideas with which he can amuse himself.

Another bad effect of commerce is that it sinks the courage of mankind, and tends to extinguish martial spirit. In all commercial countries the division of labour is infinite, and every one s thoughts are employed about one particular thing.

A man has then time to study only one branch of business, and it would be a great disadvantage to oblige every one to learn the military art and to keep himself in the practice of it. The defense of the country is therefore committed to a certain set of men who have nothing else ado, and among the bulk of the people military courage diminishes. By having their minds constantly employed on the arts of luxury, they grow effeminate and dastardly.

Part III: Of Revenue
§1: Taxes on Possession on Possession

In all [barbarous] countries we find lands appropriated to the purposes of sovereignty, and therefore little occasion for taxes and customs. We shall show that this is a bad police, and one cause of the slow progress of opulence.

All taxes may be considered under two divisions, to wit, taxes upon possessions and taxes upon consumptions. These are the two ways of making the subjects contribute to the support of government. The land tax is of the former kind, and all taxes upon commodities of the latter.

§2: Of Taxes on Consumptions

Taxes upon possessions are naturally equal, but those upon consumptions naturally unequal, as they are sometimes paid by the merchant, sometimes by the consumer, and sometimes by the importer, who must be repaid it by the consumer.

When the inhabitants of a country are in a manner prohibited by high taxes from exporting the produce of their industry, they are confined to home consumption, and their motives to industry are diminished. Taxes upon importation, on the contrary, encourage the manufacturing of these particular commodities.

To conclude all that is to be said of taxes, we may observe that the common prejudice that wealth consists in money has not been in this respect so hurtful as might have been imagined, and has even given occasion to regulations not very inconvenient. Those nations to whom we give more goods than we receive, generally send us manufactured goods; those on the contrary, from whom we receive more goods than we give, or with respect to whom the balance is in our favor, generally send us unmanufactured goods. To Russia, for example, we send fine linen and other manufactured goods, and for a small quantity of these receive, in return, great quantities of unmanufactured goods. This kind of trade is very advantageous, because goods in an unmanufactured and rude state afford employment and maintenance to a great number of persons. It is merely from the absurd notion that wealth consists in money, that the British encourage most of those branches of foreign trade, where the balance is paid in money.

Part IV: Of Arms
§1: Of Militas

In the beginning of society the defense of the state required no police, nor particular provision for it. The whole body of the people rose up to oppose any attempt that was made against them, and he who was chief in time of peace, naturally preserved his influence in time of war. But after the division of labour took place, it became necessary that some should stay at home, to be employed in agriculture and other arts, while the rest went out to war. After the appropriation of lands and the distinction of ranks were in some measure introduced, the cultivation of the ground would naturally fall to the meanest rank. The less laborious, but more honourable employment of military service would be claimed by the highest order. Accordingly we find that this was the practice of all nations in their primitive state. The Roman equites or knights were originally horsemen in the army, and no slaves or those who did not pay taxes ever went out to war. In like manner among our ancestors only they who held by what was called knight s service were employed in the defense of the state, and the ancient villains were never considered as a part of the national force.

When the improvement of arts and manufactures was thought an object deserving the attention of the higher ranks, the defense of the state naturally became the province of the lower, because the rich can never be forced to do anything but what they please.

Among a nation of hunters and shepherds, and even when a nation is advanced to agriculture, the whole body goes out together to make war. When arts and manufactures begin to advance, the whole cannot go out, and as these arts are laborious, and not very lucrative, for the reasons formerly adduced, the highest go out. After that, when arts and commerce are still farther advanced, and begin to be very lucrative, it falls to the meanest to defend the state. This is our present condition in Great Britain.

§2: Of Discipline

When the highest orders went out, a principle of honour would supply the place of discipline, but when this office fell upon the lowest order, the most severe and rigid discipline became necessary, and accordingly we find that it has been introduced into all standing armies. In general, it is necessary that they should be kept under such authority as to be more afraid of their general and officers than of the enemy. It is the fear of their officers and of the rigid penalties of the martial law, which is the chief cause of their good behaviour, and it is to this principle that we owe their valiant actions.

Part V: Of The Laws Of Nations
§Introduction

The laws of nations are such as take place either in peace or war. Those that take place in times of peace have been formerly explained, where it was shown with respect to aliens that they are entitled to security as to their persons and effects, but that they have no power to make a will, but all goes to the sovereign at their death. The laws or rules observed in time of war shall be considered.

§1: When is War Lawful?

When one nation encroaches on the property of another, or puts to death the subjects of another, imprisons them, or refuses them justice when injured, the sovereign is bound to demand satisfaction for the offence, as it is the intention of the government to protect its several members from foreign enemies, and if redress be refused, there is a foundation for war. In the same manner breach of contract, as when a debt is due by one nation to another, and payment refused, is a very just occasion of war.

Cesare Beccaria (1738-1794)

Artist: Engraved by Carlo Faucci (1766), Encyclopedia Britannica

Born to an aristocratic family in Milan on March 15, 1738, the Marchese Cesare Beccaria Bonesana was to produce perhaps the most influential text on police and jurisprudence entitled *On Crimes and Punishments*. Beccaria studied law at the University of Pavia, and received his doctor's degree by the age of twenty. He published an article dealing with the monetary disorder in Milan in 1762 and, though it was found to have serious flaws, its principles were taken into consideration by the state administration. Having made something of a name for himself, Beccaria was eager to produce another work, the result of which was his controversial 1764 treatise *On Crimes and Punishments*.

The first three editions carried neither the author's name, nor the printer's. The work, which heavily criticized the existing penal systems found throughout Europe, notably condemning torture and the death penalty, found instant popularity. The Patriotic Society of Berne awarded a gold medal to the "citizen who dared raise his voice in favor of humanity against the most deeply ingrained prejudices." The identity of this citizen was soon after revealed, and Beccaria became well known throughout the western world. Despite wide international praise for the work, the reasons for Beccaria's reluctance to take credit quickly became apparent. He came under considerable attack from traditional jurists and religious groups, with a particularly bitter denunciation coming from a Vallombrosian monk who accused Beccaria of *socialismo*. Though the term was rather ambiguous in mid-18th century, Marcello Maestro suggests Beccaria may have been the first man ever accused of being a socialist. *On Crimes and Punishments* was further assailed when it found itself on the Roman Church's Index of Condemned Books, where it would remain until the Church abolished the Index itself in 1962. Beccaria expressed fears that the book might turn him into a martyr, but he found significant support in the Verri brothers (Pietro and Alesandro), who published an apology to the book, as well as in the head of the Milan administration who intervened personally on Beccaria's behalf. The treatise was deeply influential, gaining the notice of people such as Voltaire and Thomas Jefferson, and contributed greatly to the reform of 18th century criminal law.

In 1768, the Palatine College of Milan founded a chair of law and economy specifically for Beccaria, and in 1771 he was appointed a full member of the Supreme Economic Council. In 1791, he was given the further honor of being appointed by the Emperor Leopold II to a commission looking into judicial reform. Beccaria spent the last of his years observing from a distance the pathos of the French Revolution. Beccaria succumbed to apoplexy in November 1794.

Works Referenced:

Beccaria, Cesare. *On Crimes and Punishments*. Translated with Introduction by Henry Paolucci. Bobbs-Merrill Company, Inc: Indianapolis, 1963.

Maestro, Marcello. *Cesare Beccaria and the Origins of Penal Reform*. Temple University Press: Philadelphia, 1973.

Selections from: *On Crimes and Punishments.* **Henry Paolucci (trans.) (Indianapolis: Bobbs-Merrill Educational Publishing, 1963) and (New York: Marsilio Publishers, 1966)., orig. 1764.**

§I: Introduction

If we glance at the pages of history, we will find that laws, which surely are, or ought to be, compacts of free men, have been, for the most part, a mere tool of the passion of some, or have arisen from an accidental and temporary need. Never have they been dictated by a dispassionate student of human nature who might, by bringing the actions of a multitude of men into focus, consider them from this single point of view: the *greatest happiness shared by the greatest number* (Jeremy Bentham). Happy are those few nations that have not waited for the slow succession of coincidence and human vicissitude to force some little turn for the better after the limit of evil has been reached, but have facilitated the intermediate progress by means of good laws.

§II: The Origin of Punishments, and the Right to Punish

No lasting advantage is to be hoped for from political morality if it is not founded upon the ineradicable feelings of mankind.

Laws are the conditions under which independent and isolated men united to form a society. Weary of living in a continual state of war, and of enjoying liberty rendered useless by the uncertainty of preserving it, they sacrificed a part so that they might enjoy the rest of it in peace and safety.

Some tangible motives had to be introduced to prevent the despotic spirit, which is in every man, from plunging the laws of society into its original chaos. I say 'tangible motives' because experience has shown that the multitude adopt no fixed principles of conduct and will not be released from the sway of that universal principle of dissolution which is seen to operate both in the physical and the moral universe, except for motives that directly strike the senses.

Punishments that exceed what is necessary for protection of the deposit of public security are by their very nature unjust, and punishments are increasingly more just as the safety which the sovereign secures for his subjects is the more sacred and inviolable, and the liberty greater.

§III: Consequences

The first consequence of these principles is that only the laws can decree punishments for crimes; authority for this can reside only with the legislator who represents the entire society united by a social contract. No magistrate (who is a part of society) can, with justice, inflict punishments upon another member of the same society.

The second consequence is that the sovereign, who represents the society itself, can frame only the general laws binding all members, but he cannot judge whether someone has violated the social contract... There must therefore be a third party to judge the truth of the fact.

The third consequence is this: even assuming that severity of punishments were not directly contrary to the public good and to the very purpose of preventing crimes, if it were possible to prove merely that such severity is useless, in that case also it would be contrary not only to those beneficent virtues that spring from enlightened reason which would rather rule happy men than a herd of slaves in whom a timid cruelty makes its endless rounds; it would be contrary to justice itself and to the very nature of the social contract.

§IV: Interpretations of the Laws

A fourth consequence: Judges in criminal cases cannot have the authority to interpret the laws, and the reason, again, is that they are not legislators. Such judges have not received the laws from our ancestors as a family tradition or legacy that leaves to posterity only the burden of obeying them, but they receive them, rather, from the living society, or from the sovereign representing it, who is the legitimate depositary of what actually results from the common will of all... This constitutes the natural and real authority of the laws.

For every crime that comes before him, a judge is required to complete a perfect syllogism in which the major premise must be the general law; the minor, the action that conforms or does not conform to the law; and the conclusion, acquittal or punishment. If the judge were constrained, or if he desired to frame even a single additional syllogism, the door would thereby be opened to uncertainty.

Nothing can be more dangerous than the popular axiom that it is necessary to consult the spirit of laws. It is a dam that has given way to a torrent of opinions. This truth, which seems paradoxical to ordinary minds that are struck more by trivial present disorders than by the dangerous but remote effects of false principles rooted in a nation, seems to me to be fully demonstrated. Our understanding and all our ideas have reciprocal connection; the more complicated they are, the more numerous must the ways be that lead to them and depart from them. Each man has his own point of view, and, at each different time, a different one. Thus the "spirit" of the law would be the product of a judge's good or bad logic, of his good or bad digestion; it would depend on the violence of his passions, on the weakness of the accused, on the judge's connections with him, and on all those minute factors that alter the appearances of an object in the fluctuating mind of man. Thus we see the same crimes differently punished at different times by the same court, for having consulted not the constant fixed voice of the law but the erring instability of interpretation.

When a fixed code of laws, which must be observed to the letter, leaves no further care to the judge than to examine the acts of citizens and to decide whether or not they conform to the law as written; when the standard of the just and unjust, which is to be the norm of conduct for the ignorant as well as for the philosophic citizen, is not a matter of controversy but of fact; then only are citizens not subject to the petty tyrannies of the many which are the moral cruel as the distance between the oppressed and the oppressor is less, and which are far more fatal than those of a single man, for the despotism of many can only be corrected by the despotism of one; the cruelty of a single despot is proportioned, not to his might, but to the obstacles he encounters.

§V: Obscurity of the Laws

If the interpretation of laws is an evil, another evil, evidently is the obscurity that makes interpretation necessary. And this evil would be very great indeed where the laws are written in a language that is foreign to a people, forcing it to rely on a handful of men because it is unable to judge for itself how its liberty or its members may fare—in a language that transforms a sacred and public book into something very like the private possession of a family. When the number of those who can understand the sacred code of laws and hold it in their hands increases, the frequency of crimes will be found to decrease, for undoubtedly ignorance and uncertainty of punishments add much to the eloquence of the passions.

Without writing, a society can never acquire a fixed form of government with power that derives from the whole and not from the parts, in which the laws, which cannot be altered except by the general will, are not corrupted in their passage through the mass of private interest.

We can thus see how useful the art of printing is, which makes the public, and not some few individuals, the guardian of the sacred laws. And we can see how it has dissipated the benighted spirit of cabal and intrigue, which must soon vanish in the presence of those enlightened studies and sciences, apparently despised, but really feared, by its adherents. This explains why we now see in Europe a diminishing of the atrocity of the crimes that afflicted our ancestors, who became tyrants and slaves by turns.

§VI: Imprisonment

Detention in prison is a punishment which, unlike every other, must of necessity precede conviction for crime, but this distinctive character does not remove the other which is essential—namely, that only the law determines the cases in which a man is to suffer punishment.

A man's notoriety, his flight, his nonjudicial confession, the confession of an accomplice, threats and the constant enmity of the injured person, the manifest fact of the crime, and similar evidences, are proofs sufficient to justify imprisonment of a citizen. But these proofs must be determined by the law, not by judges, whose decrees are always contrary to political liberty when they are not particular applications of a general maxim included in the public code. When punishments have become more moderate, when squalor and hunger have been removed from prisons, when pity and mercy have forced a way through barred doors, overmastering the inexorable and obdurate ministers of justice, then may the laws be content with slighter evidences as grounds for imprisonment.

A man accused of a crime, who has been imprisoned and acquitted, ought not to be branded with infamy. How many Romans accused of very great crimes, and then found innocent, were revered by the populace and honored with public offices! For what reason, then, is the fate of an innocent person so apt to be different in our time? It seems to be because, in the present system of criminal law, the idea of power and arrogance prevails over that of justice, because accused and convicted are thrown indiscriminately into the same cell, because imprisonment is rather the torment than the confinement of the accused, and because the internal power that protects the laws and the external power that defends the throne and nation are separated when they ought to be united. By means of the common sanctions of the laws, the former (internal power) would be combined with judicial authority, without, however, passing directly under its sway; the glory that attends the pomp and ceremony of a military corps would remove infamy, which, like all popular sentiments, is more attached to the manner than to the thing itself, as is proved by the fact that military prisons are, according to the common opinion, less disgraceful than the civil.

§VII: Evidences and Forms of Judgments

I speak of probability, here, with respect to crimes, when it would seem that certainty is demanded if they are to deserve punishment. But the paradox will vanish if one considers that, strictly speaking, moral certainty is never more than a probability, but a probability that is called certainty, because every man of good sense naturally gives his assent to it by force of a habit which arises from the necessity to act and is anterior to all speculation. The certainty required to prove a man guilty, therefore, is that which determines every man in the most important transaction of his life.

Most useful is the law that each man ought to be judged by his peers, for, where it is a matter of the liberty or the fortune of a citizen, the feelings which inequality inspires should be silent; neither the superiority with which the prosperous man regards the unfortunate, nor the disdain with which the inferior regards his superior, can have any place in this judgment. But when a crime involves injury to a fellow citizen, then the judges ought to be peers, half of the accused, half of the injured. In this way, by carefully balancing every private concern that might even involuntarily transform the aspect of things, nothing is heard to speak but the laws and the truth. It also accord with justice to permit the accused to refuse, on suspicion, a certain number of this judges; when this opportunity has been allowed him for a time, without opposition, the accused will seem almost to condemn himself. Let the verdicts and proofs of guilt be made public, so that opinion, which is, perhaps, the sole cement of society, may serve to restrain power and passions; so that the people may say, we are not slaves, and we are protected—a sentiment which inspires courage and which is the equivalent of a tribute to a sovereign who knows his own true interests. I shall not enter upon other specific points and precautions requiring similar regulations. I should have said nothing, were it necessary to say all.

§VIII: Witnesses

Every reasonable man, everyone, that is whose ideas have a certain interconnection and whose feelings accord with those of other men, may be a witness. The true measure of his credibility is nothing other than his interest in telling or in not telling the truth; for this reason it is frivolous to insist that women are too weak (to be good witnesses), childish to insist that civil death in a condemned man has the same effects as real death, and meaningless to insist on the infamy of the infamous, when they have no interest in lying.

Formalities and ceremonies are necessary in the administration of justice, not only because they leave nothing to be determined arbitrarily by the administrator, and because they give the populace the impression of a judgment that is not rash and partisan, but stable and regular; but also because, on men who are imitators and slaves of custom, things which impress the senses make a more lasting impression than rational arguments.

§IX: Secret Accusations

Evident, but consecrated abuses, made necessary in many nations by the weakness of the government, are secret accusations. Their customary use makes men false and deceptive.

Montesquieu has said that public accusations are more suited to a republic, in which the principle passion of citizens ought to be for the public good, than to a monarchy, where that feeling is extremely weak owing to the very nature of the government, and where the best practice is to assign commissioners who, in the name of the people, accuse the infractors of the laws. But every government, republican as well as monarchic, ought to inflict upon the false accuser the very punishment that the accused is supposed to receive.

§X: Suggestive Interrogations. Depositions

According to criminologists, interrogations should, one might say, envelop a fact spirally, but never approach it by a straight line. The reasons for this procedure are either so as not to suggest to the accused an answer that confronts him with the accusation or, perhaps, because it seems to run against the very nature for an accused person to accuse himself directly. Whether it be one or the other of these two reasons, remarkable indeed is the contradiction in the laws which couple with this usage the authorization of torture. What possible interrogation can be more suggestive than pain? The first reason is surely applicable in the case of torture, for pain will suggest obstinate silence to a strong man, enabling him thereby to exchange a greater for a lesser punishment, and to the weak it will suggest confession, so that he may free himself from present torment which is, for the moment at least, more efficacious than the fear of future pain. The second reason is also evidently relevant here, for, if a special interrogation makes an accused person confess against this natural right, spasm of torture will do so the more easily. But men are ruled much more by the difference in the names of things than by the things themselves.

§XI: Oaths

Laws and natural sentiments of man contradict one another when oaths are administered to the accused, binding him to be truthful when he can best serve his own interest by being false; as if a man could really swear to contribute to his own destruction; as if religion were not silent in most men when interest speaks. The experience of all ages has shown that men have abused this precious gift of heaven more than any other.

Why confront a man with the terrible alternative of either sinning against God or concurring in his own ruin? The law that requires such an oath commands one to be either a bad Christian or a martyr. Little by little the oath is reduced to a mere formality, and the whole force of religious feelings, which for most men are the sole pledge of honesty, is destroyed. Experience has shown how useless oaths are. Every judge can be my witness that no oath ever made any criminal tell the truth.

§XII: Torture

No man can be called guilty before a judge has sentenced him, nor can society deprive him of public protection before it has been decided that he has in fact violated the conditions under which such protection was accorded him. What right is it, then, if not simply that of might, which empowers a judge to inflict punishment on a citizen while doubt still remains as to his guilt or innocence? Here is the dilemma, which is nothing new: the fact of the crime is either certain or uncertain; if certain, all that is due is the punishment established by the laws and tortures are useless because the criminal's confession is useless; if uncertain, then one must not torture the innocent, for such, according to the laws, is a man whose crimes are not yet proved.

The law that authorizes torture is a law that says: "Men, resist pain; and if nature has created in you an inextinguishable self-love, if it has granted you an inalienable right of self-defense, I create in you an altogether contrary sentiment: a heroic hatred of yourselves; and I command you to accuse yourselves, to speak the truth even while muscles are being lacerated and bones disjointed."

Torture is an infallible means indeed —for absolving robust scoundrels and for condemning innocent persons who happen to be weak. Such are the fatal defects of this so-called criterion of truth, a criterion fit for a cannibal, which the Romans, who were barbarous themselves on many counts, reserved only for slaves, the victims of a fierce and overly praised virtue.

Of two men, equally innocent or equally guilty, the strong and courageous will be acquitted, the weak and timid condemned, by virtue of this rigorous rational argument: "I, the judge, was supposed to find you guilty of such and such a crime; you, the strong, have been able to resist the pain, and I therefore absolve you; you, the weak, have yielded, and I therefore condemn you. I am aware that a confession wrenched forth by torments ought to be of no weight whatsoever, but I will torment you again if you do not confirm what you have confessed."

The effect of torture, therefore, is a matter of temperament and calculation that varies with each man according to his strength and sensibility, so that, with this method, a mathematician could more readily than a judge resolve this problem: given the muscular force and nervous sensibility of an innocent person, find the degree of pain that will make him confess himself guilty of a given crime.

Another ridiculous pretext for torture is purgation from infamy; which is to say, a man judged infamous by the laws must confirm his deposition with the dislocation of his bones. This abuse should not be tolerated in the eighteenth century. It is believed that pain, which is a sensation, can purge infamy, which is a purely moral relationship. Is torture perhaps a crucible, and infamy, perhaps, a mixed impure substance? But infamy is a sentiment subject neither to the laws nor to reason, but to common opinion. Torture itself brings real infamy to its victims. Thus, by this method, infamy is to be removed by adding to it.

The usage [of torture] seems to have derived from religious and spiritual ideas, which exert a great influence on the thoughts of men, nations, and ages. An infallible dogma assures us that the stains contracted through our human frailty, which have not merited the eternal anger of the Grand Being, must be purged by an incomprehensible fire. Now infamy is a civil stain, and as suffering and fire remove spiritual and incorporeal stains, why should not spasm of torture remove the civil stain, which is infamy? I believe that the confession of the criminal which is exacted as essential for condemnation in certain tribunals has a similar origin, for in the mysterious tribunal of penance the confession of sins is an essential part of the sacrament.

§XIII: Prosecutions and Prescriptions

The laws should fix a definite length of time both for the defense of the accused and for the proof of crimes; the judge would become a legislator were he to decide the time necessary for the latter.

I merely indicate the principles, for a precise limitation can be fixed only for a given system of legislation and in the given circumstances of a society. I shall only add that, the advantage of moderate punishments in a nation having been demonstrated, the laws that shorten or extend the time of prescription or the time for proof according to the gravity of the crimes – thus making imprisonment itself, or voluntary exile, a part of the punishment – will provide an easy classification made up of few punishments, most of them mild, for a great number of crimes.

I distinguish two classes of crimes: the first is that of atrocious crimes, and this begins with homicide and includes all graver offences; the second is that of minor crimes. This distinction is founded on human nature. The security of one's own life is a natural right; the security of one's property is a social right. The motives that induce men to transgress their natural feeling of compassion are fewer in number than those which, because of a natural desire to be happy, induce them to violate a right which they do not find registered in their hearts, but only in the conventions of society. The considerable difference of probability in each of these two classes of crimes requires that they be governed by diverse principles. In the more atrocious crimes, which are the least common, the time for inquiry should be decreased because of the increased probability that the accused may be innocent; the time of prescription should be increased, because only a definitive sentence of innocence or guilt can remove the illusory prospect of impunity, the harm of which increases with the atrocity of crime. But in minor cases, since the probability of innocence of the accused is less, the time of inquiry should be extended, and since the harm of impunity is less, the time of prescription should also be shorter. Needless to say such a division of crimes into two classes could not be admitted were danger of impunity to decrease as much as the probability of the crimes increases.

Most men lack the vigor which is as much necessary for great crimes as for great virtues; thus it seems that the two always tend to occur simultaneously in those nations that support themselves by strenuous activity of government and of the passions that conspire to the public good rather than by their size or the constant goodness of the laws. In these, the weakened passions seem more adapted to maintain than to improve the form of government. From this an important consequence may be drawn, namely, that great crimes in a nation are always a proof of its decadence. .

§XIV: Attempts, Accomplices, Impunity

Laws do not punish intent; but surely an act undertaken with the manifest intention of committing a crime deserves punishment, though less than that which is due upon the actual execution of the crime. The importance of preventing a criminal attempt authorizes punishment, but as there may be an interval between the attempt and the execution, reservation of greater punishment for the accomplished crime may lead to repentance.

§XV: Mildness of Punishments

The purpose [of punishment] can only be to prevent the criminal from inflicting new injuries on its citizens and to deter others from similar acts. (Footnote 29: Seneca, De Clementia I, 16: "no man punishes because a sin has been committed, but that sin may not be committed. For what has passed cannot be recalled, but what is to come may be prevented.")

For a punishment to attain its end, the evil which it inflicts has only to exceed the advantage derivable from the crime; in this excess of evil one should include the certainty of punishment and the loss of the good which the crime might have produced. (Footnote 30: Considering the law of the "state of nature," Locke writes (Second Treatise, II, 12): "Each transgression may be punished to that degree and with so much severity as will suffice to make it an ill bargain to the offender, give him cause to repent, and terrify others from doing the like.")

In proportion as torments become more cruel, the spirits of men, which are like fluids that always rise to the level of surrounding objects, become callous, and the ever lively force of the passions brings it to pass that after a hundred years of cruel torments wheel inspires no greater fear than imprisonment once did. The severity of punishment of itself emboldens men to commit the very wrongs it is supposed to prevent; they are driven to commit additional crimes to avoid the punishment for a single one.

Very strong and sensible impressions are demanded for the callous spirits of a people that has just emerged from the savage state. A lightening bolt is necessary to stop a ferocious lion that turns upon the shot of a rifle. But to the extent that spirits are softened in the social state, sensibility increases and, as it increases, the force of punishment must diminish if the relation between object and sensory impression is to be kept constant. (Footnote 31: Montesquieu, Spirit, VI, 12: "Experience shows that in countries remarkable for the lenity of their laws the spirit of the inhabitants is as much affected by slight penalties as in other countries by severer punishments.")

§XVI: The Death Penalty

This useless prodigality of torments, which has never made men better, has prompted me to examine whether death is really useful and just in a well-organized government. What manner of right can men attribute to themselves to slaughter their fellow beings? Certainly not that from which sovereignty and the law derive. These (from which sovereignty and law derive) are nothing but the sum of the least portions of the private liberty of each person; they represent the general will, which is the aggregate of particular wills.

The punishment of death, therefore, is not a right, for I have demonstrated that it cannot be such; but it is the war of a nation against a citizen whose destruction it judges to be necessary or useful. If, then I can show that death is neither useful nor necessary, I shall have gained the cause of humanity.

There are only two possible motives for believing that the death of a citizen is necessary. The first: when it is evident that even if deprived of liberty he still has connections and power such as endanger the security of the nation—when, that is, his existence can produce a dangerous revolution in the established form of government. The death of a citizen thus becomes necessary when a nation is recovering or losing its liberty or, in time of anarchy, when disorders themselves take the place of laws. But while the laws reign tranquilly, in a form of government enjoying the consent of the entire nation, well defended externally and internally by force, and by opinion, which is perhaps even more efficacious than force, where executive power is lodged with the true sovereign alone, where riches purchase pleasures and not authority. I see no necessity for destroying a citizen, except if his death were the only real way of restraining others from committing crimes; this is the second motive for believing that the death penalty may be just and necessary.

It is not the intensity of punishment that has the greatest effect on human spirit, but its duration, for our sensibility is more easily and more permanently affected by slight but repeated impressions than by a powerful but momentary action. The sway of habit is universal over every sentient being; as man speaks and walks and satisfies his needs by its aid, so the ideas of morality come to be stamped upon the mind only by long and repeated impressions. It is not the terrible yet momentary spectacle of the death of a wretch, but the long and painful example of a man deprived of liberty, who, having become a beast of burden, recompenses with his labours the society he has offended, which is the strongest curb against crimes. That efficacious idea—efficacious, because very often repeated to ourselves—"I myself shall be reduced to so long and miserable a condition if I commit a similar misdeed" is far more potent than the idea of death, which men envision always at an obscure distance.

A general rule: violent passions surprise men, but not for so long, and are therefore apt to bring on those revolutions which instantly transform ordinary men either into Persians or Lacedemonians; but in a free and peaceful government the impression should be frequent rather than strong.

The death penalty becomes for the majority a spectacle and for some others an object of compassion mixed with disdain; these two sentiments rather than the salutary fear which the laws pretend to inspire occupy the spirits of the spectators. But in moderate and prolonged punishments the dominant sentiment is the latter, because it is the only one. The limit which the legislator ought to fix on the rigor of punishments would seem to be determined by the sentiment of compassion itself, when it begins to prevail over every other in the hearts of those who are the witnesses of punishment, inflicted for their sake rather than for the criminal's.

The intensity of the punishment of a life sentence of servitude, in place of the death penalty, has in it what suffices to deter any determined spirit. It has, let me add, even more. Many men are able to look calmly and with firmness upon death—some from fanaticism, some from vanity, which almost always accompanies man even beyond the tomb, some from a final and desperate attempt either to live no longer or to escape their misery. But neither fanaticism nor vanity can subsist among fetters or chains, under the rod, under the yoke, in a cage of iron, where the desperate wretch does not end his woes but merely begins them. Our spirit resists violence and extreme but momentary pains more easily than it does time and incessant weariness, for it can, so to speak, collect itself for a moment to repel the first, but the vigor of its elasticity does not suffice to resist the long and repeated action of the second.

To anyone raising the argument that perpetual servitude is as painful as death and therefore equally cruel, I will reply that, adding up all the moments of unhappiness of servitude, it may well be even more cruel; but these are drawn out over an entire lifetime, while the pain of death exerts its whole force in a moment. And precisely this is the advantage of penal servitude, that it inspires terror in the spectator more than in the sufferer, for the former considers the entire sum of unhappy moments, while the latter is distracted from the thought of future misery by that of the present moment. All evils are magnified in the imagination, and the sufferer finds compensations and consolations unknown and incredible to spectators who substitute their own sensibility for the callous spirit of a miserable wretch.

But he who foresees a great number of years, or even a whole lifetime to be spent in servitude and pain, in sight of his fellow citizens with whom he lives in freedom and friendship, slave of the laws which once afforded him protection, makes a useful comparison of all this with the uncertainty of the result of his crimes, and the brevity of the time in which he would enjoy their fruits. The perpetual example of those whom he actually sees the victims of their own carelessness makes a much stronger impression upon him than the spectacle of a punishment that hardens more than it corrects him.

The death penalty cannot be useful, because of the example of barbarity it gives men. If the passions or the necessities of war have taught the shedding of human blood, the laws, moderators of the conduct of men, should not extend the beastly example, which becomes more pernicious since the inflicting of legal death is attended with much study and formality. It seems to me absurd that the laws, which are an expression of the public will, which detest and punish homicide, should themselves commit it, and that to deter citizens from murder, they order a public one.

The happy time has not yet arrived in which truth shall be the portion of the greatest number, as error has heretofore been. And from this universal law those truths only have been exempted which Infinite Wisdom has chosen to distinguish from others by revealing them.

§XVII: Banishment and Confiscations

The loss of possessions is a punishment greater than that of banishment; in some cases, therefore, according to the crimes, all or a part of one's possessions should be forfeited, and in others, none. Forfeiture of all should follow when the banishment prescribed by the law is such that it nullifies all ties between society and a delinquent citizen; in that case, the citizen dies and the man remains. With respect to the body politic, [civil death] should produce the same effect as natural death.

§XVIII: Infamy

Infamy is a mark of public disapprobation that deprives the criminal of public esteem, of the confidence of his country, and of that almost fraternal intimacy which society inspires. It cannot be determined by law. The infamy which the law inflicts, therefore, must be the same as that which arises from the relations of things, the same that is dictated by universal morality, or by the particular morality of particular systems, which are legislators of vulgar opinions and of that particular nation.

Corporal and painful punishments should not be applied to crimes founded on pride, which derive glory and nourishment out of pain itself; far more suitable are ridicule and infamy—punishments that check the pride of fanatics with the pride of onlookers, and from the tenacity of which even truth itself can hardly work its way loose, with slow and obstinate efforts. Thus by opposing forces against forces, and opinions against opinions, the wise legislator breaks down the admiration and surprise of the populace occasioned by a false principle, the correctly deduced consequences of which tend to conceal from popular minds the original absurdity.

It is not only the arts of taste and pleasure that have as their universal principle the faithful imitation of nature, but politics itself, at least that which is true and lasting, is subject to this universal maxim, for it is nothing other than the art of properly directing and coordinating the immutable sentiments of men.

§XIX: Promptness of Punishment

The more promptly and the more closely punishment follows upon the commission of a crime, the more just and useful will it be. I say more just, because the criminal is thereby spared the useless and cruel torments of uncertainty, which increase with the vigor of imagination and with the sense of personal weakness; more just, because privation of liberty, being itself a punishment, should not precede the sentence except when necessity requires. Imprisonment of a citizen, then, is simply custody of his person until he be judged guilty; and this custody, being essentially penal, should be of the least possible duration and of the least possible severity.

§XX: The Certainty of Punishment. Mercy

The certainty of a punishment, even if it be moderate, will always make a stronger impression than the fear of another which is more terrible but combined with the hope of impunity; even the least evils, when they are certain, always terrify men's minds, and hope, that heavenly gift which is often our sole recompense for everything, tends to keep the thought of greater evils remote from us, especially when its strength is increased by the idea of impunity which avarice and weakness only too often afford.

§XXI: Asylums

Two other questions: one, whether asylums are just, and whether an international pact for reciprocal exchange of criminals is useful or not. Within the confines of a country there should be no place independent of the laws. Their power should pursue every citizen, as the shadow pursues is body. Impunity and asylum differ only in degree, and as the effectiveness of punishment consists more in the certainty of receiving it than in its force, asylums encourage crimes more than punishments deter them.

§XXII: Rewards

The other question is whether it is useful to put a price on the head of a known criminal and to make each citizen an executioner by arming his hand. The criminal is either beyond the borders of his country or within them; in the first case, the sovereign encourages citizens to commit a crime and exposes them to punishment, he himself thereby committing an injury and a usurpation of authority in the dominions of another, and in that way authorizing other nations to do the same to him. In the second case, he displays his own weakness.

To the extent that a nation becomes more enlightened, honesty and mutual confidence become necessary, and tend always to identify themselves the more with sound policy. Schemas and intrigues, dark and indirect ways, are for the most part foreseen, and the sensibility of all counterbalances that of particular individuals. Even the ages of ignorance, in which public morality inclines men to live by private standards, serve as instruction and experience for enlightened ages.

§XXIII: Proportion between Crimes and Punishments

If an equal punishment be ordained for two crimes that do not equally injure society, men will not be any more deterred from committing the greater crime, if they find a greater advantage associated with it.

It is impossible to prevent all disorders in the universal conflict of human passions. They increase according to a ratio compounded of population and the crossing of particular interests, which cannot be directed with geometric precision to the public utility. For mathematical exactitude we must substitute, in the arithmetic of politics, the calculation of probabilities. A glance at the histories will show that disorders increase with the increased interest everyone takes in such disorders; thus there is a constantly increasing need to make punishments heavier.

§XXIV: The Measure of Crimes

The true measure of crimes is the harm done to society.

§XXV: The Classification of Crimes

Some crimes directly destroy society, or the person who represents it; some injure the private security of a citizen in his life, in his goods, or in his honor; some others are actions contrary to what everyone is supposed to do or not do in view of the public good.

Any action not included between the two extremes indicated above cannot be called a "crime," or be punished as such, except by those who find their interest in applying that name. The uncertainty of these limits has produced, in nations, a morality that contradicts legislation, a number of actual legislative systems that are mutually exclusive, a host of laws that expose the wisest to the severest punishments. Thus are the terms "vice" and "virtue" rendered vague and fluctuating, and there emerges that sense of uncertainty about one's own existence which produces the lethargy and sleep that is fatal to political communities.

§XXVI: Crimes of Lese Majesty (1)

The first class of crimes, which are the gravest because most injurious, are those known as crimes of lese majesty [high treason]. Only tyranny and ignorance, confounding the clearest terms and ideas, can apply this name and consequently the gravest punishment, to crimes of a different nature, thereby making men, on this as on a thousand other occasions, victims of a word. Every crime, even of a private nature, injuries society, but it is not every crime that aims at its immediate destruction. Moral as well as physical actions have their limited sphere of activity, and are diversely circumscribed, like all movements of nature, by time and space; therefore only sophistical interpretation, which is usually the philosophy of slavery, can confound the immutable relations of things distinguished by eternal truth.

§XXVII: Crimes against Personal Security. Acts of Violence. Punishments of Nobles (2)

Inasmuch as this is the primary end of all political association [security of the society], some of the severest of punishments established by law must be assigned to any violation of the right of security acquired by every citizen.

Some crimes are attempts against the person, others against property. The penalties for the first should always be corporal punishments.

Attempts against the security and liberty of citizens are among the greatest of crimes. Within this class are included not only the assassinations and thefts committed by men of the lower classes but also those committed by noblemen and magistrates, the example of which acts with greater force and is more far-reaching, destroying the ideas of justice and duty among subjects and substituting that of the right of the strongest, equally dangerous, in the end, to those who exercise it and to those who suffer it.

To the objection that the same punishment inflicted on a nobleman and a plebian is not really the same because of the diversity of their education, and because of the disgrace that is spread over an illustrious family, I would answer that the measure of punishments is not the sensibility of the criminal, but the public inquiry, which is all the more grave when committed by a person of rank; that equality of punishments can only be extrinsic, since in reality the effect of each individual is diverse; that the disgrace of a family may be removed by the sovereign through public demonstration of benevolence toward the innocent relatives of the criminal. And who does not know that external formalities take the place of reason for the credulous and admiring populace?

§XXVIII: Injuries to Honor (3)

Personal injuries that detract from honor, that is, from the just portion of esteem which one citizen has the right to exact from others, should be punished with disgrace [infamia].

There is a remarkable contradiction between the civil laws, those jealous guardians, above all, of the life and property of each citizen, and the laws of what is called "honor," which respects opinion above everything else. This word "honor" has served as a basis for many long and brilliant argumentations, without contributing a single fixed and stable idea.

Honor is one of those complex ideas which are an aggregate not only of simple ones but of ideas equally complex which in the various aspects they present to the mind now admit and now exclude some of the diverse elements that compose them, retaining only a few of their common ideas, just as many complex algebraic quantities admit one common divisor. To find this common divisor of the various ideas that men form of honor, it is necessary to glance back rapidly to the formation of societies.

In extreme political liberty and in extreme subjection, the laws of honor disappear or become altogether confounded with the others; for, in the first case, the despotism of the laws renders the quest for the esteem of others useless; in the second, the despotism of men, nullifying civil existence, reduces everyone to a precarious and momentary personality. Honor is, therefore, one of the fundamental principles of those monarchies in which rule is a limited form of despotism; it is in them what revolutions are in despotic states—a momentary return to the state of nature, reminding the ruler of the original condition of equality.[1]

---

1 Montesquieu, *Spirit*, III, 8: "Honor is far from being the principle of despotic government: mankind being here all upon a level, no one person can prefer himself to another, and as on the other hand they are all slaves, they can give themselves not sort of preference."

§XXIX: Duels (4)

From this need for the esteem of others arose private duels, which originated precisely in the anarchy of the laws.

The best method of preventing this crime is to punish the aggressor, namely the one who has given occasion for the duel, and to acquit him who, without personal fault, has been obliged to defend what the existing laws do not assure him, that is, opinion.

§XXX: Thefts (5)

Thefts not involving violence should be punished by fine. Whoever seeks to enrich himself at the expense of others should be deprived of his own. But, since this is ordinarily the crime only of poverty and desperation, the crime of that unhappy portion of mankind to whom the right of property (a terrible and perhaps unnecessary right) has left but a bare existence, and since pecuniary punishments increase the number of criminals beyond that of the crimes, and since they deprive innocent persons of bread while taking it from rascals, the most suitable punishment will be that kind of servitude which alone can be called just—the temporary subjection of the labours and person of the criminal to the community, as repayment, through total personal dependence, for the unjust despotism usurped against the social contract.

§XXXI: Smuggling (6)

Smuggling is a real crime that injures both the sovereign and the nation, but its punishment should not involve infamy for it is itself not infamous in public opinion.

This crime arises from the law itself, for the higher the customs duty, the greater the advantage; thus the temptation and facility of smuggling increases with the boundaries to be guarded and with the reduced bulk of the prohibited merchandise. Seizure of both the prescribed goods whatever accompanies it is a very just punishment. But it would be more efficacious if the custom duty were less, for men take risks only in proportion to the advantage to be derived from success in their undertaking.

§XXXII: Debtors (7)

The good faith of contracts, the security of commerce, oblige the legislator to secure for creditors the persons of bankrupt debtors. But I think it is important to distinguish between the fraudulent and the innocent bankrupt: the first should be assigned the same punishment that counterfeiters of money receive, for to counterfeit a piece of coined metal, which is a pledge of the obligations of citizens, is not a greater crime than to counterfeit the obligations themselves. But the innocent bankrupt, who, after a rigorous examination, has demonstrated before his judge that either the malice or the misfortune of others, or events which human prudence cannot avoid, have stripped him of his possessions—

upon what barbarous pretense is he thrown into prison, deprived of the sole sad good that yet remains to him, that of mere liberty, to experience the agonies of the guilty, and, perhaps, with the desperation of violated honesty, to repent of the very innocence that permitted him to live peacefully under the tutelage of those laws which it was not in his power not to offend?—laws dictated by the powerful out of greed and suffered by the weak for the sake of that hope glittering now and then in the human heart, which makes us believe that unlucky accidents are reserved for others and only advantageous ones for us? Men, left to the sway of their most obvious feelings, love cruel laws, even though, being subject to the same themselves, it is to their own interest that they should be mild, since the fear of being injured is greater than the desire to injure.

The distinction between grave and light should be fixed by the blind and impartial laws and not by the dangerous and arbitrary prudence of judges. Fixing of limits is as necessary in politics as in mathematics, not less in measuring size.[2]

§XXXIII: Public Tranquility (8)

The night illuminated at public expense, guards stationed in the various quarters of the city, the simple and moral discourses of religion confined to the silence and to the sacred quiet of temples protected by public authority, harangues in support of private and public interests delivered in the assemblies of the nation, in the parliaments, or where the majesty of the sovereign resides—all are efficacious means for preventing any dangerous fermentation of popular passions. Together they form a principal branch of magisterial vigilance which the French call "police"; but if this magistracy should operate by means of arbitrary laws, not established by a code currently in the hands of all citizens, the door is open to tyranny which always surrounds the confines of political liberty. I find no exception to this general axiom, that every citizen should know when he is guilty of crime and when he is innocent. If censors and, in general, arbitrary magistrates are necessary in any government, the reason lies in the weakness in its constitution and not in the nature of well-ordered government. Uncertainty regarding their lot has sacrificed more victims to secret tyranny than have ever suffered from public and solemn cruelty. It inspires revulsion more than it vilifies. The true tyrant always begins by ruling over opinion, thus forestalling courage which can only shine forth in the clear light of truth, in the heat of passions, or in ignorance of danger.

---

2   Commerce and private property are not an end of the social contract but they may be a means for attaining such an end. To expose all the members of society to evils which so many circumstances are apt to produce would be a subordinating of ends to means – a paralogism of all the sciences and especially of the political, into which I fell in the preceding editions, where I said that the innocent bankrupt should be kept in custody as a pledge of his debts or employed as a slave to work for his creditors. I am ashamed of having so written. I have been accused of impiety, and should not have been. I offended the rights of humanity, and no one has reproached me for it!

§XXXIV: Political Indolence (9)

By political indolence I mean the kind which contributes nothing to society either by its work or its wealth, which acquires without ever losing, which the vulgar regard with stupid adoration and the wise with disdainful compassion for the beings who are its victims, which, lacking the incitement to active life that is necessary to protect or to increase its commodities, leaves to the passions of opinion, strong as they are, all their energy. This kind of indolence has been confused by austere moralists with the indolence of riches accumulated by industry; yet it is not the austere and limited virtue of a few censors but the laws that should define what sort of indolence is to be punished. He is not in the political sense indolent who enjoys the fruits of the vices or virtues of his own ancestors, providing, in exchange for immediate pleasures, bread and existence for industrious poverty, who carries on in peace the tacit war of indolence with opulence, instead of the uncertain and bloody one with force. Such indolence is necessary and useful to the degree that society expands and its administration contracts.

§XXXV: Suicide and Expatriation (10)

What must we think of a government that has no means other than fear for keeping men in the country to which they have been naturally attached since the earliest impressions of infancy? The surest way to keep citizens in their country is to increase the relative well-being of each of them. Just as every effort ought to be made to turn the balance of trade in our favor, so it is in the greatest interest of the sovereign and of the nation that the sum of happiness, compared with that of surrounding nations, be greater than elsewhere. The pleasures of luxury are not the principal element of this happiness, though they are a necessary remedy for the inequality that increases with a nation's progress, and are indispensable for preventing the concentration of riches in the hands of a single person.

It is demonstrated that the law which imprisons subjects in their country is useless and unjust. Punishment for suicide, then, must be equally so; therefore, although it is a fault that God may punish because he alone can punish after death, it is not a crime in man's eyes, for man's punishment, instead of falling on the criminal himself, falls on his family. To the objection that consideration of such a punishment might, nevertheless, keep a determined man from actually killing himself, my reply is that anyone who calmly renounces the advantage of life, who so hates existence here as to prefer an eternity of unhappiness, is not in the least likely to be moved by the less efficacious and more distant consideration of children and relatives.

§XXXVI: Crimes of Difficult Proof (11)

I do not pretend to diminish the just horror which these crimes merit, but having indicated their origins, I believe I can, with justice, derive a general conclusion—namely, that one cannot call any punishment of a crime just in the precise sense (that is to say, necessary) so long as the law has not made use of the best means available, in the given circumstances of a nation, to prevent it.

§XXXVII: A Particular Kind of Crime (12)

All of this should be taken as evidently proved and in conformity with the true interests of humanity, so long as it is actually practiced by someone with acknowledged authority. I speak only of the crimes that emanate from human nature and from the social contract, and not of sins, of which even the temporal punishments should be regulated according to principles other than those of a limited philosophy.

§XXXVIII: False Ideas of Utility

One source of errors and injustices are the false ideas of utility formed by legislators. False is the idea of utility that considers particular inconveniences before the general inconvenience, that commands feelings instead of exciting them, that says to logic: serve!

§XXXIX: The Spirit of the Family

The more society grows, the smaller part of the whole does each member become, and the republican sentiment diminishes proportionately if the laws neglect to reinforce it. Societies have, like human bodies, their circumscribed limits, increasing beyond which the economy is necessarily disturbed. It would seem that the size of a state ought to vary inversely with the sensibility of its constituency; otherwise, with both of them increasing, good laws would be obstructed in preventing crimes by the good they have themselves produced. A republic grown too vast can escape despotism only by subdividing and then reuniting itself as a number of federate little republics. But how is this to be realized? By a despotic dictator with the courage of Sulla and as much genius for building up as he had for destroying. Such a man, if he be ambitious, has the glory of all the ages awaiting him; if he is a philosopher, the blessings of his fellow citizens will console him for the loss of authority, even supposing him not to have become indifferent to their gratitude. To the extent that our patriotic feelings weaken, our feelings for things immediately around us grow stronger; under the most extreme despotism, therefore, friendships are more lasting, and domestic virtues, always of a low order, are the most common, or, rather, the only ones. It should now be evident to everyone how very limited the views of most legislators have been.

§XL: The Public Treasury

The judge has the power to decide what inquiries suffice for imprisonment; in order that a person may prove himself innocent he must first be declared guilty. This is what is called an *offensive prosecution*—the typical form of criminal procedure in almost every part of enlightened Europe in the eighteenth century. The true prosecution, the *informative*, that is, the impartial inquiry into the fact, which reason commands, which the military law use, which even Asiatic despotism allows in non-violent and unimportant cases, is rarely used in European tribunals. What a complicated labyrinth of strange absurdities which a happier posterity will, no doubt, find incredible! Only the philosophers of that time will be able to find, by searching in the nature of man, any verification that such a system was ever possible.

§XLI: How to Prevent Crimes

It is better to prevent crimes than to punish them. This is the ultimate end of every good legislation, which, to use the general terms for assessing the good and evils of life, is the art of leading men to the greatest possible happiness or to the least possible unhappiness.

But heretofore, the means employed have been false and contrary to the end proposed. It is impossible to reduce the turbulent activity of mankind to a geometric order, without any irregularity and confusion. As the constant and very simple laws of nature do not impede the planets from disturbing one another in their movements, so in the infinite and very contrary attractions of pleasure and pain, disturbances and disorder cannot be impeded by human laws. And yet this is the chimera of narrow-minded men when they have power in their grasp. To prohibit a multitude of indifferent acts is not to prevent crimes that might arise from them, but is rather to create new ones; it is to define by whim the ideas of virtue and vice which are preached to us as eternal and immutable. To what we should be reduced if everything were forbidden to us that might induce us to crime! It would be necessary to deprive man of the use of his senses. For one motive that drives men to commit a real crime there are a thousand that drive them to commit those indifferent acts which are called crimes by bad laws; and if the probability of crimes is proportionate to the number of motives, to enlarge the sphere of crimes is to increase the probability of their being committed. The majority of the laws are nothing but privileges, that is, a tribute paid by all to the convenience of some few.

Do you want to prevent crimes? See to it that the laws are clear and simple and that the entire force of a nation is united in their defense, and that no part of it is employed to destroy them. See to it that men fear the laws and fear nothing else. For fear of the laws is salutary, but fatal and fertile for crimes is one man's fear of another. Enslaved men are more voluptuous, more depraved, more cruel than free men. These study the sciences, give thought to the interests of their country, contemplate grand objects and imitate them, while enslaved men, content with the present moment, seek in the excitement of debauchery a distraction from the emptiness of the condition in which they find themselves.

Do you want to prevent crimes? See to it that enlightenment accompanies liberty. Knowledge breeds evils in inverse ratio to its diffusion, and benefits in direct ratio. A daring impostor, who is never a common man, is received with adorations by an ignorant people, and with hisses by an enlightened one. Knowledge, by facilitating comparisons and by multiplying points of view, brings on a mutual modification of conflicting feelings, especially when it appears that others hold the same views and face the same difficulties. In the face of enlightenment widely diffused throughout the nation, the calumnies of ignorance are silenced and authority trembles if it be not armed with reason. The vigorous force of laws, meanwhile, remains immovable, for no enlightened person can fail to approve of the clear and useful public compacts of mutual security when he compares the inconsiderable portion of useless liberty he himself has sacrificed with the sum total of liberties sacrificed by other men, which, except for the laws, might have been turned against him. Any person of sensibility, glancing over a code of well-made laws and observing that he has lost only a baneful liberty to injure others, will feel constrained to bless the throne and its occupant.

Another way of preventing crimes is to direct the interest of the magistracy as a whole to observance rather than corruption of the laws. The greater the number of magistrates, the less dangerous is the abuse of legal power; venality is more difficult among men who observe one another, and their interest in increasing their personal authority diminishes as the portion that would fall to each is less, especially in comparison with the danger involved in the undertaking. If the sovereign, with his apparatus and pomp, with the severity of his edicts, with the permission he grants for unjust as well as just claims to be advanced by anyone who thinks himself oppressed, accustoms his subjects to fear magistrates more than the laws, [the magistrates] will profit more from this fear than personal and public security will grain from it.

Another way of preventing crimes is to reward virtue. Upon this subject I notice a general silence in the laws of all the nations of our day. If the prizes offered by the academies to discoverers of useful truths have increased our knowledge and have multiplied good books, why should not prizes distributed by the beneficent hand of the sovereign serve in a similar way to multiply virtuous actions? The coin of honor is always inexhaustible and fruitful in the hands of the wise distributor.

The surest but most difficult way of preventing crimes is by perfecting education.

§XLII: Conclusion

From what has thus far been demonstrated, one may deduce a general theorem of considerable utility, tough hardly conformable with custom, the usual legislator of nations; it is this: In order for punishment not to be, in every instance, an act of violence of one or of many against a private citizen, it must be essentially public, prompt, necessary, the least possible in the given circumstances, proportionate to the crimes, dictated by the laws.[3]

---

3   National Assembly of France, "Declaration of the Rights of Man and of the Citizens," Passed on August 1789: "The law ought to impose no other penalties but such as are absolutely and evidently necessary; and no one ought to be punished, but in virtue of a law promulgated before the offense, and legally applied."

Wilhelm von Humboldt (1767-1835)

Artist: Black and white photograph after lithography (presented by: Franz Krüger del. Manufactured by lithographic company, Berlin)., Hermann Von Helmholtz Center for Cultural Technology

Wilhelm von Humboldt was born on June 23, 1767 to a German middle class family in Potsdam. His early education consisted of carefully selected tutors recruited from Berlin's enlightenment scene. He went on to study for one semester at the Prussian University at Frankurt-on-Oder, but then transferred to the University of Göttingen in 1788. There he studied classical philology, jurisprudence, natural science, and the philosophy of Immanuel Kant. Humboldt entered the Prussian civil service in Berlin, and was appointed in 1790 the position of councilor (legislator) but left a year later.

In 1792, he succeeded in publishing a series of articles, some of which appeared in Friedrich Schiller's journal, *Neue Thalia*. Two of these articles, "Ideas concerning constitutions occasioned by the new French Constitution," and "What Should be the Limits of the Government's Concern for the Well Being of its Citizens?" formed what would later become a book length manuscript. The controversial quality of the book, however, meant that it was only published posthumously in 1851, under the title *The Spheres and Duties of Government*, now often referred to as *On the Limits of State Action*. Upon its eventual publication, Humboldt's work, which argued against positive freedom and for negative freedom, came under considerable critical attack from both the traditional right as well as an emerging left. John Stuart Mill, however, used a quotation from the text as the motto for his own work, *On Liberty*.

From 1794 to 1797, Humboldt lived in Jena, serving as a philosophical advisor and critical collaborator to Schiller and Johann Wolfgang von Goethe, while simultaneously studying comparative anatomy at the University. In 1808, Humboldt accepted the position of head of the section of ecclesiastical affairs and education in the ministry of the Interior. While serving this position, Humboldt achieved a radical transformation of the Prussian educational system, instituting major reforms based on the ideal of free and universal education to all citizens. Two years later, Humboldt founded the University of Berlin, now known as the Humboldt University, which is considered an early model of the modern Western university. Humboldt was later sent to Vienna as an ambassador, and in 1819 called back to Berlin to aid in drafting the new Prussian constitution. Humboldt's liberal values clashed with the repressive measures of King Friedrich Wilhelm III, however, and he was dismissed of all duties on New Year's eve of 1819. He spent the rest of his life retired in his family estate in Tegel, concentrating on scholarly pursuits. His works would not only encompass political philosophy, but also contribute greatly to comparative linguistics and the philosophy of language. He died in Tegel on April 8, 1835.

Works Referenced:
Cowan, Marianne. *Humanist Without Portfolio: An Anthology of the Writings of Wilhelm Von Humboldt.* Wayne State University Press: Detroit, 1963.
Sweet, Paul R. *Wilhelm von Humboldt: A Biography.* 2 Vols. Ohio State University Press: Columbus, 1980.

Selections from: *The Limits of State Action* **(Indianapolis: Liberty Fund, reprint 1993) based on:** *The Sphere and Duties of Government.* **Joseph Coulthard (trans.) (London: John Chapman, 1854)., orig. 1792.**

Chapter II
Of The Individual Man, And The Highest Ends Of His Existence
The true end of Man, or that which is prescribed by the eternal and immutable dictates of reason, and not suggested by vague and transient desires, is the highest and most harmonious development of his powers to a complete and consistent whole. Freedom is the grand and indispensable condition which the possibility of such a development presupposes; but there is besides another essential,— intimately connected with freedom, it is true,—a variety of situations. Even the most free and self-reliant of men is thwarted and hindered in his development by uniformity of position. But as it is evident, on the one hand, that such a diversity is a constant result of freedom, and on the other, that there is a species of oppression which, without imposing restrictions on man himself, gives a peculiar impress of its own to surrounding circumstances; these two conditions, of freedom and variety of situation, may be regarded, in a certain sense, as one and the same. Still, it may contribute to perspicuity to point out the distinction between them.

Every human being, then, can act with but one force at the same time: or rather, our whole nature disposes us at any given time to some single form of spontaneous activity. It would therefore seem to follow from this, that man is inevitably destined to a partial cultivation, since he only enfeebles his energies by directing them to a multiplicity of objects. But we see the fallacy of such a conclusion when we reflect, that man has it in his power to avoid this one-sideness, by striving to unite the separate faculties of his nature, often singly exercised; by bringing into spontaneous co-operation, at each period of his life, the gleams of activity about to expire, and those which the future alone will kindle into living effulgence; and endeavouring to increase and diversify the powers with which he works, by harmoniously combining them, instead of looking for a mere variety of objects for their separate exercise. That which is effected, in the case of the individual, by the union of the past and future with the present, is produced in society by the mutual co-operation of its different single members; for, in all the stages of his existence, each individual can exhibit but one of those perfections only, which represent the possible features of human character. It is through such social union, therefore, as is based on the internal wants and capacities of its members, that each is enabled to participate in the rich collective resources of all the others. The experience of all, even the rudest, nations, furnishes us an example of a union thus formative of individual character, in the union of the sexes. And, although in this case the expression, as well of the difference as of the longing for union, appears more marked and striking, it is still no less active in other kinds of association where there is actually no difference of sex; it is only more difficult to discover in these, and may perhaps be more powerful for that very reason. If we were to follow out this idea, it might perhaps conduct us to a clearer insight into the phenomena of those unions so much in vogue among the ancients, and more especially the Greeks, among whom we find them countenanced even by the legislators themselves: I mean those so frequently, but unworthily, classed under the general appellation of ordinary love, and sometimes, but always erroneously, designated as mere friendship. The efficiency of all such unions as instruments of cultivation, wholly depends on the degree in which the component members can succeed in combining their personal independence with the intimacy of the common bond; for whilst, without this intimacy, one individual cannot sufficiently possess himself, as it were, of the nature of the others, independence is no less essential, in order that the perceived be assimilated into the being of the perceiver. Now, it is clear (to apply these conclusions to the respective conditions for culture,—freedom, and a variety of situations), that, on the one hand, individual energy is essential to the perceived and perceiver, into which social unions may be resolved; and, on the other, a difference between them, neither so great as to prevent the one from comprehending the other, nor so inconsiderable as to exclude admiration for that which the other possesses, and the desire of assimilating it into the perceiver's character.

This individual vigour, then, and manifold diversity, combine themselves in originality; and hence, that on which the consummate grandeur of our nature ultimately depends,—that towards which every human being must ceaselessly direct his efforts, and on which especially those who design to influence their fellow men must ever keep their eyes, is the Individuality of Power and Development. Just as this individuality springs naturally from the perfect freedom of action, and the greatest diversity in the agents, it tends immediately to produce them in turn. Even inanimate nature, which, proceeding in accordance with unchangeable laws, advances by regular grades of progression, appears more individual to the man who has been developed in his individuality. He transports himself, as it were, into the very centre of nature; and it is true, in the highest sense, that each still perceives the beauty and rich abundance of the outer world, in the exact measure in which he is conscious of their existence in his own soul. How much sweeter and closer must this correspondence become between effect and cause,—this reaction between internal feeling and outward perception,—when man is not only passively open to external sensations and impressions, but is himself also an agent!

If we attempt to confirm these principles by a closer application of them to the nature of the individual man, we find that everything which enters into the latter, reduces itself to the two elements of Form and Substance. The purest form, beneath the most delicate veil, we call Idea; the crudest substance, with the most imperfect form, we call sensuous Perception. Form springs from the union of substance. The richer and more various the substance that is united, the more sublime is the resulting form. A child of the gods is the offspring only of immortal parents: and as the blossom swells and ripens into fruit, and from the tiny germ imbedded in its soft pulp the new stalk shoots forth, laden with newly-clustering buds; so does the Form become in turn the substance of a still more exquisite Form. The intensity of power, moreover, increases in proportion to the greater variety and delicacy of the substance; since the internal cohesion increases with these. The substance seems as if blended in the form, and the form merged in the substance. Or, to speak without metaphor, the richer a man's feelings become in ideas, and his ideas in feelings, the more lofty and transcendent his sublimity; for upon this constant intermingling of form and substance, or of diversity with the individual unity, depends the perfect interfusion of the two natures which co-exist in man, and upon this, his greatness. But the force of the generation depends upon the energy of the generating forces. The consummating point of human existence is the flowering of these forces.[1] In the vegetable world, the simple and less graceful form of the fruit seems to prefigure the more perfect bloom and symmetry of the flower which it precedes, and which it is destined gradually to unfold. Everything conspires to the beautiful consummation of the blossom. That which first shoots forth from the little germ is not nearly so exquisite and fascinating. The full thick trunk, the broad leaves rapidly detaching themselves from each other, seem to require some fuller and fairer development; as the eye glances up the ascending stem, it marks the spiring grades of this development; more tender leaflets seem longing to unite themselves, and draw closer and closer together, until the central calyx of the crowning flower seems to give the sweet satisfaction to this growing desire.[2] But destiny has not blessed the tribe of plants in this the law and process of their growth. The flower fades and dies, and the germ of the fruit reproduces the stem, as rude and unfinished as the former, to ascend slowly through the same stages of development as before. But when, in man, the blossom fades away, it is only to give place to another still more exquisitely beautiful; and the charm of the last and loveliest is only hidden from our view in the endlessly receding vistas of an inscrutable eternity. Now, whatever man receives externally, is only as the grain of seed. It is his own active energy alone that can convert the germ of the fairest growth, into a full and precious blessing for himself. It leads to beneficial issues only when it is full of vital power and essentially individual. The highest ideal, therefore, of the co-existence of human beings, seems to me to consist in a union in which each strives to develope himself from his own inmost nature, and for his own sake. The requirements of our physical and moral being would, doubtless, bring men together into communities; and even as the conflicts of warfare are more honourable than the fights of the arena, and the struggles of exasperated citizens

---

1   Blüthe, Reife. Neues deutsches Museum, 1791. Junius 22, 3.
2   Goethe, über die Metamorphose der Pflanzen.

more glorious than the hired and unsympathizing efforts of mere mercenaries, so would the exerted powers of such spontaneous agents succeed in eliciting the highest and noblest energies.

And is it not exactly this which so unspeakably captivates us in contemplating the life of Greece and Rome, and which in general captivates any age whatever in the contemplation of a remoter one? Is it not that these men had harder struggles to endure with the ruthless force of destiny, and harder struggles with their fellow men? that greater and more original energy and individuality constantly encountered each other, and gave rise in the encounter to ever new and beautiful forms? Every later epoch,—and in what a rapid course of declension must this now proceed!—is necessarily inferior in variety to that which it succeeded: in variety of nature,—the boundless forests have been cleared, the vast morasses dried up; in variety of human life, by the ever-increasing intercommunication and union of all human establishments.[3] It is in this we find one of the chief causes which render the idea of the new, the uncommon, the marvellous, so much more rare,—which make affright or astonishment almost a disgrace,—and not only render the discovery of fresh and, till now, unknown expedients, far less necessary, but also all sudden, unpremeditated and urgent decisions. For, partly, the pressure of outward circumstances is less violent, while man is provided with more ample means for opposing them; partly, this resistance is no longer possible with the simple forces which nature bestows on all alike, fit for immediate application; and, in fine, partly a higher and more extended knowledge renders inventions less necessary, and the very increase of learning serves to blunt the edge of discovery. It is, on the other hand, undeniable that, whereas physical variety has so vastly declined, it has been succeeded by an infinitely richer and more satisfying intellectual and moral variety, and that our superior refinement can recognize more delicate differences and gradations, and our disciplined and susceptible character, if not so firmly consolidated as that of the ancients, can transfer them into the practical conduct of life,—differences and gradations which might have wholly escaped the notice of the sages of antiquity, or at least would have been discernible by them alone. To the human family at large, the same has happened as to the individual: the ruder features have faded away, the finer only have remained. And in view of this sacrifice of energy from generation to generation, we might regard it as a blessed dispensation if the whole human species were as one man; or the living force of one age could be transmitted to the succeeding one, along with its books and inventions. But this is far from being the case. It is true that our refinement possesses a peculiar force of its own, perhaps even surpassing the former in strength, just in proportion to the measure of its refinement; but it is a question whether the prior development, through the

---

3   Rousseau has also noticed this in his 'Emile.'

more robust and vigorous stages, must not always be the antecedent transition. Still, it is certain that the sensuous element in our nature, as it is the earliest germ, is also the most vivid expression of the spiritual.

Whilst this is not the place, however, to enter on the discussion of this point, we are justified in concluding, from the other considerations we have urged, that we must at least preserve, with the most eager solicitude, all the force and individuality we may yet possess, and cherish aught that can tend in any way to promote them.

I therefore deduce, as the natural inference from what has been argued, that reason cannot desire for man any other condition than that in which each individual not only enjoys the most absolute freedom of developing himself by his own energies, in his perfect individuality, but in which external nature even is left unfashioned by any human agency, but only receives the impress given to it by each individual of himself and his own free will, according to the measure of his wants and instincts, and restricted only by the limits of his powers and his rights.

From this principle it seems to me, that Reason must never yield aught save what is absolutely required to preserve it. It must therefore be the basis of every political system, and must especially constitute the starting-point of the inquiry which at present claims our attention.

Chapter III
On The Solicitude Of The State For The Position Welfare Of The Citizen

Keeping in view the conclusions arrived at in the last chapter, we might embody in a general formula our idea of State agency when restricted to its just limits, and define its objects as all that a government could accomplish for the common weal, without departing from the principle just established; while, from this position, we could proceed to derive the still stricter limitation, that any State interference in private affairs, not directly implying violence done to individual rights, should be absolutely condemned. It will be necessary, however, to examine in succession the different departments of a State's usual or possible activity, before we can circumscribe its sphere more positively, and arrive at a full solution of the question proposed.

A State, then, has one of two ends in view; it designs either to promote happiness, or simply to prevent evil; and in this latter case, the evil which arises from natural causes, or that which springs from man's disregard for his neighbour's rights. If it restricts its solicitude to the second of these objects, it aims merely at security; and I would here oppose this term security to every other possible end of State agency, and comprise these last under the general head of Positive Welfare. Further, the various means adopted by a State, as subservient to its purposes, affect in very different measure the extension of its activity. It may endeavour, for instance, to secure the accomplishment of these immediately, either with the aid of coercion or by the inducements of example and exhortation; or it may combine all these sources of influence in the attempt to shape the citizen's outward life in accordance with its ends, and forestal actions contrary to its intention; or, lastly, it may try to exercise a sway over his thoughts and feelings, so as to bring his *inclinations*, even, into conformity with its wishes. It will be evident, that it is single actions only that come under political supervision in the first of these cases; that this is extended in the second to the general conduct of life; and that, in the last instance we have supposed, it is the very character of the citizen, his views, and modes of thought, which are brought under the influence of State control. The actual working of this restrictive agency, moreover, is clearly least considerable in the first of these cases, more so in the second, and is most effective and apparent in the last; either because, in this, it reaches the most copious sources of action, or that the very possibility of such an influence presupposes a greater multiplicity of institutions. But however seemingly different the departments of political action to which they respectively belong, we shall scarcely find any one institution which is not more or less intimately interwoven, in its objects or its consequences, with several of these. We have but to notice, by way of illustration, the close interdependence that exists between the promotion of welfare and the maintenance of security; and further, to remember that when any influence affecting single actions only, engenders a habit through the force of repetition, it comes ultimately to modify the character itself. Hence, in view of this interdependence of political institutions, it becomes very difficult to discover a systematic division of the whole subject before us, sufficiently correspondent to the course of our present inquiry. But, in any case, it will be most immediately conducive to our design, to examine in the outset whether the State should extend its solicitude to the positive welfare of the nation, or content itself with provisions for its security; and, confining our view of institutions to what is strictly essential either in their objects or consequences, to ascertain next, as regards both of these aims, the nature of the means that may be safely left open to the State for accomplishing them.

I am speaking here, then, of the entire efforts of the State to elevate the positive welfare of the nation; of its solicitude for the population of the country, and the subsistence of its inhabitants, whether manifested directly in such institutions as poor-laws, or indirectly, in the encouragement of agriculture, industry, and commerce; of all regulations relative to finance and currency, imports and exports, etc. (in so far as these have this positive welfare in view); finally, of all measures employed to remedy or prevent natural devastations, and, in short, of every political institution designed to preserve or augment the physical welfare of the nation. For the moral welfare is not in general regarded so much for its own sake, as with reference to its bearing on security, and will therefore be more appropriately introduced in the subsequent course of the inquiry.

Now all such institutions, I maintain, are positively hurtful in their consequences, and wholly irreconcilable with a true system of polity; a system which, although conceivable only from the loftiest points of view, is yet in no way inconsistent with the limits and capacities of human nature.

1. A spirit of governing predominates in every institution of this kind; and however wise and salutary such a spirit may be, it invariably superinduces national uniformity, and a constrained and unnatural manner of action. Instead of men grouping themselves into communities in order to discipline and develope their powers, even though, to secure these benefits, they should forego a portion of their exclusive possessions and enjoyments; it is only by the actual *sacrifice* of those powers that they can purchase in this case the privileges resulting from association. The very variety arising from the union of numbers of individuals is the highest good which social life can confer, and this variety is undoubtedly merged into uniformity in proportion to the measure of State interference. Under such a system, it is not so much the individual members of a nation living united in the bonds of a civil compact; but isolated subjects living in a relation to the State, or rather to the spirit which prevails in its government,—a relation in which the undue preponderance of the State element tends already to fetter the free play of individual energies. Like causes produce like effects; and hence, in proportion as State co-operation increases in extent and efficiency, a common resemblance diffuses itself, not only through all the agents to which it is applied, but through all the results of their activity. And this is the very design which States have in view. They desire nothing so much as comfort, ease, tranquillity; and these are most readily secured when there is little or no discordancy among that which is individual. But that to which man's energies are ever urging him, and towards which he must ceaselessly direct his efforts, is the very reverse of this inertness and uniformity,—it is variety and activity. It is to these alone we are to look for the free development of character in all its vigorous and multiform diversity of phase and manifestation; and, to appeal to the inner motive of the individual man, there can be no one, surely, so far sunk and degraded, as to prefer, for himself personally, comfort and enjoyment to greatness; and he who draws conclusions for such a preference in the case of others, may justly be suspected of misconceiving the essential nobleness of human nature, and of agreeing to transform his fellow-creatures into mere machines.

2. Further, a second hurtful consequence ascribable to such a policy is, that these positive *institutions* tend to weaken the power and resources of the nation. For as the substance is annihilated by the form which is externally imposed upon it, so does it gain greater richness and beauty from that which is *internally* superinduced by its own spontaneous action; and in the case under consideration it is the form which annihilates the substance,—that which is of itself non-existent suppressing and destroying that which really is existent. The grand characteristic of human nature is *organization*. Whatever is to ripen in its soil and expand into a fair maturity, must first have existed therein as the little germ.

Every manifestation of power presupposes the existence of enthusiasm; and but few things sufficiently cherish enthusiasm as to represent its object as a present or future possession. Now man never regards that which he *possesses* as so much his own, as that which he does; and the labourer who tends a garden is perhaps in a truer sense its owner, than the listless voluptuary who enjoys its fruits. It may be, such reasoning appears too general to admit of any practical application. Perhaps it seems even as though the extension of so many branches of science, which we owe chiefly to political institutions (for the State only can attempt experiments on a scale sufficiently vast), contributed to raise the power of intellect, and collaterally, our culture and character in general. But the intellectual faculties themselves are not necessarily ennobled by every acquisition to our knowledge; and though it were granted that these means virtually effected such a result, it does not so much apply to the entire nation, as to that particular portion of it which is connected with the government. The cultivation of the understanding, as of any other of man's faculties, is in general effected by his own activity, his own ingenuity, or his own methods of availing himself of the facilities discovered by others. Now, State measures always imply more or less positive control; and even where they are not chargeable with actual coercion, they accustom men to look for instruction, guidance, and assistance from without, rather than to rely upon their own expedients. The only method of instruction, perhaps, of which the State can avail itself, consists in its declaring the best course to be pursued as though it were the result of its investigations, and in enjoining this in some way on the citizen. But, however it may accomplish this,—whether directly or indirectly by law, or by means of its authority, rewards, and other encouragements attractive to the citizen, or, lastly, by merely recommending its propositions to his attention by arguments,—it will always deviate very far from the best system of instruction. For this unquestionably consists in proposing, as it were, all possible solutions of the problem in question, so that the citizen may select, according to his own judgment, the course which seems to him to be the most appropriate; or, still better, so as to enable him to discover the happiest solution for himself, from a careful representation of all the contingent obstacles. It will be evident, in the case of adult citizens, that the State can only adopt this negative system of instruction by extending freedom, which allows all obstacles to arise, while it developes the skill, and multiplies the opportunities necessary to encounter them; but, by following out a really national system of education, it can be brought to operate positively on the early training and culture of the young. We will take occasion, hereafter, to enter on a close examination of the objection which might be advanced here in favour of these institutions; viz. that in the execution of such important designs as those to which we refer, it is of far greater moment that the thing be done, than that the person who performs it should be thoroughly instructed in his task; that the land be well tilled, than that the husbandman be just the most skilful agriculturist.

But to continue: the evil results of a too extended solicitude on the part of the State, are still more strikingly manifested in the suppression of all active energy, and the necessary deterioration of the moral character. We scarcely need to substantiate this position by rigorous deductions. The man who frequently submits the conduct of his actions to foreign guidance and control, becomes gradually disposed to a willing sacrifice of the little spontaneity that remains to him. He fancies himself released from an anxiety which he sees transferred to other hands, and seems to himself to do enough when he looks for their leading, and follows the course to which it directs him. Thus, his notions of right and wrong, of praise and blame, become confounded. The idea of the first inspires him no longer; and the painful consciousness of the last assails him less frequently and violently, since he can more easily ascribe his shortcomings to his peculiar position, and leave them to the responsibility of those who have shaped it for him. If we add to this, that he may not, possibly, regard the designs of the State as perfectly pure in their objects or execution—should he find grounds to suspect that not his own advantage only, but along with it some other bye-scheme is intended, then, not only the force and energy, but the purity and excellence of his moral nature is brought to suffer. He now conceives himself not only irresponsible for the performance of any duty which the State has not expressly imposed upon him, but exonerated at the same time from every personal effort to ameliorate his own condition; nay, even shrinks from such an effort, as if it were likely to open out new opportunities, of which the State might not be slow to avail itself. And as for the laws actually enjoined, he labours, as much as possible, to escape their operation, considering every such evasion as a positive gain. If now we reflect that, as regards a large portion of the nation, its laws and political institutions have the effect of circumscribing the grounds of morality, it cannot but appear a melancholy spectacle to see at once the most sacred duties, and mere trivial and arbitrary enactments, proclaimed from the same authoritative source, and to witness the infraction of both visited with the same measure of punishment. Further, the injurious influence of such a positive policy is no less evident in its effects on the mutual bearing of the citizens, than in those manifestations of its pernicious working to which we have just referred. In proportion as each individual relies upon the helpful vigilance of the State, he learns to abandon to its responsibility the fate and wellbeing of his fellow-citizens. But the inevitable tendency of such abandonment is to deaden the living force of sympathy, and to render the natural impulse to mutual assistance inactive: or, at least, the reciprocal interchange of services and benefits will be most likely to flourish in its greatest activity and beauty, where the feeling is liveliest that such assistance is the only thing to rely upon; and experience teaches us that those classes of the community which suffer under oppression, and are, as it were, overlooked by the Government, are always cemented together by the closest ties. But wherever the citizen becomes insensible to the interests of his fellow-citizen, the husband will contract feelings of cold indifference to the wife, and the father of a family towards the members of his household.

If men were left wholly to themselves in their various undertakings, and were cut off from all external resources, save those which their own efforts obtained, they would still, whether through their own fault and inadvertence or not, fall frequently into embarrassment and misfortune. But the happiness for which man is plainly destined, is no other than that which his own energies enable him to secure; and the very nature of such a self-dependent position furnishes him means whereby to discipline his intellect and cultivate his character. Are there no instances of such evils, I ask, where State agency fetters individual spontaneity by a too special interference? There are many, doubtless; and the man whom it has habituated to lean on foreign strength for support, is thus given up in critical emergencies to a fate which is truly far more hopeless and deplorable. For, just as the very act of struggling against misfortune, and encountering it with vigorous efforts, tends to lighten the calamity; so do baffled hopes and delusive expectations aggravate and embitter its severity tenfold. In short, to view their agency in the most favourable light, States like those to which we refer too often resemble the physician, who only retards the death of his patient in nourishing his disease. Before there were physicians, only health and death were known.

3. Everything towards which man directs his attention, whether it is limited to the direct or indirect satisfaction of his merely physical wants, or to the accomplishment of external objects in general, presents itself in a closely interwoven relation with his internal sensations. Sometimes, moreover, there co-exists with this external purpose, some impulse proceeding more immediately from his inner being; and often, even, this last is the sole spring of his activity, the former being only implied in it, necessarily or incidentally. The more unity a man possesses, the more freely do these external manifestations on which he decides emanate from the inner springs of his being, and the more frequent and intimate is the cooperation of these two sources of motive, even when he has not freely selected these external objects. A man, therefore, whose character peculiarly interests us, although his life does not lose this charm in any circumstances or however engaged, only attains the most matured and graceful consummation of his activity, when his way of life is in harmonious keeping with his character.

In view of this consideration, it seems as if all peasants and craftsmen might be elevated into artists; that is, into men who love their labour for its own sake, improve it by their own plastic genius and inventive skill, and thereby cultivate their intellect, ennoble their character, and exalt and refine their enjoyments. And so humanity would be ennobled by the very things which now, though beautiful in themselves, so often go to degrade it. The more a man accustoms himself to dwell in the region of higher thoughts and sensations, and the more refined and vigorous his moral and intellectual powers become, the more he longs to confine himself to such external objects only as furnish ampler scope and material for his internal development; or, at least, to overcome all adverse conditions in the sphere allotted him, and transform them into more favourable phases.   It is impossible to estimate a man's advance towards the Good and the Beautiful, when his unremitting endeavours are directed to this one engrossing object, the development of his inner life; so that, superior to all other considerations, it may remain the same unfailing source, the ultimate goal of all his labours, and all that is corporeal and external may seem but as its instrument and veil.

How strikingly beautiful, to select an illustration, is the historical picture of the character fostered in a people by the undisturbed cultivation of the soil! The labour they bestow on the tillage of the land, and the bounteous harvest with which it repays their industry, bind them with sweet fetters to their fields and firesides.   Their participation in the rich blessings of toil, and the common enjoyment of the ample fruits it earns, entwine each family with bonds of love, from whose gentle influence even the steer, the partner of their fatigue, is not wholly excluded.   The seed which must be sown, the fruit which must be garnered—regularly returning, as they do, their yearly increase—instil a spirit of patience, trust, and frugality.   The fact of their receiving everything immediately from the hand of benignant Nature,—the ever-deepening consciousness that, although the hand of man must first scatter the seed, it is not from human agency that the rich repletion of the harvest is derived,—the constant dependence on favourable and unfavourable skies, awaken presentiments of the existence of beings of a higher order, now instinct with dire foreboding, and now full of the liveliest joy—in the rapid alternations of fear and hope—and lead the soul to prayer and grateful praise.   The visible image of the simplest sublimity, the most perfect order, and the gentlest beneficence, mould their lives into forms of simple grandeur and tenderness, and dispose their hearts to a cheerful submission to order and law.   Always accustomed to produce, never to destroy, agriculture is essentially peaceful, and, while far beyond the reach of wrong and revenge, is yet capable of the most dauntless courage when roused to resist the injustice of unprovoked attack, and repel the invaders of its calm and happy contentment.

But, still, it cannot be doubted that freedom is the indispensable condition, without which even the pursuits most happily congenial to the individual nature, can never succeed in producing such fair and salutary influences.   Whatever man is inclined to, without the free exercise of his own choice, or whatever only implies instruction and guidance, does not enter into his very being, but still remains alien to his true nature, and is, indeed, effected by him, not so much with human agency, as with the mere exactness of mechanical routine. The ancients, and more especially the Greeks, were accustomed to regard every occupation as hurtful and degrading which was immediately connected with the exercise of physical power, or the pursuit of external advantages, and not exclusively confined to the development of the inner man.   Hence, many of their philosophers who were most eminent for their philanthropy, approved of slavery; thereby adopting a barbarous and unjust expediency, and agreeing to sacrifice one part of mankind in order to secure to the other the highest force and beauty. But reason and experience combine to expose the error which lies at the root of such a fallacy. There is no pursuit whatever, nothing with which a man can concern himself, that may not give to human nature some worthy and determinate form, and furnish fair means for its ennoblement. The manner of its performance is the only thing to be considered; and we may here lay down the general rule, that a man's pursuits re-act beneficially on his culture, so long as these, and the energies allied with them, succeed in filling and satisfying the wants of his soul; while their influence is not only less salutary, but even pernicious, when he directs his attention more exclusively to the results to which they conduce, and regards the occupation itself merely as a necessary means. For it is the property of anything which charms us by its own intrinsic worth, to awaken love and esteem, while that which only as a means holds out hopes of ulterior advantage, merely interests us; and the motives of love and esteem tend as directly to ennoble human nature, as those of interest to lower and degrade it. Now, in the exercise of such a positive solicitude as that we are considering, the State can only contemplate results, and establish rules whose observance will most directly conduce to their accomplishment.

Never does this limited point of view conduct to such pernicious issues as in those cases where moral or intellectual ends are the object of human endeavour; or, at least, where some end is regarded for itself, and apart from the consequences which are only necessarily or incidentally implied in it. This becomes evident, for instance, in all scientific researches and religious opinions, in all kinds of human association, and in that union in particular which is the most natural, and, whether we regard the State or the individual, the most vitally important, namely, Matrimony.

Matrimony, or as it may perhaps be best defined, the union of persons of both sexes, based on the very difference of sex, may be regarded in as many different aspects as the conceptions taken of that difference, and as the inclinations of the heart, and the objects which they present to the reason, assume different forms; and such a union will manifest in every man his whole moral character, and especially the force and peculiarity of his powers of sensation. Whether a man is more disposed to the pursuit of external objects, or to the exercise of the inner faculties of his being; whether reason or feeling is the more active principle in his nature; whether he is led to embrace things eagerly, and quickly abandon them, or engages slowly but continues faithfully; whether he is capable of deeper intimacy, or only loosely attaches himself; whether he preserves, in the closest union, more or less self-dependence; and an infinite number of other considerations modify, in a thousand ways, his relations in married life. Whatever form they assume, however, the effects upon his life and happiness are unmistakable; and upon the success or failure of the attempt to find or form a reality in union with the internal harmony of his nature, depends the loftier consummation or the relaxation of his being. This influence manifests itself most forcibly in those men, so peculiarly interesting in their character and actions, who form their perceptions with the greatest ease and delicacy, and retain them most deeply and lastingly. Generally speaking, the female sex may be more justly reckoned in this class than the male; and it is for this reason that the female character is most intimately dependent on the nature of the family relations in a nation. Wholly exempt as she is from most outward-occupations, and almost surrounded with those only which leave the soul undisturbed—stronger in what she can be than in what she can do—more full of expression in her calm and quiet, than in her manifested sensations—more richly endowed with all means of immediate, indefinable expression, a more delicate frame, a more moving eye, a more winning voice—destined rather, in her relations with others, to expect and receive, than to advance and approach—naturally weaker in herself, and yet not on that account, but through loving admiration of strength and greatness in another, clinging more closely—ceaselessly striving in the union to receive in common with the united one, to form the received in herself, and reproduce it moulded into new forms of creation—inspired at the same time with the courage which the solicitude of love and the feeling of strength infuse into the soul—not defying resistance, but not succumbing in endurance—Woman is, strictly speaking, nearer to the ideal of human nature than man; and whilst it is true that she more rarely reaches it, it may only be that it is more difficult to ascend by the steep, immediate path, than to approach slowly by the winding one. Now, how much such a being—so delicately susceptible, yet so complete in herself, and with whom therefore nothing is without effect—an effect that communicates itself not to a part only, but to the whole of her nature,—how much woman must be disturbed by external mis-relations, can scarcely be estimated. Hence the infinite results to society which depend on the culture of the female character. If it is not somewhat fanciful to suppose that each human excellence represents and accumulates itself, as it were, in some one species of being, we might believe that the whole treasure of morality and order is collected and enshrined in the female character. As the poet profoundly says,

"*Man strives for freedom, woman still for order.*"[4]

While the former strives earnestly to remove the external barriers which oppose his development, woman's careful hand prescribes that inner restraint within whose limits alone the fulness of power can refine itself to perfect issues; and she defines the circle with more delicate precision, in that her every sense is more faithful to her simple behests, spares her that laborious subtilizing which so often tends to enmesh and obscure the truth, and enables her to see more clearly through the intricate confusion of human relations, and fathom at once the innermost springs of human being.

---

4   Nach Freiheit strebt der Mann, das Weib nach Sitte." — Goethe's Torquato Tasso, ii. 1.

If it were not superfluous, History would afford sufficient confirmation of the truth we would establish, and exhibit unmistakably the close and invariable connection that exists between national morality and respect for the female sex. The manifest inference we would derive, however, from these considerations on the institution of Matrimony is this: that the effects which it produces are as various as the characters of the persons concerned, and that, as a union so closely allied with the very nature of the respective individuals, it must be attended with the most hurtful consequences when the State attempts to regulate it by law, or through the force of its institutions to make it repose on anything save simple inclination. When we remember, moreover, that the State can only contemplate the final results in such regulations—as, for instance, Population, Early Training, etc.—we shall be still more ready to admit the justice of this conclusion. It may reasonably be argued that a solicitude for such objects conducts to the same results as the highest solicitude for the most beautiful development of the inner man. For, after careful observation, it has been found that the uninterrupted union of one man with one woman is most conducive to population; and it is likewise undeniable that no other union springs from true, natural, harmonious love. And further, it may be observed that such love leads to no other or different results than those very relations which law and custom tend to establish, such as the procreation of children, family training, community of living, participation in the common goods, the management of external affairs by the husband, and the care of domestic arrangements by the wife. But the radical error of such a policy appears to be, that the law commands, whereas such a relation cannot mould itself according to external arrangements, but depends wholly on inclination; and wherever coercion or guidance comes into collision with inclination, they divert it still further from the proper path. Wherefore it appears to me that the State should not only loosen the bonds in this instance, and leave ampler freedom to the citizen, but, if I may apply the principles above stated (now that I am not speaking of matrimony in general, but of one of the many injurious consequences arising from restrictive State institutions, which are in this one especially noticeable), that it should entirely withdraw its active solicitude from the institution of Matrimony, and both generally and in its particular modifications should rather leave it wholly to the free choice of the individuals, and the various contracts they may enter into with respect to it. I should not be deterred from the adoption of this principle by the fear that all family relations might be disturbed, or their manifestation in general impeded; for although such an apprehension might be justified by considerations of particular circumstances and localities, it could not be fairly entertained in an inquiry into the nature of Men and States in general. For experience frequently convinces us that just where law has imposed no fetters, morality most surely binds; the idea of external coercion is one entirely foreign to an institution which, like Matrimony, reposes only on inclination and an inward sense of duty; and the results of such coercive institutions do not at all correspond to the designs in which they originate.

4. *The solicitude of a State for the positive welfare of its citizens, must further be hurtful, in that it has to operate upon a promiscuous mass of individualities, and therefore does harm to these by measures which cannot meet individual cases.*

5. *It hinders the development of Individuality*[5] In the moral life of man, and generally in the practical conduct of his actions (in as far as they are guided by the same rules), he still endeavours to keep before his eyes the highest conception of the most individual development of himself and others, is always inspired with this design, and strictly subordinates all other considerations of interest to this pure and spiritual law that he has recognized. But all the phases of human nature in which it admits of culture, consist together in a wonderful relation and interdependence; and while their mutual coherency is more strikingly manifest (if not really more intimate) in the intellectual than in the physical world, it is infinitely more remarkable in the sphere of morality. Wherefore it follows that men are not to unite themselves together in order to forego any portion of their individuality, but only to lessen the exclusiveness of their isolation; it is not the object of such a union to transform one being into another, but to open out approaches between the single natures; whatever each himself possesses, he is to compare with that which he receives by communication with others, and, while introducing modifications in his own being by the comparison, not to allow its force and peculiarity to be suppressed in the process. For as truth is never found conflicting with truth in the domain of intellect, so too in the region of morality there is no opposition between things really worthy of human nature; and close and varied unions of individual characters are therefore necessary, in order to destroy what cannot co-exist in proximity, and does not, therefore, essentially conduce to greatness and beauty, while they cherish and foster that which continues to exist without opposition or disturbance, and render it fruitful in new and more exquisite issues. Wherefore it appears to me that the principle of the true art of social intercourse consists in a ceaseless endeavour to grasp the innermost individuality of another, to avail oneself of it, and, penetrated with the deepest respect for it as the individuality of another, to act upon it,—a kind of action, in which that same respect will not allow us other means for this purpose than to manifest oneself, and to institute a comparison, as it were, between the two natures, before the eyes of the other. This art has been hitherto singularly neglected, and although such neglect might borrow a plea, perhaps, from the circumstance that social intercourse should be a refreshing recreation, and not a toilsome duty, and that, unhappily enough, it is scarcely possible to discover in the common run of men an interesting phase of individuality, yet still it seems not too much to suppose that every one will have too deep a respect for himself to seek for recreation otherwise than in an agreeable alternation of

---

5   The reader is referred to the "Prefatory Remarks" for the explanation of this hiatus.

interesting employments, or still less to look for it in that which would leave precisely his noblest faculties inactive, and too much reverence for human nature, to pronounce any single individual utterly incapable of being turned to good account, or of being in some way modified by the influence of others. He, at least, whose especial business it is to exercise an influence over his fellow-men, must not relinquish such a belief; and hence, inasmuch as the State, in its positive solicitude for the external and physical well-being of the citizen (which are closely interwoven with his inner being), cannot avoid creating hindrances to the development of individuality, we derive another reason why such a solicitude should not be conceded to it, except in the case of the most absolute necessity.

These, then, may constitute the principal hurtful consequences which flow from a positive solicitude of the State for the welfare of the citizen; and although they may be more especially implied in certain of its particular manifestations, they yet appear to me to be generally inseparable from the adoption of such a policy. It was my design hitherto to confine myself to a view of the State's solicitude for physical welfare, and I have so far accorded with this intention as to proceed strictly from this point of view alone, carefully separating everything that referred exclusively to the moral well-being. But I took occasion at the outset to mention that the subject does not admit of any accurate division; and this may serve as my excuse, if much that naturally arises from the foregoing development of the argument, applies to the entire solicitude for positive welfare in general. I have hitherto proceeded on the supposition, however, that the State institutions referred to are already established, and I have therefore still to speak of certain difficulties which present themselves in the very framing of such institutions.

6. It is certain, then, that nothing would be more conducive to the successful issue of our present inquiry, than to weigh the advantages intended by such institutions against the disadvantages necessarily inherent in their consequences, and especially against the limitations of freedom which these consequences imply. But it is always a matter of extreme difficulty to effect such a balancing of results, and perhaps wholly impossible to secure its perfect accuracy and completeness. For every restrictive institution comes into collision with the free and natural development of power, and gives rise to an infinite multiplicity of new relations; and even if we suppose the most equable course of events, and set aside all serious and unlooked-for accidents, the number of these relations which it brings in its train is not to be foreseen. Any one who has an opportunity of occupying himself with the higher departments of State administration, must certainly feel conscious from experience how few political measures have really an immediate and absolute necessity, and how many, on the contrary, have only a relative and indirect importance, and are wholly dependent on foregone measures. Now, in this way a vast increase of means is rendered necessary, and even these very means are drawn away from the attainment of the true end. Not only does such a State require larger sources of revenue, but it needs in addition an increase of artificial regulations for the maintenance of mere political security: the separate parts

cohere less intimately together—the supervision of the Government requires far more vigilance and activity. Hence comes the calculation, no less difficult, but unhappily too often neglected, whether the available resources of the State are adequate to provide the means which the maintenance of security demands; and should this calculation reveal a real misproportion, it only suggests the necessity of fresh artificial arrangements, which, in the end, overstrain the elasticity of the power—an evil from which (though not from this cause only) many of our modern States are suffering.

We must not overlook here one particular manifestation of this generally injurious agency, since it so closely affects human development; and this is, that the very administration of political affairs becomes in time so full of complications, that it requires an incredible number of persons to devote their time to its supervision, in order that it may not fall into utter confusion. Now, by far the greater portion of these have to deal with the mere symbols and formulas of things; and thus, not only men of first-rate capacity are withdrawn from anything which gives scope or stimulus to the thinking faculties, and men who would be usefully employed in some other way are diverted from their real course of action, but their intellectual powers are brought to suffer from this partly fruitless, partly one-sided employment. Wholly new sources of gain, moreover, are introduced and established by this necessity of despatching State affairs, and these render the servants of the State more dependent on the governing classes of the community than on the nation in general. Familiar as they have become to us in experience, we need not pause to describe the numerous evils which flow from such a dependence—what looking to the State for help, what a lack of self-reliance, what false vanity, what inaction even, and want. The very evils from which these hurtful consequences flow, are immediately produced by them in turn. When once thus accustomed to the transaction of State affairs, men gradually lose sight of the essential object, and limit their regard to the mere form; they are thus prompted to attempt new ameliorations, perhaps true in intention, but without sufficient adaptation to the required end; and the prejudicial operation of these necessitates new forms, new complications, and often new restrictions, and thereby creates new departments, which require for their efficient supervision a vast increase of functionaries. Hence it arises that in every decennial period the number of the public officials and the extent of registration increase, while the liberty of the subject proportionately declines. In such an administration, moreover, it follows of course that everything depends on the most vigilant supervision and careful management, since there are such increased opportunities of falling short in both; and hence we may not unjustly suppose the Government desirous that everything should pass through as many hands as possible, in order to defeat the risk of errors and embezzlement.

But according to this method of transacting affairs, business becomes in time merely mechanical, while the men who are engaged in it relapse into machines, and all genuine worth and honesty decline in proportion as trust and confidence are withdrawn. Finally, as the occupations we refer to must be vested with high importance, and must in consequence really acquire that importance in men's opinion, the idea of what is momentous or trivial, of what is dignified or contemptible, of what are essential and what are subordinate aims, must soon be wholly reversed. Admitting, in conclusion, that the actual necessity for occupations of this nature compensates, on the other hand, by many beneficial results, for the introduction of these manifold evils, I will not here dwell longer on this part of the subject, but will proceed at once to the ultimate consideration—to which all that has hitherto been educed is but the necessary prelude and preparation,—and endeavour to show how the positive solicitude of a State tends utterly to confound all just and natural points of view.

7. In the kind of policy we are supposing, then, men are neglected for things, and powers for results. A political community, organized and governed according to this system, resembles rather an accumulated mass of living and lifeless instruments of action and enjoyment, than a multitude of acting and enjoying powers. In disregarding the spontaneity of acting beings, they seem to confine their view to the attainment of happiness and enjoyment alone. But although the calculation would be just, inasmuch as the sensation of him who experiences them is the best index of happiness and enjoyment, it would still be very far below the dignity of human nature. For how could we account for it otherwise, that this very system, which aims at tranquillity, should yet, as if apprehensive of the contrary, willingly resign the highest human enjoyment? Joy is greatest in those moments in which man is sensible of having attained the highest reach of his faculties, and is most deeply conscious of the entirety of his nature. It is doubtless true that at such times also he is nearest the depth of his greatest misery; for the moment of intensity can only be succeeded by a like intensity, and the impulse to joy or despair remains ever in the hands of invincible fate. But when the feeling of the highest in human nature truly deserves the name of happiness, even pain and suffering assume another character. The inmost heart of man is the true seat of happiness or misery, nor does his feeling fluctuate with the billowy tide of circumstance on which he is borne. The system we have condemned only leads us to a fruitless struggle to escape pain. But he who truly knows the nature of enjoyment can endure and resign himself to pain, which, in spite of all, still speeds on the footsteps of the fugitive; thus he learns to rejoice unceasingly in the steady, onward march of destiny; and the prospect of greatness still sweetly allures him, whether growing up before his admiration in the present, or fleeing away from his eyes into the dimly-receding future. Thus he comes to the feeling (so rare except to the enthusiast) that even the moment in which he is most deeply sensible of destruction, may be a moment of the highest ecstasy.

Perhaps I may be charged with having exaggerated the evils here enumerated; but, allowing that they may be materially modified in their operation, according to the degree and method of State interference, I must repeat, with this reservation, that it was my task to follow out the working of that interference to its fullest and furthest consequences. With regard to the whole conduct of the inquiry, I would desire that all considerations of a general nature contained in these pages, be viewed entirely apart from the reality of actual practice. In this reality we do not often find any case fully and purely developed,—we do not see the true working of single elements, separate and by themselves. And it is not to be forgotten, in such a consideration of causes and effects, that when once noxious influences are set in operation, the course of ruin towards which they impel, progresses with rapidly accelerating strides. Just as a greater force united to a greater produces results doubly multiplied in their magnitude and importance; so does a less in conjunction with a less quickly degenerate to infinitesimal issues, which baffle the subtlest penetration to follow them in their rapid grades of declension. Should we even concede, however, that these consequences might be less fatal, the opposite theory would still approve itself the happiest in the truly inestimable blessings that must flow from the application of its principles, if that application should ever be wholly possible. For the ever-restless impulsive force inherent in the very nature of things, incessantly struggles against the operation of every pernicious institution, while it promotes as actively everything of a beneficial tendency; so that we may accept it in the highest sense as true, that the sum of evil produced at any time, even by the most determined eagerness and activity, can never equal the fair amount of good that is everywhere and at all times spontaneously effected.

I could here present an agreeable contrast of a people in the enjoyment of absolute, unfettered freedom, and of the richest diversity of individual and external relations; I could exhibit how, even in such a condition, fairer and loftier and more wonderful forms of diversity and originality must still be revealed, than even any in that antiquity which so unspeakably fascinates, despite the harsher features which must still characterize the individuality of a ruder civilization; a condition in which force would still keep pace with refinement, and even with the rich resources of revealed character, and in which, from the endlessly ramified interconnection between all nations and quarters of the globe, the very elements themselves would seem more numerous; I could then proceed to show that new force would bloom out and ripen into fruition, when every existing thing was organizing itself by its own unhindered agency; when even surrounded, as it would be, by the most exquisite forms, it transformed these present shapes of beauty into its own internal being with that unhampered spontaneity which is the cherished growth of freedom: I could point out with what delicacy and refinement the inner life of man would unfold its strength and beauty; how it would in time become the high, ultimate object of his solicitude, and how everything physical and external would be transfused into the inner moral and intellectual being, and the bond which connects the two natures together would gain lasting strength, when nothing intervened to disturb the reaction of all human pursuits upon the mind and character: how no single agent would be sacrificed to the interest of another; but while each held fast the measure of power bestowed on him, he would for that very reason be inspired with a still lovelier eagerness to give it a direction conducive to the benefit of the others: how, when every one was progressing in his individuality, more varied and exquisite modifications of the beautiful human character would spring up, and onesidedness would become more rare, as it is the result of feebleness and insufficiency; and as each, when nothing else would avail to make the other assimilate himself to him, would be more effectually constrained to modify his own being by the still continuing necessity of union with others: how, in such a people, no single energy or hand would be lost to the task of ennobling and enhancing human existence: and lastly, how through this focal concentration of energies, the views of all would be directed to this last end alone, and would be turned aside from every other object that was false or less worthy of humanity. I might then conclude, by showing how the beneficial consequences of such a constitution, diffused throughout the people of any nation whatever, would even remove an infinite share of the frightfulness of that human misery which is never wholly eradicable, of the destructive devastations of nature, of the fell ravages of hostile animosity, and of the wanton luxuriousness of excessive indulgence in pleasure. But I content myself with having limned out the more prominent features of the contrasting picture in a general outline; it is enough for me to throw out a few suggestive ideas, for riper judgments to sift and examine.

If we come now to the ultimate result of the whole argument we have been endeavouring to develope, the first principle we eliminate will be, that *the State is to abstain from all solicitude for the positive welfare of the citizens, and not to proceed a step further than is necessary for their mutual security and protection against foreign enemies; for with no other object should it impose restrictions on freedom.*

The means through which such a solicitude manifests itself in action, would now naturally present themselves for our consideration; but, as the principles we seek to establish wholly disapprove of the thing itself, it is needless to dwell on these. It may be generally observed however, in connection with this subject, that the means by which freedom is limited with a view to welfare are very various in their character, as laws, exhortations, premiums, which are direct in their operation, and immunities, monopolies, etc. and the power acquired by the sovereign as chief landowner, which are indirect; and that all of them, whether direct or indirect, or however they may differ in kind or degree, are attended with pernicious consequences. Should it be objected to these assertions that it appears somewhat strange to deny to the State a privilege which is accorded to every individual, viz. to propose rewards, to extend loans, to be a land-owner, the objection might be fairly entertained if it were possible for the State to consist of a double personality in practice, as it does in theory. In such a case it would be the same as if a private individual had secured to himself a vast amount of influence. But when we reflect (still keeping theory clear from practice) that the influence of a private person is liable to diminution and decay, from competition, dissipation of fortune, nay even death; and that clearly none of these contingencies can be applied to the State; there still remains the unassailable principle that the latter is not to meddle in anything which does not refer exclusively to security,—a principle whose force of apposition is enhanced in that it has not been supported by arguments derived from the very nature of coercion itself. A private person, moreover, acts from other motives than the State. If an individual citizen proposes premiums, which I will agree to suppose are as efficient inducements as those of the State (although this is never perhaps the case), he does so for some interest of his own. Now, from his continual intercourse with his fellow-citizens, and the equality of his condition with theirs, his interest must be closely connected with their advantage or disadvantage, and hence with the circumstances of their respective positions. The end moreover which he designs to attain is already prepared and anticipated in the present, and therefore produces beneficial results. But the grounds on which the State acts are ideas and principles, which often deceive the correctest calculations; and if the reasons be drawn from considerations of its private capacity, it may be observed that this is too often questionable, where the welfare and security of the citizen are concerned, and further, that the capacity of the citizens is never equal in the same degree. Even granting this double personality, it is then no longer the State which acts; and the very nature of such reasoning forbids its application.

The points of view from which these last considerations are suggested, and from which indeed our whole argument proceeds, have no other object than simply man's power, as such, and his internal development. Such reasoning would be justly chargeable with onesidedness if it wholly disregarded the conditions which must exist in order that that power may operate at all. And while mentioning this, we must not overlook the question that naturally arises in this place, viz. whether those very things from which we would withdraw the operation of State solicitude, could ever flourish without it and of themselves. We might here pass before us in successive review, the different kinds of handicraft, agriculture, industry, commerce, and all those distinct departments we have hitherto considered in common, and could bring in the aid of technical knowledge to exhibit the evils and advantages derivable in each case from unhindered freedom, and the abandonment of men to themselves. But, while the want of such technical insight prevents my entering on such a discussion, I am inclined to believe it no longer essential for arriving at the true merits of the question. Still, if such an investigation could be radically, and, what is especially important, historically conducted, it would not fail to be useful, in that it would tend still more convincingly to approve these ideas, and ascertain at the same time the possibility of their being put in practice, however materially modified,—for the once existing order of things in any political community would scarcely allow of their unmodified application. Leaving this inquiry however to the proper hands, I shall content myself here with a few general reflections. Every occupation, then, of whatever nature, is more efficiently performed if pursued for its own sake alone, rather than for the results to which it leads. So deeply grounded is this in human nature, that what has at first been chosen for its utility, in general becomes ultimately attractive in itself. Now this arises from nothing else than this, that action is dearer to human nature than mere possession, but action only in so far as it is spontaneous. It is just the most vigorous and energetic who would prefer inactivity to a course of labour to which they are constrained. Further, the idea of property gains proportionate strength with the idea of freedom, and it is to the feeling of property that we owe the most vigorous activity. The accomplishment of any great ultimate purpose supposes unity of plan. This requires no proof; and it is equally true of measures for the prevention of great calamities, famines, inundations, etc. But this unity might as easily proceed from national as from merely governmental arrangements. It is only necessary to extend to the nation and its different parts the freedom of entering into contracts. Between a national and a governmental institution there is always a vast and important difference. That has only an indirect—this, a direct influence; and hence with the former there is always greater freedom of contracting, dissolving, and modifying unions. It is highly probable that all State unions were originally nothing more than such national associations. And here experience shows us the fatal consequences of combining with provisions for security, the attainment of other ultimate ends. Whoever engages in this design must, for the sake of security alone, possess absolute power. But this power he extends to the execution of the remaining projects; and in proportion to its duration and the remoteness from its origin, the power of an institution increases, and the traces of the primary contract vanish. A national measure, however, only retains its proper force in so far as it adheres faithfully to this original compact and its authority. This reason alone might seem sufficient; but, granting even that the fundamental compact was rigidly observed, and that the State union was, in the strictest sense, a national association, still the will of the individuals could only be ascertained through a system of Representation; and it is impossible for the representative of a plurality to be so true an organ of all the opinions of the represented. Now the point to which the whole argument conducts us, is the necessity of securing the consent of every individual. But this very necessity renders the decision by a majority of voices impossible; and yet no other could be imagined in the case of a State union which, in regard to single objects, extended its activity to the positive welfare of the citizen. Nothing would be left to the non-consenting but to withdraw themselves from the community in order to escape its jurisdiction, and prevent the further application of a majority of suffrages to their individual cases. And yet this is almost impossible when we reflect that to withdraw from the social body is just tantamount to separating oneself from the State. We would observe, further, that it is better to enter into separate unions in single associations, than to contract them generally for undetermined future cases; and lastly, that to form associations of free men in a nation is attended with peculiar difficulty. For although this last consideration may seem prejudicial to the attainment of ultimate purposes, it is still certain that every larger association is in general less beneficial;

and it should not be forgotten that whatever is produced with difficulty gains from the very fact a more lasting vigour by the implied consolidation of forces long tested and exercised. The more a man acts for himself, the more does he develope himself. In large associations he is too prone to become an instrument merely. A frequent effect of these unions moreover is to allow the symbol to be substituted for the thing, and this always impedes true development. The dead hieroglyphic does not inspire like living nature. In place of other examples I need only instance the case of poor-laws. Does anything tend so effectually to deaden and destroy all true commiseration,—all hopeful yet unobtrusive entreaty,—all loving trustfulness of man in man? Do we not all fitly despise the beggar who rather resigns himself to be fed and nursed in an almshouse than, after sore struggling with want, to find, not a mere hand flinging him a pittance, but a tenderly sympathizing heart? I am willing to admit, in conclusion, that without the mighty masses as it were, with which we have been working in these last centuries, human progress might not have advanced with strides so rapid,— and yet perhaps not rapid alone. The fruit had been longer in expanding and maturing, but still it would really have ripened, and that with a far richer and more precious blessing. Granting this, it is needless to dwell longer on this objection. But two others remain to be tested as we proceed, viz: Whether the maintenance of security even would be possible, with those limitations of the State's activity we have here prescribed? and secondly, Whether the necessary provision of means for the manifestation of its activity, even when thus limited, does not come to necessitate a more manifold encroachment of the wheels of the State machine, into the relations of the individual citizen?

Chapter X
On The Solicitude Of The State For Security With Respect To Actions Which Directly Relate To The Agent Only. (Police Laws.)

We now come to accompany man throughout all the complex and manifold relations which his life in society presents, and shall begin with considering the simplest of these, or that in which (although in union with others) man remains strictly within the limits of what pertains to himself, and engages in nothing that refers immediately to the rights of others. It is to this aspect of the civil relations that the greater number of our so-called police, or preventive, laws are directed; since, however indefinite this expression may be, it still conveys to us the general and important idea, that such laws relate to the means of averting violations of the rights of others, while they have nothing to do with the violations of such right which are actually committed. Now they either operate to restrict actions whose immediate consequences are calculated to endanger the rights of others; or they impose limitations on those which usually end in transgressions of law; or, lastly, they may design to determine what is necessary for the preservation or efficient exercise of the political power itself. I must here overlook the fact that those regulations which do not relate to security, but are directed to the positive welfare of the citizen, are most commonly classed under this head; since it does not fall in with the system of division I have adopted. Now, according to the principles we have already determined, the State ought not to interfere with this, the simplest of human relations, except where there are just grounds for apprehending some violation of its own rights, or those of its citizens. And as to the rights of the State, it should here be borne in mind that such rights are granted only for the sake of protecting security. In no case, then, should prohibitive laws be enacted, when the advantage or disadvantage refers solely to the proprietor. Again, it is not enough to justify such restrictions, that an action should imply damage to another person; it must, at the same time, encroach upon his rights. But this second position requires explanation. Right, then, is never infringed on but when some one is deprived of a portion of what properly belongs to him, or of his personal freedom, without, or against, his will. But when, on the contrary, there occurs no such deprivation,—when one individual does not overstep the boundary of another's right, then, whatever disadvantage may accrue to the latter, there is no diminution of privilege. Neither is there any such diminution when the injury itself does not follow until he who sustains it also becomes active on his side, and, as it were, takes up the action, or, at least, does not oppose it as far as he can.

The application of these definitions is sufficiently evident, and I will only pause to mention one or two remarkable examples. According to these principles then it will be seen, that we cannot conceive the injustice of any actions which only create offence, and especially as regards religion and morals. He who utters or performs anything calculated to wound the conscience and moral sense of others, may indeed act immorally; but, so long as he is not chargeable with obtrusiveness in these respects, he violates no right. The others are free to cut off all intercourse with such a person, and, should circumstances render this impossible, they must submit to the unavoidable inconvenience of associating with men of uncongenial character; not forgetting, moreover, that the obnoxious party may likewise be annoyed by the display of peculiar traits in them. Even a possible exposure to more positively hurtful influences,—as where the beholding this or that action, or the listening to a particular argument, was calculated to impair the virtue, or mislead the reason and sound sense of others,—would not be sufficient to justify restrictions on freedom. Whoever spoke or acted thus did not therein infringe directly on the right of any other; and it was free to those who were exposed to the influence of such words and actions to counteract the evil impression on themselves with the strength of will and the principles of reason. Hence, then, however great the evils that may follow from overt immorality and seductive errors of reasoning, there still remains this excellent consequence, that in the former case the strength and resistive force of character, in the latter the spirit of toleration and diversity of view, are brought to the test, and reap benefit in the process. It is scarcely necessary to mention that in the instance I have just taken, I have confined my view to its influence on the security of the citizens.

For I have already endeavoured to exhibit the relation of such actions to national morality, and to show what may or may not be allowed to the State with regard to them, on that ground.

Since, however, there are many things of which the correct decision requires a wholly special knowledge, and since, in regard to these, security might be disturbed if any one should unthinkingly or designedly turn the ignorance of others to his own advantage, the citizen should have the option, in such cases, of applying to the State for counsel. The most striking instances of what I mean,— whether we consider the frequent necessity for such special knowledge, the difficulty attending just discrimination, or, lastly, the magnitude of the injury to be apprehended,—are furnished by those cases in which the professional services of physicians and advocates are put in requisition. Now, in order to meet the wants and wishes of the nation in these respects, it is not only advisable but necessary that the State should examine into the qualifications of those who destine themselves for such pursuits, provided they agree to submit themselves to its tests; and, furnishing them with testimonials of fitness in case of a favourable issue of the inquiry, to acquaint the citizens that they can only confide with certainty in those who have thus been proved. Beyond this, however, the State may not proceed, or withhold from those who have declined or failed in examination the exercise of their avocation, and from the public the use of their services. Neither should it be allowed to extend such supervision to any other occupations than those which are not designed to act on the internal, but only on the external life of man, and in which he is not himself required to co-operate, but only to remain passive and obedient, and where the truth or falsity of results is the only thing of importance; or, secondly, such regulations are proper in those cases where due discrimination requires the knowledge of some wholly special department, and is not attainable by the mere exercise of reason and the practical ability of judging, and further where the rarity of their occurrence renders the very seeking of advice difficult. Should the State proceed further than is prescribed by this last limitation, it falls into the danger of rendering the nation indolent, inactive, and too much inclined to repose on the knowledge and judgment of others; while, on the other hand, the very want of positive assistance invites men rather to enrich their own knowledge and experience, and knits the citizens together by a thousand intimate relations, inasmuch as they are left more exclusively dependent on each other. Should the State fail to observe the first limitation we have pointed out, that it is not to withhold a man from the free exercise of his chosen pursuit because he has not submitted himself to its tests of capability, then, besides the evils just alluded to, all those hurtful consequences will naturally follow which we exposed in detail in the beginning of this essay. It is evident then—to choose another remarkable example illustrative of our present subject—that in the case of religious teachers State regulations cannot at all be applied. For as to what points of fitness should the State examine them? In the belief of some particular dogmas? We have already fully shown that religion is in no way dependent on these. Should it ground its estimate on the degree of intellectual power in general? In the teacher of religion, whose task it is to present things to his audience in an intimate connection with their individual life, almost the sole point of importance is the relation between his reason and theirs,—a consideration which already argues such an à priori decision to be impossible. Should it judge then of moral character and integrity? For these there is no other test than that which is least adapted to the political function, viz. inquiry into the previous conduct and circumstances of the candidates, etc. Lastly, regulations of this nature—even in the cases we have ourselves approved—should, in general, only be adopted when the will of the nation demands them. For, of themselves, they are not even necessary among free men, who are developed through the very circumstance of their freedom; and further, they might be constantly liable to serious abuse. As, in general, it is not my design to examine into single objects in detail, but rather to define the fundamental principles which embrace all these in their application, I shall once more briefly indicate the only point of view from which I contemplate such regulations. The State, then, is not to concern itself in any way with the positive welfare of its citizens, and hence, no more with their life or health, except where these are imperilled by the actions of others; but it is to keep a vigilant eye on their security, though only in so far as this might suffer from the attempts of the designing to turn the ignorance of others to their own advantage. Still, in such cases of deception as that to which we refer, the victim of the imposture must necessarily have been persuaded into conviction; and as in such relations the flux and reflux of different modifying influences from one party to the other precludes the application of any general rule, and as the very liability to imposition which freedom opens out tends to discipline men's prudence and foresight, I esteem it more accordant with fundamental principles (in a theory which is necessarily removed from practical application) to confine prohibitive laws to those cases only in which actions are done without the will of another, or still more, in direct opposition to it. The general tenour of my arguments will serve to indicate the consistent treatment of other cases, should these present themselves.

While we have hitherto confined our attention only to the nature of those consequences, flowing from an action, which bring it under the operation of State supervision, we have yet to inquire whether the mere prospective possibility of such consequences is sufficient to justify the restriction of given actions, or whether this is only requisite where those consequences follow in the necessary course. Freedom may suffer if we adopt the former supposition; if the latter, security may be endangered. It is therefore sufficiently clear that a middle path should be pursued; but to give any general definition of this seems to me impossible. It is certain that the deliberation in such cases must be guided at once by considerations of the extent of the injury, and of the restrictions on freedom implied in the given law. But the proper estimation of these does not admit, properly speaking, of any general rule; and all calculations of probability are eminently fallacious. Theory therefore can only point out these moments of deliberation. In the reference to practice, I am of opinion that special circumstances should be chiefly regarded, and not so much the general cases; and that only when observation of the past and considerations of the present combine to represent a restriction as indispensable, should it ever be resolved on. The right of nature, when applied to the social life of a number of men, defines the boundary lines unmistakably. It condemns all actions in which, with his own fault, one man encroaches on the due province of another, and hence, includes all those cases in which the injury strictly arises from a blamable oversight, or where it is always associated with the action, or with such a degree of probability in the consequence, that the agent either perceives it or at least becomes accountable by overlooking it. In all other cases the injury proceeds from chance, and of course the agent is not bound to repair its effects. Any wider application than this, could only be gained from the tacit agreement of those living together; and this is again something positive. But that the State should rest here seems justly questionable; especially when we consider the importance of the injury to be apprehended, and the possibility of rendering the restriction imposed on freedom, only moderately hurtful to the citizens. In such a case it is clear that the right is undeniable on the part of the State, since it is to provide for security, not only in so far as the enforcement of reparation is concerned where right has really been violated, but also in adopting means for preventing such wrongs. A third person, moreover, can only decide according to external characteristics. It is therefore impossible for the State to wait to see whether the citizens will fail in taking due precautions against dangerous actions, neither can it rely on the probability of their foreseeing the injury: where circumstances seem to represent the apprehension as urgent, it must rather restrict actions in themselves harmless.

In view of these considerations, therefore, we may be justified in laying down the following principle: *in order to provide for the security of its citizens, the State must prohibit or restrict such actions, referring immediately to the agents alone, as imply the infringement on others' rights in their consequences, or encroach in these on their freedom or property without or against their will; and further, it must forbid or restrict these actions when the probability of such consequences is fairly to be apprehended,—a probability in which it must necessarily consider the extent of the injury feared, and on the other hand the consequences of the restriction on freedom implied in the law contemplated. Beyond this, every limitation of personal freedom is to be condemned, as wholly foreign to the sphere of the State's activity.*

Since, according to the ideas I have unfolded, the protection of the rights of others affords the only just ground for these restrictions, the necessity for them must naturally disappear when this ground no longer exists; and hence when—for instance, in most police-regulations—the danger extends only to the circuit of the community, the village, the town, as soon as such a community expressly and unanimously demands that these restrictions should be abolished. The State must then relax its efforts, and content itself with punishing such injuries only as have occurred with an intentional or culpable violation of right. For to put an end to strifes and dissensions among the citizens is the only true interest of the State; and to the promotion of this, the will of single citizens, even though they are themselves the parties injured, should never be allowed to oppose obstacles. If we suppose a community of enlightened men,—fully instructed in their truest interests, and therefore mutually well-disposed and closely united together,—we can easily imagine how voluntary contracts with a view to their security, would be entered into among them; contracts, for example, that this or that dangerous occupation or manufacture should be carried on only in certain places and at certain times, or even should be wholly prohibited. Agreements of this kind are infinitely to be preferred to any State arrangements. For as it is the very persons who enter into such contracts who are most conscious of their necessity, and feel directly the advantage or disadvantage accruing from them, it is clear that they will not be easily formed without an evident want of such agreements; that they will be far more rigidly observed, being voluntarily made; that however considerable the restrictions they entail, they will have a less hurtful influence on the character, being the results of spontaneous activity; and that, lastly, springing as they would from a certain spirit of benevolence and enlightenment, would still further contribute in their turn to increase and diffuse both. The best efforts of the State should therefore aim at bringing men into such a condition by means of freedom, that associations would arise with greater facility, and so supply the place of political regulations in these and manifold similar instances.

I have not made any mention here of such laws as impose positive duties on the citizens, or the sacrifice or performance of anything either for the State or for each other, though there are such laws everywhere among us. But, apart from that application of his powers which every citizen, where it is necessary, owes to the State (concerning which I shall have to speak hereafter), I do not esteem it good that the State should compel any one to do anything to gratify the wish or further the interests of another, even though he should receive the amplest compensation. For as everything and every pursuit, from the infinite diversity of human dispositions and desires, confers on each such various and inestimable benefits, and as these benefits may likewise vary infinitely in interest, importance, and necessity, the decision as to which good of the one, and which of the other, should be chosen as equivalent (though its difficulty should not deter us from it), is always attended with something harsh, and seems like passing sentence on the feelings and individuality of another. For this reason, moreover, that we cannot make any exact substitution except where the things in question are exactly of the same kind, real compensation is often utterly impossible, and can scarcely even be determined by a general rule.

In addition to these injurious consequences of the best of laws of this kind, there is always, moreover, an implied facility of possible abuse.

Further, the consideration of security (which alone rightly prescribes the sphere of State agency) does not render such regulations generally necessary, since every case in which this necessity occurs must be strictly exceptional: men, moreover, become more kindly disposed towards each other, and more prompt to render mutual assistance, the less they feel their self-love and sense of freedom to be wounded by an actual right of coercion on the part of others; and even though the mere humour and wholly groundless obstinacy of a man may happen to thwart an excellent undertaking, such an event is not sufficient to require that the power of the State should be thrown into the contest. In the physical world, it does not shatter every rock to pieces that juts out on the path of the wanderer. Obstacles serve to stimulate energy, and discipline forethought; none uselessly obstruct, save those which arise from human injustice; but that obstinacy is not such an impediment which may indeed be bent by the force of laws in single cases, but can only be removed by the blessed influences of freedom. These reasons, of which a brief summary is all that can be given here, seem yet sufficient to make us yield to iron necessity alone; and the State should content itself with securing to men their natural right to sacrifice the freedom and property of another in order to avert their own ruin.

Lastly, there are many police laws framed to meet actions which are performed, it is true, within the limits of the agent's right, but that not his exclusively, it being shared in conjunction with others. In such cases, restrictions on freedom are evidently far less questionable; as in property that is common, every joint proprietor has the right of gainsay. Such common property we have, for instance, in roads, in rivers flowing through different properties, in squares and streets of towns.

It might appear that the cases here mentioned do not so much belong to the present chapter as to the next, since they concern actions which refer immediately to others. But I have not here considered the case in which a physician actually treats a patient, or a lawyer really undertakes a suit; but only of the choice of a means of gaining a livelihood in these respects. I only propose the question whether the State should restrict such a choice; and this choice alone does not relate directly to any one.

Jeremy Bentham (1748-1832)

Artist: Henry Pickersgill (exhibited 1829), National Portrait Gallery, London

Born on February 15, 1748, Jeremy Bentham was very early identified as a prodigy. With his mother dying at the age of ten, Bentham's childhood was described by himself as gloomy and monotonous. He received his early education at the Westminster school and was sent to Queen's College, Oxford in 1760, at the age of twelve. Bentham finished his Bachelor's in 1763 and his Masters in 1776. Trained as a lawyer, Bentham was called to the bar in 1769, but rebelled against what he saw as an over-complicated legal system that was incomprehensible to all but trained lawyers. Deeply impressed with the English publication of Cesare Beccaria's *On Crimes and Punishments*, in which Bentham likely first encountered the phrase, 'the greatest happiness for the greatest number,' he decided to write about the law as it ought to be instead of practice law as it was. In the mid 1770s, Bentham wrote a long critique of Sir William Blackstone's *Commentaries on the Laws of England*, considered an authoritative work at the time, and a piece of this critique was published in 1776 as *A Fragment of Government*. Published anonymously, it generated a good deal of interest until its authorship was later revealed and sales dropped.

A 1780s visit to Russia saw Bentham shift his focus to more practical issues, dealing with what today would be termed penology, public administration, social policy, and economics. While at Krichev Bentham wrote the *Panopticon*, an architectural design for a prison or workhouse. The Panopticon was greeted with some interest in London, but plans to construct the inspection house were scrapped, and in 1813, the British Parliament voted to compensate Bentham for its non-implementation at £23,000. Excited by the French Revolution, Bentham had also sent several essays, including his idea of the inspection house, to France. The Panopticon went as far as being put before the National Assembly, and for Bentham's efforts he was made an honorary citizen of France in 1792.

With an inheritance from his father's death and the compensation from the scrapping of the Panopticon, Bentham spent his later years financially comfortable and academically productive. He developed a system of moral principles upon which many of his social reforms rested, and is generally attributed the architect of the philosophical doctrine of utilitarianism which holds that a correct act or policy can be determined by looking for that which achieves the greatest happiness for the greatest number of people. Utilitarianism would be further developed by John Stuart Mill. Bentham's notoriety as a philosopher and legal reformer is matched by his request to be enshrined in the "Auto-Icon," after his death. In June of 1832, Bentham passed and, as he requested, his body was preserved and displayed at the University College, London.

Works Referenced:
Dinwiddy, John. *Bentham*. Oxford University Press: New York, 1989.
Mack, Mary P. *Jeremy Bentham: An Odyssey of Ideas (1748-1792)*. Heinmann Educational Books Ltd: London, 1962.
Plamenatz, John. *The English Utilitarians*. Basil Blackwood and Mott Ltd: London and Oxford, 1949.

**Selections from *The Panopticon Writings* (London: Verso., reprint 1995).,
orig. 1787**

Letter I: Idea of the Inspection Principle
It occurred to me, that the plan of a building, lately contrived by my brother, for
purposes in some respects similar, and which, under the name of the *Inspection
House*, or the *Elaboratory*... I have accordingly obtained some drawings relative
to it, which I here enclose. Indeed I look upon it as capable of applications of
the most extensive nature; and that for reasons which you will soon perceive. To
say all in one word, it will be found applicable, I think, without exception, to all
establishments whatsoever, in which, within a space not too large to be covered
or commanded by buildings, a number of persons are meant to be kept under
inspection. No matter how different, or even opposite the purpose: whether
it be that of punishing the incorrigible, guarding the insane, reforming the
vicious, confining the suspected, employing the idle, maintaining the helpless,
curing the sick, instructing the willing in any branch of industry, or training
the rising race in the path of education: in a word, whether it be applied to the
purposes of perpetual prisons in the room of death, or prisons for confinement
before trial, or penitentiary-houses, or houses of correction, or work-houses, or
manufactories, or mad-houses, or hospitals, or schools. It is obvious that, in all
these instances, the more constantly the persons to be inspected are under the
eyes of the persons who should inspect them, the more perfectly will the purpose
X of the establishment have been attained. Ideal perfection, if that were the
object, would require that each person should actually be in that predicament,
during every instant of time. This being impossible, the next thing to be wished
for is, that, at every instant, seeing reason to believe as much, and not being able
to satisfy himself to the contrary, he should *conceive* himself to be so... To cut
the matter as short as possible, I will consider it at once in its application to such
purposes as, being most complicated, will serve to exemplify the greatest force
and variety of precautionary contrivance. Such are those which have suggested
the idea of *penitentiary-houses*: in which the objects of *safe custody, confinement,
solitude, forced labour,* and *instruction*, were all of them to be kept in view. If all
these objects can be accomplished together, of course with at least equal certainty
and facility may any lesser number of them.

Letter II: Plan for a Penitentiary Inspection-House
Before you look at the plan, take in words the general idea of it.

The building is circular.

The apartments of the prisoners occupy the circumference. You may call
them, if you please, the *cells*.

These *cells* are divided from one another, and the prisoners by that means
secluded from all communication with each other, by *partitions* in the form

of *radii* issuing from the circumference towards the centre, and extending as many feet as shall be thought necessary to form the largest dimension of the cell.

The apartment of the inspector occupies the centre; you may call it if you please the *inspector's lodge*.

It will be convenient in most, if not in all cases, to have a vacant space or *area* all round, between such centre and such circumference. You may call it if you please the *intermediate* or *annular* area.

About the width of a cell may be sufficient for a *passage* from the outside of the building to the lodge.

Each cell has in the outward circumference, a *window*, large enough, not only to light the cell, but, through the cell, to afford light enough to the correspondent part of the lodge.

The inner circumference of the cell is formed by an iron *grating*, so light as not to screen any part of the cell from the inspector's view.

Of this grating, a part sufficiently large opens, in form of a *door*, to admit the prisoner at his first entrance; and to give admission at any time to the inspector or any of his attendants.

To cut off from each prisoner the view of every other, the partitions are carried on a few feet beyond the grating into the intermediate area: such projecting parts I call the *protracted partitions*.

It is conceived, that the light, coming in in this manner through the cells, and so across the intermediate area, will be sufficient for the inspector's lodge. But, for this purpose, both the windows in the cells, and those corresponding to them in the lodge, should be as large as the strength of the building, and what shall be deemed a necessary attention to economy, will permit.

To the windows of the lodge there are *blinds*, as high up as the eyes of the prisoners in their cells can, by any means they can employ, be made to reach.

To prevent *thorough light*, whereby, notwithstanding the blinds, the prisoners would see from the cells whether or not any person was in the lodge, that apartment is divided into quarters, by *partitions* formed by two diameters to the circle, crossing each other at right angles. For these partitions the thinnest materials might serve; and they might be made removable at pleasure; their height, sufficient to prevent the prisoners seeing over them from the cells. Doors to these partitions, if left open at any time, might produce the thorough light. To prevent this, divide each partition into two, at any part required, setting down the one-half at such distance from the other as shall be equal to the aperture of a door.

These windows of the inspector's lodge open into the intermediate area, in the form of *doors*, in as many places as shall be deemed necessary to admit of his communicating readily with any of the cells.

Small *lamps*, in the outside of each window of the lodge, backed by a reflector, to throw the light into the corresponding cells, would extend to the night the security of the day.

To save the troublesome exertion of voice that might otherwise be necessary, and to prevent one prisoner from knowing that the inspector was occupied by another prisoner at a distance, a small *tin tube* might reach from each cell to the inspector's lodge, passing across the area, and so in at the side of the correspondent window of the lodge. By means of this implement, the slightest whisper of the one might be heard by the other, especially if he had proper notice to apply his ear to the tube.

With regard to *instruction*, in cases where it cannot be duly given without the instructor's being close to the work, or without setting his hand to it by way of example before the learner's face, the instructor must indeed here as elsewhere, shift his station as often as there is occasion to visit different workmen; unless he calls the workmen to him, which in some of the instances to which this sort of building is applicable, such as that of imprisoned felons, could not so well be. But in all cases where directions, given verbally and at a distance, are sufficient, these tubes will be found of use. They will save, on the one hand, the exertion of voice it would require, on the part of the instructor, to communicate instruction to the workmen without quitting his central station in the lodge; and, on the other, the confusion which would ensue if different instructors or persons in the lodge were calling to the cells at the same time. And, in the case of hospitals, the quiet that may be insured by this little contrivance, trifling as it may seem at first sight, affords an additional advantage.

A *bell,* appropriated exclusively to the purposes of *alarm,* hangs in a *belfry* with which the building is crowned, communicating by a rope with the inspector's lodge.

The most economical, and perhaps the most convenient, way of *warming* the cells and area, would be by flues surrounding it, upon the principle of those in hot-houses. A total want of every means of producing artificial heat might, in such weather as we sometimes have in England, be fatal to the lives of the prisoners; at any rate, it would often times be altogether incompatible with their working at any sedentary employment. The flues, however, and the fire-places belonging to them, instead of being on the outside, as in hot-houses, should be in the inside. By this means, there would be less waste of heat, and the current of air that would rush in on all sides through the cells, to supply the draught made by the fires, would answer so far the purpose of ventilation. But of this more under the head of Hospitals.

Letter III: Extent for a Single Building
Betwixt every other two cells, at the end of the partition which divides them, a hollow shaft or tunnel is left in the brick-work of the exterior wall; which tunnel, if there be several stories to the building, is carried up through all of them.

Into this tunnel is inserted, under each cell, the bottom of an EARTHEN PIPE (like those applied in England to the tops of chimneys) glazed in the inside. The upper end, opening into the cell, is covered by a seat of cast-iron, bedded into the brick-work; with an aperture, which neither by its size nor shape shall be capable of admitting the body of a man. To gain the tunnel from the inside of the cell, the position of this pipe will of course be slanting. At the bottom of the tunnel, on the outside of the building, an arched opening, so low as scarcely to be discernible, admits of the filth being carried away. No one, who has been at all attentive to the history of prisons, but must have observed how often escapes have been effected or attempted through this channel.

A slight screen, which the prisoner might occasionally interpose, may perhaps not be thought superfluous. This, while it answers the purpose of decency, might be so adjusted as to prevent his concealing from the eye of the inspector any forbidden enterprise.

For each cell, the whole apparatus would not come to many shillings: a small consideration for a great degree of security. In this manner, without any relaxation of the discipline, the advantages of cleanliness, and its concomitant health, may be attained to as great a degree as in most private houses.

It would be regarded, perhaps, as a luxury too great for an establishment of this kind, were I to venture to propose the addition of a water-pipe all around with a cock to it in each cell. The clear expense would, however, not be quite so great as it might seem: since by this means a considerable quantity of attendance would be saved. To each prisoner, some allowance of water must necessarily be afforded, if it were only to drink, without regard to cleanliness To forward that allowance by hand to two or three hundred prisoners in so many different apartments, might perhaps be as much as one man could do if constantly employed. For the raising the water by pumps to necessary elevation, the labour of the prisoners would suffice.

As to the materials, brick, as every body knows, would be the cheapest in ***, and either brick or stone, in every other part of England. Thus much as to the shell. But in a building calculated for duration, as this would be, the expense of allowing the same materials to the floors, and laying them upon arches, would, I imagine, not be deemed an unsuitable one, especially when the advantage of a perfect security from fire is taken into account.

As to the *cells*, they will of course be more or less spacious, according to the employment which it is designed should be carried on in them.

As to the *whole building*, if it be too small, the circumference will not be large enough to afford a sufficient number of cells: if too large, the depth from the exterior windows will be too great; and there will not be light enough in the lodge.

As to this individual building of my brother's, the dimensions of it were determined by the consideration of the most convenient scantlings of the timbers, (that being in his situation the cheapest material), and by other local considerations. It is to have two stories, and the diameter of the whole building is to be 100 feet out and out.

Merely to help conception, I will take this size for an example of such a building as he would propose for England.

Taking the diameter 100 feet, this admits of 48 *cells*, 6 feet wide each at the outside, walls included; with a *passage* through the building, of 8 or 9 feet.

I begin with supposing two stories of cells.

In the *under* story, thickness of the walls 25 feet.

From thence, clear *depth* of each cell from the window to the grating, 13 feet.

From thence to the ends of the *partition walls*, 3 feet more; which gives the length of the *protracted partitions*.

Breadth of the *intermediate area*, 14.

Total from the outside of the building to the *lodge*, 32 1/2 feet. The double of this, 65 feet, leaves for the *diameter of the lodge*, 35 feet; including the thickness of its walls.

In the *upper story*, the *cells* will be but 9 feet deep; the difference between that and the 13 feet, which is their depth in the under story, being taken up by a *gallery* which surrounds the protracted partitions.

This gallery supplies, in the upper story, the place of an intermediate area on that floor; and by means of *steps*, which I shall come to presently, forms the communication between the upper story of cells to which it is attached, and the lower story of the cells, together with the intermediate area and the lodge.

The spot most remote from the place where the light comes in from, I mean the *centrical* spot of the building and of the lodge, will not be more than 50 feet distant from that place; a distance not greater, I imagine, than what is often times exemplified in churches; even in such as are not furnished in the manner of this building, with *windows* in every part of the exterior boundary. But the inspector's windows will not be more than about 32 1/2 feet from the open light.

It would be found convenient, I believe, on many accounts, and in most instances, to make *one story of the lodge* serve for *two stories* of the *cells*; especially in any situation where ground is valuable, the number of persons to be inspected large, the room necessary for each person not very considerable, and frugality and necessity more attended to than appearance.

For this purpose, the *floor* of the *ground story of the lodge* is elevated to within about 4 1/2 feet of the floor of the *first story* of the cells. By this means, the inspector's eye, when he stands up, will be on, or a little above, the level of the floor of the above mentioned upper story of the cells; and, at any rate, he will command both that and the ground story of the cells without difficulty, and without change of posture.

As to the *intermediate area*, the floor of it is upon a level, not with the *floor* of the *lodge*, but with that of the *lower story* of the cells. But at the *upper* story of the cells, its place, as I have already mentioned, is supplied by the above-mentioned *gallery*; so that the altitude of this area from the floor to the ceiling is equal to that of both stories of the cells put together.

The floor of the lodge not being on a level with either story of the cells, but between both, it must at convenient intervals be provided with flights of *steps*, to go *down* to the ground story of the cells by the intermediate area, and *up* to the first floor of the cells by the gallery. The ascending flights, joined to the *descending*, enable the servants of the house to go to the upper story of the cells, without passing through the apartment of the inspector.

As to the *height* of the whole, and of the several parts, it is supposed that 18 feet might serve for *the two stories of cells*, to be inspected, as above, by *one story* of the *lodge*. This would hold 96 persons.

36 feet for four stories of *cells*, and two of the lodge: this would hold 192 persons.

54 feet for six stories of the cells, and three of the lodge: this would hold 288 persons.

And 54 feet, it is conceived, would not be an immoderate elevation.

The drawings which, I believe, will accompany this, suppose *four* for the number of stories of the cells.

You will see, under the head of hospitals, the reasons why I conceive that even a less height than 9 feet, deducting the thickness of a floor supported by arches, might be sufficient for the cells.

The *passage* might have, for its *height*, either the height of one story, or of two stories of the cells, according as the number of those cells was two or four. The part over the passage might, in either case, be added to the lodge, to which it would thereby give a communication, at each end, with the world without doors, and ensure a keeper against the danger of finding himself a prisoner among his prisoners.

Should it be thought, that, in this way, the lodge would not have light enough, for the convenience of a man of a station competent to the office, the deficiency might be supplied by a void space left in that part, all the way up. You may call it if you please the *central area*. Into this space windows may open where they are wanted, from the apartments of the lodge. It may be either left *open* at the top, or covered with a *sky-light*. But this expedient, though it might add, in some respects, to the convenience of the lodge, could not but add considerably to the quantity and expense of the building.

On the other hand, it would be assistant to ventilation. Here, too, would be a proper place for the *chapel*: the prisoners remaining in their cells, and the windows of the lodge, which is almost all window, being thrown open. The advantages derivable from it in point of light and ventilation depending upon its being kept vacant, it can never be wanted for any profane use. It may therefore, with the great propriety, be allotted to divine service, and receive a regular consecration. The *pulpit* and *sounding-board* may be moveable. During the term of service, the sky-light, at all other times kept as open as possible, might be shut.

Letter IV: The Principle Extended to Uncovered Areas

In my two last letters, I gave you such idea as it was in my power to give you by words, of this new plan of construction, considered in its most *simple* form. A few more with regard to what further *extensions* it may admit of.

The utmost number of persons that could be stowed in a single building of this sort, consistently with the purposes of each several institution, being ascertained, to increase the number, that of the buildings must of course be increased. Suppose two of these *rotundas* requisite: these two might, *by a covered gallery* constructed upon the same principles, be consolidated into one inspection-house. And by the help of such a covered gallery, *the field of inspection* might be dilated to any extent.

If the number of rotundas were extended to *four*, a regular uncovered area might in that way be enclosed; and being surrounded by covered galleries, would be commanded in this manner from all sides, instead of being commanded only from one.

The area thus enclosed might be either *circular* like the buildings, or *square*, or *oblong*, as one or other of those forms were best adapted to the prevailing ideas of beauty or local convenience. A chain of any length, composed of inspection-houses adapted to the same or different purposes, might in this way be carried round an area of any extent.

On such a plan, either one inspector might serve for two or more rotundas, or if there were one to each, *the inspective force*, if I may use the expression, would be greater in such a compound building, than in any of the number singly taken, of which it was composed; since each inspector might be relieved occasionally by every other.

In the uncovered area thus brought within the field of inspection, out-door employments, or any employments requiring a greater covered space than the general form of construction will allow, might be carried on upon the same principle. A kitchen-garden might then be cultivated for the use of the whole society, by a few members of it at a time, to whom such an opportunity of airing and exercising themselves would be a refreshment and indulgence.

Many writers have expatiated with great force and justice, on the unpopular and unedifying cast of that undistinguishing discipline, which, in situation and treatment, confounds the lot of those who *may* prove innocent, with the lot of those who *have been* proved to be guilty. The same roof, it has been said, ought not to enclose persons who stand in predicaments so dissimilar. In a combination of inspection-houses, this delicacy might be observed without any abatement of that vigilance with regard to safe custody, which in both cases is equally indispensable.

Letter V: Essential Points of the Plan

It may be of use, that among all the particulars you have seen, it should be clearly understood what circumstances are, and what are not, essential to the plan. The essence of it consists, then, in the *centrality* of the inspector's situation, combined with the well-known and most effectual contrivances for *seeing without being seen*. As to the *general form* of the building, the most commodious for most purposes seems to be the circular: but this is not an absolutely essential circumstance. Of all figures, however, this, you will observe, is the only one that affords a perfect view, and the same view, of an indefinite number of apartments of the same dimensions: that affords a spot from which, without any change of situation, a man may survey, in the same perfection, the whole number, and without so much as a change of posture, the half of the whole number, at the same time: that, within a boundary of a given extent, contains the greatest quantity of room: - that places the centre at the least distance from the light: - that gives the cells most width, at the part where, on account of the light, most light may, for the purposes of work, be wanted: - and that reduces to the greatest possible shortness the path taken by the inspector, in passing from each part of the field of inspection to every other.

You will please to observe, that though perhaps it is the most important point, that the persons to be inspected should always feel themselves as if under inspection, at least as standing a great chance of being so, yet it is not by any means the only one. If it were, the same advantage might be given to buildings of almost any form. What is also of importance is, that for the greatest proportion of time possible, each man should actually be under inspection. This is material in all cases, that the inspector may have the satisfaction of knowing, that the discipline actually has the effect which it is designed to have: and it is more particularly material in such cases where the inspector, besides seeing that they conform to such standing rules as are prescribed, has more or less frequent occasion to give them such transient and incidental directions as will require to be given and enforced, at the commencement at least of every course of industry. And I think, it needs not much argument to prove, that the business of inspection, like every other, will be performed to a greater degree of perfection, the less trouble the performance of it requires.

Not only so, but the greater chance there is, of a given person's being at a given time actually under inspection, the more strong will be the persuasion - the more intense, if I may say so, the feeling, he has of his being so. How little turn so ever the greater number of persons so circumstanced may be supposed to have for calculation, some rough sort of calculation can scarcely, under such circumstances, avoid forcing itself upon the rudest mind. Experiment, venturing first upon slight transgressions, and so on, in proportion to success, upon more and more considerable ones, will not fail to teach him the difference between a loose inspection and a strict one. It is for these reasons, that I cannot help looking upon every form as less and less eligible, in proportion as it deviates from the *circular*.

A very material point is, that room be allotted to the lodge, sufficient to adapt it to the purpose of a complete and constant habitation for the principal inspector or head-keeper, and his family. The more numerous also the family, the better; since, by this means, there will in fact be as many inspectors, as the family consists of persons, though only one be paid for it. Neither the orders of the inspector himself, nor any interest which they may feel, or not feel, in the regular performance of his duty, would be requisite to find them motives adequate to the purpose. Secluded oftentimes, by their situation, from every other object, they will naturally, and in a manner unavoidably, give their eyes a direction conformable to that purpose, in every momentary interval of their ordinary occupations. It will supply in their instance the place of that great and constant fund of entertainment to the sedentary and vacant in towns - the looking out of the window. The scene, though a confined, would be a very various, and therefore, perhaps, not altogether an unamusing one.

Letter VI: Advantages of the Plan

I flatter myself there can now be little doubt of the plan's possessing the fundamental advantages I have been attributing to it: I mean, the *apparent omnipresence* of the inspector (if divines will allow me the expression,) combined with the extreme facility of his *real presence*.

A collateral advantage it possesses, and on the score of frugality a very material one, is that which respects the *number* of the inspectors requisite. If this plan required more than another, the additional number would form an objection, which, were the difference to a certain degree considerable, might rise so high as to be conclusive: so far from it, that a greater multitude than ever were yet lodged in one house might be inspected by a single person; for the trouble of inspection is diminished in no less proportion than the strictness of inspection is increased.

Another very important advantage, whatever purposes the plan may be applied to, particularly where it is applied to the severest and most coercive purposes, is, that the *under* keepers or inspectors, the servants and subordinates of every kind, will be under the same irresistible control with respect to the *head* keeper or inspector, as the prisoners or other persons to be governed are with respect to *them*. On the common plans, what means, what possibility, has the prisoner of appealing to the humanity of the principal for redress against the neglect or oppression of subordinates in that rigid sphere, but the *few* opportunities which, in a crowded prison, the most conscientious keeper *can* afford - but the none at all which many a keeper *thinks* fit to give them? How different would their lot be upon this plan!

In no instance could his subordinates either perform or depart from their duty, but he must know the time and degree and manner of their doing so. It presents an answer, and that a satisfactory one, to one of the most puzzling of political questions - *quis custodiet ipsos custodes?* And, as the fulfilling of his, as well as their, duty would be rendered so much easier, than it can ever have been hitherto, so might, and so should any departure from it be punished with the more inflexible severity. It is this circumstance that renders the influence of this plan not less beneficial to what is called *liberty*, than to necessary coercion; not less powerful as a control upon subordinate power, than as a curb to delinquency; as a shield to innocence, than as a scourge to guilt.

Another advantage, still operating to the same ends, is the great load of trouble and disgust which it takes off the shoulders of those occasional inspectors of a higher order, such as *judges* and other *magistrates*, who, called down to this irksome task from the superior ranks of life, cannot but feel a proportionable repugnance to the discharge of it. Think how it is with them upon the present plans, and how it still must be upon the best plans that have been hitherto devised! The cells or apartments, however constructed, must, if there be nine hundred of them (as there were to have been upon the penitentiary-house plan,) be opened to the visitors, one by one. To do their business to any purpose, they must approach near to, and come almost in contact with each inhabitant; whose situation being watched over according to no other than the loose methods of inspection at present practicable, will on that account require the more minute and troublesome investigation on the part of these occasional superintendents. By this new plan, the disgust is entirely removed, and the trouble of going into such a room as the lodge, is no more than the trouble of going into any other.

Were *Newgate* upon this plan, all Newgate might be inspected by a quarter of an hour's visit to Mr. Akerman.

Among the other causes of that reluctance, none at present so forcible, none so unhappily well grounded, none which affords so natural an excuse, nor so strong a reason against accepting of any excuse, as the danger of *infection* - a circumstance which carries death, in one of its most tremendous forms, from the seat of guilt to the seat of justice, involving in one common catastrophe the violator and the upholder of the laws. But in a spot so constructed, and under a course of discipline so insured, how should infection ever arise? Or how should it continue? Against every danger of this kind, what private house of the poor, one might almost say, or even of the most opulent, can be equally secure?

Nor is the disagreeableness of the task of superintendence diminished by this plan, in a much greater degree than the efficacy of it is increased. On all others, be the superintendent's -visit ever so unexpected, and his motions ever so quick, time there must always be for preparations blinding the real state of things. Out of nine hundred cells, he can visit but one at a time, and, in the meanwhile, the worst of the others may be arranged, and the inhabitants threatened, and tutored how to receive him. On this plan, no sooner is the superintendent announced, than the whole scene opens instantaneously to his view.

In mentioning inspectors and superintendents who are such by office, I must not overlook that system of inspection, which, however little heeded, will not be the less useful and efficacious: I mean, the part which individuals may be disposed to take in the business, without intending, perhaps, or even without thinking of, any other effects of their visits, than the gratification of their own particular curiosity. What the inspector's or keeper's family are with respect to him, that, and more, will these spontaneous visitors be to the superintendent, - assistants, deputies, in so far as he is faithful, witnesses and judges should he ever be unfaithful, to his trust. So as they are but there, what the motives were that drew them thither is perfectly immaterial; whether the relieving of their anxieties by the affecting prospect of their respective friends and relatives thus detained in durance, or merely the satisfying that general curiosity, which an establishment, on various accounts so interesting to human feelings, may naturally be expected to excite.

You see, I take for granted as a matter of course, that under the necessary regulations for preventing interruption and disturbance, the doors of these establishments will be, as, without very special reasons to the contrary, the doors of all public establishments ought to be, thrown wide open to the body of the curious at large - the great *open committee* of the tribunal of the world. And who ever objects to such publicity, where it is practicable, but those whose motives for objection afford the strongest reasons for it?

Letter VII: Penitentiary-Houses-Safe Custody

A Penitentiary-house, more particularly is (I am sorry I must correct myself, and say, was to have been) what every prison might, and in some degree at least ought to be, designed at once as a place of safe custody, and a place of labour. Every such place must necessarily be, whether designed or not, and hospital – a place where sickness will be found at least, whether provision be or be not made for its relief. I will consider this plan in its application to these three distinguishable purposes.

Against *escapes* and in particular on the part of felons of every description, as well before as after conviction, persons from the desperateness of whose situation attempts to escape are more particularly to be apprehended, it would afford, as I dare say you see already, a degree of security, which, perhaps, has been scarce hitherto reached by conception, much less by practice. Overpowering the guard requires an union of hands, and a concert among minds. But what union, or what concert, can there be among persons, no one of whom will have set eyes on any other from the first moment of his entrance? Undermining walls, forcing iron bars, requires commonly a concert, always a length of time exempt from interruption. But who would think of beginning a work of hours and days, without any tolerable prospect of making so much as the first motion towards it unobserved? Such attempts have been seldom made without the assistance of implements introduced by accomplices from without. But who would expose themselves even to the slightest punishment, or even to the mortification of the disappointment, without so much as a tolerable chance of escaping instantaneous detection? - Who would think of bringing in before the keeper's face, so much as a small file, or a phial of *aqua fortis*, to a person not prepared to receive any such thing, nor in a condition to make use of it? Upon all plans hitherto pursued, the thickest walls have been found occasionally unavailing: upon this plan, the thinnest would be sufficient - a circumstance which must operate, in a striking degree, towards a diminution of the expense.

* * *

In this view I am sure you cannot overlook the effect which it would have in rendering unnecessary that inexhaustible fund of disproportionate, too often needless, and always unpopular severity, not to say torture – the use of *irons*. Confined in one of these cells, every motion of the limbs, and every muscle of the face exposed to view, what pretence could there be for exposing to this hardship the most boisterous malefactor? Indulged with perfect liberty within the space allotted to him, in what worse way could he vent his rage, than by beating his head against the walls? and who but himself would be a sufferer by such folly? Noise, the only offence by which a man thus engaged could render himself troublesome (an offence, by the bye, against which irons themselves afford no security,) might, if found otherwise incorrigible, be subdued by *gagging* - a most natural and efficacious mode of prevention, as well as punishment, the prospect of which would probably be for ever sufficient to render the infliction of it unnecessary. Punishment, even in its most hideous forms, loses its odious character, when bereft of that uncertainty, without which the rashest desperado would not expose himself to its stroke...

Letter X: Choice of Trades Should Be Free

The general notion seemed to be, that as the people were to be made to work for their punishment, the works to be given to them should be somewhat which they would not like; and, in that respect, it looks as if the consideration of punishment, with its appendage of reformation, had kept the other of economy a little behind the curtain. But I neither see the great danger nor the great harm of a man's liking his work too well; and how well so ever he might have liked it elsewhere, I should still less apprehend his liking the thought of having it to do there. Supposing no sage regulations made by any body to nail them to this or that sort of work, the work they would naturally fall upon under the hands of a contractor would be that, whatever it might be, by which there was most money to be made; for the more the prisoner-workman got, the more the master could get out of him; so that upon that point I should have little fear of their not agreeing. Nor do I see why labour should be the less reforming for being profitable. On the contrary, among working men, especially among working men whom the discipline of the house would so effectually keep from all kinds of mischief, I must confess I know of no test of reformation so plain or so sure as the improved quantity and value of their work...

Letter XIII: Means of Extracting Labour

Understanding thus much of his situation, my contractor, I conceive, notwithstanding the checks you have seen, will hardly think it necessary to ask me how he is to manage to persuade his boarders to set to work. - Having them under this regimen, what better security he can wish for of their working, and that to their utmost, I can hardly imagine. At any rate, he has much better security than he can have for the industry and diligence of any ordinary journeyman at large, who is paid by the day, and not by the piece. If a man won't work, nothing has he to do, from morning to night, but to eat his bad bread and drink his water, without a soul to speak to. If he will work, his time is occupied, and he has his meat and his beer, or whatever else his earnings may afford him, and not a stroke does he strike but he gets something, which he would not have got otherwise. This encouragement is necessary to his doing his utmost: but more than this is not necessary. It is necessary every exertion he makes should be sure of its reward; but it is not necessary that such reward be so great, or any thing near so great, as he might have had, had he worked elsewhere. The confinement, which is his punishment, preventing his carrying the work to another market, subjects him to a monopoly; which the contractor, his master, like any other monopolist, makes, of course, as much of as he can. The workman lives in a poor country, where wages are low; but in a poor country, a man who is paid according to his work will exert himself at least as much as in a rich one. According to Mr. Arthur Young, and the very cogent evidence he gives, he should work more: for more work that intelligent traveler finds always done in dear years than in plentiful ones: the earnings of one day affording, in the latter case, a fund for the extravagance of the next. But this is not all. His master may fleece him, if he pleases, at both ends. After sharing in his profits, he may again take a profit upon his expense. He would probably choose to employ both expedients together. The tax upon earnings, if it stood alone, might possibly appear liable to be evaded in some degree, and be frustrated in some cases, by a confederacy between the workmen and their employers out of doors; the tax upon expenditure, by their frugality, supposing that virtue to take root in such a soil; or in some instances, perhaps, by their generosity to their friends without doors. The tax upon earnings would probably not be laid on in an open way, upon any other than the *good* hands; whose traffic must be carried on, with or without his intervention, between them and their out-of-door employers. In the trades which he thought proper to set up of himself for his *capable* hands, his *promising* hands, and his *drones*, the tax might be levied in a more covert way by the lowering of the price paid by him, in comparison of the free prices given out of doors for similar work. Where he is sure of his men, as well with regard to their disposition to spend as with regard to their inability to collude, the tax upon expenditure, without any tax upon profits open or covert, would be the least discouraging: it would be the least discouraging for the present, as the earnings would sound greater to their ears; and with a view to the future, as they would thereby see (I mean such of them as had any hopes of releasement) what their earnings might at that happy period be expected to amount to, in reality as well as in name?

Letter XV: Prospect of Saving from this Plan

Many are the data with which a man ought to be furnished (and with not one of which am I furnished) before he pretended to speak upon any tolerable footing of assurance with regard to the advantage that might be expected in the view of pecuniary economy from the inspection plan. On the one hand, the average annual amount of the present establishments, what ever they are (for I confess I do not know,) for the disposal of convicts: The expected amount of the like average with regard to the measure which I have just learnt has been resolved upon for sending colonies of them to New South Wales, including as well the maintenance of them till shipped, as the expense of the transportation, and the maintenance of them when they are got there: - On the other hand, the capital proposed to have been expended in the building and fitting up the experimental penitentiary-house:-The further capital proposed to have been expended in the furniture of it: - The sum proposed to have been allowed per man for the maintenance of the prisoners till the time when their labour might be expected to yield a produce. These points and a few others being ascertained, I should then be curious to know what degree of productiveness, if any would be looked upon as giving to the measure of a penitentiary-house, either of any construction or of this extraordinary one, the pre-eminence upon the whole over any of the other modes of disposal now in practice or in contemplation. Many distinct points for the eye to rest upon in such a scale will readily occur: - 1st, The produce might be barely sufficient to pay the expense of feeding; - 2d, It might farther pay the expense of clothing; - 3d, It might farther pay the expense of guarding and instructing, viz. the salaries or other emoluments of the numerous tribe of visitors, governors, jailors, task-masters, &c. in the one case, and of the contractor and his assistants in the other; - 4th, It might farther pay the wear and tear of the working-stock laid in; - 5th, It might farther pay the interest of the capital employed in the purchase of such stock; - 6th, It might farther pay the interest of the capital laid out in the erecting and fitting up the establishment in all its parts, at the common rate of interest for money laid out in building; - 7th, It might farther pay, at the ordinary rate, the interest of the money, if any, laid out in the purchase of the ground. Even at the first mentioned and lowest of these stages, I should be curious to compare the charge of such an institution with that of the least chargeable of those others that are as yet preferred to it. When it had arisen above the last, then, as you see, and not till then, it could be said to yield a profit, in the sense in which the same thing could be said of any manufacturing establishment of a private nature...

Letter XVI: Houses of Correction

I will not pester you with further niceties applicable to the difference between houses of correction, and work-houses, and poor-houses, if any there should be, which are not work-houses; between the different modes of treatment that may be due to what are looked upon as the inferior degrees of dishonesty, to idleness as yet untainted with dishonesty, and to blameless indigence. The law herself has scarcely eyes for these microscopic differences. I bow down, therefore, for the present at least, to the counsel of so many sages, and shrink from the crime of being 'wiser than the law.

Letter XVII: Prisons for Safe Custody Merely

A word or two respecting the condition of *offenders before conviction*: or, if that expression should appear to include a solecism, of persons accused, who either for want of bail, or as charged with offences not billable, have hitherto been made, through negligence or necessity, to share by anticipation so much of the fate of convicts, as imprisonment more or less rigid may amount to.

To persons thus circumstanced, the inspection principle would apply, as far as *safe custody* was concerned, with as much advantage as to convicts. But as there can be no ground for punishing them any otherwise than in so far as the *restraint* necessary for safe custody has the effect of punishment, there can be as little ground for subjecting them to *solitude*, unless where that circumstance should also appear necessary, either to safe custody, or to prevent that mental infection, which novices in the arts of dishonesty, and in debauchery, the parent of dishonesty, are so much in danger of contracting from the masters of those arts. In this view, therefore, the *partitions* might appear to some an unnecessary ingredient in the composition of the building; though I confess, from the consideration just alleged, they would not appear in that light to me. Communication must likewise be allowed to the prisoners with their friends and legal assistants, for the purpose of settling their affairs, and concerting their defence.

As forced labour is punishment, labour must not here be forced. For the same reason, and because the privation of such comforts of any kind as a man's circumstances allow him, is also punishment, neither should the free admission of such comforts, as far as is consistent with sobriety, be denied; nor, if the keeper is permitted to concern himself in any part of the trade, should he be permitted to make a greater profit than would be made by other traders.

But amongst persons of such description, and in such a multitude~ there will always be a certain number, nor that probably an inconsiderable one, who will possess no means of subsistence whatever of their own. These then will, in so far, come under a predicament not very dissimilar to that of convicts in a penitentiary-house. Whatever works they may be capable of, there is no reason why subsistence should be given to them, any more that to persons free from suspicion and at large, but as the price for work, supposing them able to perform it. But as this ability is a fact, the judgment of which is a matter of great nicety, too much it may be thought by far to be entrusted to such hands, if to any, some allowance must therefore be made them *gratis*, and that at least as good a one as I recommended for the penitentiary-house. In order to supply the defects of this allowance, the point then will be, to provide some sort of work for such, who not having trades of their own which they can work at, are yet willing to take work, if they can get it. If to find such work might be difficult, even in a house of correction, on account of the shortness of the time which there may be for learning work, for the same reason it should be still more difficult in a prison appropriated to safe custody before conviction, at least in cases where, as it will sometimes happen, the commitment precedes the trial but a few days. If on the ground of being particularly likely to have it in his power to provide work, the contracting keeper of a penitentiary-house should be deemed the fittest person for the keeping of a *safe-custody house* (for so I would wish to call it, rather than a prison,) in other respects he might be thought less fit, rather than more so. In a penitentiary-house, he is an extortioner by trade: a trade he must wholly learn, every time he sets his foot in a safe-custody house, on pain of such punishment as unlicensed extortioners may deserve. But it by no means follows, because the keeper of a penitentiary-house has found one, or perhaps half-a-dozen sorts of work, any of which a person may make himself tolerably master of in the course of a few months, that he should be in possession of any that might be performed without learning, or learnt in a few days. If, therefore, for frugality's sake, or any other convenience, any other establishments were taken to combine with that of a safe-custody house, a house of correction would seem better suited to such a purpose, than a penitentiary-house. But without considering it as matter of necessity to have recourse to such shifts, the eligibility of which might depend upon local and other particular considerations, I should hope that employments would not be wanting, and those capable of affording a moderately good subsistence, for which a man of ordinary faculties would be as well qualified the first instant, as at the end of seven years. I could almost venture to mention examples, but that the reasons so often given stop my pen.

Letter XVIII: Manufactories

After so much as has been said on the application of our principle to the business of manufactories, considered as carried on by forced labour, you will think a very few words more than sufficient, in the view of applying it to manufactories carried on upon the ordinary plan of freedom.

The centrality of the presiding person's situation will have its use at all events; for the purpose of direction and order at least, if for no other. The concealment of his person will be of use, in as far as control may be judged useful. As to partitions, whether they would be serviceable in the way of preventing distraction, or disserviceable by impeding communication, will depend upon the particular nature of the particular manufacture. In some manufactories they will have a further use, by the convenience they may afford for ranging a greater number of tools than could otherwise be stowed within the workman's reach. In nice businesses, such as that of watch-making, where considerable damage might result from an accidental jog or a momentary distraction, such partitions, I understand, are usual.

Whatever be the manufacture, the utility of the principle is obvious and incontestable, in all cases where the workmen are paid according to their *time.* Where they are paid by the piece, there the interest which the workman has in the value of his work supersedes the use of coercion, and of every expedient calculated to give force to it. In this case, I see no other use to be made of the inspection principle, than in as far as instruction may be wanted, or in the view of preventing any waste or other damage, which would not of itself come home to the workman, in the way of diminishing his earnings, or in any other shape.

Were a manufactory of any kind to be established upon this principle, the *central lodge* would probably be made use of as the competing-house: and if more branches than one were carried on under the same roof, the accounts belonging to each branch would be kept in the corresponding parts of the lodge. The lodge would also serve as a sort of temporary store-room, into which the tools and materials would be brought from the work-houses, and from whence they would be delivered out to the workmen all around, as well as finished work received, as occasion might require.

Letter XIX: Mad-Houses

That any of the receptacles at present subsisting should be pulled down only to make room for others on the inspection principle, is neither to be expected nor to be wished. But, should any buildings that may be erected in future for this purpose be made to receive the inspection form, the object of such institutions could scarce fail of receiving some share of its salutary influence. The powers of the insane, as well as those of the wicked, are capable of being directed either against their fellow-creatures or against themselves. If in the latter case nothing less than perpetual chains should be availing, yet in all instances where only the former danger is to be apprehended separate cells, exposed, as in the case of prisons, to inspection, would render the use of chains and other modes of corporal sufferance as unnecessary in this case as in any. And with regard to the conduct of the keepers, and the need which the patients have to be kept, the natural, and not discommendable jealousy of abuse would, in this instance as in the former ones, find a much readier satisfaction than it could anywhere at present.

Letter XX: Hospitals

If any thing could still be wanting to show how far this plan is from any necessary connexion with severe and coercive measures, there cannot be a stronger consideration than that of the advantage with which it applies to *hospitals*; establishments of which the sole object is the relief of the afflicted, whom their own entreaties have introduced. Tenacious as ever of the principle of o*mnipresence*, I take it for granted that the whole tribe of medical curators - the *surgeon*, the *apothecary*, the *matron*, to whom I could wish to add even the *physician*, could the establishment be but sufficient to make it worth his while, find in the inspection-lodge and what apartments might be added above it, their constant residence. Here the physician and the apothecary might know with certainty that the prescription which the one had ordered and the other made up, had been administered at the exact time and in the exact manner in which it was ordered to be administered. Here the surgeon would be sure that his instructions and directions had been followed in all points by his pupils and assistants. Here the faculty, in all its branches, might with the least trouble possible watch as much as they chose to watch, of the progress of the disease, and the influence of the remedy. Complaints from the sick might be received the instant the cause of the complaint, real or imaginary, occurred; though, as misconduct would be followed by instant reprehension, such complaints must be proportionably rare.

The separation of the cells might be in part, continued either for comfort, or for decency. Curtains, instead of grating, would give the patients, when they thought fit, the option of being seen. Partitions of greater solidity and extent might divide the fabric into different wards, confining infection, adapting themselves to the varieties of disease, and affording, upon occasion, diversities of temperature.

In hot weather, to save the room from being heated, and the patients from being incommoded by the sun, *shades* or awnings might secure the windows towards the south.

* * *

From the same reasoning it will follow, that the *circular* form demanded as the best of all by the inspection principle, must, in a view to ventilation, have in a considerable degree the advantage over *rectilinear*; and even, were the difference sufficiently material, the inspection principle might be applied to his oval with little or no disadvantage. The form of the inspection lodge might in this case follow that of the containing building; and that central part, so far from obstructing the ventilation, would rather, as it should seem, assist it, increasing the force of the current by the compressure.

It should seem also, that to a circular building, the central lodge would thus give the same aptitude to ventilation, which the Doctor's oval form possesses of itself.

To save his patients from catching cold while the current is passing through the room, the Doctor allows to each a short screen, like the head of a cradle, to be rested on the bed.

Here the use of the tin *speaking-tubes* would be seen again, in the means they would afford to the patient, though he were equal to no more than a whisper, of conveying to the lodge the most immediate notice of his wants, and receiving answers in a tone equally unproductive of disturbance.

Something I could have wished to say on the important difference between the general and comparatively immaterial impurity resulting merely from the *phlogiston*, and the various particular impurities constituted by the various products of *putrefaction*, or by the different matters of the various *contagions*. Against these very different dangers, the mode and measure of precaution might admit of no small difference. But this belongs not necessarily to the subject, and you would not thank me, any more than gentlemen of the faculty who understand it better than I, or gentlemen at large who would not wish to understand it.

An hospital built and conducted upon a plan of this kind, of the success of which everybody might be an observer, accessible to the patients' friends, who, without incommoding or being incommoded, might see the whole economy of it carried on under their eye, would lose, it is to be hoped, a great part of those repelling terrors, which deprive of the benefit of such institutions many objects whom prejudice, in league with poverty, either debars altogether from relief, or drives to seek it in much less eligible shapes. Who knows but that the certainty of a medical attendance, not occasional, short-lived, or even precarious, as at present, but constant and uninterrupted, might not render such a situation preferable even to home, in the eyes of many persons who could afford to pay for it? and that the erection of a building of this kind might turn to account in the hands of some enterprising practitioner?

A *prison*, as I observed in a former letter, includes an hospital. In prisons on this construction, every cell may receive the properties of an hospital, without undergoing any change. The whole prison would be perhaps a better hospital than any building known hitherto by that name. Yet should it be thought of use, a few cells might be appropriated to that purpose; and perhaps it may be thought advisable that some cases of infection should be thrown out, and lodged under another roof.

But if infection in general must be sent to be *cured* elsewhere, there is no spot in which infection originating in negligence can, either in the *rise* or *spread* of it, meet with such obstacles as here. In what other instance as in this, will you see the interests of the governor and the governed in this important particular, so perfectly confounded and made one? - those of the keeper with those of the prisoners - those of the medical curator with those of the patients? Clean or unclean, safe or unsafe, he runs the chance that they do: if he lets them poison themselves, he lets them poison *him*. Encompassed on all sides by a multitude of persons, whose good or bad condition depends upon himself, he stands as a hostage in his own hands for the salubrity of the whole.

Letter XXI: Schools

To the first of these applications the most captious timidity, I think, could hardly fancy an objection: concerning the hours of study, there can, I think, be but one wish, that they should he employed in study. It is scarce necessary to observe that gratings, bars, and bolts, and every circumstance from which an inspection-house can derive a terrific character, have nothing to do here. All play, all chattering - in short, all distraction of every kind, is effectually banished by the central and covered situation of the master, seconded by partitions or screens between the scholars, as slight as you please. The different measures and casts of talent, by this means rendered, perhaps for the first time, distinctly discernible, will indicate the different degrees of attention and modes of culture most suitable to each particular disposition; and incurable and irreproachable dullness or imbecility will no longer be punished for the sins of idleness or obstinacy. That species of fraud at Westminster called *cribbing*, a vice thought hitherto congenial to schools, will never creep in here. That system of premature corruption, in which idleness is screened by opulence, and the honour due to talents or industry is let out for hire, will be completely done away; and a nobleman may stand as good a chance of knowing something as a common man.

Nor, in point of present enjoyment, will the scholars be losers by the change. Those sinkings of the heart at the thoughts of a task undone, those galling struggles between the passion for play and the fear of punishment, would there be unknown. During the hours of business, habit, no longer broken in upon by accident, would strip the master's presence of its terrors, without depriving it of its use. And the time allotted for study being faithfully and rigidly appropriated to that service, the less of it would serve.

The separate spaces allotted for this purpose would not in other respects be thrown away. A bed, a bureau, and a chair, must be had at any rate; so that the only extraordinary expense in building would be for the *partitions*, for which a very slight thickness would suffice. The youth of either sex might by this means sleep, as well as study, under inspection, and alone - a circumstance of no mean importance in many a parent's eye.

In the Royal Military School at Paris, the bed-chambers (if my brother's memory does not deceive him) form two ranges on the two sides of a long room; the inhabitants being separated from one another by *partitions*, but exposed alike to the view of a master at his walks, by a kind of a *grated window* in each door. This plan of construction struck him, he tells me, a good deal, as he walked over that establishment (about a dozen years ago, was it not?) with you; and possibly in that walk the foundation was laid for his Inspection-House. If he there borrowed his idea, I hope he has not repaid it without interest. You will confess some difference, in point of facility, betwixt a state of incessant walking and a state of rest; and in point of completeness of inspection, between visiting two or three hundred persons one after another, and seeing them at once.

In stating what this principle *will* do in promoting the progress of instruction in every line, a word or two will be thought sufficient to state what it will *not* do. It *does* give every degree of efficacy which can be given to the influence of *punishment* and *restraint*. But it does nothing towards correcting the oppressive influence of punishment and restraint, by the enlivening and invigorating influence of *reward*. That noblest and brightest engine of discipline can by no other means be put to constant use in schools, than by the practice which at Westminster, you know, goes by the name of *challenging* - an institution which, paying merit in its fittest and most inexhaustible coin, and even uniting in one impulse the opposite powers of reward and punishment, holds out dishonour for every attention a boy omits, and honour for every exertion he can bestow.

With regard to the extending the range of inspection over every moment of a boy's time, the sentiments of mankind might not be altogether so unanimous. The notion, indeed, of most parents is, I believe, that children cannot be too much under the master's eye; and if man were a consistent animal, none who entertain that notion but should be fonder of the principle the farther they saw it pursued. But as consistency is of all human qualities the most rare, it need not at all surprise us, if, of those who in the present state of things are most anxious on the head of the master's omnipresence, many were to fly back and change their note, when they saw that point screwed up at once to a pitch of perfection so much beyond whatever they could have been accustomed to conceive.

* * *

Would happiness be most likely to be increased or diminished by this discipline? - Call them soldiers, call them monks, call them machines: so they were but happy ones, I should not care. Wars and storms are best to read of, but peace and calms are better to enjoy. Don't be frightened now, my dear *****, and think that I am going to entertain you with a course of moral philosophy, or even with a system of education. Happiness is a very pretty thing to feel, but very dry to talk about; so you may unknot your brow, for I shall say no more about the matter. One thing only I will add, which is, that whoever sets up an inspection-school upon the tiptop of the principle, had need to be very sure of the master; for the boy's body is not more the child of his father's, than his mind will be of the master's mind; with no other difference than what there is between command on one side and subjection on the other.

Some of these fine queries which I have been treating you with, and finer still, Rousseau would have entertained us with; nor do I imagine he would have put his Emilius into an inspection-house; but I think he would have been glad of such a school for his Sophia.

* * *

I hope no critic of more learning than candor will do an inspection-house so much injustice as to compare it to Dionysius' ear. The object of that contrivance was, to know what prisoners said without their suspecting any such thing. The object of the inspection principle is directly the reverse: it is to make them not only suspect, but be assured, that whatever they do is known, even though that should not be the case. Detection is the object of the first: prevention, that of the latter. In the former case the ruling person is a spy; in the latter he is a monitor. The object of the first was to pry into the secret recesses of the heart; the latter, confining its attention to overt acts, leaves thoughts and fancies to their proper ordinary, the court above.

Patrick Colquhoun (1745-1820)

Born in Dumbarton on March 14, 1745, Patrick Colquhoun was orphaned at a young age. Before turning sixteen he was sent to the colony of Virginia where he often associated with legal minds. In 1766, however, Colquhoun suffered a deterioration of health, and returned home to take up residence in Glasgow. When the American Revolution broke out in 1776, Colquhoun contributed to the formation of a Glasgow regiment to fight the rebels. Much of his life was devoted to business exploits, trading linen, and lobbying avidly for local industries. In 1797, he was awarded an honorary LL.D. by the University of Glasgow, and went on to conduct business with the then Prime Minister, Lord North.

Colquhoun was also responsible for the establishment of a Chamber of Commerce and Manufactures in Glasgow, which he also chaired. He was made Lord Provost of Glasgow in 1782, and appointed city Magistrate in London from 1792 until 1818. He earned a good deal of attention for his work, *Wealth, Power and Resources of the British Empire*, published in 1814. Colquhoun provided estimates of national income, and wrote on the dichotomies between productive and unproductive labour.

As Magistrate, Colquhoun was also deeply concerned with crime prevention. His works included treatises on police, social reform, welfare, moral regulation and civic education with the primary aim of disciplining the labouring poor. Along with *Treatise of the Police of the Metropolis* (1797), therefore, Colquhoun also published works such as *New and Appropriate System of Education for the Labouring People* in 1806, a pamphlet that was highly influential in its time.

In 1798, Colquhoun was successful in convincing the West India Planters Committees and the West India Merchants to fund a force designed to curb crime on the River Thames. Colquhoun sought to deter theft with the creation of the Thames River Police, using 50 men to supervise thousands of workers who were suspected of theft from their own employers. Though met with hostility, Colquhoun proclaimed success for his police project, arguing he had saved over one hundred thousand pounds worth of stolen goods. Word of Colquhoun's success travelled quickly with the help of his own account of the experiment: *Treatise on the Commerce and Police of the River Thames* (1800). The police force was soon transformed into a public agency, inspiring similar projects throughout the Western world and solidifying Colquhoun's reputation as the architect of the modern police. He died on April 25, 1820.

Works Referenced:
Critchley, Thomas A. *A History of Police in England and Wales.* Patterson Smith: New Jersey, 1972.
Yeats, Grant David. *A Biographical Sketch of the Life and Writings of Patrick Colquhoun.* G. Smeeton: London, 1818.

Selections from: *Treatise on the Police of the Metropolis* **(London: J. Mawman, 1800)., orig. 1795.**

Preface
Police in this country may be considered as a new science; the properties of which consist not in the Judicial Powers which lead to Punishment, and which belong to Magistrates alone; but in the Prevention and Detection of Crimes, and in those other functions which relate to internal regulations for the well ordering and comfort of civil society.

Chapter I: General View of Existing Evils
In developing the causes which have produced that want of security, which it is believed prevails in no other civilized country in so great a degree as in England, it will be necessary to examine how far the System of Criminal Jurisprudence has been, hitherto, applicable to the prevention of crimes.

The severity of the punishment, which at present attaches to crimes regarded by mankind as of an interior nature, and which affect property in a trivial manner, is also deserving the most serious attention. It is only necessary to be acquainted with the modern history of the criminal prosecutions, trials, acquittals, and pardons in this country, in order to be completely convicted that the progressive increase of delinquents, and the evils experienced by society from the multitude of petty crimes, result in a great measure from this single circumstance.

It would by no means difficult to form such a plan of Police as should establish many useful restrictions, for the purpose of checking and embarrassing these criminal people; so as to render it extremely difficult, if not impracticable for them, in many instances, to carry on their business without the greatest hazard of detection.

If the evil is to be cured at all, it must be by the promotion and encouragement of an active principle, under proper superintendence, calculated to prevent every class of dealers, who are known to live partly or wholly by fraud, from pursuing those illegal practices; which nothing but a watchful Police, aided by a correct system of restraints, can possibly effect.

The system now suggested, is calculated to prevent, if possible, the seeds of villainy from being sown: or, if sown, to check their growth in the bud, and never permit them to ripen at all.

The want of security which the public experiences with regard to life and property, and the inefficacy of the Police in preventing crimes are to be attributed principally to the following causes:

The imperfections in the Criminal Code; and in many instances, its deficiency with respect to the mode of punishment: as well as to the want of many other regulations, provisions, and restraints, applicable to the present state of society,

The laws are armed against the powers of Rebellion, but are not calculated to oppose its principle.

Doubtless, the fundamental principle of good legislation is, rather to prevent crimes than to punish.—If a mathematical expression may be made use of, relative to the good and evil of human life, it is the art of conducting men to the maximum of happiness and the minimum of misery.

Chapter III: The Cause and Progress of Small Thefts
The rapid growth of this Evil within the last twenty years, and the effect it has upon the morals of menial servants and others, who must in the nature of things have a certain trust committed to them, is a strong reason why some effectual remedy should be administred as speedily as possible.

The following particulars, extracted from Mr. Middleton's *View of the Agriculture of Middlesex*, will enable the reader to form some judgment of the extent of the mischief, and the cause from which it originates; producing and increasing that band of plunderers, of which the Metropolis itself has ultimately been at once the Nurse and the Victim.

Although these suggestions may appear harsh, and some of them may admit of more extended discussion, yet they certainly deserve very serious consideration, as do also the following observations on the commons and waste lands with which this kingdom still abounds; and on the general character of servants and labourers; the latter of which afford but too melancholy a confirmation of many opinions which the author of this treatise has thought it his duty to bring forward to the public eye.

On estimating the value of the commons in Middlesex, including every advantage that can be derived from them in pasturage, locality of situation, and the barbarous custom of turbary, it appears that they do not produce to the community, in their present state, more than four shilling per Acre! On the other hand, they are, in many instances, of real injury to the public, by holding out a lure to the poor man; by affording him materials wherewith to build his cottage, and ground to erect it upon; together with firing, and the run of his poultry and pigs for nothing.

In short, the Commons of this Country are well known to be the constant resort of footpads and highwaymen, and are literally and proverbially a public nuisance.

The labourers of this country are ruined in morals and constitution by the public houses. It is a general rule, that the higher their wages, the less they carry home, and consequently the greater is the wretchedness of themselves and their families. Comforts in a cottage are mostly found where the man's wages are low, at least so low as to require him to labour six days a week.

If his master has business in hand that requires particular dispatch, he will then, more than at any other time, be absent from his work, and his wife and children will experience the extreme of hunger, rags and cold.

Gentlemen's Servants are mostly a bad set, and the great number kept in this country, is the means of the rural labourers acquiring a degree of idleness and insolence unknown in places more remote from the Metropolis.

Chapter IV: On Burglaries and Highway Robberies

The criminal and unfortunate individuals, who compose the dismal catalogue of highwaymen, footpad-robbers, burglars, pick-pockets, and common thieves, in and about this Metropolis, may be divided into the three following classes:

1. Young men of some education, who having acquired idle habits of abandoning business, or by being bred to no profession, and having been seduced by this idleness to indulge in gambling and scenes of debauchery and dissipation, at length impoverished and unable to purchase their accustomed gratifications, have recourse to the highway to supply immediate wants.

2. Tradesmen and others, who having ruined their fortunes and business by gaming and dissipation, sometimes as a desperate remedy, go upon the road.

But these two classes are extremely few in number, and bear no proportion to the lower and more depraved part of the fraternity of thieves.

1. (1) Servants, hostlers, stable and post-boys out of place; who, preferring what they consider as idleness, have studied the profession of thieving. (2) Persons who being imprisoned for debts, assaults, or petty offences, have learned habits of idleness and profligacy in goals. (3) Idle and disorderly mechanics and labourers, who having on this account lost the confidence of their masters or employers, resort to thieving, as a means of support; from all whom the notorious and hackneyed thieves generally select the most trusty and daring to act as their associates. (4) Criminals tried and acquitted of offences charged against them, of which class a vast number is annually let loose upon society. (5) Convicts discharged from prison and the hulks, after suffering the sentence of the Law: too often instructed by one another in all the arts and devices which attach to the most extreme degree of human depravity, and in the perfect knowledge of the means of perpetrating crimes, and of eluding justice.

Without friends, without character, and without the means of subsistence, what are these unhappy mortals to do?—they are no sooner known or suspected, than they are avoided—No person will employ them, even if they were disposed to return to the paths of honesty; unless they make use of fraud and deception, by concealing that they have been the inhabitants of a prison, or of the hulks.

At large upon the world, without food or raiment, and with the constant calls of nature upon them for both, without a home or any asylum to shelter them from the inclemency of the weather, what is to become of them?

If some plan of employment is not speedily devised, to which all persons of this description may resort, who cannot otherwise subsist themselves in an honest way; and if the police of the Metropolis is not greatly improved, by the introduction of more energy, and a greater degree of system and method in its administration; it is much to be feared, that no existing power will be able to keep them within bounds.

It is in vain to say the laws are sufficient.—They are indeed abundantly voluminous, and in many respects very excellent, but they require to be revised, consolidated, modernized, and adapted in a greater degree to the prevention of existing evils, with such regulations as would ensure their due execution not only in every part of the Capital, but also in all parts of the Kingdom.

If, by wise regulations, it were possible to embarrass and disturb the extensive trade carried on by all the concealed receivers, who are the particular class having connection with the professed thieves, a very great check would be given to public depredations.

Chapter VI: On Gaming and The Lottery

A mistaken sense of what constitutes human happiness, fatally leads the mass of the people who have the means of moving in any degree above the middle ranks of life, into circles where Faro Tables and other games at hazard are introduced in private families:--Where the least recommendation (and sharpers spare no pains to obtain recommendations) is a passport to all who can exhibit a genteel exterior; and where the young and the inexperienced are initiated in every propensity tending to debase human character; while they are thought to view with contempt every acquirement, connected with the duties which lead to domestic happiness, or to those qualifications which can render either sex respectable in the world.

If a legislative regulation could also be established, extending certain restrictions to the members of the different *Friendly Societies* situated within the Bills of Morality with regard to Fraudulent Lottery Insurances, above seventy thousand families would be relieved from the consequences of this insinuating evil; which has been so fatal to the happiness and comfort of a vast number of tradesmen and artisans, as well as inferior classes of labourers.

At present, the temptation to follow these fraudulent practices is so great, from the productive nature of the business, that unless some new expedient be resorted to, no well-grounded hope can be entertained of lessening the evil in any material degree.

It is clear to demonstration that the present system is founded on a principle not less erroneous than mischievous; and, therefore, it cannot too soon be abandoned; especially since it would appear that the revenue it produces might be preserved, with the incalculable advantage to the nation of preserving, at the same time, the morals of the people, and turning into a course of industry and usefulness the labour of many thousand individuals, who, instead of being, as at present, pests in society, might be rendered useful members of the state.

Chapter VII: On the Coinage of Counterfeit Money

In contemplating and in developing the causes of the vast accumulation and increase of base money, which has thus deluged the country of late years, the evil will be found to have proceeded chiefly from the want of a new coinage—of laws, applicable to the new tricks and devices practiced by the coiners—of proper checks upon fraudulent circulation—of rewards for the detection and apprehension of offenders—and of a sufficient fund to ensure the prompt execution of the law, by a vigorous and energetic police, directed not only to the execution of apposite laws in the detection and punishment of offenders, but also to the means of prevention.

In suppressing great evils, strong and adequate powers must be applied, and nothing can give force and activity to these powers, but the ability to reward liberally all persons engaged in the public service, either as police officers, or as temporary agents for the purpose of detecting atrocious offenders.

Chapter IX: On Plunder in the Dock-Yards:

Having thus traced the outlines of such remedies [that are (1) a general police system, (2) a local police for the dock-yards, (3) legislative regulations proposed in aid of the general and local police system] for the protection of his Majesty's Naval, Victualling, Ordnance and other stores, as certainly require Legislative Regulations; it remains now to consider, what other measures may appear necessary, within the limits of the authority with which the Lords Commissioners of the Admiralty are invested, for the purpose of rendering the preventive system complete. Those which have occurred to the author of this work will be classed under the following heads:

(4) regulations respecting the sale of old stores

(5) the abolition of the perquisite of chips

(6) the abolition of fees and perquisites of every description; to be recompensed by a liberal increase of salaries

(7) an improved mode of keeping accounts

(8) an annual inventory of stores on hand. (p. 273)

The abolition of fees and perquisites, and an increase of salaries: It has been observed, and it is a circumstance much to be lamented, that in too many instances, where individuals have pecuniary transactions with any of the Departments of Government, a dereliction of principle is apparent which does not extend to the general intercourse of society, and hence arises the necessity of stronger guards, where the Public interest is concerned; and nothing appears to be better calculated to counteract this baneful propensity in the human mind than the total abolition of fees and perquisites. (pp. 282-283).

The suggestions now offered are in the best train of being adopted, by the total abolition of fees and perquisites, and a liberal increase of salary in lieu of the reduction of income, which such an arrangement will occasion: Such salaries as will secure to the nation those inestimable advantages which always result from rectitude of conduct, zeal, accuracy, and fidelity, in the discharge of public trusts committed to subordinate officers. It is by this and other wise and practicable arrangements, that a confidence is to be established, "that the resources of the state will not only last our time," but extend to many generations; while the improvement of public morals will contribute, in an eminent degree, to the happiness and prosperity of the country.

Chapter XI: On the Origin of Criminal Offences

When by means of strong constitutions, they survive the shocks which nature has sustained in its progress to maturity under the influence of habits so exceedingly depraved, they are restrained by no principle of morality or religion, and only wait for opportunities, to plunge into every excess and every crime.

The bad and immoral education of apprentices to mechanical employments.

1. The number of individuals in various occupations among the lower and middling ranks of life who from their own mismanagement and want of industry, or attention to their business, are suddenly broke down, and in some degree excluded from the regular intercourse with society.

2. The situation of idle and profligate menial servants out of place, and destitute of the means of obtaining situations from the loss of character.

3. The deplorable state and condition of the lower order of the Jews in the Metropolis, who are of the Society of the Dutch Synagogue. Totally without education, and very seldom trained to any trade or occupation by which they can earn their livelihood by manual labour.

4. The deprave morals of the Aquatic labourers and others employed on the wharfs and quays, and in ships, vessels, and craft, upon the River Thames; and from the want, until lately, of an appropriate Preventive System to check these depredations.

5. The want of a proper control over persons of loose conduct and dishonest habits, who have opened shops for the purchase and sale of Old Iron, and other metals—old stores—rags—old furniture—old building materials, and second hand wearing apparel, and other goods—and also cart-keepers for the collection and removal of these articles from place to place.

6. Ill-regulated Public Houses, conducted by men of loose conduct and depraved morals—since it is in these receptacles that the corruption of morals originates.

Chapter XII: The Origin of Crimes: Female Prostitution

"Government," says the benevolent Hanway, "originates from the love of order.—Watered by Police it grows up to maturity, and in course of time spreads a luxuriant comfort and security.—Cut off its branches, and the mere trunk, however strong it may appear, can afford no shelter."

Chapter XIII: The Origin of Crimes Continued: State of the Poor

The system which prevails in the Metropolis, with respect to these unfortunate individuals who are denominated the Casual Poor, will be found on minute inquiry to be none of the least considerable of the causes, which lead to the corruption of morals, and to the multiplication of minor offences in particular.

Such is frequently the situation of the more decent and virtuous class of the labouring people, who come to seek employment in the Metropolis. The more profligate who pursue the same course have generally other resources. Where honest labour is not to be procured, they connect themselves with those who live by petty or more atrocious offences, and contribute in no small degree to the increase of the general phalanx of delinquents. The young female part of such families too often become prostitutes, while the males pursue acts of depredation upon the Public, by availing themselves of the various resources, which the defects in the Police system allow.

It is not primary aid that will heal this gangrene: this Corruption of Morals. There must be the application of a correct System of Police calculated to reach the root and origin of the evil.—Without System, Intelligence, Talents, and Industry, united in all that relates to the affairs of the Poor, millions may be wasted as millions have already been wasted, without bettering their condition. In all the branches of the Sciences of Political Economy, there is none which requires so much skill and knowledge of men and manners, as that which relates to this particular object: and yet, important as it is to the best interests of the Community, the management of a concern, in which the very foundation of the national prosperity is involved, is suffered to remain, as in the rude ages, when Society had not assumed the bold features of the present period,--in the hands of changeable, and in many instances, unlettered agents; wholly incompetent to a task at all times nice and difficult in the execution, and often irksome and inconvenient.

By the poor we are not to understand the whole mass of the people who support themselves by labour; for those whose necessity compels them to exercise their industry, become by their poverty the actual pillars of the state.

Labour is absolutely requisite to the existence of all Governments; and as it is from the poor only that labour can be expected, so far from being an evil, they become, under proper regulations, an advantage to every country, and highly deserve the fostering care of every government. It is not poverty, therefore, that is in itself an evil, while health, strength, and inclination, afford the means of subsistence, and while work is to be had by all who seek it.—the evil is to be found only in indigence, where the strength fails, where disease, age, or infancy deprives the individual of the means of subsistence, or where he knows not how to find employment when willing and able to work.

In this view the poor may be divided into five classes:

1. The useful poor: who are able and willing to work—who have already been represented as the pillars of the state, and who merit the utmost attention of all governments, with a direct and immediate view of preventing their poverty from descending unnecessarily into indigence.

2. The vagrant poor: who are able but not willing to work, or who cannot obtain employment in consequence of their bad character. This class may be said to have descended from poverty into beggary, in which state they become objects of peculiar attention, since the state suffers not only the loss of their labour, but also of the money which they obtain by the present ill-judged mode of giving charity.

3. The indigent poor: who from want of employment, sickness, losses, insanity or disease, are unable to maintain themselves. In attending to this description of poor, the first consideration ought to be to select those who are in a state to re-occupy their former station among the labouring poor; and to restore them to the first class as soon as possible, by such relief as should enable them to resume their former employments, and to help themselves and families.

4. The aged and infirm: who are entirely past labour, and have no means of support. Where an honest industrious man has wasted his strength in labour and endeavors to rear a family, he is well entitled to an asylum to render the evening of his life comfortable. For this class the gratitude and the humanity of the Community ought to provide a retreat separate from the profligate and vagrant poor.

5. The infant poor: who from extreme indigence, or the death of parents, are cast upon the public for nurture. Their moral and religious education is of the last importance to the community. They are the children of the public, and if not introduced into life, under circumstances favorable to the interest of the state, the error in the system becomes flagrant. (p. 370).

The error is not in the original design, which is wise and judicious. The 43d of Elizabeth authorizes an assessment to be made for three purposes:

1st To purchase raw materials to set the poor to work, who could not otherwise dispose of their labour.

2nd. To usher into the world, advantageously, the children of poor people, by binding them apprentices to some useful employment.

3rd. To provide for the lame, impotent and blind, and others, being poor and not able to work.

Nothing can be better imagined that the measures in the view of the very able framers of this act: but they did not discover that to execute such a design required powers diametrically opposite to those which the law provided.

That a public institution shall be established in the Metropolis, with three Chief Officers, who shall be charged with the execution of that branch of the police, which relates to street beggars, ad those classes of poor who have no legal settlements in the metropolis, and who now receive casual relief from the different parishes, where they have fixed their residence for the time;--and that these principal officers, (who may be stilled commissioners for inquiring into the cases and causes of the distress of the poor in the metropolis) should exercise the following functions:

1. to charge themselves with the relief and management of the whole of the casual poor, who at present receive temporary aid from the different parishes, or who ask alms in any part of the Metropolis or its Suburbs.

2. to provide work-rooms in various central and convenient situations in the Metropolis, where persons destitute of employment may receive a temporary subsistence for labour. To superintend these work-houses, and become responsible for the proper management.

3. to be empowered to give temporary relief to prop up sinking families, and to prevent their descending from poverty to indigence, by arresting the influence of despondency, and keeping the spirit of industry alive.

4. to assist in binding out the children of the poor, or the unfortunate, who have seen better days, and preventing the females from the danger of becoming prostitutes, or the males from contracting loose and immoral habits, so as if possible to save them to their parents, and to the state.

5. to open offices of inquiry in different parts of the Metropolis, where all classes of indigent persons, who are not entitled to parochial relief, will be invited to resort, for the purpose of being examined, and relieved according to the peculiar circumstance of the case.

6. to exercise the legal powers, through the medium of constables, for the purpose of compelling all mendicants, and idle destitute bays and girls who appear in the streets, to come before the commissioners for examination; that those whose industry cannot be made productive, or who cannot be put in a way to support themselves without alms, may be passed to their parishes, while means are employed to bind out destitute children to some useful occupation.

7. to keep a distinct register of the cases of all mendicants or distressed individuals, who may seek advice and assistance, and to employ such means for alleviating misery, as the peculiar circumstances may suggest—never losing sight of indigence, until an asylum is provided for the helpless and infirm, and also until the indigent, who are able to labour, are placed in a situation to render it productive.

8. that these commissioners shall report their proceedings annually, to his Majesty in Council, and to parliament; with abstracts showing the numbers who have been examined—how disposed of—the earning of the persons at the different work-rooms—the annual expense of the Establishment; together with a general view of the advantages resulting from it; with the proofs of these advantages.

As well as several other respectable living characters, who have particularly turned their thoughts to the subject of the poor, the public are not only already much indebted, but from this prolific resource of judgment, talents, and knowledge, much good might be expected, if ever the period shall arrive when the revision of the Poor Laws shall engage the attention of the legislature.

Chapter XIV: On the Detection of Offenders

Nothing can certainly be better calculated for complete protection against acts of violence in the streets, than the system of a well-regulated Stationary Watch; composed of fit and able bodied men, properly controlled and superintended: and from the number of persons already employed, independent of private watchmen, it would seem only to be necessary to lay down apposite legislative rules, with respect to age or ability, character, wages, rewards for useful services, and general superintendence, in order to establish that species of additional security which would operate as a more effectual means of preventing crimes within the Metropolis.

Let the same system of moderate rewards also be extended to beadles [footnote: beadles are, in many instances, employed at present as local superintendents of the watch, within their respective parishes] for useful public service actually performed, as is proposed with regard to officers of justice, watchmen, and patrols; and much good will arise to the community, without any great additional expense.

For the purpose of establishing a complete and well-connected system of detection, some means ought certainly to be adopted, more closely to unite the city and Police Magistrates, that they may, in a greater degree, go hand in hand in all matters regarding the general interest of the Metropolis and its environs; making the suppression of crimes one common cause, and permitting no punctilio, regarding jurisdiction, to prevent the operation of their united energy in the prompt detection of offenders. This, from the extended state of commerce and society, and the great increase of property, is now rendered a measure in which the inhabitants of the whole Metropolis, as well as the adjacent villages, have a common interest. It is an evil which affects all ranks, and calls aloud for the speedy adoption of some effectual remedy.

Chapter XVI: On the System of Punishments

In the course of the present century, several of the old sanguinary modes of punishment have been either, very properly, abolished by acts of parliament, or allowed, to the honor of humanity, to fall into disuse:--such as burning alive (particularly women) cutting off hands or ears, slitting nostrils, or branding in the hand or face; and among lesser punishments, fallen into disuse, may be mentioned the ducking-stool.

The punishment of death for felony has existed since the reign of Henry I. nearly 700 years.—Transportation is commonly understood to have been first introduced, in 1718, by the act of the 4th George I.; and afterwards enlarged by the Act 6th of George I., which allowed the court a discretionary power to order felons who were by law entitled to their clergy, to be transported to the American plantations for seven or fourteen years, according to circumstances.

Since that period the mode of punishment has undergone several other alterations; and many crimes which were formerly considered of an inferior rank, have been rendered capital; which will be best elucidated by the following Catalogue of Offences divided into six classes according to the Laws now in force.

1. Crimes punishable by the Deprivation of Life; and where upon the conviction of the offenders, the sentence of death must be pronounced by the fudge.

2. Crimes denominated Single Felonies; punishable by Transportation, Whipping, Imprisonment, the Pillory, and Hard Labour in Houses of Correction, according to the nature of offence.

3. Offences denominated Misdemeanors, punishable by Fine, Imprisonment, Whipping, and the Pillory.

4. Idle and disorderly persons, punishable with one month's imprisonment.

5. Rogues and Vagabonds, punishable by six months' imprisonment.

6. Incorrigible rogues, punishable with two years imprisonment and whipping, or transportation for seven years if they break out of prison.

After maturely considering the enormous expense, and the total inefficacy of the System of Hulks, aided by the new lights which have been thrown upon the subject by the important documents called for by the Select Committee on finance, it appears clear to demonstration, that it would be for the interest of the country to abandon the present system; and the author heartily joins in the opinion expressed by those respectable members of the Legislature—"That our principal places of confinement, and modes of punishment, so far from the conversion and reformation of the criminal, tend to send him forth at the expiration of the period of his imprisonment more confirmed in vice; and that the general tendency of our economical arrangements upon this subject, is ill calculated to meet the accumulating burdens, which are the infallible result of so much error in the system of police."

Chapter XVII: Criminal Police of the Metropolis

When the police system was first established in 1792, the public mind became impressed with an idea that the chief, if not the only object of the institution was to prevent robberies, burglaries, and other atrocious offences; and that the suppression of those crimes, which bore hardest upon society, and were most dreaded by the police at large, was to be the result. These expectations showed, that neither the powers nor authorities granted by the Act of Parliament, nor the other duties imposed upon the Magistracy of the Police, were understood. For this Statute, useful as it certainly is in a very high degree in many other respects, does not contain even a single regulation applicable to the prevention of crimes; except that which relates to the apprehension of suspected characters, found in the avenues to public places, with intent to commit felony, who are liable to be punished as rogues and vagabonds,--and even this provision does not extend to the city of London.

Contemplating the various existing evils detailed in this work, and which form so many prominent features of Police, requiring the constant and watchful eye of the Magistrate, it seems clear to demonstration, that unless official duties become the sole business and pursuit of the parties engaged in them, the Public interest must suffer; and (although imperceptible in their progress), crimes will increase and multiply: at a time when the comfort, happiness, and security of society, require that they should be diminished.

To understand the police of the Metropolis to that extent which is necessary to direct and superintend its general operations, it must be acted upon practically; and those who undertake the superintendence and management alluded to, must be men able, intelligent, prudent, and indefatigable: devoting their whole attention to this object alone. Clerks might be continually employed with great advantage in entering and posting up under the proper heads, such new information as should be appointed for receiving such intelligence from all proper and well-informed persons, who might choose to offer the same; so far as such information related to public wrongs, and offences against the peace, safety, and well-being of society.

Chapter XIX: Municipal Police of the Metropolis

The number of inhabitants of this great Metropolis, occupying these various houses and buildings, may, under all circumstances, be rationally estimated at one million at least; for whose accommodation, convenience, and security, the following institutions have been formed, namely,--for education, for promoting good morals, for useful and fine arts, for objects of charity and humanity, for distributing justice, for punishing offenders. (p. 569).

The Metropolis of the Empire having been extended so far beyond its ancient limits;--every parish, hamlet, liberty, or precinct, now contiguous to the cities of

London and Westminster, may be considered as a separate Municipality, where the inhabitants regulate the police of their respective districts, under the authority of a great variety of different Acts of Parliament; enabling them to raise money for paving the streets, and to assess the householders for the interest thereof, as well as for the annual expense of watching, cleansing, and removing nuisances and annoyances. These funds, as well as the execution of the powers of the different Acts are placed in the hands of trustees, of whom in many instances, the Church Wardens, or Parish Officers for the time being, are members ex officio; and by these different bodies, all matters relative to the immediate safety, comfort and convenience of the inhabitants are managed and regulated.

Selections from: *Treatise On Indigence.* Chapter 3 (pp. 79-109) (London: J. Hatchard)., orig. 1806

Chapter III. Board of General And Internal Police
The best security against *indigence, vagrancy, and criminal offences*, will be found in promoting and exciting religious and moral habits among the inferior classes of the community; and it is none of the least of the consolations which attend the present discussion, that the means exist whereby such a favourable turn may be given to the minds of at least a large proportion of the labouring people in every part of the British dominions. Although it is much to be lamented that the lower orders in England are too generally prone to dissolute and immoral propensities, yet no people in Europe, from a characteristic good nature are more easily governed, or better disposed to be led and directed, by gentle means, in all matters tending to the improvement of their condition, although they will not be driven. Many have been improvident, and have descended into indigence more from deficient education, from the temptations which assail them, from the habit of frequenting and almost living in alehouses from the first dawn of manhood, and from the want of religious and moral instruction in early life, than from any vicious principle in the mind. An attention to their condition by the higher ranks of society, and still more by those who compose the executive government of the country, can scarcely fail, if properly directed, to give a new and favourable turn to their character and dispositions. And here a question arises, how is this great desideratum to be accomplished?

A problem so difficult in the police of any civilized country can only be solved by a previous review of the most prominent evils which afflict society, and by a dispassionate inquiry into the means which the legislature has adopted to prevent them, or to check their progress. It has been shown that above one million of individuals, in a country containing less than nine millions of inhabitants, have descended into a state of indigence, requiring either total or partial support from the public, to the amount of nearly £4,300,000 a year. It appears, notwithstanding this great pecuniary sacrifice, that misery, mendacity, and vagrancy prevail to a great extent; and that, including the voluntary aids of the benevolent and humane, the total burdens applicable to *temporary or permanent distress* and to *indigence, misery, mendicity, and vagrancy*, may be estimated at £8,000,000 a year. It further appears that mendicity, vagrancy, female prostitution, and criminal offences, notwithstanding the means which have been pursued, still continue to afflict society with the discouraging prospect of a gradual, and, in the event of peace, a *rapid increase*, and with little expectation of any diminution.

The cause of these evils may be traced principally to *one source*. There exists in this country nothing in the shape of a *systematic superintending police*, calculated to check and prevent the growth and progress of vicious habits, and other irregularities incident to civil society. By the term *police* we are to understand *all those regulations in a country which apply to the comfort, convenience, and safety of the inhabitants*, whether it regards their security against the calamity of indigence, or the effects produced by moral and criminal offences. In discussing subjects of this nature, it is astonishing how much the mind is bewildered for want of a clear conception of the proper division of statistical labour. The duties of *magistrates* are always confounded with those belonging to *police*, without considering that they are separate and distinct: and that the functions of those to whom it ought to be assigned to conduct the police system terminate the moment the exercise of the magisterial duties becomes necessary. The moral, political, or criminal offence, which it was the object of the police to prevent, *is then committed*; and *then* and not till *then*, are magistrates authorized to interfere.

It is indeed true that there is a species of police applicable to the poor, and in some few instances to the prevention of moral and criminal offences; but the latter scarcely exists any where but on the statute-books; and while it partakes in no respect of the true features of *useful police*, it is without proper springs to put the system in motion. Indeed the whole of the national police is without that watchful and superintending agency which is indispensably necessary to produce a preventive effect; and to cause is chiefly to be attributed the great increase of indigence, vagrancy, and crimes.

Boards have long been established for conducting the affairs of the revenue, because the intricacy of the subject, and the minute attention to a very complicated system, required the constant attention of able and intelligent individuals. Commissioners have also been appointed in a variety of instances to audit and examine the public accounts, and to disclose abuses which have taken place in the different departments of Government; but the most important, the most laborious, and the most arduous and intricate branch of statistical inquiry, *the regulation of the national police*, has been assigned to no responsible subordinate agency. No effectual means have been established (the Board of Agriculture excepted) for the purpose of ascertaining useful and minute facts in different branches, of political economy, applicable to the pressures which exist, or may exist, in various parts of the country. No talents have been employed to consider and arrange these facts, if in any instance they have been partially obtained, with a view to suggest a remedy for existing evils. It is the duty of no individual to look to the education of the children of the poor, or to the progress of morals, whether they advance or retrograde; to investigate accurately the various causes of indigence, the management of those to whom it is assigned to relieve, check, and prevent it, or the nature and extent of moral and criminal offences, in all their various ramifications, so as to form an accurate opinion of the proper measures to be pursued, with a view to improve the condition of society in general.

The evils which have been detailed in the progress of this work, are certainly very excessive; and it has been long evident to every enlightened member of the community, that attempts towards a remedy ought not to be delayed; but the pressure perhaps has never been so generally felt as of late years, since the parochial rates for the maintenance of the indigent have so rapidly increased, disclosing through this and other mediums a corresponding increase of vagrancy, idleness, and a general corruption of morals.

In order, however, to discover an effectual remedy, there are innumerable minute facts to be ascertained before any accurate judgment can be formed of the best means of ameliorating the condition of the poor.

An intelligent and respectable author (Mr. Ruggles), while he approves of the ground-work, as established by the 43d of Elizabeth, asserts, *"That the poor laws, which regulate seven millions of people, form a vague, unconnected, and inconsistent piece of patch-work; that the management should be the same as a prudent man would exercise in the conduct of his own affairs; that the poor are a large family, and the legislature the master."*

Admitting the conclusion to be just, it follows of course, that as the structure of the legislature cannot admit of the exercise of the functions of a master, this task must be committed to an agency, representing that august body, and responsible for the due execution of the duties assigned.

Great doubts appear to be justly entertained of the wisdom or policy of disturbing a system so thoroughly identified with the constitution of the country. It is, however, unquestionably susceptible of great improvements. The funds now raised by assessments, and collected by the various classes of individuals who conduct the affairs of 14,611 parishes and places, and the economy of 1970 workhouses, and who deal out relief to above a million of paupers[1] yearly, have become so gigantic as to exceed in their amount the whole aggregate revenues of several of the kingdoms of Europe, which, heretofore at least, held a considerable rank with respect to the power of consequence. They exceed the revenues of Denmark and Sweden nearly threefold; while the general assessments, applicable to all purposes, exceed even the whole revenues of Old Spain, containing ten millions of people.

Independent of other considerations, the changes which have taken place in the state of society have rendered the system too extensive for the species of management which the legislature originally provided. The portion of intelligence applied to this complicated machine is too scanty, and the duties to be performed

---

1   In 1785, according to Mr. Coxe, the revenue of Denmark amounted to £1,5,000 sterling. The revenue of Sweden—1,443,574. According to Mr. M'Arthur, the revenue of Old Spain, before the war, about 5,000,000. According to Mr. Tooke, the revenue of Russia is estimated at 8,500,000.

are besides often as assigned to men who are not only unwilling labourers, but much occupied in the paramount duty of providing for the support of their own families; and even those whose superior education renders them more competent to so difficult a task, and who are disposed to execute it with zeal, fidelity, and intelligence, are not seldom soured or disgusted by the opposition they experience in all attempts to challenge unequal assessments, or to reform existing abuses; and being unable to enforce such necessary improvements, they have no alternative but to abandon the pursuit, and leave the parochial affairs to the management of interested juntos, who out-vote all that attempt to oppose their own system, however erroneous and expensive it may be.

Such improvements, therefore, as may be suggested by individuals of greater intelligence and more extensive information are rejected, and the proposers considered as innovators and intruders. In all such cases there is no remedy, because there is no adequate control or superintending authority to which an appeal can be made.

In the general distribution of the funds assigned for the relief of the indigent, there is seldom much discrimination. There is no time for minute inquiry,-- the object is to get rid of the unfortunate applicant in the easiest manner. The management and mode of giving relief often vary as much as the parishes are different from one another. The general economy is often irregular, ill digested and not seldom the effect of momentary impulse: the result is, that parish officers', thus guided by no fixed principle, are sometimes right and often wrong. Established regulations are frequently changed, according to the caprice or conceited opinion of a new officer, who adopts a theory of his own, equally erroneous with that of his predecessor. Some are anxious to acquire credit by diminishing the rates, which reduces virtuous indigence often to great and unnecessary distress; while others, careless and improvident of money not their own, give encouragement to vice and idleness by a profuse and indiscriminate distribution.

Other instances occur, where paupers requiring relief, are sent from one repulsive officer to another, until at length, wearied out by fruitless attendance, and unskilled in the art of impudent importunity, which characterizes *vicious* indigence, or disgusted by the contumely and abuse with which they are loaded, they retire to their miserable abodes, if they have any, and pine and die by inches for want of sufficient sustenance.

Various other reasons could be assigned why a general superintending authority has become indispensably necessary. The system (metaphorically considered) may be compared to a ship at sea without a rudder, or a complicated machine divested of the mechanical powers necessary to produce a regular or correct motion.

Combining the immense expenditure which attaches to the relief of the indigent with the other disbursements connected with objects of police, criminal offences and punishments, exclusive of what is expended in roads, bridges, militia-men's families, soldiers' baggage, &c. extending upon the whole to about £4,581,600 sterling[2] yearly, and involving in the general details innumerable items requiring investigation and control, but still more, embracing objects more immediately and closely connected with the best interests of society, *"that of regulating the economy and improving the morals of the poor, and thereby ameliorating their condition: by the adoption of measures calculated to prevent moral, political, and criminal offences;"*—it should seem, that the first measure to be adopted is to place this great and important department of *general and internal police*, under the superintendence of a board, composed of the most able and intelligent individuals that can be found in the country, to be under the control of His Majesty's principal secretary of state for the home department, to whom the legislature must look forward from time to time for such reports and suggestions as shall ultimately produce the most perfect legislative system which human wisdom can devise, aided by an accurate knowledge of facts, and by judgments matured by practice and experience in all the various branches of internal police.

In order more clearly to elucidate the great advantages which are likely to result to the country by the establishment of such a board, in reducing the national expenditure and in improving the condition of society in general, it is only necessary to give the following brief detail of the:

Functions Proposed

I

That a *board of general and internal police* should be established, nearly on the plan so strongly recommended to Parliament by the Select Committee on Finance, in their twenty-eighth Report, made in the year 1798, but with functions considerably extended, so as to embrace all objects in any degree connected with the casualties of life or a retrograde state of morals, producing *indigence, vagrancy,* or *criminal offences*; with an immediate view to the adoption of the best and most

---

2	Expense applicable solely to the poor in 1803	£4,267,965
	Expense applicable to prisons, houses of correction, prisoners' trials, witnesses, coroners' expenses, rewards, vagrants, &c. from the county rate, about	150,000
	Expenses applicable to convicts, as reported to the House of Commons, in hulks and New South Wales	120,036
	Expense of rewards to persons apprehending offenders and bringing them to conviction	9,650
	Other expenses applicable to establishments in the metropolis	34,000
		£4,581,651

effectual measures which *intelligence, labour,* and *investigation,* aided by a *thorough knowledge of facts,* can suggest, for the purpose of increasing the productive labour of the country, encouraging industry, checking idleness and vagrancy, and securing the peaceful subject (as far as circumstances will permit) against the injuries arising from criminal offences. With this particular view, to take cognizance of the affairs of paupers in every parish in the kingdom, under certain limitations hereafter explained; and to be authorized to apply for information to the resident ministers, parochial officers, and high constables, on the following points:

1. The number of indigent persons totally supported, specifying their respective ages, former occupations, state of health, the number and ages of their children, whether maintained in or out of a workhouse; the number of adults and youths employed in labour, the species of labour; the children employed in schools of industry, the nature of the labour they perform, and the profit arising from the labour of both, after deducting the cost of raw materials and all other expenses. The causes which have produced indigence, applicable to each class, whether innocent or culpable; the period they remained chargeable; the yearly expense incurred; the place of birth; the character of husband or wife, or of individuals if unmarried. Whether blind, lame, decrepit, or from insanity or any other cause incapable of labour; with such other queries as may be thought pertinent: the whole to be arranged in the form of a table, with columns to be filled up by the persons to whom they are transmitted.

2. A similar table, exhibiting the names, ages, and occupations of the paupers removed: the reasons assigned for such removals, the parish to which removed, the distance and the specific expense applicable to each removal.

3. A table, exhibiting in columns the whole aggregate expenses of the parish, in lodging, clothing, food, medical assistance, removals, law charges, expense of public meetings, and all other disbursements, arranged under distinct heads.

4. A table, showing the rental of the parish, the rate assessed, whether on rack rent or reduced, to what extent reduced; the number of persons who actually pay the assessment, and the amount; the number liable to pay who are excused, the ground of exemption, rental, and the sum to which the assessments would amount of the persons so exempted, also the number of persons totally exempted.

5. A table, exhibiting in columns the specific food of different kinds usually consumed by the poor, detailing each article comprising their common diet and beverage, with the expense, according to the prices for the time being, calculated to be consumed by a single person; by a man and his wife; by a family comprising a man, wife, and one child – two children – three children – four children – five children.

6. A table, showing the usual rent paid for houses, cottages, or lodgings, for the different classes of the poor, according to their families.

7. A table, showing the usual earnings of mechanics and labourers, divided into classes, according to their respective occupations.

8. A table, showing the number of apprentices in each parish, arranged according to the agricultural, mechanical, and other employments in which they are engaged, and distinguishing the male from the female apprentices; also the number of the youth of both sexes not bound out to masters.

9. A table, showing the resource for employment in each parish, arising from *agricultural labour, handicraft labour, manufactures, trade, shipping, canals, mines,* or other public works; stating whether there is an abundance or a scarcity of labour, and if scarce, the cause of such scarcity, and the number of labourers and handicrafts out of employment for the time being, and of what class and description.

10. The number of schools for the education of children of the poor in the parish; the wages paid for education; the number of children educated; the number above six years uneducated, with the reason, whether from inability of parents or any other cause.

11. The general state of morals in the parish; whether the inferior classes are generally sober and industrious, or the reverse, or in what degree and proportion.

12. The number of vagrants or mendicants who are in the habits of asking alms in the parish assigning reasons why they are permitted to do so.

13. A return, from the high constable, of the number of vagrants passed, by contract or otherwise, and the expense incurred on their account.

14. That, on receiving the said returns, the commissioners, or two or more assigned to the pauper department, shall systematize and digest them, and, from the minute facts thus disclosed, shall once in every year report the results to His Majesty's principal secretary of state, with such propositions for the improvement of the pauper system, as the facts disclosed shall suggest to their minds to be proper.

15. That the commissioners shall in the meantime be authorized to suggest such regulations for the general economy and management of the pauper police in each parish, as shall appear to them to be best calculated to *relieve the indigent requiring assistance, to prop up the industrious poor ready to descent into indigence,* from sickness or other casualties, and generally to offer such advice as shall not only tend to correct abuses in the management of the pauper system, but also to ameliorate, as far as possible, the condition of the labouring people in every part of England and Wales.

II

That, as the prevention of indigence depends in so great a degree on the morals of the labouring people, the commissioners shall be authorized to call upon the clerks of the peace of the different counties for lists of the names of persons licensed to sell ale, beer, and other liquors, in each parish, with the sign of the house, whether an inn, tavern, coffeehouse, hotel, or common alehouse, and to establish rules and orders for the proper conduct of such houses, varying the same according to circumstances and locality.[3]

III

With a view also to the establishment of a system for the prevention of criminal offences, generally the offspring of idleness and loose and immoral conduct; and to prevent the extensive operation of the existing facilities and temptations which are afforded by the numerous purchasers of stolen goods, and the consequent loss of character producing indigence; the commissioners shall be likewise authorized to call for a return of all the following classes of dealers in each parish in the kingdom.

1. Purchaser s of second-hand household goods, for sale.

2. Wholesale purchasers of rags and unserviceable cordage, for sale to paper-makers.

3. Retail purchasers of rags and unserviceable cordage, for sale to paper-makers.

4. Purchasers of second-hand apparel, made-up piece-goods, and remnants, for sale.

5. Walking itinerant purchasers of second-hand apparel and other articles, for sale.

6. Purchasers of second-hand naval stores, for sale.

7. Wholesale purchasers of second-hand metals, for sale.

8. Retail purchasers of second-hand metals, for sale.

9. Purchasers of second-hand building materials, for sale.

10. Pawnbrokers, in town and country.

11. Persons keeping slaughtering-houses for horses and other animals not food for man.

12. Collar-makers, fell-mongers, and others slaying and skinning horses in the country.

13. Dealers in horses, and persons who buy horses to sell for profit.

14. Persons (not employed in His Majesty's mint) setting up and working any engine for cutting round blanks, or any stamping-press, fly rolling mill, or other instrument for flatting, stamping, or marking metals or bank notes, or which, with the assistance of any matrix, stamp, die, or plate, will stamp coin, or bank notes.

---

3   Vide Appendix, No. I. for a copy of the rules and orders for regulating alehouses, which were framed by the author about fourteen years ago, and since adopted in many of the licensing divisions in the metropolis.

15. Hawkers and pedlars, including all petty hawkers, duffers, and all descriptions of itinerants selling small wares.

16. Hackney-coaches in the metropolis, and the names and places of abode of all hackney-coachmen who ply in the night-time.

For the purpose of establishing that species of control which the present state of society has rendered necessary to preserve the privileges of innocence, the commissioners to be authorized to grant licenses to the sixteen classes of persons hereinbefore mentioned, to receive such license-duties as shall be authorized by Parliament. Licenses to persons residing twenty miles from the metropolis to be granted by the justices at their special meetings, once in every year for the licensing of alehouses. And the commissioners to be authorized to establish a system of control, applicable to each of the said occupations, and to lay down rules according to which the same should be conducted.

IV

The commissioners shall cause to be published once every week a *Police Gazette*, to be edited by a fit person under their control and responsibility, which shall be confined totally and exclusively to the following objects, with an immediate view to excite in the minds of the labouring people a strong sense of moral virtue, loyalty, and love of their country; to forewarn the unwary, and to arrest the hands of evil-doers by appropriate admonitions, introduced in plain and familiar language, upon the following.

Plan
I

Each Gazette to contain a short abstract of some existing act of Parliament, divested of technical phraseology; selecting those which are particularly applicable to religious, moral, and criminal offences, and to masters and servants in various trades: to carts and other carriages on the highways; to combinations among journeymen, in various trades; to masters and apprentices, detailing the duties of each; the leading features of the pawnbroker's act, with the interest which may be legally taken; also the acts respecting hawkers and pedlars, and all others calculated to guard the lower classes against fraud and imposition; with suitable short commentaries on each abstract, with a view to apprise them of the penalties they incur by offending against each respective law, and of the advantages which will result to them from a strict obedience, particularly to those laws which regard the defence of their country against the enemy—the advantages they derive in their own country in privileges and in assistance during distress, above what is to be found in any other nation in the world.

II

Occasional short essays, conveyed in familiar language, enlivened and rendered interesting by the introduction of *narrative,* as often as circumstances will admit, on the following subjects:

Criminal Offences

1. On treason ⎱ Disloyalty to the king.
2. On sedition ⎰
3. On combinations of workmen.
4. On mobs and unlawful assemblies.
5. On fighting and breaches of the peace.
6. On cheating.
7. On receiving stolen goods.
8. On stealing in any way from masters or others.
9. Stealing turnips, potatoes, or other vegetables.
10. Stealing corn on pretence of gleaning.
11. Stealing horses, cattle, sheep, pigs, or poultry.
12. Stealing fence-rails or brushwood.
13. Housebreaking.
14. Highway robbery.
15. Footpad robbery.
16. Rape, or violation of female chastity.
17. Wilful burning houses, barns, or stacks.
18. Manslaughter
19. Wounding or maiming any person.
20. Murder.

Occasional observations on the horrors of a gaol; on punishments—whipping, the pillory, the hulks, transportation, and public execution.

Religious and moral Duties

1. On breaches of the Lord's Day and regular attendance at church.
2. On providence and economy.
3. On industry, honesty, and truth.
4. On sloth and idleness, and lounging in alehouses.
5. On lying and dissimulation.
6. Duties of a good husband.
7. Duties of a good wife.
8. On a good example to children and apprentices.
9. On a religious and moral education to children.
10. On the duty of providing for a family.
11. On the duty of children to parents.

12. On the duty of parents to children.

13. On frugal housewifery.

14. On the duty of masters to apprentices.

15. On the duty of apprentices to masters.

16. On the advantages of a good character.

17. On the disadvantages of a bad character.

18. On female chastity.

19. On the infamy of female seduction.

20. On frugality and sobriety.

21. On frugal cookery, with occasional receipts.

22. On patience under adversity.

23. On the government of the passions.

24. On the commendable pride of rearing a family without parish assistance.

III

Occasional essays on the great advantages arising from a provident care of the earnings of labour during early life, and the benefits to be obtained by entering into friendly societies, and thereby making a provision against hurts, accidents, sickness, want of work, infirmity, and old age: to be placed in various points of view, repeated frequently, and exemplified by narratives of the benefits others have derived from these institutions, in preventing them from falling into the degraded state of paupers.

IV

Occasional extracts from the Reports of the Society for bettering the Condition of the Poor, and other works, showing the happiness enjoyed by the industrious cottager, labourer, and handicraft, contrasted with the misery attached to the idle and dissolute.

V

To introduce the following articles of police information, viz.

1. A list and description of deserters from the army, navy, marines, and militia, mentioning the penalties incurred for harbouring deserters, and the rewards allowed for apprehending them, with suitable observations, to be occasionally introduced, showing the evils arising from desertion.

2. Advertisements for the apprehension of different offenders, describing their persons and the rewards for apprehending them.

3. A summary view of the offences tried at the general and quarter sessions of the peace in each county, city, and town, in England and Wales, showing the number of persons convicted, the punishments inflicted, the number of

acquittals and discharges by gaol delivery, without mentioning names.

4. A summary view of the higher offences tried at the assizes in each county, twice a year, in England and Wales, showing in like manner the convictions, punishments, and discharges by gaol delivery.

5. The number of convicts sent for punishment to the hulks, with appropriate observations.

6. The number of convicts sent to New South Wales, with proper remarks.

7. An account of the different malefactors, stating their behaviour at the place of execution, with commentaries suited to the comprehension of the vulgar, tending to operate as warnings, and to excite a dread of crimes.

In order to bring these Police Gazettes under the notice and inspection of all classes likely to benefit by their circulation, or in a manner advantageous to the nation at large, that they should be distributed in the following manner:

1. One copy to each of the great officers of state.	Estimated number of papers weekly
2. Once copy to each of the acting resident magistrates in each county, city, town, and place.	
3. Once copy to the high sheriff of each country in England and Wales.	
4. One copy to the high constable in each hundred or licensing division.	
5. One copy to each public office in the metropolis.	
6. One copy to each of the public offices in Birmingham and Manchester, &c.	25,000
7. One copy to the clerks of the peace in each county.	
8. One copy to the minister, churchwardens, and overseers of each parish.	
9. One copy to each public house licensed to sell ale, beer, and other liquors, in England and Wales, that they may be seen and perused by all the labouring people, who frequent licensed alehouses; the number of which is here estimated at	50,000
Total	75,000

As these papers will contain nothing of what is denominated *news*, although much that will be infinitely more beneficial in disseminating useful information, calculated to improve the morals of the people, no stamp will be required, and they may be afforded at an expense of not more than one penny halfpenny weekly for each paper.

It will be the duty of the commissioners to receive information, and to correspond with the magistrates in every county, city, and corporate and other town, in England and Wales, respecting all matters connected with the functions assigned to them; and to receive from the justices in sessions, a periodical return of the state of all gaols and houses of correction, specifying in a table, according to a form to be prescribed, the number of prisoners, their offences, the manner in which they are employed in houses or correction, the diet and clothing, the expense incurred in each year, the raw materials purchased, the manufactured articles sold, the profit derived from the labour of the prisoners, the salaries of the gaoler, chaplain, surgeon, and other persons employed, and all other information necessary to enable the board to form a complete judgment as to the improvements necessary to be recommended by an accurate inspection of each return, and by comparing one return with another.

VI

It will be the duty of the commissioners to avail themselves of the practical experience they may acquire, by suggesting from time to time to His Majesty's principal secretary of state, such improvements in the system of *pauper police*, and in all the branches of *the general police of the country,* as may appear to them to be necessary, assigning their reasons for such amendments, in a detailed report, for the ultimate consideration of Parliament.

VII

It will be the duty of the commissioners to keep a distinct alphabetical register of all idle, suspicious, and criminal persons, with their description, who are reported to them from time to time to be at large, and in the course of committing offences in any part of the country, that there may be a centre point of intelligence, for the purpose of detecting and apprehending such persons, thus in the course of committing depredations upon the peaceful subject.

VIII

It will be the duty of the commissioners to collect and receive the revenues applicable to the fiscal branches placed under their management, and, after deducting the expenses, to pay the surplus into the receipt of His Majesty's Exchequer; following such orders in this respect as they may receive from the lords commissioners of the Treasury, to whom the receipts and disbursements shall be reported quarterly.

Many other sources of revenue, arising from useful police regulations, might be placed under the management of this central board, which would prove in a certain degree productive, without being felt as a burden, while they operated powerfully in checking frauds and penal offences, without at all abridging the liberty of the useful part of the community.

It is here to be observed, that nothing is proposed that has the least tendency to disturb, alter, or amend the existing statutory system, with respect to the management of paupers, or even to control that management in the smallest degree. The functions of the commissioners are of a nature merely *inquisitorial,* except in as far as advice and suggestion extend. The object is, in the first instance, to acquire that stock of knowledge and accurate and minute information, which may ultimately lead to those improvements, which shall be the result of deep reflection, on the various important statistical facts, which would through this medium be disclosed: without such previous information it would be an act of great temerity to attempt any reform; since, in order to render the system complete, a great variety of collateral as well as direct measures will be necessary, but above all, that paramount watchful superintendence which shall guide and direct this very complicated machine.

There exist in the metropolis, and almost in every large town in the kingdom, certain suspicious and dangerous trades; the uncontrolled exercise of which, by persons of loose conduct, is known to contribute in a very high degree to the multiplication of crimes, from the facilities held out by the purchase of articles which may be pilfered, with scarcely and chance of detection; but which would be otherwise secure, did not such facilities for the ready and immediate disposal exist.

The power, therefore, proposed to be vested in the central board, to call for a return of the number of persons exercising these trades, and to regulate them by means of licenses, is a measure strongly recommended six years ago by the Select Committee of the House of Commons,[4] than which nothing can operate more powerfully as a barrier against those temptations which lead to criminal offences. It will admit of a considerable extension after the system is fully matured, and when thus aided by a centre point and superintending agency, would go very far towards the prevention at least of minor crimes; since, upon this foundation, a superstructure may be gradually raised that would do much to preserve and secure the privilege of innocence, and to check the growing corruption of morals, and the numerous temptations to the commission of petty offences.

The habit of frequenting alehouses, so universal among the inferior orders of society (which of late years extends in no inconsiderable degree to *women* and *youths* as well as men), renders it of great importance to the morals of

---

4   See the twenty-eighth Report of the Select Committee on Finance, 1798.

the people, that rules and orders (varied in some respects according to local circumstances) should be enforced with respect to publicans of every description; and the proposed commissioners, as the general guardians of the morals of the people, seem to be the proper source from which such regulations should issue, since otherwise, in many instances, omissions would take place, and uniformity could not be expected. Many improvements could be suggested with regard to publicans, favourable to health and good morals, which it would be the province of the central board, after facts were ascertained, to offer to the consideration of Parliament.

The proposed Police Gazette, from its extensive circulation, from the matter it would contain, and from the general and unexampled diffusion of good instruction and useful information, conveyed to all ranks of the community, but particularly the labouring classes of the people, could not fail to operate powerfully with respect to the improvement of morals, since it would be every where accessible, operating as an incentive to virtue and industry, and as an antidote to vice and idleness.

It is thus that the manners and moral habits of the adults, comprising the labouring classes, are gradually to be improved. It is by this species of attention that they are to be persuaded of the advantages resulting from industry, frugality, and temperance. It is by these and other measures, suggested in the course of this work, that the number of paupers are to be reduced, indigence raised in many instances to a state of independent poverty, vagrancy lessened, and moral and criminal offences, which so much swell the calendars of delinquency, greatly diminished. It is by such gentle and indirect means that the stock of the national industry is to be increased, and the parochial assessments brought within a moderate compass.

The great object is first to establish a *foundation, a rallying point, a centre of action, a fixed responsible agency,* a resource of *talents, knowledge, application,* and *industry,* equal, if possible, to the difficult task of improving the condition of society in all those ramifications, where a gangrene either exists, or is threatened.

1. By diminishing the number of the innocent indigent by judicious and timely props.

2. By restoring the culpable indigent to at least an useful condition in society, by a variety of combined regulations, applicable to persons discharged from prisons and unable to obtain work for want of character:--to others, under similar circumstances, in point of character, who have not been imprisoned:--to unfortunate females, abandoned by the world and degraded by prostitution:--to the race of gypsies and others imitating their manners: to vagrants of all descriptions:--and finally, to the means of diminishing the temptations and resources which are rendered so prolific for the commission of moral and criminal offences.

And thus, by an all-pervading system of well-regulated police, having its chief seat or central point in the metropolis, and from thence maintaining a close and connected chain of correspondence, by receiving information and communicating the same with regularity and promptitude to all parts of the kingdom, by a permanent authority, competent (in consequence of the continually accumulating fund of information and experience so collected and preserved) to report to His Majesty in Parliament such measures as shall in any degree be conducive to the great objects of the institution—*The improvement of the condition of the labouring people—the increase of the productive labour of the country—the more effectual prevention of moral and criminal offences—to the lessening the demand for punishment—the diminution of the public burdens attached to pauper and criminal police, by turning the hearts and arresting the hands of evildoers—by forewarning the unwary, and preserving in innocence the untained;* thus returning to police its genuine character, unmixed with those judicial powers which lead to punishment, and properly belong to magistracy alone.

Georg W.F. Hegel (1770-1831)

Artist: Jakob Schlesinger (1831), Alte Nationalgalerie Berlin, A I 556

Born on August 27, 1770 in Stuttgart, G.W.F. Hegel was the son of a middle class civil servant. Hegel lived through a time of remarkable upheaval throughout continental Europe. He witnessed and attempted to provide an account for the Industrial revolution, the French Revolution, the Terror, the Napoleonic Wars, as well as the restructuring of the European Empires and the rise of nationalism. Legend holds that he wrote his first notable work, The Phenomenology of Spirit, while hearing gunfire from the Battle of Jena in October 1806.

After completing his education as a seminary student, Hegel briefly served as a family tutor but then joined the University of Jena in 1800. When Napoleon conquered the city six years later, the University was shut down, and Hegel turned to editing newspapers before accepting a post of high school headmaster and lecturer. He remained an active spectator of the current affairs, reading English and French newspapers, and publishing articles on political issues. In 1816, he was offered a professorship in the University of Heidelberg, and was soon after appointed to the highly prestigious chair of philosophy at the University of Berlin in 1818. Reform movements in Prussia followed the Napoleonic occupation, and the state was veering away from absolutism in favor of constitutionalism. Less progressive states such as Austria and Russia were highly suspicious of Prussia, and in 1819, the cause for reform was defeated. The resulting censorship on academic publications and the removal of so-called 'demagogues' from universities saw the arrest of some of Hegel's own students and assistants.

Hegel's career was meteoric and he was considered an intellectual giant of his time. Along with the *Phenomenology of Spirit*, Hegel's major works included the *Science of Logic*, *Encyclopedia of the Philosophical Sciences*, and *Philosophy of Right*. Hegel developed themes that continue to bear on the philosophical and social sciences including his conception of alienation, historical dialectic, and the inherent freedom and rationality of the modern world. Hegel's work has often been misinterpreted. He has thus been labeled at various times: a reactionary, an absolutist, and a totalitarian. Hegel's work is also deeply suspicious of the conception of freedom grounded on radical individuality. This suspicion has appealed to both the right and left. Hegel's death came unexpectedly and at the height of his career, falling victim to a choleric outbreak in 1831.

Works Referenced:
Hegel, G.W.F. *Elements of the Philosophy of Right.* Edited with Introduction by Allen W. Wood. Cambridge University Press, Cambridge, 1991.
Hegel G.W.F. *Introduction to the Philosophy of History.* Translated with Introduction by Leo Rauch. Hackett Publishing Company, Indianapolis and Cambridge, 1988.
Mueller, Gustav E. *Hegel: The Man, His Vision and Work.* Pageant Press, Inc: New York, 1968.
Pinkard, Terry. *Hegel: A Biography.* Cambridge University Press: Cambridge, 2000.

Selections from: *Philosophy of Right.* **T. M. Knox (trans.) (Amherst NY: Prometheus., reprint 1996) and (Oxford University Press, 1967)., orig. 1821.**

B. Administration of Justice

§209. The relatedness arising from the reciprocal bearing on one another of needs and labour to satisfy these is first of all reflected into itself as infinite personality, as abstract right. But it is this very sphere of relatedness – a sphere of education, which gives abstract right the determinate existence of being something universally recognised, known, and willed, and having a validity and an objective actuality mediated by this known and willed character.

Remark: It is part of education, of thinking as the consciousness of the single in the form of universality, that the ego comes to be apprehended as a universal person in which all are identical. A man counts as a man in virtue of his manhood alone, not because he is a Jew, Catholic, Protestant, German, Italian, &c. This is an assertion which thinking ratifies and to be conscious of it is of infinite importance. It is defective only when it is crystallised, e.g. as a cosmopolitanism in opposition to the concrete life of the state.

Addition: From one point of view, it is through the working of the system of particularity that right becomes an external compulsion as a protection of particular interests. Even though this result is due to the concept, right none the less only becomes something existent because this is useful for men's needs. To become conscious in thought of his right, man must be trained to think and give up dallying with mere sensation. We must invest the objects of our thought with the form of universality and similarly we must direct our willing by a universal principle. It is only after man has devised numerous needs and after their acquisition has become intertwined with his satisfaction, that he can frame laws for himself.

§210. The objective actuality of the right consists, first, in its existence for consciousness, in its being known in some way or other; secondly, in its possessing the power which the actual possesses, in its being valid, and so also in its becoming known as universally valid.

(a) Right as Law

§211. The principle of rightness becomes the law (*Gesetz*) when, in its objective existence, it is posited (*gesetzt*), i.e. when thinking makes it determinate for consciousness and makes it known as what is right and valid; and in acquiring this determinate character, the right becomes positive law in general.

Remark: To posit something as universal, i.e. to bring it before consciousness as universal, is, I need hardly say, to think (compare Remarks to §§ 13 and 21). Thereby its content is reduced to its simplest form and so is given its final determinacy. In becoming law, what is right acquires for the first time not only the form proper to its universality, but also its determinacy. Hence making a law is not to be represented as merely the expression of a rule of behaviour valid for everyone, though that is one moment in legislation; the more important moment, the inner essence of the matter, is knowledge of the content of the law in its determinate universality.

Since it is only animals which have their law as instinct, while it is man alone who has law as custom, even systems of customary law contain the moment of being thoughts and being known. Their difference from positive law consists solely in this, that they are known only in a subjective and accidental way, with the result that in themselves they are less determinate and the universality of thought is less clear in them. (And apart from this, knowledge of a system of law either in general or in its details, is the accidental possession of a few.) The supposition that it is customary law, on the strength of its character as custom, which possesses the privilege of having become part of life is a delusion, since the valid laws of a nation do not cease to be its customs by being written and codified – and besides, it is as a rule precisely those versed in the deadest of topics and the deadest of thoughts who talk nowadays of 'life' and of 'becoming part of life'. When a nation begins to acquire even a little culture, its customary law must soon come to be collected and put together. Such a collection is a legal code, but one which, as a mere collection, is markedly formless, indeterminate, and fragmentary. The main difference between it and a code properly so-called is that in the latter the principles of jurisprudence in their universality, and so in their determinacy, have been apprehended in terms of thought and expressed. English national law or municipal law is contained, as is well known, in statutes (written laws) and in so-called 'unwritten' laws. This unwritten law, however, is as good as written, and knowledge of it may, and indeed must, be acquired simply by reading the numerous quartos which it fills. The monstrous confusion, however, which prevails both in English law and its administration is graphically portrayed by those acquainted with the matter. In particular, they comment on the fact that, since this unwritten law is contained in court verdicts and judgments, the judges are continually legislators. The authority of precedent is binding on them, since their predecessors have done nothing but give expression to the unwritten law; and yet they are just as much exempt from its authority, because they are themselves repositories of the unwritten law and so have the right to criticise previous judgments and pronounce whether they accorded with the unwritten law or not.

A similar confusion might have arisen in the legal system of the later Roman Empire owing to the different but authoritative judgments of all the famous jurists. An Emperor met the situation, however, by a sensible expedient when, by what was called the Law of Citations, he set up a kind of College of the jurists who were longest deceased. There was a President, and the majority vote was accepted.

No greater insult could be offered to a civilised people or to its lawyers than to deny them ability to codify their law; for such ability cannot be that of constructing a legal system with a novel content, but only that of apprehending, i.e. grasping in thought, the content of existing laws in its determinate universality and then applying them to particular cases.

Addition: The sun and the planets have their laws too, but they do not know them. Savages are governed by impulses, customs, and feelings, but they are unconscious of this. When right is posited as law and is known, every accident of feeling vanishes together with the form of revenge, sympathy, and selfishness, and in this way the right attains for the first time its true determinacy and is given its due honour. It is as a result of the discipline of comprehending the right that the right first becomes capable of universality. In the course of applying the laws, clashes occur, and in dealing with these the judge's intelligence has its proper scope; this is quite inevitable, because otherwise carrying out the law would be something mechanical from start to finish. But to go so far as to get rid of clashes altogether by leaving much to the judge's discretion is a far worse solution, because even the clash is intrinsic to thought, to conscious thinking and its dialectic, while the mere fiat of a judge would be arbitrary.

It is generally alleged in favour of customary law that it is 'living', but this vitality, i.e. the identity between the subject and what the law provides, is not the whole essence of the matter. Law (*Recht*) must be known by thought, it must be a system in itself, and only as such can it be recognised in a civilised country. The recent denial that nations 'have a vocation to codify their laws' is not only an insult; it also implies the absurdity of supposing that not a single individual has been endowed with skill enough to bring into a coherent system the endless mass of existing laws. The truth is that it is just systematisation, i.e. elevation to the universal, which our time is pressing for without any limit. A similar view is that collections of judgments, like those available in a *Corpus Juris,* are far superior to a code worked out in the most general way. The reason alleged is that such judgments always retain a certain particularity and a certain reminiscence of history which men are unwilling to sacrifice. But the mischievousness of such collections is made clear enough by the practice of English law.

§212. It is only because of this identity between its implicit and its posited character that positive law has obligatory force in virtue of its rightness. In being posited in positive law, the right acquires determinate existence. Into such existence there may enter the contingency of self-will and other particular circumstances and hence there may be a discrepancy between the content of the law and the principle of rightness.

Remark: In positive law, therefore, it is the legal which is the source of our knowledge of what is right, or, more exactly, of our legal rights (*Rechtens*). Thus the science of positive law is to that extent an historical science with authority as its guiding principle. Anything over and above this historical study is matter for the Understanding and concerns the collection of laws, their classification on external principles, deductions from them, their application to fresh details, &c. When the Understanding meddles with the nature of the thing itself, its theories, e.g. of criminal law, show what its deductive argumentation can concoct.

The science of positive law has not only the right, but even the inescapable duty, to study given laws, to deduce from its positive data their progress in history, their applications and subdivisions, down to the last detail, and to exhibit their implications. On the other hand, if, after all these deductions have been proved, the further question about the rationality of a specific law is still raised, the question may seem perverse to those who are busied with these pursuits, but their astonishment at it should at least stop short of dismay.

With this Remark, compare what was said in the Remark to § 3 about 'understanding' the law.

§213. Right becomes determinate in the first place when it has the form of being posited as positive law; it also becomes determinate in content by being applied both to the material of civil society (i.e. to the endlessly growing complexity and subdivision of social ties and the different species of property and contract within the society) and also to ethical ties based on the heart, on love and trust, though only in so far as these involve abstract right as one of their aspects (see § 159) – Morality and moral commands concern the will on its most private, subjective, and particular side, and so cannot be a matter for positive legislation. Further material for the determinate content of law is provided by the rights and duties which have their source in the administration of justice itself, in the state, and so forth.

Addition: In the higher relationships of marriage, love, religion, and the state, the only aspects which can become the subject of legislation are those of such a nature as to permit of their being in principle external. Still, in this respect there is a wide difference between the laws of different peoples. The Chinese, for instance, have a law requiring a husband to love his first wife more than his other wives. If he is convicted of doing the opposite, corporal punishment follows. Similarly, the legislation of the ancients in earlier times was full of precepts about uprightness and integrity which are unsuited by nature to legal enactment because they fall wholly within the field of the inner life. It is only in the case of the oath, whereby things are brought home to conscience, that uprightness and integrity must be taken into account as the substance of the matter.

§214. But apart from being applied to particular instances, right by being embodied in positive law becomes applicable to the single case. Hence it enters the sphere where quantity, not the concept, is the principle of determination. This is the sphere of the quantitative as such, of the quantitative as that which determines the relative value in exchange of *qualia*. In this sphere, the concept merely lays down a general limit, within which vacillation is still allowed. This vacillation must be terminated, however, in the interest of getting something done, and for this reason there is a place within that limit for contingent and arbitrary decisions.

Remark: The purely positive side of law lies chiefly in this focusing of the universal not merely on a particular instance, but on an isolated case, i.e. in its *direct* application. Reason cannot determine, nor can the concept provide any principle whose application could decide whether justice requires for an offence (i) a corporal punishment of forty lashes or thirty-nine, or (ii) a fine of five dollars or four dollars ninety-three, four, &c., cents, or (iii) imprisonment of a year or three hundred and sixty-four, three, &c., days, or a year and one, two, or three days. And yet injustice is done at once if there is one lash too many, or one dollar or one cent, one week in prison or one day, too many or too few.

Reason itself requires us to recognise that contingency, contradiction, and show have a sphere and a right of their own, restricted though it be, and it is irrational to strive to resolve and rectify contradictions within that sphere. Here the only interest present is that something be actually done, that the matter be settled and decided somehow, no matter how (within a certain limit). This decision pertains to abstract subjectivity, to formal self-certainty, which may decide either by simply holding to its power (within that limit) of settling the matter by merely terminating deliberation and thereby dismissing it out of hand, or else by adopting some reason for decision such as keeping to round numbers or always adopting, say thirty-nine.

It is true that the law does not settle these ultimate decisions required by actual life; it leaves them instead to the judge's discretion, merely limiting him by a maximum and minimum. But this does not affect the point at issue, because the maximum and minimum are themselves in every instance only round numbers once more. To fix them, therefore, does not exempt the judge from making a finite, purely positive, decision, since on the contrary such a decision is still left to him by the necessities of the case.

Addition: There is one essential element in law and the administration of justice which contains a measure of contingency and which arises from the fact that the law is a universal prescription which has to be applied to the single case. If you wished to declare yourself against this contingency, you would be talking in abstractions. The measure of a man's punishment, for example, cannot be made equivalent to any determination of the concept of punishment, and the decision made, whatever it be, is from this point of view arbitrary always. But this contingency is itself necessary, and if you argue against having a code at all on the ground that any code is incomplete, you are overlooking just that element of law in which completion is not to be achieved and which therefore must just be accepted as it stands.

(b) Law determinately existent

§215. If laws are to have a binding force, it follows that, in view of the right of self-consciousness (see § 132 and the Remark thereto) they must be made universally known.

Remark: To hang the laws so high that no citizen could read them (as Dionysius the Tyrant did) is injustice of one and the same kind as to bury them in row upon row of learned tomes, collections of dissenting judgments and opinions, records of customs, &c., and in a dead language too, so that knowledge of the law of the land is accessible only to those who have made it their professional study. Rulers who have given a national law to their peoples in the form of a well-arranged and clear-cut legal code or even a mere formless collection of laws, like Justinian's – have been the greatest benefactors of their peoples and have received thanks and praise for their beneficence. But the truth is that their work was at the same time a great act of justice.

Addition: The legal profession, possessed of a special knowledge of the law, often claims this knowledge as its monopoly and refuses to allow any layman to discuss the subject. Physicists similarly have taken amiss Goethe's theory about colours because he did not belong to their craft and was a poet into the bargain. But we do not need to be shoemakers to know if our shoes fit, and just as little have we any need to be professionals to acquire knowledge of matters of universal interest. Law is concerned with freedom, the worthiest and holiest thing in man, the thing man must know if it is to have obligatory force for him.

§216. For a public legal code, simple general laws are required, and yet the nature of the *finite* material to which law is applied leads to the further determining of general laws *ad infinitum*. On the one hand, the law ought to be a comprehensive whole, closed and complete; and yet, on the other hand, the need for further determinations is continual. But since this antinomy arises only when universal principles, which remain fixed and unchanged, are applied to particular types of case, the right to a complete legal code remains unimpaired, like the right that these simple general principles should be capable of being laid down and understood apart and in distinction from their application to such particular types.

Remark: A fruitful source of complexity in legislation is the gradual intrusion of reason, of what is inherently and actually right, into primitive institutions which have something wrong at their roots and so are purely historical survivals. This occurred in Roman law, as was remarked above (see Remark to § 180), in medieval feudal law, &c. It is essential to notice, however, that the very nature of the finite material to which law is applied necessarily entails an infinite progress in the application to it of principles universal in themselves and inherently and actually rational.

It is misunderstanding which has given rise alike to the demand – a morbid craving of German scholars chiefly – that a legal code should be something absolutely complete, incapable of any fresh determination in detail, and also to the argument that because a code is incapable of such completion, therefore we ought not to produce something 'incomplete', i.e. we ought not to produce a code at all. The misunderstanding rests in both cases on a misconception of the nature of a finite subject-matter like private law, whose so-called 'completeness' is a perennial approximation to completeness, on a misconception of the differences between the universal of reason and the universal of the Understanding, and also in the application of the latter to the material of finitude and atomicity which goes on for ever. – *Le plus grand ennemi du Bien, c'est le Meilleur* is the utterance of true common sense against the common sense of idle argumentation and abstract reflection.

Addition: Completeness means the exhaustive collection of every single thing, pertaining to a given field, and no science or branch of knowledge can be complete in this sense. Now, if we say that philosophy or any one of the sciences is incomplete, we are not far from holding that we must wait until the deficiency is made up, since the best part may still be wanting. But take up this attitude and advance is impossible, either in geometry, which seems to be a closed science although new propositions do arise, or in philosophy, which is always capable of freshness in detail even though its subject is the universal Idea. In the past, the universal law always consisted of the ten commandments; now we can see at once that not to lay down the law 'Thou shalt not kill', on the ground that a legal code cannot be complete, is an obvious absurdity. Any code could be still better – no effort of reflection is required to justify this affirmation; we can think of the best, finest, and noblest as still better, finer, and nobler. But a big old tree puts forth more and more branches without thereby becoming a new tree; though it would be silly to refuse to plant a tree at all simply because it might produce new branches.

§217. The principle of rightness passes over in civil society into law. My individual right, whose embodiment has hitherto been immediate and abstract, now similarly becomes embodied in the existent will and knowledge of everyone, in the sense that it becomes recognised. Hence property acquisitions and transfers must now be undertaken and concluded only in the form which that embodiment gives to them. In civil society, property rests on contract and on the formalities which make ownership capable of proof and valid in law.

Remark: Original, i.e. direct, titles and means of acquisition (see §§ 54 ff.) are simply discarded in civil society and appear only as isolated accidents or as subordinated factors of property transactions. It is either feeling, refusing to move beyond the subjective, or reflection, clinging to its abstract essences, which casts formalities aside, while the dry-as-dust Understanding may for its part cling to formalities instead of the real thing and multiply them indefinitely.

Apart from this, however, the march of mental development is the long and hard struggle to free a content from its sensuous and immediate form, endow it with its appropriate form of thought, and thereby give it simple and adequate expression. It is because this is the case that when the development of law is just beginning, ceremonies and formalities are more circumstantial and count rather as the thing itself than as its symbol. Thus even in Roman law, a number of forms and especially phrases were retained from old-fashioned ceremonial usages, instead of being replaced by intelligible forms and phrases adequately expressing them.

Addition: Law and the right are identical in the sense that what is implicitly right is posited in the law. I possess something, own a property, which I occupied when it was ownerless. This possession must now further be recognised and posited as mine. Hence in civil society formalities arise in connection with property. Boundary stones are erected as a symbol for others to recognise. Entries are made in mortgage and property registers. Most property in civil society is held on contract, and contractual forms are fixed and determinate. Now we may have an antipathy to formalities of this kind and we may suppose that they only exist to bring in money to the authorities; we may even regard them as something offensive and a sign of mistrust because they impair the validity of the saying: 'A man is as good as his word.' But the formality is essential because what is inherently right must also be posited as right. My will is a rational will; it has validity, and its validity should be recognised by others. At this point, then, my subjectivity and that of others must be set aside and the will must achieve the security, stability, and objectivity which can be attained only through such formalities.

§218. Since property and personality have legal recognition and validity in civil society, wrongdoing now becomes an infringement, not merely of what is subjectively infinite, but of the universal thing which is existent with inherent stability and strength. Hence a new attitude arises: the action is seen as a danger to society and thereby the magnitude of the wrongdoing is increased. On the other hand, however, the fact that society has become strong and sure of itself diminishes the external importance of the injury and so leads to a mitigation of its punishment.

Remark: The fact that an injury to one member of society is an injury to all others does not alter the conception of wrongdoing, but it does alter it in respect of its outward existence as an injury done, an injury which now affects the mind and consciousness of civil society as a whole, not merely the external embodiment of the person directly injured. In heroic times, as we see in the tragedy of the ancients, the citizens did not feel themselves injured by wrongs which members of the royal houses did to one another.

Implicitly, crime is an infinite injury; but as an existent fact it must be measured in quantity and quality (see § 96), and since its field of existence here has the essential character of affecting an idea and consciousness of the validity of the laws, its danger to civil society is a determinant of the magnitude of a crime, or even one of its qualitative characteristics.

Now this quality or magnitude varies with the state of civil society; and this is the justification for sometimes attaching the penalty of death to a theft of a few pence or a turnip, and at other times a light penalty to a theft of a hundred or more times that amount. If we consider its danger to society, this seems at first sight to aggravate the crime; but in fact it is just this which has been the prime cause of the mitigation of its punishment. A penal code, then, is primarily the child of its age and the state of civil society at the time.

Addition: It seems to be a contradiction that a crime committed in society appears more heinous and yet is punished more leniently. But while it would be impossible for society to leave a crime unpunished, since that would be to posit it as right, still since society is sure of itself, a crime must always be something idiosyncratic in comparison, something unstable and exceptional. The very stability of society gives a crime the status of something purely subjective which seems to be the product rather of natural impulse than of a prudent will. In this light, crime acquires a milder status, and for this reason its punishment too becomes milder. If society is still internally weak, then an example must be made by inflicting punishments, since punishment is itself an example over against the example of crime. But in a society which is internally strong, the commission of crime is something so feeble that its annulment must be commensurable with its feebleness. Harsh punishments, therefore, are not unjust in and by themselves; they are related to contemporary conditions. A criminal code cannot hold good for all time, and crimes are only shows of reality which may draw on themselves a greater or lesser degree of disavowal.

(c) The Court of Justice

§219. By taking the form of law, right steps into a determinate mode of being. It is then something on its own account, and in contrast with particular willing and opining of the right, it is self-subsistent and has to vindicate itself as something universal. This is achieved by recognising it and making it actual in a particular case without the subjective feeling of private interest; and this is the business of a public authority – the court of justice.

Remark: The historical origin of the judge and his court may have had the form of a patriarch's gift to his people or of force or free choice; but this makes no difference to the concept of the thing. To regard the introduction of a legal system as no more than an optional act of grace or favour on the part of monarchs and governments (as Herr von Haller does in his *Restauration der Staatswissenschaft*) is a piece of the mere thoughtlessness which has no inkling of the point at issue in a discussion of law and the state. The point is that legal and political institutions are rational in principle and therefore absolutely necessary, and the question of the form in which they arose or were introduced is entirely irrelevant to a consideration of their rational basis.

At the other extreme from Herr von Haller's point of view is the barbarous notion that the administration of justice is now, as it was in the days when might was right, an improper exercise of force, a suppression of freedom, and a despotism. The administration of justice must be regarded as the fulfilment of a duty by the public authority, no less than as the exercise of a right; and so far as it is a right, it does not depend upon an optional delegation to one authority by the individual members of society.

§220. When the right against crime has the form of revenge (see § 102), it is only right implicit, not right in the form of right, i.e. no act of revenge is justified. Instead of the injured party, the injured universal now comes on the scene, and this has its proper actuality in the court of law. It takes over the pursuit and the avenging of crime, and this pursuit consequently ceases to be the subjective and contingent retribution of revenge and is transformed into the genuine reconciliation of right with itself, i.e. into punishment. Objectively, this is the reconciliation of the law with itself; by the annulment of the crime, the law is restored and its authority is thereby actualised. Subjectively, it is the reconciliation of the criminal with himself, i.e. with the law known by him as his own and as valid for him and his protection; when this law is executed upon him, he himself finds in this process the satisfaction of justice and nothing save his own act.

§221. A member of civil society has the right *in judicio stare* and, correspondingly, the duty of acknowledging the jurisdiction of the court and accepting its decision as final when his own rights are in dispute.

Addition: Since any individual has the right *in judicio stare,* he must also know what the law is or otherwise this privilege would be useless to him. But it is also his *duty* to stand his trial. Under the feudal system, the nobles often refused to stand their trial. They defied the court and alleged that the court was wrong to demand their appearance. Feudal conditions, however, contravened the very idea of a court. Nowadays monarchs have to recognise the jurisdiction of the court in their private affairs, and in free states they commonly lose their case.

§222. In court the specific character which rightness acquires is that it must be demonstrable. When parties go to law, they are put in the position of having to make good their evidence and their claims and to make the judge acquainted with the facts. These steps in a legal process are themselves rights, and their course must therefore be fixed by law. They also constitute an essential part of jurisprudence.

Addition: A man may be indignant if a right which he knows he has is refused him because he cannot prove it. But if I have a right, it must at the same time be a right posited in law. I must be able to explain and prove it, and its validity can only be recognised in society if its rightness in principle is also made a posited rightness in law.

§223. These steps in a legal process are subdivided continually within no fixed limits into more and more actions, each being distinct in itself and a right. Hence a legal process, in itself in any case a means, now begins to be something external to its end and contrasted with it. This long course of formalities is a right of the parties at law and they have the right to traverse it from beginning to end. Still, it may be turned into an evil, and even an instrument of wrong, and for this reason it is by law made the duty of the parties to submit themselves to the simple process of arbitration (before a tribunal of arbitrators) and to the attempt to reconcile their differences out of court, in order that they – and right itself, as the substance of the thing and so the thing really at issue – may be protected against legal processes and their misuse.

Remark: Equity involves a departure from formal rights owing to moral or other considerations and is concerned primarily with the content of the lawsuit. A court of equity, however, comes to mean a court which decides in a single case without insisting on the formalities of a legal process or, in particular, on the objective evidence which the letter of the law may require. Further, it decides on the merits of the single case as a unique one, not with a view to disposing of it in such a way as to create a binding legal precedent for the future.

§224. Amongst the rights of the subjective consciousness are not only the publication of the laws (see § 215) but also the possibility of ascertaining the actualisation of the law in a particular case (the course of the proceedings, the legal argument, &c.) – i.e. the publicity of judicial proceedings. The reason for this is that a trial is implicitly an event of universal validity, and although the particular content of the action affects the interests of the parties alone, its universal content, i.e. the right at issue and the judgment thereon, affects the interests of everybody.

Remark: If the members of the bench deliberate amongst themselves about the judgment which they are to deliver, such deliberations express opinions and views still personal and so naturally are not public.

Addition: It is straightforward common sense to hold that the publicity of legal proceedings is right and just. A strong reason against such publicity has always been the rank of justices; they are unwilling to sit in public and they regard themselves as a sanctuary of law which laymen are not to enter. But an integral part of justice is the confidence which citizens have in it, and it is this which requires that proceedings shall be public. The right of publicity depends on the fact that (i) the aim of the court is justice, which as universal falls under the cognisance of everyone, and (ii) it is through publicity that the citizens become convinced that the judgment was actually just.

§225. By the judgment of the court, the law is applied to a single case, and the work of judgment has two distinct aspects: first, ascertainment of the nature of the case as a unique, single, occurrence (e.g. whether a contract, &c., &c., has been made, whether a trespass has been committed, and if so by whom) and, in criminal cases, reflection to determine the essential, criminal, character of the deed (see Remark to § 119); secondly, the subsumption of the case under the law that right must be restored. Punishment in criminal cases is a conception falling under this law. Decisions on these two different aspects are given by different functionaries.

Remark: In the Roman judicial system, this distinction of functions appeared in that the Praetor pronounced judgment on the assumption that the facts were so and so, and then appointed a special *judex* to inquire into the facts.

In English law, it is left to the insight or option of the prosecutor to determine the precise character of a criminal act (e.g. whether it is murder or manslaughter) and the court is powerless to alter the indictment if it finds the prosecutor's choice wrong.

§226. First, the conduct of the entire process of inquiry, secondly, the detailed stages of the action between the parties (these stages themselves being rights – see § 222), and then also the second of the aspects of the work of judgment mentioned in the previous paragraph, are all a task which properly belongs to the judge at law. He is the organ of the law, and the case must be prepared for him in such a way as to make possible its subsumption under some principle; that is to say, it must be stripped of its apparent, empirical, character and exalted into a recognised fact of a general type.

§227. The first aspect of the work of judgment, i.e. the knowledge of the facts of the case as a unique, single, occurrence, and the description of its general character, involves in itself no pronouncement on points of law. This is knowledge attainable by any educated man. In settling the character of an action, the subjective moment, i.e. the agent's insight and intention (see the Second Part), is the essential thing; and apart from this, the proof depends not on objects of reason or abstractions of the Understanding, but only on single details and circumstances, objects of sensuous intuition and subjective certainty, and therefore does not contain in itself any absolute, objective, probative factor. It follows that judgment on the facts lies in the last resort with subjective conviction and conscience (*animi sententia*), while the proof, resting as it does on the statements and affidavits of others, receives its final though purely subjective verification from the oath.

Remark: In this matter it is of the first importance to fix our eyes on the type of proof here in question and to distinguish it from knowledge and proof of another sort. To establish by proof a rational category, like the concept of right itself, means to apprehend its necessity, and so demands a method other than that requisite for the proof of a geometrical theorem. Further, in this latter case, the figure is determined by the Understanding and made abstract in advance according to a rule. But in the case of something empirical in content, like a fact, the material of knowledge is a given sensuous intuition and subjective sense-certainty, and statements and affidavits about such material. It is then a question of drawing conclusions and putting two and two together out of depositions of that kind, attestations and other details, &c. The objective truth which emerges from material of this kind and the method appropriate to it leads, when attempts are made to determine it rigidly and objectively, to half-proofs and then, by further sincere deductions from these – deductions which at the same time involve formal illogicality – to extraordinary punishments. But such objective truth means something quite different from the truth of a rational category or a proposition whose content the Understanding has determined for itself abstractly in advance. To show that, since the strictly legal character of a court covers competence to ascertain this sort of truth about empirical events, it thereby properly qualifies a court for this task and so gives it an inherent exclusive right to perform it and lays on it the necessity of performing it – that is the best approach to settling the question of how far decisions on points of fact, as well as on points of law, should be ascribed to courts as strictly juristic bodies.

Addition: No grounds can be adduced for supposing that the judge, i.e. the legal expert, should be the only person to establish how the facts lie, for ability to do so depends on general, not on purely legal, education. Determination of the facts of the case depends on empirical details, on depositions about what happened, and on similar perceptual data, or again on facts from which inferences can be drawn about the deed in question and which make it probable or improbable. Here then, it is an assurance which should be required, not truth in the higher sense in which it is always something eternal. Here such assurance is subjective conviction, or conscience, and the problem is: What form should this assurance take in a court of law? The demand, commonly made in German law, that a criminal should confess his guilt, has this to be said for it, that the right of self-consciousness thereby attains a measure of satisfaction; consciousness must chime in with the judge's sentence, and it is only when the criminal has confessed that the judgment loses its alien character so far as he is concerned. But a difficulty arises here, because the criminal may lie, and the interest of justice may be jeopardised. If, on the other hand, the subjective conviction of the judge is to hold good, some hardship is once more involved, because the accused is no longer being treated as a free man. Now the middle term between these extremes is trial by jury, which meets the demand that the declaration of guilt or innocence shall spring from the soul of the accused.

§228. When judgment is pronounced – so far as the function of judgment is the subsumption under the law of the case whose nature has been settled – the right due to the parties on the score of their self-consciousness is preserved in relation to the law because the law is known and so is the law of the parties themselves, and in relation to the *subsumption*, because the trial is public. But when a verdict is given on the particular, subjective, and external facts of the case (knowledge of which falls under the first of the aspects described in § 225), this right is satisfied by the confidence which the parties feel in the subjectivity of those who give the verdict. This confidence is based primarily on the similarity between them and the parties in respect of their particularity, i.e. their social position, &c.

Remark: The right of self-consciousness, the moment of subjective freedom, may be regarded as the fundamental thing to keep before us in considering the necessity for publicity in legal proceedings and for the so-called jury-courts, and this in the last resort is the essence of whatever may be advanced in favour of these institutions on the score of their utility. Other points of view and reasoning about their several advantages and disadvantages may give rise to an argumentative exchange, but reasoning of this kind, like all deductive reasoning, is either secondary and inconclusive, or else drawn from other and perhaps higher spheres than that of advantage. It may be the case that if the administration of justice were entirely in the hands of professional lawyers, and there were no lay institutions like juries, it would in theory be managed just as well, if not better. It may be so, but even if this possibility rises by general consent to probability, or even certainty, it still does not matter, for on the other side there is always the right of self-consciousness, insisting on its claims and dissatisfied if laymen play no part.

Owing to the character of the entire body of the laws, knowledge both of what is right and also of the course of legal proceedings may become, together with the capacity to prosecute an action at law, the property of a class which makes itself an exclusive clique by the use of a terminology like a foreign tongue to those whose rights are at issue. If this happens, the members of civil society, who depend for their livelihood on their industry, on their own knowledge and will, are kept strangers to the law, not only to those parts of it affecting their most personal and intimate affairs, but also to its substantive and rational basis, the right itself, and the result is that they become the wards, or even in a sense the bondsmen, of the legal profession. They may indeed have the right to appear in court in person and to 'stand' there (*in judicio stare*), but their bodily presence is a trifle if their minds are not to be there also, if they are not to follow the proceedings with their own knowledge, and if the justice they receive remains in their eyes a doom pronounced *ab extra*.

§229.   In civil society, the Idea is lost in particularity and has fallen asunder with the separation of inward and outward. In the administration of justice, however, civil society returns to its concept, to the unity of the implicit universal with the subjective particular, although here the latter is only that present in single cases and the universality in question is that of *abstract* right. The actualisation of this unity through its extension to the whole ambit of particularity is (i) the specific function of the Police, though the unification which it effects is only relative; (ii) it is the Corporation which actualises the unity completely, though only in a whole which, while concrete, is restricted.

Addition: In civil society, universality is necessity only. When we are dealing with human needs, it is only right as such which is steadfast. But this right – only a restricted sphere – has a bearing simply on the protection of property; welfare is something external to right as such. This welfare, however, is an essential end in the system of needs. Hence the universal, which in the first instance is the right only, has to be extended over the whole field of particularity. Justice is a big thing in civil society. Given good laws, a state can flourish, and freedom of property is a fundamental condition of its prosperity. Still, since I am inextricably involved in particularity, I have a right to claim that in this association with other particulars, my particular welfare too shall be promoted. Regard should be paid to my welfare, to my particular interest, and this is done through the Police and the Corporation.

C. The Public Authorities

§230.   In the system of needs, the livelihood and welfare of every single person is a possibility whose actual attainment is just as much conditioned by his caprices and particular endowment as by the objective system of needs. Through the administration of justice, offences against property or personality are annulled. But the right actually present in the particular requires, first, that accidental hindrances to one aim or another be removed, and undisturbed safety of person and property be attained; and secondly, that the securing of every single person's livelihood and welfare be treated and actualised as a right, i.e. that particular welfare as such be so treated.

(a) Police [or the public authority]

§231.   Inasmuch as it is still the particular will which governs the choice of this or that end, the universal authority by which security is ensured remains in the first instance, (a) restricted to the sphere of contingencies, and (b) an external organisation.

§232.   Crime is contingency as subjective willing of evil, and this is what the universal authority must prevent or bring to justice. But, crime apart, the subjective willing which is permissible in actions lawful *per se* and in the private use of property, also comes into external relation with other single persons, as well as with public institutions, other than law-courts, established for realising a common end. This universal aspect makes private actions a matter of contingency which escapes the agent's control and which either does or may injure others and wrong them.

§233. There is here only a possibility of injury; but the actual non-occurrence of injury is at this stage not just another contingency. The point is that the actions of individuals may always be wrongful, and this is the ultimate reason for police control and penal justice.

§234. The relations between external existents fall into the infinite of the Understanding; there is, therefore, no inherent line of distinction between what is and what is not injurious, even where crime is concerned, or between what is and what is not suspicious, or between what is to be forbidden or subjected to supervision and what is to be exempt from prohibition, from surveillance and suspicion, from inquiry and the demand to render an account of itself. These details are determined by custom, the spirit of the rest of the constitution, contemporary conditions, the crisis of the hour, and so forth.

Addition: Here nothing hard and fast can be laid down and no absolute lines can be drawn. Everything here is personal; subjective opinion enters in, and the spirit of the constitution and the crisis of the day have to provide precision of detail. In time of war, for instance, many a thing, harmless at other times, has to be regarded as harmful. As a result of this presence of accident, of personal arbitrariness, the public authority acquires a measure of odium. When reflective thinking is very highly developed, the public authority may tend to draw into its orbit everything it possibly can, for in everything some factor may be found which might make it dangerous in one of its bearings. In such circumstances, the public authority may set to work very pedantically and embarrass the day-to-day life of people. But however great this annoyance, no objective line can be drawn here either.

§235. In the indefinite multiplication and interconnection of day-to-day needs, (a) the acquisition and exchange of the means to their satisfactions – satisfaction which everyone confidently expects to be possible of attainment without hindrance, and (b) the endeavours made and the transactions carried out in order to shorten the process of attainment as much as possible, give rise to factors which are a common interest, and when one man occupies himself with these his labour is at the same time done for all. The situation is productive too of contrivances and organisations which may be of use to the community as a whole. These universal activities and organisations of general utility call for the oversight and care of the public authority.

§236. The differing interests of producers and consumers may come into collision with each other; and although a fair balance between them on the whole may be brought about automatically, still their adjustment also requires a control which stands above both and is consciously undertaken. The right to the exercise of such control in a single case (e.g. in the fixing of the prices of the commonest necessaries of life) depends on the fact that, by being publicly exposed for sale, goods in absolutely universal daily demand are offered not so much to an individual as such but rather to a universal purchaser, the public; and thus both the defence of the public's right not to be defrauded, and also the management of goods inspection, may lie, as a common concern, with a public authority. But public care and direction are most of all necessary in the case of the larger branches of industry, because these are dependent on conditions abroad and on combinations of distant circumstances which cannot be grasped as a whole by the individuals tied to these industries for their living.

Remark: At the other extreme to freedom of trade and commerce in civil society is public organisation to provide for everything and determine everyone's labour – take for example in ancient times the labour on the pyramids and the other huge monuments in Egypt and Asia which were constructed for public ends, and the worker's task was not mediated through his private choice and particular interest. This interest invokes freedom of trade and commerce against control from above; but the more blindly it sinks into self-seeking aims, the more it requires such control to bring it back to the universal. Control is also necessary to diminish the danger of upheavals arising from clashing interests and to abbreviate the period in which their tension should be eased through the working of a necessity of which they themselves know nothing.

Addition: The oversight and care exercised by the public authority aims at being a middle term between an individual and the universal possibility, afforded by society, of attaining individual ends. It has to undertake street-lighting, bridge-building, the pricing of daily necessaries, and the care of public health. In this connection, two main views predominate at the present time. One asserts that the superintendence of everything properly belongs to the public authority, the other that the public authority has nothing at all to settle here because everyone will direct his conduct according to the needs of others. The individual must have a right to work for his bread as he pleases, but the public also has a right to insist that essential tasks shall be properly done. Both points of view must be satisfied, and freedom of trade should not be such as to jeopardise the general good.

§237. Now while the possibility of sharing in the general wealth is open to individuals and is assured to them by the public authority, still it is subject to contingencies on the subjective side (quite apart from the fact that this assurance must remain incomplete), and the more it presupposes skill, health, capital, and so forth as its conditions, the more is it so subject.

§238 . Originally the family is the substantive whole whose function it is to provide for the individual on his particular side by giving him either the means and the skill necessary to enable him to earn his living out of the resources of society, or else subsistence and maintenance in the event of his suffering a disability. But civil society tears the individual from his family ties, estranges the members of the family from one another, and recognises them as self-subsistent persons. Further, for the paternal soil and the external inorganic resources of nature from which the individual formerly derived his livelihood, it substitutes its own soil and subjects the permanent existence of even the entire family to dependence on itself and to contingency. Thus the individual becomes a son of civil society which has as many claims upon him as he has rights against it.

Addition: To be sure, the family has to provide bread for its members, but in civil society the family' is something subordinate and only lays the foundations; its effective range is no longer so comprehensive. Civil society is rather the tremendous power which draws men into itself and claims from them that they work for it, owe everything to it, and do everything by its means. If man is to be a member of civil society in this sense, he has rights and claims against it just as he had rights and claims in the family. Civil society must protect its members and defend their rights, while its rights impose duties on every one of its members.

§239. In its character as a universal family, civil society has the right and duty of superintending and influencing education, inasmuch as education bears upon the child's capacity to become a member of society. Society's right here is paramount over the arbitrary and contingent preferences of parents, particularly in cases where education is to be completed not by the parents but by others. To the same end, society must provide public educational facilities so far as is practicable.

Addition: The line which demarcates the rights of parents from those of civil society is very hard to draw here. Parents usually suppose that in the matter of education they have complete freedom and may arrange everything as they like. The chief opposition to any form of public education usually comes from parents and it is they who talk and make an outcry about teachers and schools because they have a faddish dislike of them. Nonetheless, society has a right to act on principles tested by its experience and to compel parents to send their children to school, to have them vaccinated, and so forth. The disputes that have arisen in France between the advocates of state supervision and those who demand that education shall be free, i.e. at the option of the parents, are relevant here.

§240. Similarly, society has the right and duty of acting as trustee to those whose extravagance destroys the security of their own subsistence or their families. It must substitute for extravagance the pursuit of the ends of society and the individuals concerned.

Addition: There was an Athenian law compelling every citizen to give an account of his source of livelihoods Nowadays we take the view that this is nobody's business but his own. Of course every individual is from one point of view independent, but he also plays his part in the system of civil society, and while every man has the right to demand subsistence from it, it must at the same time protect him from himself. It is not simply starvation which is at issue; the further end in view is to prevent the formation of a pauperised rabble. Since civil society is responsible for feeding its members, it also has the right to press them to provide for their own livelihood.

§241. Not only caprice, however, but also contingencies, physical conditions, and factors grounded in external circumstances (see § 200) may reduce men to poverty. The poor still have the needs common to civil society, and yet since society has withdrawn from them the natural means of acquisition (see § 217) and broken the bond of the family – in the wider sense of the clan (see § 181) – their poverty leaves them more or less deprived of all the advantages of society, of the opportunity of acquiring skill or education of any kind, as well as of the administration of justice, the public health services, and often even of the consolations of religion, and so forth. The public authority takes the place of the family where the poor are concerned in respect not only of their immediate want but also of laziness of disposition, malignity, and the other vices which arise out of their plight and their sense of wrong.

§242 Poverty and, in general, the distress of every kind to which every individual is exposed from the start in the cycle of his natural life has a subjective side which demands similarly subjective aid, arising both from the special circumstances of a particular case and also from love and sympathy. This is the place where morality finds plenty to do despite all public organisation. Subjective aid, however, both in itself and in its operation, is dependent on contingency and consequently society struggles to make it less necessary, by discovering the general causes of penury and general means of its relief, and by organising relief accordingly.

Remark: Casual almsgiving and casual endowments, e.g. for the burning of lamps before holy images, &c., are supplemented by public almshouses, hospitals, street-lighting, and so forth. There is still quite enough left over and above these things for charity to do on its own account. A false view is implied both when charity insists on having this poor-relief reserved solely to private sympathy and the accidental occurrence of knowledge and a charitable disposition, and also when it feels injured or mortified by universal regulations and ordinances which *are obligatory*. Public social conditions are on the contrary to be regarded as all the more perfect the less (in comparison with what is arranged publicly) is left for an individual to do by himself as his private inclination directs.

§243. When civil society is in a state of unimpeded activity, it is engaged in expanding internally in population and industry. The amassing of wealth is intensified by generalising (a) the linkage of men by their needs, and (b) the methods of preparing and distributing the means to satisfy these needs, because it is from this double process of generalisation that the largest profits are derived. That is one side of the picture. The other side is the subdivision and restriction of particular jobs. This results in the dependence and distress of the class tied to work of that sort, and these again entail inability to feel and enjoy the broader freedoms and especially the intellectual benefits of civil society.

§244. When the standard of living of a large mass of people falls below a certain subsistence level – a level regulated automatically as the one necessary for a member of the society – and when there is a consequent loss of the sense of right and wrong, of honesty and the self-respect which makes a man insist on maintaining himself by his own work and effort, the result is the creation of a rabble of paupers. At the same time this brings with it, at the other end of the social scale, conditions which greatly facilitate the concentration of disproportionate wealth in a few hands.

Addition: The lowest subsistence level, that of a rabble of paupers, is fixed automatically, but the minimum varies considerably in different countries. In England, even the very poorest believe that they have rights; this is different from what satisfies the poor in other countries. Poverty in itself does not make men into a rabble; a rabble is created only when there is joined to poverty a disposition of mind, an inner indignation against the rich, against society, against the government, &c. A further consequence of this attitude is that through their dependence on chance men become frivolous and idle, like the Neapolitan lazzaroni for example. In this way there is born in the rabble the evil of lacking self-respect enough to secure subsistence by its own labour and yet at the same time of claiming to receive subsistence as its right. Against nature man can claim no right, but once society is established, poverty immediately takes the form of a wrong done to one class by another. The important question of how poverty is to be abolished is one of the most disturbing problems which agitate modern society.

§245. When the masses begin to decline into poverty, (a) the burden of maintaining them at their ordinary standard of living might be directly laid on the wealthier classes, or they might receive the means of livelihood directly from other public sources of wealth (e.g. from the endowments of rich hospitals, monasteries, and other foundations). In either case, however, the needy would receive subsistence directly, not by means of their work, and this would violate the principle of civil society and the feeling of individual independence and self-respect in its individual members. (b) As an alternative, they might be given subsistence indirectly through being given work, i.e. the opportunity to work. In this event the volume of production would be increased, but the evil consists precisely in an excess of production and in the lack of a proportionate number of consumers who are themselves also producers, and thus it is simply intensified by both of the methods (a) and (b) by which it is sought to alleviate it. It hence becomes apparent that despite an excess of wealth civil society is not rich enough, i.e. its own resources are insufficient to check excessive poverty and the creation of a penurious rabble.

Remark: In the example of England we may study these phenomena on a large scale and also in particular the results of poor-rates, immense foundations, unlimited private beneficence, and above all the abolition of the Guild Corporations. In Britain, particularly in Scotland, the most direct measure against poverty and especially against the loss of shame and self-respect – the subjective bases of society – as well as against laziness and extravagance, &c., the begetters of the rabble, has turned out to be to leave the poor to their fate and instruct them to beg in the streets.

§246. This inner dialectic of civil society thus drives it – or at any rate drives a specific civil society – to push beyond its own limits and seek markets, and so its necessary means of subsistence, in other lands which are either deficient in the goods it has over-produced, or else generally backward in industry, &c.

§247. The principle of family life is dependence on the soil, on land, *terra firma*. Similarly, the natural element for industry, animating its outward movement, is the sea. Since the passion for gain involves risk, industry though bent on gain yet lifts itself above it; instead of remaining rooted to the soil and the limited circle of civil life with its pleasures and desires, it embraces the element of flux, danger, and destruction. Further, the sea is the greatest means of communication, and trade by sea creates commercial connections between distant countries and so relations involving contractual rights. At the same time, commerce of this kind is the most potent instrument of culture, and through it trade acquires its significance in the history of the world.

Rivers are not natural boundaries of separation, which is what they have been accounted to be in modern times. On the contrary, it is truer to say that they, and the sea likewise, link men together. Horace is wrong when he says:

deus abscidit prudens Oceano dissociabili terras. [vain was the purpose of the god in severing the lands by the estranging ocean.]

Remark: The proof of this lies not merely in the fact that the basins of rivers are inhabited by a single clan or tribe, but also, for example, in the ancient bonds between Greece, Ionia, and Magna Graecia, between Brittany and Britain, between Denmark and Norway, Sweden, Finland, Livonia, &c., bonds, further, which are especially striking in contrast with the comparatively slight intercourse between the inhabitants of the littoral and those of the hinterland. To realise what an instrument of culture lies in the link with the sea, consider countries where industry flourishes and contrast their relation to the sea with that of countries which have eschewed sea-faring and which, like Egypt and India, have become stagnant and in the most frightful and scandalous superstition. Notice also how all great progressive peoples press onward to the sea.

§248. This far-flung connecting link affords the means for the colonising activity – sporadic or systematic – to which mature civil society is driven and by which it supplies to a part of its population a return to life on the family basis in a new land and so also supplies itself with a new demand and field for its industry.

Addition: Civil society is thus driven to found colonies. Increase of population alone has this effect, but it is due in particular to the appearance of a number of people who cannot secure the satisfaction of their needs by their own labour once production rises above the requirements of consumers. Sporadic colonisation is particularly characteristic of Germany. The emigrants withdraw to America or Russia and remain there with no home ties, and so prove useless to their native land. The second and entirely different type of colonisation is the systematic; the state undertakes it, is aware of the proper method of carrying it out and regulates it accordingly. This type was common amongst the ancients, particularly the Greeks. Hard work was not the business of the citizens in Greece, since their energy was directed rather to public affairs. So if the population increased to such an extent that there might be difficulty in feeding it, the young people would be sent away to a new district, sometimes specifically chosen, sometimes left to chance discovery. In modern times, colonists have not been allowed the same rights as those left at home, and the result of this situation has been wars and finally independence, as may be seen in the history of the English and Spanish colonies. Colonial independence proves to be of the greatest advantage to the mother country, just as the emancipation of slaves turns out to the greatest advantage of the owners.

§249. While the public authority must also undertake the higher directive function of providing for the interests which lead beyond the borders of its society (see § 246), its primary purpose is to actualise and maintain the universal contained within the particularity of civil society, and its control takes the form of an external system and organisation for the protection and security of particular ends and interests *en masse*, inasmuch as these interests subsist only in this universal. This universal is immanent in the interests of particularity itself and, in accordance with the Idea, particularity makes it the end and object of its own willing and activity. In this way ethical principles circle back and appear in civil society as a factor immanent in it; this constitutes the specific character of the Corporation.

(b) The Corporation

§250. In virtue of the substantiality of its natural and family life, the agricultural class has directly within itself the concrete universal in which it lives. The class of civil servants is universal in character and so has the universal explicitly as its ground and as the aim of its activity. The class between them, the business class, is essentially concentrated on the particular, and hence it is to it that Corporations are specially appropriate.

§251. The labour organisation of civil society is split, in accordance with the nature of its particulars, into different branches. The implicit likeness of such particulars to one another becomes really existent in an association, as something common to its members. Hence a selfish purpose, directed towards its particular self-interest, apprehends and evinces itself at the same time as universal; and a member of civil society is in virtue of his own particular skill a member of a Corporation, whose universal purpose is thus wholly concrete and no wider in scope than the purpose involved in business, its proper task and interest.

§252. In accordance with this definition of its functions, a Corporation has the right, under the surveillance of the public authority, (a) to look after its own interests within its own sphere, (b) to co-opt members, qualified objectively by the requisite skill and rectitude, to a number fixed by the general structure of society, (c) to protect its members against particular contingencies, (d) to provide the education requisite to fit others to become members. In short, its right is to come on the scene like a second family for its members, while civil society can only be an indeterminate sort of family because it comprises everyone and so is farther removed from individuals and their special exigencies.

Remark: The Corporation member is to be distinguished from a day labourer or from a man who is prepared to undertake casual employment on a single occasion. The former who is, or will become, master of his craft, is a member of the association not for casual gain on single occasions but for the whole range, the universality, of his personal livelihood.

Privileges, in the sense of the rights of a branch of civil society organised into a Corporation, are distinct in meaning from privileges-proper, in the etymological sense. The latter are casual exceptions to universal rules; the former, however, are only the crystallisation, as regulations, of characteristics inherent in an essential branch of society itself owing to its nature as particular.

§253. In the Corporation, the family has its stable basis in the sense that its livelihood is assured there, conditionally upon capability, i.e. it has a stable capital (see § 170) – In addition, his nexus of capability and livelihood is a *recognised* fact, with he result that the Corporation member needs no external marks beyond his own membership as evidence of his skill and his regular income and subsistence, i.e. as evidence that he is a somebody. It is also recognised that he belongs to a whole which is itself an organ of the entire society, and that he is actively concerned in promoting the comparatively disinterested end of this whole. Thus he commands the respect due to one in his social position.

Remark: The institution of Corporations corresponds, on account of its assurance of capital, to the introduction of agriculture and private property in another sphere (see Remark to § 203).

When complaints are made about the luxury of the business classes their passion for extravagance – which have as their concomitant creation of a rabble of paupers (see § 244) – we must not forget that besides its other causes (e.g. increasing mechanisation of labour) this phenomenon has an ethical ground, as was indicated above. Unless he is a member of an authorised Corporation (and it is only by being authorised that an association becomes a Corporation), an individual is without rank or dignity, his isolation reduces his business to mere self-seeking, and his livelihood and satisfaction become insecure. Consequently, he has to try to gain recognition for himself by giving external proofs of success in his business, and to these proofs no limits can be set. He cannot live in the manner of his class, for no class really exists for him, since in civil society it is only something common to particular persons which really exists, i.e. something legally constituted and recognised. Hence he cannot achieve for himself a way of life proper to his class and less idiosyncratic.

Within the Corporation the help which poverty receives loses its accidental character and the humiliation wrongfully associated with it. The wealthy perform their duties to their fellow associates and thus riches cease to inspire either pride or envy, pride in their owners, envy in others. In these conditions rectitude obtains its proper recognition and respect.

§254. The so-called 'natural' right of exercising one's skill and thereby earning what there is to be earned is restricted within the Corporation only in so far as it is therein made rational instead of natural. That is to say, it becomes freed from personal opinion and contingency, saved from endangering either the individual workman or others, recognised, guaranteed, and at the same time elevated to conscious effort for a common end.

§255. As the family was the first, so the Corporation is the second ethical root of the state, the one planted in civil society. The former contains the moments of subjective particularity and objective universality in a substantial unity. But these moments are sundered in civil society to begin with; on the one side there is the particularity of need and satisfaction, reflected into itself, and on the other side the universality of abstract rights. In the Corporation these moments are united in an inward fashion, so that in this union particular welfare is present as a right and is actualised.

Remark: The sanctity of marriage and the dignity of Corporation membership are the two fixed points round which the unorganised atoms of civil society revolve.

Addition: The consideration behind the abolition of Corporations in recent times is that the individual should fend for himself. But we may grant this and still hold that corporation membership does not alter a man's obligation to earn his living. Under modern political conditions, the citizens have only a restricted share in the public business of the state, yet it is essential to provide men – ethical entities – with work of a public character over and above their private business. This work of a public character, which the modern state does not always provide, is found in the Corporation. We saw earlier [Addition to § 184] that in fending for himself a member of civil society is also working for others. But this unconscious compulsion is not enough; it is in the Corporation that it first changes into a known and thoughtful ethical mode of life. Of course Corporations must fall under the higher surveillance of the state, because otherwise they would ossify, build themselves in, and decline into a miserable system of castes. In and by itself, however, a Corporation is not a closed caste; its purpose is rather to bring an isolated trade into the social order and elevate it to a sphere in which it gains strength and respect.

§256. The end of the Corporation is restricted and finite, while the public authority was an external organisation involving a separation and a merely relative identity of controller and controlled The end of the former and the externality and relative identity of the latter find their truth in the absolutely universal end and its absolute actuality. Hence the sphere of civil society passes over into the state.

Remark: The town is the seat of the civil life of business. There reflection arises, turns in upon itself, and pursues its atomising task; each man maintains himself in and through his relation to others who, like himself, are persons possessed of rights. The country, on the other hand, is the seat of an ethical life resting on nature and the family. Town and country thus constitute the two moments, still ideal moments, whose true ground is the state, although it is from them that the state springs.

The philosophic proof of the concept of the state is this development of ethical life from its immediate phase through civil society, the phase of division, to the state, which then reveals itself as the true ground of these phases. A proof in philosophic science can only be a development of this kind.

Since the state appears as a result in the advance of the philosophic concept through displaying itself as the true ground [of the earlier phases], that show of mediation is now cancelled and the state has become directly present before us. Actually, therefore, the state as such is not so much the result as the beginning. It is within the state that the family is first developed into civil society, and it is the Idea of the state itself which disrupts itself into these two moments. Through the development of civil society, the substance of ethical life acquires its infinite form, which contains in itself these two moments: (1) infinite differentiation down to the inward experience of independent self-consciousness, and (2) the form of universality involved in education, the form of thought whereby mind is objective and actual to itself as an organic totality in laws and institutions which are its will in terms of thought.

About the Editors

George S. Rigakos is associate professor of law, criminology and political economy at Carleton University. He has published widely on public and private policing, risk theory, and critical realism. His most recent books are: *The New Parapolice: Risk Markets and the Commodified of Social Control* (University of Toronto Press, 2002) and *Nightclub: Bouncers, Risk and the Spectacle of Consumption* (McGill-Queen's University Press, 2008).

John L. McMullan is professor of sociology and criminology at Saint Mary's University. His wide-ranging research includes the social effects of the gaming industry, corporate criminality in the Westray Mine disaster, critical criminology, and eighteenth to nineteenth century British policing. His books include: *News, Truth and Crime: The Westray Disaster and its Aftermath* (Fernwood, 2006) and *The Canting Crew: London's Criminal Underworld, 1550-1700* (Rutgers University Press, 1984).

Joshua Johnson is a Master's student at Carleton University where he studies political theory. His research interests include alienation, mortality, and discourses of social control in both ancient and modern political thought. His work has appeared in *Innovations: A Journal of Politics*.

Gulden Ozcan is currently a doctoral student in sociology at Carleton University. She completed her B.A. in political science and international relations at Baskent University (Ankara, Turkey) in 2005 and her M.A. in political economy at Carleton University in 2007. Her interests are Marxist theory, policing, exploitation, and critical social theory.

9 780981 280707